Child Welfare Social Work

An Introduction

Philip Popple
University of North Carolina, Charlotte

Francine Vecchiolla
Springfield College, Massachusetts

PEARSON

Boston   New York   San Francisco
Mexico City   Montreal   Toronto   London   Madrid   Munich   Paris
Hong Kong   Singapore   Tokyo   Cape Town   Sydney

Series Editor: Patricia Quinlin
Series Editorial Assistant: Sara Holliday
Marketing Manager: Laura Lee Manley
Editorial Production Service: Omegatype Typography, Inc.
Manufacturing and Composition Buyer: Andrew Turso
Electronic Composition: Omegatype Typography, Inc.
Cover Administrator: Kristina Mose-Libon

For related titles and support materials, visit our online catalog at
www.ablongman.com.

Between the time website information is gathered and then published, it is not unusual for some sites to have closed. Also, the transcription of URLs can result in typographical errors. The publisher would appreciate notification where these errors occur so that they may be corrected in subsequent editions.

Library of Congress Cataloging-in-Publication Data

Popple, Philip R.
    Child welfare social work : an introduction / Philip Popple and Francine Vecchiolla.
      p.   cm.
    Includes bibliographical references and index.
    ISBN 0-205-27490-0 (alk. paper)
    1. Child welfare. 2. Social work with children 3. Social case work with children. I. Vecchiolla, Francine J. II. Title.

HV713.P58 2007
362.7—dc22
                                                        2005053483

Printed in the United States of America

10 9 8 7 6 5 4 3 2 1   11 10 09 08 07 06

Photo Credits: pp. 1, 10, 14, 53, 61, 64, 78, 85, 91, 93, 119, 126, 134, 145, 148, 151, 169, 175, 181, 187, 191, 208, 210, 217, 231, 254, 258, 262, 271, 277, 282, and 286, © Harry Cutting Photography—www.harrycutting.com; p. 29, CULVER PICTURES; p. 32, Fototeca Storica Nazionale/Getty Images; p. 41, Kansas State Historical Society; p. 192, Rebecca Turner; p. 242, George Dodson/Pearson Education/PH College.

From P. R. P.

To my three sets of grandkids—Katie, Annie, and John; Abby and Benjamin; Megan, Lauren, and Kaitlyn—with the wish that all children were so loved and cared for

From F. J. V.

With many thanks to my husband, Duncan Reid, whose encouragement and sage advice I will always value, and to our son, Trevor, whose creativity and compassion are an inspiration for the future

Contents

Contents

Preface

At the current time, child welfare social work is, in the words of businesspeople, a "growth industry." After a number of years of deprofessionalizing child welfare via the declassification of social work positions in child welfare agencies, these agencies are turning to schools of social work with pleas for help.

There are a number of reasons for the renewed interest of child welfare agencies in professionally trained personnel. The first is the explosive growth in abuse and neglect referrals over recent decades, with the accompanying increases in caseload sizes, foster home placements, and demand for preventive services—all combining to create a need for better-trained staff. Another factor is the number of legal challenges that have been filed by groups such as the American Civil Liberties Union's Children's Rights Project, which have, in every case, resulted in court orders to improve services. One of the components of the directives to improve services has generally been to upgrade the professional qualifications of child welfare staff. Finally, most large city newspapers now have a reporter assigned to the child welfare beat, which means agency problems are quickly subjected to public scrutiny, with the result that mistakes are nearly always accompanied by cries for better-trained staff.

Schools of social work, for their part, have finally begun to recognize that child welfare is a central concern and responsibility of the social work profession. Strangely, this has not always been the case. Until fairly recently, the child welfare agency was viewed by schools of social work as a place where truly professional social work practice was difficult, if not impossible, and a job in such an agency was seen as a stop gap for any graduate—to be taken only until a job in a mental health agency opened up. Fortunately, beginning with the NEW Partnership initiatives that began in the 1970s and continuing on to the federally funded Title IVE child welfare education collaboratives, this is no longer the case. Education for child welfare practice is now a central concern of virtually every undergraduate department and graduate school of social work in the United States.

This increased emphasis on child welfare by social work education has been accompanied by the need for up-to-date, relevant, user-friendly educational materials. We have written *Child Welfare Social Work: An Introduction* to help meet that need.

Plan of the Book

We begin this book with three chapters that provide a general description of child welfare. Chapter 1, Child Welfare as a Field of Social Work and Public Policy, describes the field of practice with an emphasis on various perspectives for viewing child welfare and on some of the features that contribute to Americans' conflicted attitudes toward protecting children. Chapter 2, Child Welfare in the United States: A Brief History, provides a straightforward description of the historical development of child welfare services, from apprenticeship and orphanages through the Adoption and Safe Families Act. Chapter 3, Families and Children Served by Child Welfare Agencies, written by A. Suzanne Boyd, Carole A. Winston, and Marianne Berry, looks at the current American social environment for families and children and at the many influences and stresses that bring increasing numbers of them into contact with the child welfare system.

Chapters 4 and 5 are intended as an introduction to critical practice issues in child protective services. Chapter 4, Risk Factors and Risk Assessment in Child Welfare, was contributed by Diane DePanfilis. Although the content of this chapter is a bit more technical and advanced than that of other chapters, it is included because of our belief that valid and reliable risk assessment is the key to unlocking the puzzle of effective child welfare practice. Chapter 5, Assessing and Intervening with Families, was contributed by Ineke Way and Marlys Staudt. Included in this chapter are descriptions and discussions of the major theories of the etiology of maltreatment; the means of assessing and prioritizing families' needs; an application of systems theory to families; and the use of tools including genograms, ecomaps, and culturagrams. Also presented is an introduction to major intervention methods, including multifamily group therapy, parent training, social support groups, and intensive family-centered crisis services.

Chapters 6 through 9 describe a continuum of child welfare services based on the degree and length of state involvement with affected families. Chapter 6, Universal Services for Children and Families, written with the help of Joseph Gianesin, describes what are referred to in the social policy literature as *institutional programs* and in the practice literature as *preventive social work*. These programs, of which there are far too few in the United States, recognize the complexity of successful child-rearing in modern society and seek to provide services to all families to enable them to effectively care for their own children. In Chapter 7, Services to Families and Children at Home, Joseph Gianesin and Joyce Lee Taylor help us describe the United States' residual child welfare system by discussing the child welfare services provided to families that are determined to have problems great enough to require formal intervention but not so severe as to warrant removal of the children. The services discussed in this chapter include ongoing child protective supervision, wraparound services, homemaker services, and family preservation models. In Chapter 8, Services to Families and Children with the Children in Substitute Care, Rebecca Turner discusses services for children and families with problems severe enough to warrant removal of the children from the home, including temporary foster care, termination of parental rights, concurrent planning, and therapeutic foster care. Her presentation is bolstered by the results of a previously unpublished quality assurance study of therapeutic foster care. In Chapter 9, Services for Children Who Cannot Go Home, Joan R. Rycraft discusses services for children for whom it has been determined that they will never be able to return to their families of origin. Rycraft includes in her discussion adoption services, long-term care for children unlikely to be adopted, independent-living programs provided when these children age out of the foster care system, and finally, the Chafee Foster Care Independence Act.

The final three chapters return to some general child welfare issues. Chapter 10, Doing Child Welfare, describes what the job of a child welfare worker is actually like. It is based on an extensive ethnographic study of child welfare workers in one midwestern city as well as other data describing the child welfare worker's day-to-day job. Chapter 11, Other Key Players in the Child Welfare System, contributed by Joyce Lee Taylor, Michael Schultz, and Jessica Noel, discusses the contributions of other professionals with whom child welfare workers interact. Included are discussions of mandated reporters, legal system professionals, and other service providers, with an emphasis on multidisciplinary teams. Finally, Chapter 12, Concluding Thoughts on the Practice of Child Welfare, presents a few of our thoughts on the current state of child welfare practice.

Acknowledgments

As with any project of this scope, we, the authors, have incurred debts to many people and institutions. Philip Popple would like to express gratitude for both the financial support and intellectual stimulation provided by the University of California at Berkeley/California Social Work Education Center (CALSWEC)/U.S. Children's Bureau Child Welfare Fellows Program, in which he participated from 1996 through 1999. Chapter 10 is a direct result of the research he conducted during this fellowship. Special thanks is due to Dr. Nancy Dickinson, who was then Executive Director of CALSWEC and is now Executive Director of the Jordan Institute for Families at the University of North Carolina at Chapel Hill, and to Dr. Sherrill Clark, who was the Child Welfare Fellows Program Coordinator and has since assumed the position of Executive Director of CALSWEC. Two contributors to this volume, Drs. Rebecca Turner and Marianne Berry, were also fellows in this program, and Dr. Turner's chapter is partially based on her fellowship project. Two other fellows, Drs. Monit Cheung and Ellen Whipple, served as reviewers of this manuscript, and the final version is much improved based on their critical reading and comments. Additional research support was provided by a President's Research Grant awarded to Professor Popple by Western Michigan University. Gratitude is also due to Professor Popple's graduate research assistants who helped with Chapter 10: Cris Fisher, Denise Hartsough, and Trish Heyn.

Francine Vecchiolla would like to thank Dr. Philip Popple, first and foremost, for his leadership. This book would not have been undertaken were it not for his vision. The Child Welfare League of America and the Connecticut Department of Children and Youth Services, by whom Dr. Vecchiolla was employed, influenced her thinking about the importance of multidisciplinary approaches and comprehensive community-based public/private partnerships. Special thanks is extended to a colleague, Dr. Diane DePanfilis, for accepting the invitation to participate in this project. Our shared experiences with the National Center on Child Abuse and Neglect and with Action for Child Protection, along with Dr. DePanfilis's work on risk assessment, made her the ideal choice for a chapter on this topic. Two contributors and colleagues are acknowledged with gratitude: Dr. Joseph Gianesin, of Springfield College School of Social Work, for sharing his knowledge about vulnerable children from a systems and practice perspective, and Joyce Lee Taylor, Associate Commissioner of the Connecticut Department of Children and Families, for lending her expertise about the current challenges in public child welfare. Research support on selected chapters was provided by Professor Vecchiolla's graduate assistants, including Sandra Johnson, Glenn Little, and Jennifer Rossario. Graduate social work students in child welfare courses at Springfield College School of Social Work are acknowledged for sharing practice experiences and in particular for their dedication to improving the child welfare field of practice.

We would like to thank the following reviewers for their comments on the manuscript: Venessa Brown, Southern Illinois University, Edwardsville; Monique Bush, Indiana University; Monit Cheung, University of Houston; and Ellen Whipple, Michigan State University.

Finally, both of the authors would like to express gratitude to Barbara Lawing, who provided the content editing of this volume. Her skill at not only correcting the usual problems with spelling and grammar but also at smoothing out the sometimes jarring changes in style and tone of the multiple authors contributed immeasurably to the readability of the final version of this work.

CHAPTER 1

Child Welfare as a Field of Social Work and Public Policy

It is 10:00 P.M., and Robert, a long-time child welfare supervisor, has changed the channel to watch *NYPD Blue*. His wife, Kathy, a pharmacist, looks up with a pained expression; she thinks the show is lowbrow and distasteful, and the jumpy editing style gives her a headache. In spite of her view, though, she will usually sit with Robert while he watches his

his show. Generally, she reads a magazine and falls asleep before the second round of commercials.

In the episode this night, one of the veteran female detectives is introduced to another female detective who's been assigned as her new partner. Then, a young woman with wild hair, disheveled clothes, and the nervous mannerisms of a cocaine addict enters the squad room and blurts out, "I need to see a detective. My baby is missing."

The two detectives look at each other, eyebrows rising in alarm, and one says, "Okay, how long has your baby been missing?"

The woman replies, "I don't know. It depends on how you look at it. Either a few hours or a few years."

The detectives roll their eyes and one snaps, "Come on back here. We've got to straighten this out." During the questioning, the woman's fidgeting increases and she says, "You see, I just got out of the joint. I was in for three years on a drug charge. But I'm clean now and want to get my life back. I left my baby with a friend, and when I went to get her, she said that she doesn't have her anymore."

One of the detectives asks, "Why did you leave her with a friend? Why didn't you call social services for help?"

The mother answers, "Oh, no. I didn't want the government involved! They came out once and accused me of abusing my daughter and threatened to take her away."

She explains that her friend offered to take care of the child until she got out of prison.

A detectives asks, "Didn't you write to her when you were in prison to see how your baby was doing?" The mother says that she wrote two or three times, but her friend never answered.

The detectives go to the apartment of the friend, who, predictably, has a very different story. She says the mother left the baby with her "for a couple of hours" and never returned. Pointing to the torn curtains, threadbare carpet, and peeling paint, she says, "Does it look like I can afford another kid?" She says she found another friend to care for the child but doesn't think the child is there any longer.

The detectives follow the trail of the child from one crummy-looking apartment and drugged-out-looking person to another, until they get to a residence on a leafy street with a doorman and a security guard. They are buzzed up to the apartment and then greeted by a well-dressed woman who appears to be in her thirties. They enter the apartment and find a clean, spacious room with toys, games, and stuffed animals all over the place. In the middle is an apparently happy and healthy little girl.

One of the detectives says, "Is this your daughter?"

"Yes."

"Is she your natural child?"

"No, we adopted her three years ago."

"We'll need to see some documentation of that: the adoption decree, her new birth certificate, something official like that."

Suddenly, the woman's face crumples like a soufflé pulled from the oven too soon.

"Oh, God," she says. "We never actually adopted her. She was being cared for by this really horrible woman, and she asked if we would take care of her. She left the baby, and we never heard from her again. My husband and I had been trying to get pregnant, with no luck. We'd about given up hope, so we applied to adopt, and every agency told us it would take years. Then this woman appeared with this beautiful child and just gave her to us. I thought she was a gift from God. Please don't take her from me."

The detectives look at each other, then at the woman, and one says, "Hang on. Don't do anything rash. We'll get back to you."

At this point in the show, Robert notices that Kathy is not reading her magazine and has not fallen asleep. Her eyes are wide with alarm. "They wouldn't really take that little girl away from the only parents she has ever known, would they?"

"Well, yeah," Robert says, drawing on his ten years of experience working for the state child welfare department. "Those people have absolutely no legal claim on the child, and no one knows a thing about them. They look happy, healthy, and prosperous, but they could be the Steinbergs for all anyone knows" (referring to the infamous case of the New York City lawyer and his book editor wife who were arrested, convicted, and imprisoned for the abuse and murder of their informally adopted daughter).

"But after they studied the home," Kathy says, "they would return the child there if everything looked okay, wouldn't they?"

"No, the court would insist that the child welfare department make 'reasonable efforts' to reunite the girl with her birth mother."

"How long would that take? I mean, a few months is an eternity to a child that age. The birth mother is obviously never going to be able to actually care for the child. When could the 'real' parents get her back?"

Robert sighs and says, "It could take years, and before it is done, it is not at all unlikely that the child will be ruined."

Kathy jumps off the couch and says, "I don't want to watch this. I'm going to bed. I don't see why you insist on watching this stupid show anyway."

That child welfare should be the subject of television drama is not surprising. What's more dramatic than life, death, sex, violence, relationships, betrayal, abuse, exploitation, crime, mystery, pain, and guilt? All of these topics are central to child welfare. And television executives are well aware that they translate to top ratings. Prime-time episodes of *NYPD Blue, Third Watch, Boston Public,* and *Judging Amy* often tackle the thorny issues of child welfare.

The real world of child welfare social work is no less dramatic than its TV representation, but—no surprise—it is much more complex and infinitely messier. In the TV world, situations look clear and unambiguous. The issues are portrayed as black and white, right and wrong, good and evil. Nice people love children, protect them, nurture them, supervise them, and when necessary, firmly but lovingly discipline them. Bad people beat children, burn them, exploit them, and sexually molest them. On TV, the appropriate remedies in cases where children are mistreated are presented so they seem clear and simple: Turn the perpetrators over to the criminal justice system for stern punishment, and turn the children over to the social welfare system to be placed in warm and loving homes that will compensate for their unfortunate beginnings. In the real world of child welfare, of course, things don't go quite this way.

Definition of Child Welfare

Even the term *child welfare* is not simple or unambiguous. It originally described a general and wide range of activities to do with the well-being of children. Included in the "child welfare" entry in volume one of the *Social Work Yearbook,* published in 1929, are services for delinquent children, detention homes, child development research, parent education, visiting teachers, psychiatric clinics for children, compulsory education, vocational guidance, social hygiene (whatever that is), physically handicapped children, mentally defective children, dependent children, and neglected children (Ellis, 1929). In recent years, due to the publicity that has focused attention on the problem of child abuse and neglect, the term has been narrowed to mean almost exclusively *child protective services,* or services to protect children from maltreatment from their primary caretakers. Social policy scholars Kamerman and Kahn (1990) make these observations with some regret:

> Most child welfare activities of public agencies are [now] largely directed toward the problem of child abuse and neglect. Agency efforts focus on investigating reports and protecting children when allegations are verified. Few resources remain for troubled families who do not fall under the purview of CPS [child protective services]. In many jurisdictions, there are few supportive services or treatment options for these families. Agencies often turn away parents with out-of-control or defiant children. Services for latency or early adolescent children also are limited. Chronic multi-problem cases in troubled families often are overlooked. In fact, if a case is not marked by dramatic events, it may receive only token processing and resources. . . . Most agencies focus almost exclusively on child and family crises. Chronic parenting problems are ignored. (p. 10)

The nineteenth edition of the *Social Work Yearbook* (1995), now called the *Encyclopedia of Social Work,* illustrates Kamerman and Kahn's point, offering a narrowed definition of *child welfare* as services "designed to assist abused, neglected, or at-risk children and their families" (Liederman, 1995, p. 424).

Very few people in the field of child welfare social work, including the authors of this text, believe that the narrowing of the definition of child welfare has been a good thing. It has resulted in resources being diverted away from needed supportive and developmental services for children and families into services only for those in crisis. The result is that situations that start out fairly minor, such as a defiant teenager, a family with unsafe housing, or a crumbling marriage—situations that could be remedied with appropriate supportive services—become serious cases of abuse and neglect because needed services were not provided.

We agree that the restricting of child welfare to services for only the most serious cases is an undesirable development, but we also agree with the old proverb that "It is better to light a candle than to curse the darkness." Social policy in the United States currently defines *child welfare* as services for children who are victims of abuse and neglect, and social work is the profession responsible for implementing this policy. Therefore, in this book, we provide coverage of services for families and children in situations where abuse and neglect has occurred or is suspected of having occurred. We would like to see the definition of child welfare broadened again to encompass a wider range of services, but until that happens, we will play the hand we have been dealt. We accept and use the restricted definition of child welfare to mean child protective services.

Definition of Child Maltreatment

If we are going to define *child welfare* as services to protect maltreated children, then we also need to define *maltreatment,* another task that is not easy or clear. First, we must recognize that definitions of child maltreatment are rooted in time and place. Many childrearing practices that were considered acceptable in the past—for example, a frontier schoolmaster caning a wayward pupil—are now not only unacceptable but illegal. Conversely, some practices that were considered abusive or neglectful in the past—for example, choosing to educate your children at home instead of sending them to a formal school—are now considered perfectly acceptable. Moreover, practices such as female circumcision that are deemed acceptable in other areas of the world are considered horribly abusive in the United States, while spanking a child in a manner considered reasonable here constitutes abuse and is illegal in Sweden.

There is also the matter of fringe religious groups and subcultural groups that follow practices outside the mainstream definition of appropriate child care. The most common examples are cases where families deny medical care to children for religious reasons. Situations involving these citizens create a dilemma for social workers, who usually pride themselves on being culturally sensitive and accepting of diversity. Korbin (1987) has summed up this problem:

> Failure to allow for cultural perspective . . . promotes an ethnocentric position in which one's own . . . cultural beliefs and practices are presumed superior to all others. Nevertheless, a stance of extreme cultural relativism, in which all judgments . . . are suspended . . . may justify a lesser standard of care for some children. (p. 24)

Social workers have tended to take a middle-of-the-road position on cultural differences in definitions of maltreatment. Relatively innocuous practices—such as that of Vietnamese immigrant parents engaging in coin rubbing, a practice that often leaves bruises on a child—have generally been ignored under the rubric of cultural sensitivity. Practices with more serious consequences, however—such as withholding medical treatment for severe conditions—have resulted in the imposition of state authority by social workers.

Although there are many perspectives on the definition of child maltreatment, the legal definition is the important one for child welfare social workers, for they operate under legal sanction. The current legal definition is contained in the 1974 Child Abuse Prevention and Treatment Act (CAPTA). It has been reauthorized and amended several times, most recently by the Keeping Children and Families Safe Act of 2003. According to CAPTA, child maltreatment means

 the physical or mental injury, sexual abuse or exploitation, negligent treatment, or maltreatment of a child by a person who is responsible for the child's welfare, under circumstances which indicate that the child's health or welfare is harmed or threatened thereby, as determined in accordance with regulations prescribed by the Secretary. (Section 5106g)

The definition goes on to define "a person who is responsible for the child's welfare" to include employees of residential care facilities and any staff person of any organization providing out-of-home care.

CAPTA is a federal law, but the laws that actually authorize intervention into homes by child welfare social workers are state laws, so it is necessary to look at the definitions of maltreatment contained in state statutes. While there are many similarities among state definitions, there are also many differences. Wells (1996) has looked at the state laws and observes this:

> Some states emphasize that physical abuse or neglect is defined by the presence of serious injury. Other states explicitly include or exclude a variety of conditions, such as a positive drug toxicology in a newborn, truancy or educational neglect, children being left alone, head lice, and parents' behavior not resulting in specific observable harm to the child. (p. 347–348)

Because all of the laws, federal and state, leave many terms undefined—for example, *serious injury, educational neglect, sexual abuse, negligent treatment*—there have been a number of attempts to achieve greater precision. Probably the best to date resulted from an effort by the National Center on Child Abuse and Neglect to develop definitions that provide a valid basis for collecting data on the incidence of child maltreatment. A summary of the National Center's definitions is provided in Figure 1.1.

In the final analysis, the definition of child maltreatment is always going to be somewhat subjective. Defining child maltreatment is similar to defining pornography, in that it is going to involve the vague test of whether the average person applying community standards would consider an act to be abusive or neglectful. As U.S. Supreme Court Justice Potter Stewart said regarding pornography, "I shall not today attempt further to define the kinds of material I understand to be embraced . . . [b]ut I know it when I see it" (Vacobellis v. Ohio, 1964). Social workers end up in the difficult and uncomfortable spot of having to accurately read community standards and uniformly and accurately apply them.

The Size of the Problem

Child maltreatment is a difficult phenomenon to describe with precise numbers, for several reasons. First, child maltreatment is something that people try to cover up. Ordinarily, a crime is added to statistical records when a victim (or eyewitness) reports the incident. Child maltreatment, on the other hand, gets noted statistically *only if someone reports it*. For this reason, the problem of child maltreatment is seen as analogous to an iceberg, where only a portion is visible and most of it remains hidden (NCCAN, 1988).

Note: An earlier version of this section appears in Philip R. Popple and Leslie Leighninger, *Social Work, Social Welfare, and American Society,* 6th ed. (Boston: Allyn & Bacon, 2005).

| FIGURE 1.1 | Incidents Defined as Child Maltreatment |

Specifically what types of incidents are considered to be sufficiently serious to warrant intervention? A useful list was developed as part of the *National Study of the Incidence and Severity of Child Abuse and Neglect.* The forms of maltreatment identified identified are:

Physical Assault with Bodily Injury

1. Assault with implement (knife, strap, cigarette, etc.)
2. Assault without implement (hitting with fist, biting, etc., or means of assault unknown)

Sexual Exploitation

3. Intrusion (acts involving penile penetration—oral, anal, or genital; e.g., rape, incest)
4. Molestation with genital contact
5. Other or unknown

Other Abusive Treatment

6. Verbal or emotional assault (threatening, belittling, etc.)
7. Close confinement (tying, locking in closet, etc.)
8. Other or unknown

Refusal of Custody

9. Abandonment
10. Other (expulsion, refusal to accept custody of runaway, etc.)

Inattention to Remedial Health Care Needs

11. Refused to allow or provide needed care for diagnosed condition or impairment
12. Unwarranted delay or failure to seek needed care

Inattention to Physical Needs

13. Inadequate supervision
14. Disregard of avoidable hazards in home (exposed wiring, broken glass, etc.)
15. Inadequate nutrition, clothing, or hygiene
16. Other (reckless disregard of child's safety: driving while intoxicated, etc.)

Inattention to Educational Needs

17. Knowingly "permitting" chronic truancy
18. Other (repeatedly keeping child home, failing to enroll, etc.)

Inattention to Emotional/Developmental Needs

19. Inadequate nuturance/affection (e.g., failure to thrive)
20. Knowingly "permitting" maladaptive behavior (delinquency, serious drug/alcohol abuse, etc.)
21. Other

Other

22. Involuntary neglect (due to hospitalization, incarceration, etc.)
23. General neglect (more than two of codes 13–16)

Source: Children's Bureau, U.S. Department of Health and Human Services, *Study Findings, National Study of the Incidence and Severity of Child Abuse and Neglect,* Appendix A, "Data Forms for Child Protective Services Agencies" (Microfiche, September 1988), 50.

Another problem in gaining precise numbers to describe the problem of child maltreatment relates to the previous discussion of the lack of a clear, precise, and universally recognized definition of child maltreatment. This problem has been addressed and, although not totally solved, is moving toward resolution with a set of definitions and statistical reporting procedures being formulated by the federal government called the National Child Abuse and Neglect Data System (NCANDS). The following sections are based on NCANDS reports, and while they do not provide a perfect description, they do help us approximate the size and nature of the problem.

Number of Children Involved

According to NCANDS (2003) reports, 3,058,129 children were investigated by state protective services agencies in 2002 as suspected victims of maltreatment. This figure works out to a rate of approximately 36.6 children per 1,000 U.S. child population. After investigation, 771,791 of these cases were substantiated. An additional 121,803 were *indicated,* a term that means there was enough evidence to warrant suspicion but no actual proof of the allegation. These numbers represent only those cases known to state protective service agencies—the part of the iceberg that is above the water, so to speak. Thus, they represent a substantial underrepresentation of the actual incidence, but how much of an underrepresentation is anyone's guess.

Types of Maltreatment

The NCANDS (2001) data on types of maltreatment are summarized in Figure 1.2. As the graph shows, neglect is by far the most frequently reported type of maltreatment (56 percent of reports). An interesting study by Drake and Johnson-Reid (2000) found that regardless of the reason for an original referral, subsequent referrals were most likely to be for neglect. This leads to the conclusion that neglect is probably present as a secondary problem in nearly all child maltreatment referrals.

Gender

The NCANDS (2001) data show that reports of maltreatment are fairly evenly divided between boys and girls. In 2001, 48 percent of substantiated reports involved boys and 51.5 percent involved girls. The proportion of reports involving girls has

FIGURE 1.2   **Types of Child Maltreatment (Percentages of victims who experienced abuse and neglect, 1999)**

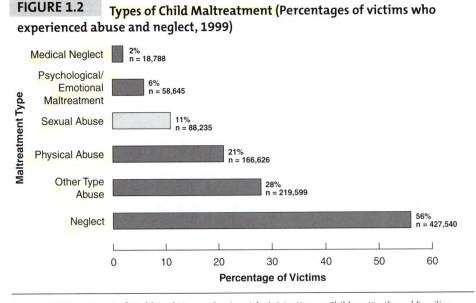

Source: U.S. Department of Health and Human Services Administration on Children, Youth, and Families, *Child Maltreatment 1999: Reports from the States to the National Child Abuse and Neglect Data System* (Washington, DC: U.S. Government Printing Office, 2001).

been increasing in recent years, up from 51.1 percent in 1983, because of the increase in sexual abuse referrals, which predominantly involve female victims.

Social Class

Although it is true that child maltreatment occurs in all social classes, the data indicate that it is most common among families in lower socioeconomic levels. In a 1969 survey of abusive families, Gil (1970) found that nearly 60 percent had been on public assistance at some time and that slightly more than 34 percent were receiving welfare at the time of the report. Today, more than half of the children removed from their homes because of abuse and neglect come from families receiving TANF (i.e., public assistance). Looking at data from the most recent National Incident Study, Lindsey (2004, p. 181) has observed that the likelihood of fatalities and severe injuries to children is highly correlated with poverty. The rate of severe injuries for families with annual incomes below $15,000 was 22 times greater than that for families with incomes above $30,000. The rate for fatalities was 60 times greater for poor families.

These figures have often been rejected, based on the theory that poor people are more susceptible to being reported to public agencies than middle-class people and thus that the figures reflect reporting bias, rather than an actual relationship between socioeconomic class and child maltreatment. However, social scientists have concluded that although poor people may be slightly overreported, it is probable that a greater proportion of poor children are maltreated (Pelton, 1989, pp. 37–42).

Race/Ethnicity

Studies of child maltreatment have consistently found that minority groups are overrepresented. Although approximately 24 percent of the child population of the United States is made up of minority group members, the NCANDS (2001) data indicate that 44 percent of the substantiated reports of abuse and neglect in 2001 involved minority group children. It is generally thought, however, that these figures represent differences in social class, rather than race/ethnicity. One study conducted by the American Humane Association found that when income was controlled for, the maltreatment rate for nonwhite children was actually slightly lower than that for white children (Mayhall & Norgard, 1983, p. 101).

Age

Maltreatment occurs throughout childhood, but clearly, the younger a child is, the greater the danger of serious harm. In the most recent analysis of the NCANDS (2001) data, children in the age group of birth to 3 years accounted for 28 percent of the victims. Overall, the rate of victimization was inversely related to the age of the child.

Trend

Probably the most significant finding of the national studies is not the absolute level of reporting but the extent to which reporting has increased over time. The NCANDS (2001) data show an increase in reports from 2,086,000 in 1986 (34 children per 1,000)

Younger children are at the greatest risk for maltreatment.

to 3,058,129 in 2001 (51 children per 1,000). It is doubtful that these figures represent anywhere near this large an increase in the actual *number* of children being maltreated. Rather, the figures probably reflect factors that increase the likelihood that incidents will be reported, such as the allocation of more federal money for reporting; the strengthening of state reporting laws (physicians, teachers, social workers, and other professionals who work with children are now required to report in all states); the redesign of state social service intake systems; the implementation of 24-hour hotline systems; and the massive public awareness campaigns of the 1970s. The rate of increase in estimates of child maltreatment began to slow in 1990 and appeared to have leveled off by 1994.

Disciplinary Perspectives on Child Maltreatment

In the winter of 1994, the police conducted a drug raid on the apartment of Maxine Melton on Keystone Street on Chicago's West Side. Shapiro (1999) describes what they found:

> There were nineteen children in the apartment.[1] They were crammed, four and five together, on two stained and sheetless mattresses or on the living room floor, near the

---

1. The number of children involved eventually increased to 28; some of the children were not there that particular night (*Chicago Tribune*, February 15, 2004).

radiator, huddled under piles of dirty clothes, under a dirty blanket. They slept in their diapers or underwear. One slept on the floor naked. The children stank of filth. The youngest child was a few months old, and all the rest were under nine, except for a fourteen-year-old who weighed two hundred and eighty pounds and suffered from respiratory problems.

The teenage boy began trying to clean the house, clearing the floor with a snow shovel, hoping that things would not look so bad. Soiled diapers were shoved in the corner. Excrement and toilet paper clogged the single toilet. The bathroom light was out, and the faucet leaked cold water. There was no hot water. There were no towels, soap, or shampoo, and only a single roll of toilet paper. The kitchen sink was piled with dishes caked with spaghetti sauce. The stove was broken and thick with grease. Its door hung open. Cans of lard and some Kool-Aid sat in the pantry. Dripping water stained the bathroom sink black. Cockroaches ran across the floor and in and out of the open boxes of rice and cereal in the pantry. The plaster ceiling was cracked, and the green walls were pocked with holes. . . .

In the living room [police] watched a child sitting on the floor, sharing a chicken neckbone with a dog. In one of the bedrooms, they found the father of one of Maxine's children, lying on a king-size bed, watching television.

Five of the children were Maxine's. Eleven were the children of her four sisters . . . [who] had moved in with their children. So too had Denise Turner, the sister of Maxine's boyfriend, and her three children, one of whom, a four-year-old boy, suffered from cerebral palsy and whose skin was scarred with what the police suspected were cigarette burns. The other mothers were out. Maxine did not know where they had gone, except for her sister Diane, who was, at that moment, in labor at Bethany Hospital. (p. 1)

The Melton case received national attention because a freelance photographer happened to be on the scene and took dramatic videotape footage that he sold to the television networks. The case was consequently followed for years by the press and was the subject of at least one book. Other than the widespread public interest, however, as any child welfare social worker could tell you, the case was not at all unusual.

The question that comes up whenever there is a case like this is, How do we explain situations like that of the Melton sisters and their children? Are the Meltons sick and in need of treatment by physicians and psychologists? Are they evil and in need of spiritual guidance by clergy? Are they simply criminals who should be arrested and jailed? Or are they victims of an unjust and repressive social and economic system that places overwhelming burdens on them without providing resources and opportunities for help? Like the blind men describing different parts of the elephant, the answer depends on whose perspective you use.

The Law Enforcement Perspective

The *law enforcement approach* to child welfare emphasizes the criminal aspect of the problem and calls for the investigation of incidents, the arrest and trial of those responsible, and imprisonment, if the parties are found guilty. As will be discussed in some detail in Chapter 2, the origins of child protective services are in law enforcement. The earliest child welfare workers were deputized agents who had the power to arrest suspects. This was natural and logical because assault on or neglect of a child was a crime. Early in the last century, the primary responsibility for child protection was delegated from law enforcement to social work. Critics of the child welfare system often lament this development, which they attribute to weak-minded liberalism that does not want to hold people accountable for their actions.

The real reason child welfare evolved from a function of law enforcement to a social work function had nothing to do with liberalism. The change was a pragmatic one. Two problems quickly became apparent with the law enforcement approach. The first was that if you arrest and jail a parent or caretaker, you still have the problem of what to do with the child and then what to do when the parent is released from jail and resumes caring for the child. Law enforcement agencies and personnel are neither equipped for nor interested in dealing with these aspects of cases. The second problem that became apparent was that even in cases in which the parents were so deficient that the courts terminated their rights so their child could be placed in some form of adoption or long-term care, there was no way to prevent them from having more children. Every experienced child welfare worker can regale you with stories of working with parents and finally having to go to court to terminate their rights, only to have the parents turn up again five years later with a new set of children, which means having to repeat the whole process.

The evolution of child welfare from law enforcement to social work has not been an unmixed blessing. Two significant problems remain. The first is that social workers, by training and by inclination, are not criminal investigators. Moreover, parents being investigated for child maltreatment are generally not cooperative subjects. They realize they are being investigated for acts that can have criminal or civil consequences, so they try to cover up what they have done. A social worker can easily miss clues and evidence that a trained and experienced criminal investigator would pick up on; the social worker therefore sometimes fails to substantiate a case of abuse and neglect that should have been substantiated. The second problem is that the child welfare social worker is forced to play two roles. First, the social worker arrives at the parents' house wearing an investigator's hat and proceeds to act in what is easily perceived as an intrusive and insulting manner; the worker maybe even takes the parents to court or removes the children. Then later, the social worker comes back wearing a social worker's hat and wants to help the parents; he or she even talks about building a productive relationship with the family. No wonder parents often do not trust social workers or their agencies.

In rural areas, where there is only one child welfare worker to do everything, there is no way around this problem of dual roles. In larger areas, agencies generally deal with the problem by separating the investigation phase of the case process from efforts to help the parents solve the problems that led to agency intervention. As will be discussed in Chapter 10, a case will be assigned to an intake/investigation social worker until the case is either closed as unsubstantiated or substantiated and opened for ongoing service. At the point it is opened, it will be assigned to a new social worker, who will work with the parents to develop a plan to solve the family's problems. This procedure helps to a certain extent, but the problem remains that the new social worker represents the same agency that has accused, investigated, and concluded that the parents are doing something wrong. Thus, the problem of conflicting roles remains. This problem has led to calls to return the investigative phase of child welfare cases to law enforcement agencies and to involve social work agencies only after cases have been investigated and substantiated (Costin, Karger, & Stoesz, 1996; Lindsey, 2004).

The Medical/Psychological Perspective

The medical approach to child maltreatment originated, appropriately enough, with the development of accurate and reliable diagnostic indicators of nonaccidental injuries to children. Prior to around 1950, if a child had an injury or a developmental problem, regardless of how suspicious, authorities had little choice but to accept whatever explanation the parents offered.

In 1946, radiologist John Caffey linked observed series of long bone fractures in children with what he termed some "unspecified origin." Although Caffey (1946) suspected that some intentional infliction of injury might have been related to these fractures, he stopped short of actually specifying abuse as the causal agent. After nine more years of research, Caffey changed his attribution of "unspecified trauma" to "misconduct and deliberate injury" as the primary causative agent of the injuries that his X-rays were revealing.

After physicians developed reliable ways to diagnose nonaccidental injuries to children, they moved toward trying to understand and treat the underlying causes of injuries, causes they assumed to be psychological. They applied the same model to the behavioral problems as they had to the physical problems, an approach known as the *medical*, or *disease, model of deviance*. According to Conrad and Schneider (1992), it "locates the source of deviant behavior within the individual, postulating a physiological, constitutional, organic, or, occasionally, psychogenic agent or condition that is assumed to cause the behavioral deviance" (p. 35). In 1955, P. V. Wooley and W. A. Evans investigated the home situations of a sample of children displaying injuries of unexplained origins and found that the infants "came invariably from unstable households with a high incidence of neurotic or frankly psychotic behavior on the part of at least one adult" (p. 22). In 1960, a pediatrician, C. Henry Kempe (Kempe, Silverman, & Steele, 1962), put together the evidence amassed by radiologists and pediatricians, who were also beginning to be suspicious of parental explanations of strange illnesses and injuries among small children. He coined the term *battered child syndrome* to identify a cluster of nonaccidental injuries to small children.

The conceptualization of child maltreatment as a disease resulted in literally dozens of theoretical schemes developed by physicians, psychologists, social workers, and allied social scientists to attempt to explain and understand this phenomenon. These schemes have ranged from psychoanalytic theory (i.e., reactivation by the child of unresolved conflicts relating to the Oedipal situation, sibling rivalry, sexual identification—a reactivation that threatens the precarious emotional equilibrium of the parents [Kadushin, 1965]), to cognitive behavioral theory (i.e., people who maltreat children believe in harsh discipline, have a negative outlook on life, and have

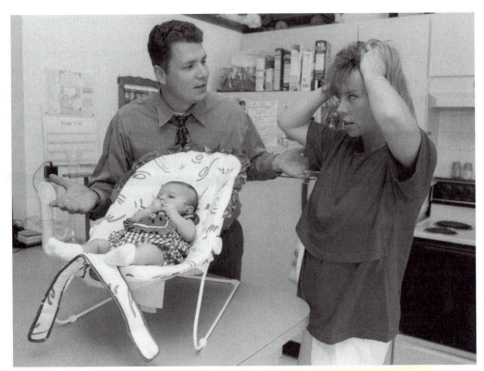

Childrearing problems sometimes result from intrarole conflict, meaning that the parents can't reach agreement on who is supposed to do what for the child.

unrealistic expectations of their children's behavior and accomplishments [Winton & Mara, 2001]), to social exchange theory (i.e., people abuse children when the costs are lower than the rewards and controls are absent; people neglect children when the costs of properly caring for them are greater than the costs of not doing so [Gelles & Cornell, 1990]), and many others.

One theory that has been very influential in child welfare social work was developed by social worker and psychologist Alfred Kadushin (Kadushin & Martin, 1988) using concepts from role theory. Kadushin conceptualizes child welfare problems as a result of eight categories of problems in the role network of parents, children, and community:

1. *Parental role unoccupied.* For any of a large number of reasons, one or both parents are not present in a child's life.
2. *Parental incapacity.* The parent is present and may want to fulfill his or her role requirements but is prevented from doing so by physical, mental, or emotional inadequacy, or by lack of knowledge or training.
3. *Role rejection.* The parent, often because he or she did not want a child in the first place, either consciously or unconsciously rejects the parental role, resulting in varying degrees of failure in role performance.
4. *Intrarole conflict.* In a two-parent family, the parents are in conflict regarding role definitions. They fail to reach agreement about who is supposed to do what

for and with the child. For example, a child is frequently not picked up from school because each parent assumes it is the other's job.

5. *Interrole conflict.* The parent or parents are unable to discharge their childrearing responsibilities because of competition with other social roles. For example, a small child is often left alone until late at night because both parents are at their respective offices finishing up projects.

6. *Role transition problems.* There is a significant change in a parent's role resulting from the death or disability of a spouse, divorce, entering or leaving the job market, or any number of other life changes. Even in strong families, problems result from these role transitions. In families with marginal abilities, such changes can cause serious parenting problems.

7. *Child incapacity or disability.* An exceptional child places exceptional demands on parents. Even the most capable, organized, and well-adjusted parents are greatly taxed by the needs of a child with a physical or mental disability or emotional disturbance. Parents or caretakers whose abilities and resources are marginal will often be unable to meet the challenge.

8. *Deficiency of community resources.* Parents are sometimes unable to adequately fulfill their roles because of a lack of community resources. For example, a parent with a minimum-wage job is going to have a hard time finding adequate and affordable child care arrangements.

The bible of the medical/psychological perspective on any type of deviance is the *Diagnostic and Statistical Manual of Mental Disorders (DSM-IV-Text Revision)*, published by the American Psychiatric Association (2000). For physicians, psychologists, and social workers to collect reimbursement from government agencies and insurance companies for services performed, they must find a diagnosis in the *DSM-IV-TR* to use as the basis of the claim. The authors of the manual classify the problem of child maltreatment as pathological. They do not, however, maintain that child maltreatment constitutes an independent category of mental illness. Rather, they assert that the clinical symptoms seen in child maltreatment cases are already represented by existing disorders such as posttraumatic stress disorder and major depression. The manual does list, under "V" codes, specific disorders related to child maltreatment, including physical abuse of a child, sexual abuse of a child, and neglect of a child. (The V codes are not considered major mental illnesses and diagnoses.)

The medical/psychological perspective on child maltreatment is currently the most widely accepted approach and the perspective adopted by most child welfare social workers. Critics say this perspective places too much responsibility on parents and caretakers, defining them as being in some way sick or otherwise deficient while placing too little responsibility on the social environment in which the problem occurs. These critics expound what is known as a *structural explanation.*

The Structural Perspective

The law enforcement perspective and the medical/psychological perspective both proceed from the assumption that child maltreatment results from and is the responsibility of individuals, generally the child's parents, who have some degree of involvement with the child. The structural perspective looks at factors external to the child and parents to explain the problem. Beckett (2003) observes that child maltreatment takes place within a social context:

> To fully understand child abuse we need to look beyond the particular individuals in-volved, or the particular family, and think about the workings of a society in which individuals and families are only tiny parts. We need to think of things like the way that relationships between adults and children are constructed in this society, for ex-ample, and about the power differences between men and women. Why is it that more abusers are men than women, for example? When looking at abuse involving black children or black adults, we need to consider the question of racism, as well as being aware of the possibility of different norms and expectations. (pp. 19–20)

Structural theorists identify poverty as the primary cause of child maltreatment. Poverty, they say, relates to child maltreatment on two levels: societal and individ-ual. First, consider the level of the whole society. The fact that in 2002, more than 12 million American children lived in poverty—more than 5 million in families with incomes less than one-half of the official poverty line—is seen as an indictment of our whole society for child maltreatment. In Europe, a term that has become popular is *social exclusion,* meaning the poor are excluded from participating as full members of society, with too little access to activities and resources necessary for adequate childrearing.

Second, poverty is seen as a causative agent in child maltreatment on the indi-vidual level. Poor people often cannot afford the things necessary for adequate child care and thus are accused of maltreatment, even though they are doing the best job possible. Examples are numerous. Poor parents are forced to live in unsafe housing because it is all they can afford. Single parents working at minimum wage leave their children home alone because they cannot afford day care or place their children in cheap, unlicensed day care. In order to make ends meet, a poor parent takes in a boarder of unknown character, who may turn out to be a threat to the children. All of these things can subject a parent to charges of child neglect. Parenting is viewed by adherents to the structural perspective as a "catch 22" for poor parents: The par-ent who doesn't keep a job is viewed as neglectful in not supporting the child; the parent who works but does not earn enough to pay for adequate child care is viewed as neglectful for not making better child care arrangements.

Structural theorists recognize that a poor parent has few options for escaping the pressures of parenting: He or she cannot hire a babysitter, cannot send the kids to summer camp, cannot send them to a movie for the afternoon, cannot say yes to a child's demands for money to pay for activities and things the child sees other chil-dren enjoying. The parent gets angry and frustrated, perhaps to the point of abusing the child. The structural perspective maintains that this abuse could be prevented if the community provided more support to its poorest families.

The Social Work Perspective

Social workers have been involved in developing all the perspectives discussed thus far, but when we speak of the *social work perspective* on child maltreatment, we must remember that social work is the profession designated by society to actually manage cases of child maltreatment—that is, to do something about the problem at the individual level.

Police can investigate cases, jail parents and take their kids to the local emergency shelter or foster home, and go on to the next case. Courts can try parents and place them on probation, send them to jail, remove custody of the children, and then turn the whole mess over to the child welfare agency. Physicians can diagnose a case, treat the physical symptoms, and refer the case to the child welfare agency, at which point their involvement is done. Psychologists can test the parents and children, spend 50 minutes a week doing therapy with them, and send them back to the child welfare social worker at the end of each session. However, the ultimate responsibility for managing child welfare cases resides with child protective social workers; thus, their perspective on the problem of child maltreatment has to be pragmatic. During the 100-plus years that social workers have been dealing with child abuse and neglect, the following elements of a coherent perspective have been developed.

CHILD SAFETY   The major responsibility, the number-one rule, of child welfare is to protect children from harm. This is a difficult rule to follow because, as will be discussed in Chapter 4, we do not have any really good, valid, and reliable ways of deciding just how much risk a child is experiencing. Child welfare agencies are criticized much more frequently for leaving children in homes that turn out to be dangerous, even lethal, than for removing children from homes that really aren't very dangerous. The professional response has been that agencies probably err more on the side of removing children who could have safely stayed in the home than on the side of leaving them in a dangerous situation, an approach that has been described by critics as "When in doubt, pull 'em out." O'Conner (2001) has criticized this tendency and encourages social workers to accept that

> mistakes are an inescapable component of the human condition. And insofar as they are inescapable, insofar as they are a function of the limits of human intelligence and strength, they are not morally culpable, no matter how tragic their consequences. No one can be blamed when their best efforts are not enough. We can only be morally culpable when we truly have a choice, when there is something that we could do to help a child, and we know that we could do it, but we simply don't. (p. 317)

The problem is, child welfare social workers are all too aware that if they leave a child in a home—a home they erroneously identify as safe—and the child comes to harm, they will be held morally culpable by the community, in spite of having expended their best efforts.

FAMILY FOCUS   Years of experience have taught social workers three truths about cases of child maltreatment. The first is that although the parents may have done awful things, in most cases, they are not awful people. The vast majority of parents involved in the child welfare system are not abusers or killers; they are simply people who are overwhelmed by problems, who have few resources, and who often have serious personal limitations. As a result, they have great difficulty keeping their children fed, clothed, schooled, and safe. In most cases, they recognize that they have problems and sincerely want to be good parents. The second truth social workers have realized is that nearly all the mistreated children they come in contact with still love their parents and, if removed, want to go home. The third truth is that, except in the rare case of a healthy infant who can be quickly freed for adoption, the alternatives we have to offer children are not much, if indeed any, better than the situations we remove them from.

Given these observations, social workers have concluded that in most cases of child maltreatment, the best plan is this one: Work with the family to improve its level of functioning, and believe that with sufficient help and support the vast majority of parents will have the desire and capacity to care for their children and keep them safe. Shireman (2003) summarizes the social work perspective: "There is no dichotomy between the welfare of the child and the welfare of the family. Every child grows best in his or her own family, if the family can provide proper care. Any policy that supports family life supports the welfare of children." (p. 5).

CULTURAL SENSITIVITY AND COMPETENCE   In the past, protective service intervention with a family was too often a social control activity fueled by hostility toward the practices of minority groups. In the early 1900s, a substantial disproportion of protective service investigations were of families of recent immigrants. In Italian neighborhoods in New York and Boston, a popular game among children was called "cruelty agent." Basically a game of hide-and-seek, the twist was that the person who was "it" pretended to be an agent from the Association for the Prevention of Cruelty to Children (the predecessor to today's child welfare agency, covered in Chapter 2). When this child found the children who were hiding, they pretended they were being taken away from their homes, never to be seen again. Obviously, the people in these neighborhoods considered child protective services to be a culturally insensitive, intrusive, and dangerous force.

Things have changed a great deal in the past 100 years. Child welfare social work now considers cultural competence a major value and professional skill. The ability to speak the languages of other cultures, especially Spanish, is useful to a social worker, and knowledge of and respect for alternative ways of childrearing and family life are considered essential. If a social worker finds a family practicing a culturally different style of childrearing, yet empirical evidence gives no cause to think the practice will result in any absolute harm to the child, the practice is to be tolerated.

There is no clearer example of how the approach of the child welfare system to minority cultures has changed than that of the system's approach to American Indian children. In the not so distant past, these children were frequently removed from their families and sent to Bureau of Indian Affairs' boarding schools, where the primary intent was to stamp out the influence of the child's culture and replace it with the culture of the dominant white Christian society. In 1978, Congress enacted the Indian Child Welfare Act, which was based on the belief that "there is no resource more vital to the continued existence and integrity of the Indian Tribe than their children" and that "an alarmingly high percentage of Indian families are broken up by the removal, often unwarranted, of their children . . . by non-tribal public and private agencies" (Pecora, Whittaker, Maluccio, Barth, & Plotnick, 2000). Through a number of provisions, the act ensures that the culture of the Indian family and their children is respected and protected.

The Role of Child Welfare Social Work in U.S. Society

A number of years ago, there was a long-running TV series called *Mission Impossible*. More recently, there was a movie by the same name, starring Tom Cruise. The premise for these programs was a supersecret government intelligence agency that took on jobs that, while not actually impossible (for the Impossible Mission Force always managed to get them done), were so difficult that they *seemed* impossible.

Carrying out the task of child welfare in U.S. society involves dilemmas, contradictions, and just plain old problems that make it seem like an impossible mission. Primary among the problems are (1) deeply held values that give conflicting messages, (2) society's residual approach to social welfare, (3) preferences for both a family-centered and a child-centered approach to child protection, and (4) unrealistic expectations of what the state can accomplish on behalf of maltreated children.

Conflicting Value Systems

The task of protecting children is mission impossible enough, but U.S. society makes the job even more difficult by placing it at the intersection of two deeply held values—values that are contradictory in this context. The first is our humanitarian–moral orientation, which compels us to take care of those in need and protect the weak when they are mistreated. Williams (1970), in an analysis of American society, concludes that caring for one another, particularly those who are perceived as less fortunate and suffering through no fault of their own, is a key value. This value is behind all our efforts to set up systems to intervene in situations and to correct conditions leading to child suffering.

The second value system that affects our mandate to protect children is the American belief in freedom from unnecessary government interference in our lives. We tend to think the power of the government should be limited. The saying used to be, "We only want government to protect our shores and deliver our mail." With the advent of successful private competitors to the postal service, this can probably be shortened to only wanting government to protect our shores. In any case, we certainly don't want the government involved in our families.

These conflicting value systems create a damned-if-you-do-and-damned-if-you-don't situation for child protective services. Agencies that move aggressively to protect children by removing them from situations deemed to be dangerous are accused of interfering in the private lives of families and oppressing people merely because they are poor.[2] Agencies that work with a family and do not remove a child who ends up being abused are criticized for failing to act in an aggressive and authoritative enough

---

2. See, for example, R. Wexler, "Take the child and run: Tales from the age of ASFA," *New England Law Review*, 36 (October 2002), 129–152; Alliance for Family Rights, *How the state can kidnap your children legally* (New Hampton, NH: Author, no date); and S. Evans, "Presumed abusive: Parents feel mistreated by the system," *Washington Post*, October 13, 1991, pp. B1 & B7.

manner to protect the child.[3] In other words, the child welfare agency that places emphasis on working with families to help them keep their children gets accused of violating our basic humanitarian value of protecting the weak and suffering. And the agency that acts to remove the child to a better place to live is accused of overstepping its bounds and violating our fundamental value of minimal government interference in people's personal lives. Child welfare agencies simply have to live with the reality that, at best, they will be able to please some of the people some of the time.

Child Welfare Based on a Residual Model

In their classic work *Industrial Society and Social Welfare*, Wilensky and Lebeaux (1958) identified two basic societal approaches to social welfare, which they labeled *institutional* and *residual*. Here's their description of the first type:

> [The institutional approach] implies no stigma, no emergency, no "abnormalcy" [on the part of those receiving services]: Social welfare becomes accepted as a proper, legitimate function of modern industrial society in helping individuals achieve self-fulfillment. The complexity of modern life is recognized. The inability of the individual to provide for himself, or to meet all his needs in family and work settings, is considered a "normal" condition; and the helping agencies achieve "regular" institutional status. (pp. 139, 140)

In other words, the institutional conception recognizes that life in modern society is so complex that nearly everyone will need help in dealing with the problems of daily living and that the level of help needed will be beyond the capacity of the basic social institutions of family, church, and market economy. Families cannot provide 100 percent of the care needed by their children; the economy cannot provide 100 percent employment for the entire population at all times; and families and churches cannot care for all the elderly, now that people are living many years past retirement and an ever-increasing proportion of the population is elderly. Social welfare is viewed as a first-line, permanent social institution.

Wilensky and Lebeaux describe the other approach to social welfare, the *residual conception,* as follows:

> [The residual approach is] based on the premise that there are two "natural" channels through which an individual's needs are properly met: the family and the market economy. These are the preferred structures of supply. However, sometimes these institutions do not function adequately: family life is disrupted, depressions occur. Or sometimes the individual cannot make use of the normal channels because of old age or illness. In such cases, according to this idea, a third mechanism of need fulfillment is brought into play—the social welfare structure. This is conceived as a residual agency, attending primarily to emergency functions, and is expected to withdraw when the regular social structure—the family and the economic system—is again working

---

3. See, for example, R. Gelles, *The book of David, How preserving families can cost children's lives* (New York: Basic Books, 1996); KCTS/TV, *The unquiet death of Eli Creekmore* (New York: Filmmakers Library, 1989); R. L. Jones & R. Smothers, "Boys death called new sign of lapses in child welfare system," *New York Times,* March 4, 2004, p. B5.

properly. Because of its residual, temporary, substitute characteristic, social welfare thus conceived often carries the stigma of "dole" or "charity." (p. 139)

In this conception, social welfare is not an institution but an emergency backup system. If the other institutions of society could be made to perform properly—the family to care for its children, the church to care for the less fortunate, and the economy to provide enough jobs for everyone—then social welfare programs would not be necessary.

The child welfare system in the United States is based entirely on the residual model. A child care situation has to become so bad that the child is in actual danger before services are offered to help with the problem. We will discharge an 18-year-old single mother with newborn asthmatic twins from the hospital to an un–air conditioned ghetto apartment in July, with no job and no family to help, and wave "Bye" and say "You be a good mother, now." Two weeks later, when she shows up in the emergency room with the twins in respiratory distress, malnourished, with fleabites, we will declare that she is a bad mother and offer services to try to fix the situation.

Many families with a mentally ill child—even middle-class families with health insurance—have found it necessary to feign abuse or neglect so the state will take custody of the child and provide the services the family cannot afford. It is estimated that one in five families with mentally ill children in the United States has surrendered custody in exchange for treatment of the child (Barovick, 2002). Gutkind (1993) has chronicled the life of the Scanlon family, a family that was nearly destroyed by a mentally ill daughter before the state finally took custody when her middle-class parents could no longer afford her care. He reflects on the results of a residual system:

> How much suffering and misery might have been avoided if the Scanlons had received the respite care for which they were so desperate—just a way to get out of the house a couple of times a week for a quiet dinner without worrying about "World War III" at home? How would their lives have been altered if a caseworker had been available to help Meggan focus upon her studies after school, to help her go to sleep at a reasonable hour without disturbing her parent's privacy, to even awaken her in the morning and help her prepare for school? It is quite possible that after a few months of such intense intervention, at a cost of $5,000 to $6,000, Meggan and her parents could have learned to handle the medications that Meggan had been taking, combined with . . . family therapy, would have been more fruitful. [The state psychiatric hospital] might have been inevitable destination, but surely one needn't attempt the most drastic, last-resort problem-solving approach first. (p. 234)

Because of our residual approach to child protection, by the time a case enters the system, the possibility of significantly improving the situation is slim, for the damage to child and family often is already too great.

Child-Centered versus Family-Centered Approaches to Child Welfare

The problems we have been discussing have led to two opposing views of the proper approach for state intervention with families where child maltreatment is alleged. The first approach is a traditional approach, with roots in the nineteenth-century child-saving movement, and is known as *child-centered policy.* This approach advocates more aggressive government intervention and more emphasis on the permanent removal of children from parents who are deemed to be inadequate.

The leading contemporary advocate of this approach is Richard Gelles, Dean of the University of Pennsylvania School of Social Work and a nationally renowned expert on family violence. An interdisciplinary center has been established at Penn to promote this approach (Hughes, 1999). Gelles's arguments are most cogently laid out in a book in which he traces the death of a child he calls David, who was under the supervision of a state child welfare agency that left him in the care of his parents. The child was eventually murdered by his mother. Gelles (1996) writes:

> Although David had twice been reported as being abused, he remained with his parents. David's death can be traced to the doctrine that requires social service agencies such as the Department of Children and Their Families to make "reasonable efforts" to keep or reunite abused and neglected children with their biological parents. It can also be traced to the larger ideology behind "reasonable efforts," the sacrosanct belief that children *always* (or nearly always) are better off with their biological parents. (p. 9)

Gelles goes on to say that the problem with the U.S. child welfare system

> is a persistent unwillingness to put children *first* . . . both by supporting families so that abuse will not occur in the first place and by absolutely guaranteeing the future safety and developmental integrity of children who have been abused and neglected. (pp. 171–172)

The other approach to providing child welfare services is the *family-centered,* or *family preservation, approach.* It argues that children should be removed from their parents' care only under the most dire of circumstances and even then not until every possible effort has been made to prevent removal. The argument in support of this approach has several related parts. The first is that while there are children who are subjected to severe abuse (and the state should certainly act to protect them from harm), the vast majority of cases involve neglect, rather than abuse—neglect that results from poverty and other external problems. Therefore, the family preservationists argue, we should leave these children in their own homes and work to help their parents obtain the resources they need to adequately care for their children. This approach has the bonus effect of freeing up time and resources for work with the children who do have to be removed.

The second part of the argument for family-based services is child safety. Advocates argue that, far from ensuring a child's safety by foster care placement, we actually place most children in greater danger. Wexler (2002, p. 137), for example, points to national data on child abuse fatalities that show that a child is twice as likely to die of abuse in foster care than in the general population. The third argument for family-based services is the data we discussed earlier on how poorly children who grow up in foster care turn out. The final argument for family-based services is based on data indicating that children who receive intensive services in their homes are as safe as those placed in foster care and that the cost of delivering the services is much less than the cost of placement (Berry, 1992).

Several organizations advocate for a family-based approach to child welfare. The Family Preservation Institute at New Mexico State University, publisher of *Family Preservation Journal*, represents professional social workers and other social scientists. The National Resource Center on Family Based Services is supported by the Administration on Children, Youth, and Families of the U.S. Department of Health and Human Services. Two foundations, the Casey Family Foundation and the Edna McConnell Clark Foundation, have devoted significant resources to promoting family-based services. In addition, there is an independent advocacy group devoted to the promotion of family-based services: the National Coalition for Child Protection Reform. Interestingly, this group seems to have little or no contact with other groups that advocate family-based services. The reason seems to be that the coalition distrusts the professional advocacy groups, thinking them to be part of what Wexler (the coalition's executive director) refers to as the "child welfare establishment." The professional groups say Wexler often comes across as more of an apologist for maltreating parents than an advocate for their children. In any case, it's too bad the groups do not work together, since their agendas are very similar.

To understand these two approaches—child based and family based—we must note the two types of risk faced by a child who is referred to protective services. The first is the risk of harm to the child if left in a home with dangerous or inadequate parents, and the second is the risk of harm to the child if removed from the home when the removal is not absolutely necessary. As we have mentioned in several places, children who are removed from their homes are at risk of abuse and neglect in their new placements, and even children in good placements are still at risk for the serious adjustment and developmental problems of people who grow up in foster care. Child welfare workers at both policy and practice levels tend to be very risk aversive and seek the least risky (though not always the best) plan for a child. O'Connor (2001), in a history of foster care, concluded his work with an interesting observation on risk that social workers would do well to ponder:

> To make a risk-free decision about what to do with this child—or any child—the caseworker would have to combine the wisdom of Solomon with the omniscience of a deity, . . . which is to say there are no risk-free decisions in child welfare. All decisions are based, at least in part, on hunches, educated guesses, superstition, and prejudice. They have to be. And mistakes, inevitably, get made—not just regarding the initial disposition of the child but in every phase of foster care. Even the best trained, most intelligent, diligent, compassionate, and experienced caseworker, with all the best services at her fingertips, can decide to return children to parents who will kill them, or to keep children away from parents whose problems might easily be solved if they were not so distraught at the forced breakup of their family. (p. 322)

As discussed earlier, the vast majority of social workers in child welfare (with the notable exception of those at the University of Pennsylvania) are firmly in the camp of the family-based services group. Years of experience have revealed that for the majority of children referred for protective services, their own homes can usually be made safe, that is where they want to be, and their parents genuinely want to be good parents. For all these reasons, the child's own home is probably the best of a choice of bad alternatives.

The Reality of What Government Intervention Can Accomplish

In most people's minds, child welfare conjures an image of a beautiful infant who has been mistreated by evil, no-good parents. They envision a solution: The state swoops in, removes the child from its evil parents, and places the child in a good home for a happy-ever-after life. While this type of situation does occur, it is rare. The vast majority of cases are much more complex, the children are already seriously damaged when they enter the system, and the amount of good the state can do is limited.

Shapiro (1999) says this fundamental problem in child protective services is the result of

> a debilitating myth that lies at the heart of the state's failure [to help maltreated children], the myth that the state can save a child, that it can give that child an ideal life in which the past, awful as it might have been, does not exist. The state tries to do this by severing the relationship between a child and the parents who failed him. That well-intentioned but naïve mistake sets in motion many of the other mistakes the state makes when it tries to help children. (p. xii)

There is evidence that the children who come into the child welfare system are increasingly troubled by physical and mental illness. Shapiro asserts that "local child welfare agencies can do little to assist these children because virtually all the money they get from Washington must be spent on housing and feeding them" (p. xiv). There is evidence that even when agencies do have money, many children, by the time they enter the system, are so disturbed that the agencies have no great success. It is estimated that Los Angeles County spends $276,000 per child per year at MacLaren Children's Center, a shelter that houses 156 of Los Angeles's most troubled young people. The center is supposed to provide only 30 days of care while a child is evaluated and treated and a suitable long-term placement found. But many of the children stay for more than a year, and second, third, and even fourth stays are common. Humes (2003) reports, "The children tend to be so ill, violent, and difficult to control after years of abuse that better-equipped facilities—including mental hospitals, which can use drugs and physical restraints—frequently refuse them outright or bounce them back to the center at the first opportunity" (p. 65).

Social workers have long been aware that foster care is a far from ideal place for children to grow up. Two recent studies—one by the Pew Commission (2004) and one by the Chapin Hall Center for Children (Courtney, Terao, & Bost, 2004)—have reconfirmed just how great the problems are. Foster care is supposed to be a temporary situation, but the studies found that many children languish in foster care for five or more years. Each year, 20,000 children "age out" of foster care—that is, reach their eighteenth birthdays and legally become adults without first returning to their own homes. The statistics describing the lives of these young people can only be described as grim: They experience mental health problems at three times the rate of a comparable national sample; one-quarter have been tested or treated for sexually transmitted diseases, more than four times the rate of the national sample; two-thirds of the males and one-half of the females have been arrested, convicted of a crime, or sent to a correctional facility; nearly 40 percent fail to graduate from high school and over one-half read at below the seventh-grade level; and nearly 40 percent end up on welfare (Heyman & Fowler, 2002).

One true characteristic of Americans is that we don't like problems that can't be solved. And while we are willing to devote resources and energy to a problem for a period of time, if our money and efforts do not yield a cure, we quickly become disillusioned and want to move on to some other task. Unfortunately, the problems of child welfare cannot be cured, no matter how we view them: as an aggregate problem or individual situations. The best we can do is manage the problems, try to make the lives of children and families a little better, deal with problems of child maltreatment so extended families and neighbors do not have to, and understand all the while that there will be only few examples we can hold up to the world as triumphs. The problems faced by child welfare are not the quick-fix kind Americans like to tackle, which makes the task of child welfare lonely work.

A Final Word

Remember our friends Robert and Kathy, who were watching TV at the beginning of the chapter? Well, Kathy should have stayed up to see the end of the *NYPD Blue* episode, for she would have liked it.

In the last scene, the detectives have called the young mother in and once again have her in the interview room. One says to her, "We're sorry to have to tell you this, but your daughter is dead. She was sent to live with a family in Ohio and she caught pneumonia and died. You could be in big trouble for failing to make better arrangements for your daughter, but we're going to cut you a break. If you get out of here and never mention this to anyone, we won't tell your probation officer and you won't go back to prison. But you can't ever tell anyone about this and you can't ever ask anyone about your daughter."

The mother looks distraught and then demonstrates her total unworthiness as a parent by saying, "Well, can you give me a letter or something for the welfare office. I mean, there must be a death benefit or something that I am eligible for."

The detectives look disgusted and tell her, "Just get out of here, and never say anything to anyone."

Fortunately or unfortunately, as we have tried to demonstrate in this chapter, child welfare is never so clear and simple. In the real world, the police, as representatives of the state, would have had to refer the situation to child protective services. The agency would have first looked at the case to determine if it fit the definition of child maltreatment. They would have assessed the case in terms of law enforcement: Were any crimes committed, and if so, should the perpetrators be pursued? Next, they would have applied the medical/psychological approach: Is anything wrong with the child, her informal foster parents, or her biological mother, and if so, what resources and services are necessary to fix the problems? The structural perspective would enter the equation when someone, probably the biological mother's lawyer, accused the state of sending the mother to prison knowing she had a child yet did nothing to ensure the child was well taken care of.

Overlaying the whole case would be whether the child welfare agency believed in child-centered or family-centered services. A child-centered agency would probably have placed the child, perhaps with the family with whom she had been living, and required that the biological mother jump through all sorts of hoops before they would agree to place the child in her care. A family-centered agency would have tried to return the child to the biological mother and provide whatever services in whatever intensity were necessary to enable her to provide a home for the child.

No matter which choices the child welfare agency made, a number of points would have been clear: Nothing was simple, no choice was obvious, and no matter what was done, not everyone would be happy.

REFERENCES

American Psychiatric Association. (2000). *Diagnostic and statistical manual of mental disorders* (IV-Text revision). Washington, DC: Author.

Barovick, H. (2002, October 28). The secret sacrifice. *Time,* 52.

Beckett, C. (2003). *Child protection: An introduction.* London: Sage.

Berry, M. (1992). An evaluation of family preservation services: Fitting agency services to family needs. *Social Work, 37,* 314–321.

Caffey, J. (1946, August) Multiple fractures of the long bones of infants suffering from chronic subdural hematoma. *American Journal of Roentology, 56,* 163–173.

Child Abuse Prevention and Treatment Act (CAPTA) as amended by Keeping Children and Families Safe Act of 2003, 42 U.S.C.A. Sec. 5106g.

Conrad, P., & Schneider, J. W. (1992). *Deviance and medicalization: From badness to sickness.* Philadelphia: Temple University Press.

Costin, L. B., Karger, H. J., & Stoez, D. (1996). *The politics of child abuse.* New York: Oxford University Press.

Courtney, M., Terao, S., & Bost, N. (2004). *Midwest evaluation of the adult functioning of former foster youth: Conditions of youth preparing to leave care.* Chicago: Chapin Hall Center for Children.

Drake, B., & Johnson-Reid, M. (2000, October). *Recidivism in child protective services.* Paper presented at the George Warren Brown School of Social Work Seventy-fifth Anniversary Conference, St. Louis, MO.

Ellis, M. B. (1929). Child welfare. In F. S. Hall (Ed.), *Social work yearbook* (pp. 68–70). New York: Russell Sage Foundation.

Gelles, R. J. (1996). *The book of David: How preserving families can cost children's lives.* New York: Basic Books.

Gelles, R. J., & Cornell, C. P. (1990). *Intimate violence in families* (2nd ed.). Newbury Park, CA: Sage.

Gil, D. (1970). *Violence against children: Physical abuse in the United States.* Cambridge, MA: Harvard University Press.

Gutkind, L. (1993). *Stuck in time: The tragedy of childhood mental illness.* New York: Henry Holt.

Heyman, J. D., & Fowler, J. (2002, January 20). Sink or swim: At 18, most foster kids are pushed out of the system. *People, 59,* 66.

Hughes, S. (1999, May/June). The children's crusaders. *Pennsylvania Gazette*, 22–28.

Humes, E. (2003, January). The unwanted. *Los Angeles Magazine, 48*, 64–73.

Kadushin, A. (1965). Introduction of new orientations in child welfare research. In M. Norris & B. Wallace (Eds.), *The known and unknown in child welfare research: An appraisal* (pp. 28–39). New York: Child Welfare League of America.

Kadushin, A., & Martin, J. (1988). *Child welfare services*. New York: Macmillan.

Kamerman, S. B., & Kahn, A. (1990). If CPS is driving child welfare—where do we go from here? *Public Welfare, 48*, 9–13.

Kempe, C. H., Silverman, F. N., Steele, B. F., Droegemueller, W., & Silver, H. K. (1962, July). The battered child syndrome. *Journal of the American Medical Association, 181*, 17–24.

Korbin, J. (1987). Child abuse and neglect: The cultural context. In R. E. Helfer & C. H. Kempe (Eds.), *The battered child* (4th ed., pp. 23–41). Chicago: University of Chicago Press.

Liederman, D. (1995). Child welfare overview. In R. L. Edwards (Ed.), *Encyclopedia of social work* (19th ed., pp. 424–432). Washington, DC: NASW Press.

Lindsey, D. (2004). *The welfare of children* (2nd ed.). New York: Oxford University Press.

Mayhall, P. D., & Norgard, K. E. (1983). *Child abuse and neglect: Sharing responsibility*. New York: John Wiley and Sons.

National Center on Child Abuse and Neglect. (1988). Levels of recognition of child abuse and neglect. In *Study of national incidence and prevalence of child abuse and neglect—1988*. Washington, DC: Government Printing Office.

National Child Abuse and Neglect Data System (NCANDS), U.S. Department of Health and Human Services; Administration on Children, Youth and Families. (2003). *Child maltreatment 2001*. Washington, DC: Government Printing Office.

O'Conner, S. (2001). *Orphan trains: The story of Charles Loring Brace and the children he saved and failed*. Boston: Houghton Mifflin.

Pecora, P., Whittaker, J. K., Maluccio, A., Barth, R. P., & Plotnick, R. P. (2000). *The child welfare challenge: Policy, practice, and research*. New York: Aldine de Gruyter.

Pelton, L. H. (1981). Child abuse and neglect: The myth of classlessness. In L. H. Pelton (Ed.), *The social context of child abuse and neglect* (pp. 22–38). New York: Human Sciences Press.

Pelton, L. H. (1989). *For reasons of poverty: A critical analysis of the public child welfare system in the United States*. New York: Praeger.

Pew Commission on Children in Foster Care. (2004). *Fostering the future: Safety, permanence and well-being for children in foster care*. Washington, DC: Author.

Popple, P. R. & Leighninger, L. (2005). *Social work, social welfare, and American society* (6th ed.). Boston: Allyn & Bacon.

Purdum, T. S. (1987, November 3). Manhattan couple are charged in beating of 6-year-old daughter. *New York Times*, 1.

Shapiro, M. (1999). *Solomon's sword: Two families and the children the state took away*. New York: Times Books.

Shireman, J. (2003). *Critical issues in child welfare*. New York: Columbia University Press.

Trattner, W. I. (1999). *From poor law to welfare state: A history of social welfare in America* (6th ed.) New York: Free Press.

Trice, D. T. (2004, February 15) Rescued from neglect, 5 brothers find hope. *Chicago Tribune*, 1.

Vacobellis v. Ohio, 378 U.S. 184, 197 (1964).

Wells, S. J. (1995). Child abuse and neglect overview. In R. L. Edwards (Ed.) *Encyclopedia of social work* (19th ed., pp. 346–352). Washington, DC: NASW Press.

Wexler, R. (2002, October). Take the child and run: Tales from the age of ASFA. *New England Law Review, 36*, 129–152.

Wilensky, H. L., & Lebeaux, C. N. (1958). *Industrial society and social welfare.* New York: Russell Sage Foundation.

Williams, R. (1970). *American society: A sociological interpretation* (3rd ed., pp. 454–500). New York: Alfred A. Knopf.

Winston, M. A., & Mara, B. A. (2001). *Child abuse and neglect: Multidisciplinary approaches.* Boston: Allyn & Bacon.

Wooley, P. V., & Evans, W. A. (1955, September). Significance of skeletal lesions in infants resembling those of traumatic origin. *Journal of the American Medical Association, 181*, 17–24.

CHAPTER **2**

Child Welfare in the United States: A Brief History

In April 1874, the *New York Times* was reporting to an outraged city. Neighbors had reported to a church worker that 6-year-old Mary Ellen Wilson was in need of help. They reported that "her present custodians have been in the habit of beating her cruelly, the marks of which are visible on her person; that her punishment was so cruel and frequent as to attract the attention of the residents in the vicinity, . . . that not only was she cruelly beaten, but rigidly confined" (April 10, 1874). Upon investigation, it was established that she had been beaten with a long cane and a braided leather whip, and she had been cut with a pair of scissors (April 11, 1874).

The police removed Mary Ellen from her home and arrested her primary caretaker, Mrs. Connolly. At Mrs. Connolly's trial, the *Times* reported that the judge "would have been satisfied if the jury had found her guilty of [a] higher offense. . . . As a punishment to herself, but more as a warning to others, he would sentence her to the extreme penalty of the law—one year in the Penitentiary at hard labor. The prisoner heard her sentence without moving a muscle, and preserved the same hard, cruel expression of countenance displayed by her during the trial, while conveyed to the Tombs" (April 14, 1874).

Horrified by this case in specific, the *Times* was encouraged by it in general. The case provided an opportunity for Henry Bergh, founder of the Society for the Prevention of Cruelty to Animals, to "enlarge his sphere of usefulness." The *Times* reported that the case provided evidence that "Mr. Bergh does not confine the humane impulse of his heart to smoothing the pathway of brute creation toward the grave or elsewhere, but he embraces within the sphere of his kindly efforts the human species also" (April 28, 1874). The *Times* saw in this a sign that U.S. society was entering an era in which children would be protected from the cruelty and ineptness of their parents.

Fast forward more than 100 years to 1987, and once again, the *Times* is reporting to an outraged city. The paper has reported that the police, responding to a 911 call, went to the apartment of Joel Steinberg and Hedda Nussbaum. Upon arrival, they found 6-year-old Elizabeth battered and barely breathing and a younger boy "in urine soaked clothes and tethered by twine in a playpen in the dark and filthy apartment" (November 31, 1987). The children were removed from the home and the parents arrested. A few days later, Elizabeth, known as Lisa, died as a result of her injuries.

The parents were charged with murder, and the father was eventually sentenced to life in prison. The *Times* expressed horror in specific and in general. In article after article, they questioned why the system that had begun in response to Mary Ellen Wilson had failed to protect Lisa Steinburg (November 4, 1987; November 5, 1987; November 6, 1987; November 7, 1987). With shock and dismay, the paper reported the New York City Human Resources Commissioner as saying, "I don't think a government agency is responsible every time something goes wrong in a person's private life" (November 9, 1987).

Some people believe that "If you do not know your history, you are doomed to repeat it." That is probably not true. However, it is certain that if you do not know your history, you will miss the chance to learn anything from it and, as a consequence, will probably repeat your mistakes.

With the practice of child welfare in this twenty-first century, we are desperately in need of lessons. The two series of *New York Times* stories poignantly illustrate our history. Our commitment to protect children has turned into a much more complex, difficult, and expensive mission than we ever could have imagined. Moreover, we have lost our innocence and are facing what has become a nightmare of complexities.

In this chapter, we present the history of child welfare organized in a roughly chronological fashion but a chronology in which certain themes clearly emerge like the threads of a tapestry. The first theme, the one that provides the unifying background for the tapestry, is child welfare as an issue of social order. Regardless of whether we care about children, view children as beings with innate rights, or are concerned with the problems of children's families, children must be attended to at a certain level to prevent social chaos. Children without care and supervision tend to roam the streets and countryside. They beg, steal, prostitute themselves, and engage in a remarkable range of generally dangerous and unpleasant behaviors. From the earliest point in history, it has been necessary to pay some attention to the welfare of children in order to safeguard the welfare of everyone else.

The second thread in the tapestry is the emergence of a changing conception of *childhood*. In the earliest definitions, childhood was not even viewed as a separate stage of life worthy of mention. Even after childhood was defined, many years passed before children were viewed as individuals with rights independent of their fathers. Obviously, until recognition of childhood as a particular stage of life, a stage that entailed some rights to care and protection, child welfare was not even a blip on the social radar screen.

Once childhood and its associated rights were recognized, the third thread emerged. This thread dealt with the rights of children and the responsibility of society to protect those rights. Throughout history, the family was considered a sacred sphere, and except in cases of capital murder, the intervention of government or any other outsiders was unthinkable.

Once we accept the right of, even the necessity for, outside intervention in the family, the two final threads appear simultaneously: What services should be provided to mistreated children, and who should be responsible for providing them? Should services be provided by the government or by private groups? And where does child welfare fit into the profession of social work? The question of which services we should provide was quickly followed by which services we could afford to provide.

A good number of years have passed since we accepted our right and responsibility to protect children, and now in this twenty-first century, we come face to face with twin realities. First, we have barely scratched the surface of the knowledge needed to effectively intervene in children's lives. Second, the problem is huge and the solution costly—much more so than we anticipated.

We can view these themes in a rough chronology, so long as we keep in mind that one does not disappear as the next appears. Once a theme emerges, it stays with us, in ever-changing form, with the next one layered upon it, making the problem of child welfare ever more complex. The social definition of childhood is constantly being reevaluated. Our beliefs regarding the rights of children—vis-à-vis the rights of parents, vis-à-vis the right of society to intervene—have been the subject of constant debate since they emerged in the past century. The public and private split in responsibility for children's services changes frequently and not always in the same direction. There are frequent shifts in how the profession of social work is believed to relate to child welfare, in particular public child welfare. And finally, we have been debating proper intervention approaches for most of a century, and the major things we have learned are how complex the questions are and how little we really know.

Child Welfare as a Problem of Social Order

Prior to the nineteenth century, there was little concern for the well-being of children, aside from concern over the threat that children without supervision posed to the social order. People were concerned with children to the extent that children roaming

The apprenticeship system partially solved the problem of what to do with dependent children prior to the twentieth century.

the streets and countryside, free from parental supervision, created a number of social problems—mostly, crime and begging—which interfered with the welfare of adults. The two major social responses to the problem of children without care and supervision were apprenticeship and the poorhouse.

The Apprenticeship System

Dependent children were a part of colonial America almost from the time of the first settlers. Some children were sent to America because they had no parents, and others became orphans in the course of the voyage or shortly thereafter when their parents succumbed to the rigors of pioneer life. The colonial settlers dealt with these children through the *apprenticeship, or indenture, system*, which they transplanted from England. Under this system, an adult entered into a contract with a child's parents or, in the case of an orphan, with a governmental unit generally known as "overseers of the poor." The adult, known as the *master*, agreed to provide the child with food, clothing, shelter, a rudimentary education, and training in the skills of a trade. Boys generally learned the trade of their masters, while girls usually learned housekeeping skills in their masters' homes. The children were expected to work for their masters until they reached the agreed-upon age in return for the care and training they received. The apprenticeship system served a social welfare function by solving the problem of what to do with dependent children. It was, however, fundamentally an economic arrangement. An indenture agreement typically included some protection against cruelty, but that protection was minimal and fit the standards of the time. Historian LeRoy Ashby (1997) quotes an author of the time: "If one beats a child until it bleeds," according to a common-law rule of thumb, "then it will remember the words of its master. But if one beats it to death, then the law applies" (pp. 6–7).

In the nineteenth century, the indenture system began to decline. In the early 1800s, apprenticeship ceased to be seen as an appropriate arrangement for children from the middle class and became almost exclusively a response to poor children. In the mid 1800s, the level of care that masters were expected to provide began to increase. Masters were required to provide children with more formal schooling than had been required in the past. Also, as the industrial system replaced independent craftsmen, the use of apprenticeship as a means of job training declined. By the end of the century, indenture contracts were rare.

The Poorhouse

As apprenticeship declined as an efficient response to child dependency, the first response was to treat orphans in the same manner as other dependent people: place them in county poorhouses. An influential report written in 1824 by New York's Secretary of State John Yates confidently asserted that the poorhouse could rescue children who would otherwise "grow up in filth, idleness, ignorance and disease, and . . . become early candidates for prison or the grave" (Ashby, 1997, p. 23). The report stated that 2,604 children were living in poorhouses New York.

It was not long before reformers began to criticize poorhouses as a response to child dependency. The thrust of the criticism was that in poorhouses, children grew up in the company of elderly, alcoholic, sick, insane, and feeble-minded people. A visiting committee of the New York State Charities Aid Association described the plight of children in the Westchester County Poorhouse in 1873 as follows:

> The children, about sixty in number, are in the care of a pauper woman, whose daughter and whose daughter's child, both in the poorhouse, make her one of three generations of paupers. The daughter assists in the care of the children. She has a contagious disease of the eyes, which is, apparently, communicated to them. The children are neither properly clothed nor fed; but saddest of all is to see the stolid look gradually stealing over the faces of these little ones, as all joy of their lives is starved out of them. (Bremner, 1971, p. 251)

With conditions such as these, it is not surprising that a call for reform began. The Charities Aid Association report continued:

> To think what these children must grow up to, what they must become, if they are not soon removed from this atmosphere of vice. . . . Alas! We know only too well what becomes of children who live and grow up in the poorhouses. (Bremner, 1971, p. 251)

In response to the scandal of children growing up in poorhouses in New York, an Act to Provide for the Better Care of Pauper and Destitute Children was passed in 1875. This act made it unlawful for any child over 3 and under 16 years of age to be committed to a county poorhouse, "unless such child is an unteachable idiot, an epileptic or paralytic, or . . . otherwise defective, diseased, or deformed, so as to render it unfit for family care" (Bremner, 1971, p. x). As with apprenticeship, the poorhouse approach declined as the conception of children and childhood changed.

The Emergence of Concern for Children

Historian Catherine Ross (1980) notes, regarding the history of child maltreatment, "The crucial historical questions include what behavior toward children people in the past viewed as correct, and how communities responded when adults mistreated children" (p. 63). Shocking to our modern sensibilities is the observation that until the nineteenth century, nearly any behavior toward children by a parent or other authorized caretaker was viewed automatically as correct. When children were mistreated, even by the standards of the day, the community response usually was to turn a blind eye.

Childhood Prior to Industrialization

The relative lack of concern with the protection of children prior to modern times is noted in two related factors: the perception of the nature of childhood and beliefs regarding the rights of parents. Childhood was perceived generally as an inconvenient period of life that one simply had to get through in order to begin the duties of living as an adult. Adults tended to view children as noisy animals who should, to the greatest extent possible, stay out of sight of their parents and other adults. An early author on childhood explained, "Only time can cure a person of childhood and youth, which are truly ages of imperfection in every respect" (Aries, 1962, p. 130). Children in Europe and probably even more so in colonial America were viewed as products of original sin and were suspected of being possessed of an inherently sinful nature. One of the primary tasks expected of parents and other caretakers was the suppression of this sinful nature—for the child's own good, as well as for the good of society. Harsh discipline was not only viewed as acceptable, but to fail to severely punish a child was seen as a dereliction of parental duty. When King Louis XIII of France, born in 1601, was a small child, his father wrote to his caretakers; "You do not send word that you have whipped my son. I wish and command you to whip him every time he is obstinate or misbehaves" (Ross, 1980, pp. 65–66). In colonial America, Puritan parents sometimes sent their children to be raised by servants because they feared that they loved the children too much to provide proper parenting—namely, being willing to subject the children to severe physical punishment.

Prior to industrialization, not only was severe physical punishment considered appropriate but parents were accorded the right to do almost anything they wished with their children. In ancient Greece, a child was the absolute property of the father, who, on the fifth day after birth, would decide whether the child would live or die. If the father did not want the child, perhaps due to poverty or often because the child was female and therefore considered of little value, the child was killed, generally through exposure. Under Roman law, the father had the power of life or death over his children into adulthood under the legal principle of *patria potestas* (i.e., the state as the ultimate parent to all citizens) (Thomas, 1972, pp. 294–295).

Some restrictions were placed on the rights of parents well before the advent of industrialization, but these were minimal. In Rome, the doctrine of *patria potestas* evolved so that no child could be killed before the age of 3, and infanticide against male children was prohibited, since the state valued male children as future soldiers. Later, all infanticide was prohibited, although it remained permissible to sell a child into slavery. The development and increasing influence of Judaism, Christianity, and Islam led to a significant decrease in the acceptance of infanticide. The early Christian church preached against infanticide, and the church became a place where a desperate mother could abandon her infant with the knowledge that the clergy would find a place for the child with someone in the parish.

In colonial America, the doctrine of *paren patrias* theoretically gave the government the right to intervene in the relations between parents and children. This, in fact, rarely happened, and when it did, the intervention was generally not aggressive. Ashby (1997) reports:

> In all of colonial New England's court, . . . only one natural father faced child abuse charges. The Essex County court convicted Michael Emerson of "cruel and excessive beating of his daughter." He had kicked the 11-year-old and beaten her with a stick used to thresh grain. Even then, the court reduced his fine six months later and settled for a bond of good behavior. (p. 13)

In colonial America, the main duty of parenthood was seen as teaching children discipline, the value of hard work, and the rudiments of a trade. Harsh discipline was often necessary for this task, and modern concepts of nurturing were not in evidence. Hacsi (1995) observes that the modern welfare system " is populated by children who are deemed neglected by standards of child care that would have seemed very strange to colonial parents" (p. 164).

Just how bad the plight of children actually was prior to industrialization is not really clear, although there is little doubt that it was bad by modern standards. Some scholars of childhood, such as psychohistorian Lloyd deMause and psychologist Gertrude Williams, assert that childhood prior to modern times was a hellish nightmare. DeMause (1975) says,

> A child's life prior to modern times was uniformly bleak. Virtually every tract from antiquity to the modern century recommended the beating of children. We found no examples from this period in which a child wasn't beaten, and hundreds on instances of not only beating, but battering, beginning in infancy. (p. 85)

Williams (1980a) states,

> Since time immemorial children have been treated with incredible cruelty. . . . Children have been tortured, burned, worked to death, terrorized, and flogged daily in order to "discipline" them, dipped in ice water and rolled in the snow in order to "harden" them, and buried alive with their dead parents. (p. 9)

On the other hand, there are those who argue that childhood was probably not so bad. Excessive cruelty to children may have been relatively infrequent, at least in colonial Puritan communities, according to historian John Demos (1986), because of "the twin principles of mutual support and mutual surveillance" (p. 84). It is clear, however, that children had few rights, parents had near total power, and the state chose rarely if ever to intervene on behalf of children. For example, between 1633 and 1802 in Plymouth, Massachusetts, not a single court case concerned violence against children (Pleck, 1987, p. 13).

The Changing Conception of Childhood

The way children were perceived and feelings about social responsibility for children underwent a radical transformation during the nineteenth century. However, the reasons are not entirely clear. It appears that three interrelated trends contributed to this transformation: (1) the lengthening of childhood, (2) a gradually changing conception of childhood, and (3) the breakdown of the ability of traditional social institutions—the family, the church, and the indenture system—to manage child dependency.

THE LENGTHENING OF CHILDHOOD   Before industrialization, childhood was relatively short because in rural agricultural environments, children became economically useful and began to fulfill adult roles at young ages. On a farm, where most children grew up, a 5 or 6-year-old would be a productive part of the family: gathering eggs, weeding the garden, and taking lunch to the workers in the fields. Children's economic value quickly exceeded their costs. Higgeson wrote in his 1629 *New England Plantation* (cited in Bossard & Boll, 1960) that "little children here by setting of corne may earn much more than their own maintenance" (p. 613). Sociologists Bossard and Boll add that "children, little children, worked hard. But adults worked hard too. Hard work was a colonial necessity for both. The struggle for existence in the New World was a stern reality" (p. 614).

In a similar fashion, the level of technology in the shops and homes where urban children were apprenticed was such that many useful tasks could be accomplished by even a small child. Thus, children both on farms and in urban areas became productive and assumed adult functions at an early age. Today's definition of *childhood*—a lengthy period of immaturity and dependence before the assumption of adult responsibilities—did not exist until well into the 1800s.

THE DEVELOPMENT OF A CHANGED CONCEPTION OF CHILDHOOD   Prior to the nineteenth century, children were viewed, at best, as miniature adults. In many homes, they were thought of as products of original sin, possessed of evil impulses, and likely to run wild if not strictly controlled. Few people felt that children needed protection or that they had any right to protection.

During the 1800s in the United States, a marked change in the attitude toward children began. The change in attitude evolved into a conception of children as beings who had unique needs and the right to have those needs fulfilled to a reasonable extent. Zelizer (1985) documents in her book *Pricing the Priceless Child* how during the nineteenth century, the concept of the "useful" child who made a valuable contribution to the family economy gradually evolved into the "useless" child of the twentieth century: the child who is economically worthless, in fact, very costly to the family, but is considered to be emotionally priceless. The reasons for this transformation included the decline in useful tasks that could be performed by children in a maturing industrial economy, the decline of the birth and death rates, and the rise of the compassionate family.

THE BREAKDOWN OF THE ABILITY OF THE EXTENDED FAMILY AND THE CHURCH TO MANAGE CHILD DEPENDENCY   Before the Industrial Revolution, which took hold in the United States during the mid-nineteenth century, family and child problems were more or less adequately dealt with by the basic social institutions of the extended family and the church, supplemented by the practice of indenture. An orphaned child would generally be taken in by a member of the extended family or a church family, or the child would be placed in an apprenticeship. If the parents were mentally or physically ill, the extended family, church, or community would step in to ensure that the child's care did not sink too far below an adequate level.

With the onset of heavy industrialization, the family, church, and community were no longer able to handle child dependency. An ever-increasing number of people lived in cities far from their extended families. In addition, they were marginally involved in church, if at all, and many had little knowledge of or concern for their neighbors. The first visible symptom of the breakdown in the ability of the family and the church to handle child dependency was a vast and rapid increase in the number of homeless children. Fry (1974) notes,

> The numbers were immense. At a time when New York City's population was around five hundred thousand, the police estimated that there were ten thousand homeless children wandering about. Later, after close observation [social workers] came to the conclusion that the number ran as high as thirty thousand. (p. 4)

This large number of children was, of course, cause for concern. Fry continues,

> Ragged, verminous, barefoot, the vagrant children slept where they could: in door ways, under stairways, in privies, on hay barges, in discarded packing boxes, and piles of rubbish in alleys and littered back yards. The older boys often became members of street gangs who terrified respectable citizens when they weren't bashing one another's head in; many of the girls were accomplished streetwalkers by the time they were twelve or thirteen years old. (p. 5)

The Beginning of Children's Services

As the nineteenth century unfolded, childhood lengthened as a result of industrialization. A child had to be older to do the work of an urbanized industrial age. We can trace the beginnings of our child welfare system to this period, when the question of childhood and social problem management came into focus due to the many homeless children perceived as threats to social stability.

A parallel change was occurring in how the citizenry viewed childhood. People began to see children as beings with innate value and unique needs—and with certain rights to have those needs fulfilled. Once children were recognized as having some rights and society began to accept responsibility for acting toward children in accord with those rights, the problem of child welfare became infinitely more complex. Three great movements developed in the 1800s to address the concern for children: orphanages, child protective services, and foster family care.

The Development of Orphanages

The first major response targeted specifically at the problem of child dependency was the development of *orphanages*. A few orphanages had been established prior to the nineteenth century: a home for girls in New Orleans established by the Ursuline Sisters in 1729; the Bethesda House for Boys founded near Savannah, Georgia, in 1740; and the Charleston Orphans Home, opened in 1790 in Charleston, South Carolina. These early orphanages were, for the most part, anomalies, established in response to specific events such as plagues and Indian wars. They did not constitute a social movement. But shortly after the turn of the nineteenth century, the number of orphanages and the number of residents in them increased at a rapid rate.

The idea of the orphanage and the rapid spread of orphanages resulted primarily from two factors: the decline of the indenture system and a belief in the institution as a way of handling social problems. This era saw the establishment of large prisons to deal with crime, poorhouses to deal with the destitute, and specialized schools such as those for the blind and deaf. These were congregate settings where the environments could be strictly controlled and, theoretically at least, the problems adjusted.

Early criticism of the poorhouse as a response to child dependency did not in any way constitute an attack on the belief in institutions as desirable solutions for social problems. Rather, the preferred solution of critics was to remove children from poorhouses and place them in specialized children's institutions. Thus, the orphanages developed. In the United States, 150 private orphanages were established between 1820 and 1860: 11 in the 1820s, 36 in the 1830s, 39 in the 1840s, and 64 in the 1850s. The growth was temporarily slowed by the Civil War but then resumed at an even faster rate, with 600 orphanages in operation by the 1890s (Ashby, 1997, p. 28). The number of children residing in these facilities grew from 200 in 1790 to 123,000 in 1910 (Downs & Sherraden, 1983, p. 275). The number of children residing in these facilities continued to grow until well into the twentieth century. By the mid 1930s, the children's home population reached its high point, housing approximately 144,000 children. From this time, the population of orphanages declined—to 95,000 in 1951, 63,000 in 1970, and continually less thereafter.

A significant point to be made about orphanages in the United States is that, contrary to their name, they housed relatively few true orphans. From about 1880 to 1900, 45 percent of the population of the Albany Orphan Asylum had two living parents, 45 percent were "half-orphans" (had one living parent), and only about 10 percent were actually orphans (Dulberger, 1996, p. 10). Orphanages were, more than anything else, a response to poverty. Until passage of the Social Security Act in 1935, little financial assistance was available for parents in crisis. In fact, during the last years of the nineteenth century, assistance to poor people, both in cash and in kind (known as "outdoor relief"), was almost nonexistent, due to fears that assistance would cause the poor to lose motivation to work. Therefore, when faced with unemployment, parents often had little choice but to request placement for their children (Crenson, 1998).

Although orphanages were undoubtedly major improvements over poorhouses, they were still far from ideal places for children to grow up. The problems became really serious in the late 1800s, when the number of children housed in orphanages exploded due to a combination of factors, prominently the almost total elimination of outdoor relief. The need was such that St. Agatha's Home opened in New York City in 1884 and within a year had a population of 124. That same year, the 29 orphanages in New York City housed nearly 15,000 children (Ashby, 1997, p. 68).

The large size of these institutions, combined with the meager resources, resulted in settings that were generally rigid and impersonal. One critic complained, "The child is reared by the bell. The bell rings in the morning to rise, the bell rings to dress, the bell rings for prayers" (Ashby, 1997, p. 65). One of the leading critics of institutional care, Charles Loring Brace (quoted in Fry, 1974), felt that

> the impersonal custodial care of an institution . . . not only stunted children, it destroyed them. . . . The regimentation did little to build self-reliance, to prepare the child for practical living. . . . Institutional life, like charity handouts, perpetuated pauperism and . . . both were dismal failures when it came to helping people to learn to stand on their own. (p. 6)

Although orphanages were undoubtedly rigid and institutional, it would be unfair to paint them and the large numbers of workers in them as characteristically cold and uncaring. Evidence indicates that the people who ran orphanages empathized with poor parents to a greater extent than others working in charity. Superintendents often saw poor parents as victims of bad luck, rather than examples of moral shortcomings. Ashby (1997) notes,

> Although the managers of a Brooklyn institution asserted in 1867 that intemperance and lack of character ruined some poor people, they insisted that unexpected tragedies such as unemployment, death, and illness were more typically the source of problems. Rather than blame destitute, struggling parents, a number of asylum directors agreed to shelter their children until the return of better times. (pp. 66–67)

As just one example, Dulberger (1996) studied the history of the Albany Orphan Asylum and found records indicating that one of its superintendents, Albert Fuller, corresponded with parents of residents to the rate of more than 125 letters per day. Many of his letters consisted of standard phrases such as "Your children are well and are getting along first rate. They are standing at my side as I write to you and they send ever so much love" (p. 17). Dulberger noted further that "most letters included also a phrase or sentence or two of a personal nature regarding the individual child—his or her health, schooling, behavior, emotional adjustment, or joy over the receipt of a gift from a parent" (p. 17). Parents were free to correspond with their children and were allowed to visit. There were generally few restrictions and little red tape to slow down the return of a child, once the parents were able to resume their responsibility.

The concept of the orphanage as the major social response to child dependency was doomed from the beginning. Not only were the institutions impersonal, custodial, and rigid, but other problems soon developed. Although the number of institutions grew at a fast rate, the number of dependent children grew at an even faster pace. The overflow either ended up in county poorhouses or, more likely, became "street Arabs" living on their own.

Axinn and Levin (1975) explain that another problem resulted from the fact that institutions were designed to take care of children for a relatively short period of time, "during which education and reeducation for orderly living were provided. Having satisfactorily completed this period of rehabilitation, the male child was placed out by the institution as an apprentice in a particular trade or occupation; the female child was indentured as a domestic servant" (p. 95). The period of time that dependent children needed care lengthened with the spread of compulsory public education and the decline of the apprentice system. The pressure on the overcrowded institutions increased: As children stayed longer, the institutions could care for fewer children.

An Alternative to Institutionalization: The Emigration Movement

From the beginning, orphanages faced serious limitations as a solution to the problem of child dependency:

1. The orphanages were large, impersonal, and artificial environments that did not enhance and often damaged child development.
2. The numbers of children needing care grew at a greater rate than orphanage capacity.
3. Orphanages did not have sufficient resources to adequately care for their charges or to expand to meet the growing need.
4. A number of children, such as the very young, simply did not fit the "institutional placement" category.

These problems led to the *emigration movement* and eventually to modern foster care. Both schemes placed children in private homes to be cared for as members of families.

The first widespread effort to place children with private families was emigration, also known as the "orphan trains." While probably not the originator of the concept, the first person to put it into practice effectively was the Reverend Charles Loring Brace, who founded the New York Children's Aid Society (CAS) in 1853. Brace's basic idea was to take homeless children from the streets of New York—where they had few options other than begging, crime, and vice and therefore were a serious social problem—and transport them to rural regions of the U.S. to live with farm families. There, they would be assets, since even small children could be useful on a farm. Brace (1872) and his associates advertised their plan and found the response to be immediate and astounding. He recalled:

> Most touching of all was the crowd of little ones who immediately found their way to the office. Ragged young girls who had nowhere to lay their heads; children driven

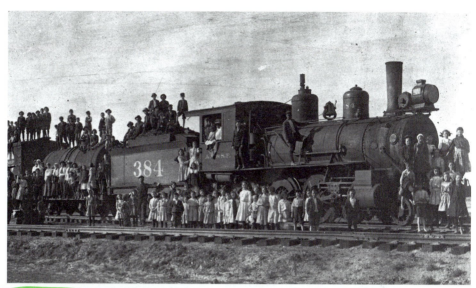

The orphan trains represented the first step away from orphanages and toward the modern system of foster care.

from drunkards' homes; orphans who slept where they could find a box or stairway; boys cast out by stepmothers or stepfathers; newsboys whose incessant answer to our question, "Where do you live?" rang in our ears—"Don't live nowhere!" . . . All this motley throng of infantile misery and childish guilt passed through our doors, telling their simple stories of suffering and loneliness and temptation. (pp. 88–89)

The CAS gathered homeless children in shelters in New York City. When a large enough group was gathered, they sent them by train to towns in the West. Agents of the society preceded the train into each town to organize a local placement committee of prominent citizens and to advertise the location and date that the children would be available for placement. When the day arrived, local families would inspect the children, and families who were deemed suitable by both the society's agent and the local committee could select one or more of them. *Suitable* generally meant that the family was Protestant, self-supporting, and had no members with criminal records or who were known to drink excessively. The prospective parents promised to take good care of the children and to provide them with a Christian home and an education.

The Children's Aid Society was able to make a significant dent in the number of children in New York City orphanages. By 1873, the CAS was placing more than 3,000 children per year. Its peak year was 1875, when a total of 4,026 children were placed. By 1929, the year the last orphan train rolled, a total of 200,000 children had emigrated from New York to western states (Popple & Leighninger, 2004).

Although an innovative organization for its time, the Children's Aid Society had serious problems both in terms of its philosophy and its technique, and shortly after it began its work, criticisms began to surface. In terms of philosophy, Brace and his organization were anti-urban, anti-immigrant, and anti-Catholic. The sum of these characteristics made the CAS antifamily. In contrast to the orphanages—which tended to work closely with a child's family, generally encouraged parent/child contact, and were happy to return a child to the parents as soon as possible—the CAS sought to sever ties between children and parents as well as to get children out of the city and onto a farm. Brace viewed farm life as ideal for child development. In the society's annual report, he stated that "for an outcast or homeless or orphan child, not tainted with bad habits, the best possible place of shelter and education, better than any prison or public institution, was the farmer's home" (quoted in McOllough, 1988, p. 145).

The CAS worked from the assumption that the parents of dependent or neglected children were morally inadequate and viewed its role as rescuing these children both from the parents and the city. Catholics accused the CAS of snatching Catholic children off the streets of New York and sending them out of the city to be reared in Protestant homes. Although there is no evidence that the CAS sought out Catholic children as a matter of policy, it is clear that when a Catholic child came under the agency's care, the child was placed in a Protestant home, which the staff considered a victory for the child.

The most serious criticism of the CAS regarded the techniques it employed to make and then to follow up (actually, in most cases, not to follow up) the placement. Critics charged that the placement process was overly casual and characterized by a lack of study of prospective homes. In 1894, Hasting Hart, Secretary of the Minnesota State Board of Charities, made a careful study of the children placed in that state. He found that 58 percent of the placements made by the CAS had turned out badly. Hart concluded that the primary reasons for the high failure rate were that the children had been hastily placed and that there had not been sufficient supervision of the placements to afford the children reasonable protection (Bruno, 1946, pp. 59–60). This high failure rate was supported by data from agencies that did do careful follow-up on their placements. For example, children under the care of the Pennsylvania Children's Aid Society for more than a year often were placed in four or more homes (Clement, 1979, p. 410).

By the turn of the century, many states were so disenchanted with Brace's work that they passed laws prohibiting the CAS from making placements unless a bond was first posted with the state to reimburse it should the placement break down and the child become a public charge. However, by this time, Brace's whole philosophy and method of child placement was rapidly being replaced by the modern concept of foster family care.

The Development of Protective Services

The orphanages and placement societies of the nineteenth century were mainly a response to the problem of dependent children—children needing care mostly due to the poverty of their parents. Toward the end of the century, a new problem had been discovered: *neglect*, a broad term referring to mistreated children and including abuse as well as neglect. Interestingly, the awareness and concern regarding this problem was slightly preceded by concern with the abuse and neglect of animals. In 1866, Henry Bergh founded the Society for the Prevention of Cruelty to Animals. He quickly succeeded in getting laws passed prohibiting the neglect and abuse of animals and empowering the society's agents to actually make arrests and issue subpoenas.

It was to Bergh and his society that a charity worker turned with her concern about the treatment of Mary Ellen Wilson, the 8-year-old girl described earlier, who was being abused and neglected by her stepparents. Bergh, acting through his attorney, Elbridge Gerry, agreed to help and, amid much publicity, was successful in prosecuting and jailing the stepparents and placing the child. Media coverage of the Wilson case caused a flood of public opinion and resulted in the passage in New York in 1875 of "an Act of the incorporation of societies for the prevention of cruelty to children." Like animal protection agents, employees of these new societies were empowered to "prefer a complaint before any court or magistrate having jurisdiction for the violation of any law relating to or affecting children" (Williams, 1980, p. 77).

In 1877, the American Humane Association was incorporated. Six years later, there were societies in 37 cities, and Gerry (1882) made this report:

> In New York City alone 604 complaints were received, 569 convictions secured, and 1,161 children were rescued. In Pennsylvania, 900 complaints were received and 2,212 children were rescued. In Massachusetts, 712 complaints were received and 1,350 children rescued. In Wisconsin, 399 complaints were received and 164 children rescued. In California, 409 complaints were received, 681 cases examined, and 81 convictions secured. (p. 640)

By 1900, the membership of the American Humane Association included 150 anticruelty or humane societies throughout the United States. Most dealt with both child and animal protection, but about 20 restricted their activities to the protection of children.

The societies for the prevention of cruelty to children viewed themselves as child rescue agencies, not charitable organizations. Like law enforcement agencies (which they were, for all practical purposes), the societies investigated cases of abuse, neglect, and exploitation. If a complaint was substantiated, criminal charges were initiated against the perpetrators and custody papers filed. The Thirty-First Annual Report of the American Humane Association, issued in 1907, stated that the societies were never intended to reform children or families. Rather, they were

> a hand affixed to the arm of the law by which the body politic reaches out and enforces the law. The arm of the law seizes the child when it is in an atmosphere of impurity, or in the care of those who are not fit to be entrusted with it, wrenches the child out of these surroundings, brings it to the court, and submits it to the decision of the court. (quoted in Bremner, 1971, p. 214)

Once they gained custody of the child, agents would place the child in a home or institution and close the case. Only in cases of lost or kidnapped children did the society ever consider reuniting the children with their parents.

The Development of Concern for Families

As the problem of child dependency grew and early simplistic attempts to remedy the problem—namely, orphanages and placing out—created as many problems as they solved, the focus of child savers began to change. A gradually increasing number of people began to think that the child's own family should be the focus of services: Rather than rescue the child from the family, it made more sense to rescue the family for the child. This emerging perspective led to the development of two major approaches: foster care and public assistance.

FOSTER CARE   Although the Children's Aid Society program had many flaws, the basic idea of placing dependent children in a family setting caught on and had a tremendous impact on child welfare practice. Toward the end of the nineteenth century, members of the newly emerging social work profession—notably, John Finley of the New York State Charities Aid Association, Charles Birtwell of the Boston Children's Aid Society, and Homer Folks of the Children's Aid Society of Pennsylvania— began to develop systematic and sound administrative procedures for child placement. The system they developed was called *boarding out*. This practice later became known as *foster care*.

Although placing out (orphan trains) and boarding out (foster homes) were similar, with the basic idea that a home placement was superior to an institutional placement, they had several major differences. For instance, proponents of placing out strongly opposed any kind of financial payment to the families or the children. They believed that people should care for children out of Christian charity and love for kids and that introducing money into the relationship might result in people taking on the task for the wrong reason. They were also concerned that as soon as any family began to receive payment, every family would expect this and the supply of free homes would dry up. Advocates of boarding out believed that children should be cared for in their own homes and communities to the greatest extent possible. This generally meant finding homes in cities. Because children were not economic assets for families in cities, as they were on farms, it was necessary to provide some kind of subsidy in order for families to be able to afford to take on an additional family member.

Other differences between boarding out and placing out related to the placement process, supervision of the placement, and involvement of the child's family of origin. The Children's Aid Society had a casual approach to placing children, with virtually no study being made of prospective homes. Their trust in the goodness of people could perhaps be interpreted as naïve, but others in children's work did not share their assumptions. For example, Dulberger (1996) found that "during his tenure as superintendent of the Albany asylum, Albert Fuller noted on more than one occasion that oftentimes very 'peculiar people' made application for children, many who ought never to have them" (p. 16).

The developers of boarding out established thorough investigative protocols to be followed prior to a child being placed in a home. These agencies believed that because they were paying for the placement, they had a right to demand that the family meet and adhere to high standards. Conversely, a child in a placing-out program was rarely if ever visited by a representative of the agency to see that all was well and to help with any problems. In boarding-out agencies, each child was assigned an ongoing worker, who visited regularly and kept thorough records. Perhaps the most significant difference between the approaches was that the boarding-out placement was generally made in the child's own community, with the intention of involving the child's family of origin and eventually returning the child to the family, if such a plan became feasible.

The Massachusetts system of boarding out children challenged existing ideas about child placement. As Ashby (1997) has noted,

> Paid fostering offered a novel alternative, especially for young children who otherwise had no value economically. A fee for parenting meant that even the unproductive child could still be a good bargain. Just maybe, too, as child welfare reformer C. H. Pemberton hoped, the child in its new home might "awaken a sentiment" that would encourage the family to keep it after the payments ended. (p. 74)

Charles Loring Brace scoffed at such expectations as utter nonsense. In his opinion, paid fostering vulgarized the home placement movement, turning a humanitarian ideal into a crass business arrangement. Nonetheless, after the turn of the century, aided by the establishment of the juvenile court and the 1935 Social Security Act, both of which made public funds available to pay for foster care, the paid system eventually evolved to dominate child placement practice.

With the development of new procedures by the advocates of boarding out, foster care spread quickly after the turn of the century. The movement received a boost in 1909, when the report from the first White House Conference on Children gave support to the foster care movement by declaring that

> home life is the most important thing for the child, and whenever the home was in any way adequately suitable the child should be brought up in its own home. . . . When it was impracticable for the child to be brought up in its own home, the next best thing was to provide a foster home, which must be watched over to carefully protect the rights of the child in order that it might still enjoy the advantages of home life." (quoted in Hart, 1909, p. 464)

PUBLIC ASSISTANCE To a certain extent, child welfare has always been a function of government. Poorhouses were supported out of public funds; however, due to a prevailing philosophy about the proper role of government, as well as the low level of funds available, the involvement of government was minimal. With the massive increase in child dependency in the latter half of the nineteenth century, that philosophy began to change. States began to heavily support the care of children by establishing public institutions, providing subsidies to private orphanages, and paying for children's board with private families. The approaches that states employed varied widely: New York provided subsidies for private institutions; Michigan refused to give public money for private care, instead building a state orphanage at Coldwater; Ohio passed a law in 1866 that allowed each county to impose taxes to support a county level home for dependent children under 16 and Massachusetts chose to subsidize the care of children in private foster homes (Ashby, 1997).

Until the present century, government involvement in private life tended to be anti-family. The philosophy was that a family that was unable to support itself financially was, ipso facto, inadequate, morally suspect, and probably not a fit place to raise children. In her study of the relations between government and family of that period, Vandepol (1982) discovered the following:

Public authorities generally dismantled families on relief. . . . The power of local authorities, in particular the elected selectmen and overseers of the poor, to reorganize destitute families would startle those who regard modern government power as arbitrary or excessive. The practice of terminating parental custody and removing children from families persisted as the dominant method of caring for dependent children until the 20th century. (p. 222)

As we have seen, poverty has been the major reason that children throughout history have been classified as dependent and neglected. Those children who were placed in poorhouses and orphanages, who served as apprentices, and who were sent west on orphan trains were, in nearly all cases, poor children. Following the turn of the twentieth century, the sentiment began to develop, encouraged by leaders such as C. Carl Carstens, that support should be provided to parents (actually, to mothers) for the support of children in the home to prevent a family breakup.

Two reasons explain the development of this idea. The first was a changing conception of childhood and the importance of home life—and the role of motherhood within it—that developed during the late 1800s. This phenomenon has been termed the *cult of domesticity.* People began to recognize the dismantling of a family as a serious matter. A second factor in the new way of seeing things was simply practical cost analysis. As the cost of substitute placement of children began to increase at a rapid rate, civic leaders began to look for a more cost-efficient method of dealing with the problem of child dependency. Many began to recognize that it would perhaps be cheaper to subsidize poor children in their own homes than to provide substitute care.

These ideas came to a head at the 1909 White House Conference on Children, convened by President Theodore Roosevelt. The 200 children's advocates convened at this conference released a report that contained a major philosophical statement and a major policy recommendation. The philosophical statement said, "Home life is the highest and finest product of civilization" (Trattner, 1999, p. 215). The policy change the advocates supported recommended that "no child should be separated from its family for reasons of poverty alone" (Trattner, 1999, p. 215).

Following the White House Conference, advocates for poor children began to successfully lobby for state welfare laws that became known as *mothers'* or *widows' pensions.* These terms were borrowed from the powerful and popular industrial insurance movement that was successfully lobbying for workers' compensation, unemployment insurance, and retirement programs as measures to ensure workers against the risks of industrial employment. The name *mothers' pension* implied that women with children were productive workers of a sort and as such had a right to insurance against widowhood, the primary threat to their livelihood, just as men had a right to insurance against industrial accident. The first mothers' pension laws were passed in Missouri and Illinois in 1911. Within two years, similar laws were passed in 17 additional states, and by 1919, 39 states had mothers' pension programs.

Although mothers' pension programs established an important precedent for the development of public assistance, it was not until the Great Depression of the 1930s that state and federal governments actually began to play a major role. Mothers' pension programs were always highly selective and as a result quite small; in 1930, for example, fewer than 3 percent of female-headed households received benefits under these programs (Handler & Hasenfeld, 1991, p. 71). The Depression shocked Americans into the realization that small local and state programs were not sufficient to deal with the massive economic problems of an urban industrial society. When the Depression hit, private agencies such as children's homes almost immediately ran out of money in response to the huge number of impoverished parents who needed a place to leave their children. These agencies turned to state and local governments, who in turn fell into financial peril and consequently turned to the federal government for help.

The realization that private agencies and state and local governments could not cope with the economic crisis resulted in the passage of the Social Security Act in 1935. This act, the first comprehensive social welfare legislation in the nation's history, included Aid to Dependent Children (ADC), a program established to serve single mothers with small children—basically, the same group the states had targeted with mothers' pension laws. This program was later called Aid to Families with Dependent Children (AFDC) in recognition of the fact that mothers, as well as their children, were receiving assistance.

The Professionalization and Institutionalization of Child Welfare

The massive increase in the need for children's services, along with the realization that something had to be done to preserve social order and help dependent children, took center stage in the United States during the early 1900s, a time that has come to be called the *progressive era*. It was characterized by what historian Robert Wiebe (1967) has called "a search for order in a distended society." There were two major characteristics of this search for order. First, there was an increased belief that government should be larger and should take responsibility for the management of social concerns, including social problems such as poverty and child dependency. Second, as a wide variety of new professions emerged, society became willing to look to these professions for solutions to social problems. During this era, child welfare became a responsibility of both the new profession of social work and of various levels of government.

Child Welfare Becomes a Part of Professional Social Work

Social work became a profession in New York City in the late nineteenth century. The Charity Organization Society began developing the methods for the emerging specialization of social casework. The social workers in that organization, along with other progressive social workers, established the first school of social work, and the Russell Sage Foundation was founded with a particular emphasis on promoting scientific social work. However, New York was also the center of the old custodial law enforcement approach to child protection work—the placing-out approach to child care—and as such was the center of resistance to attempts to reform child welfare methods. It was in the city of Boston that social reformers began to recognize the value of applying the new methods of scientific charity to the field of child protection and thus pave the way for the eventual professionalization of child welfare.

The first concern of Boston's child welfare reformers was child placement. Charles Birtwell, a young summa cum laude graduate of Harvard, began work in the Boston Children's Aid Society (BCAS) in 1885 as an assistant visiting agent and in 1887 became the organization's general secretary (what is now called the *executive director*). Birtwell shared Charles Loring Brace's anti-institutional bias, but unlike Brace, he opposed separating children from their families except when no other option was available. When separation was necessary, he believed in maintaining contact between the children and family to the greatest extent possible. That notion was part of the philosophy of the BCAS (1887), as stated by Birtwell: "It has always been borne in mind that the sundering of family ties—the separation of a child from a father or mother, or the scattering of brothers and sisters—is a serious matter, requiring for its justification grave reasons and evident advantage" (p. 11). He was also critical of the generally sloppy placement process and the lack of effective supervision of placements that characterized the work of the New York CAS.

Under Birtwell's leadership, BCAS developed sound methods of child placement that today form the basis of modern foster home procedures. Five principles guided the BCAS:

1. Family care was considered preferable to institutional care in the great majority of cases.
2. The child's family was to be involved to the greatest extent possible.
3. All relevant areas of a placement family's qualifications, including numerous character references, were checked before a placement decision was made.
4. Placement was viewed as temporary, with the intention of returning the child to the parents as soon as they were able to resume care.
5. The child and family were closely supervised following placement.

Families were asked to voluntarily grant temporary custody to the agency and were expected to financially contribute as much as they could of the costs of care—in many cases, 100 percent. Birtwell (BCAS, 1887) said, "Almost invariably the unfortunate father or mother, and often relatives outside of the immediate family, when informed of a suited boarding place at a low charge for board, have gladly made effort to provide for the children in this natural, self-respectful way" (p. 13).

The BCAS did not assume that simply because a family expressed a desire to have a child and appeared to be Christian, they would be suitable foster parents. Besides an elaborate procedure for studying the prospective family, including the checking of references provided by the family, the society selected other references—people the society thought could give an objective assessment.

Boston was also the site of the professionalization of child protection. The Massachusetts Society for the Prevention of Cruelty to Children was founded in 1880 under direct influence of the New York society. Like the New York society, the Massachusetts society began as primarily a law enforcement agency. In 1906, this approach came to an end, apparently with some stiff resistance from agency staff. The president of the society, progressive reformer Grafton Cushings (Massachusetts Society for the Prevention of Cruelty to Children, 1907), reported the following to the board of directors and members of the society:

> The traditional policy of the Massachusetts Society for the Prevention of Cruelty to Children is the prosecution of offenders against children and the taking of children from immoral or unhealthy surroundings, and placing them in homes or institutions. . . . There is no attempt to discover the cause of the condition which make action by the Society necessary, and therefore, no endeavor to prevent a recurrence of these conditions. In other words, there is no "social" work done. It is all legal or police work. A Society for the Prevention of Cruelty to Children thus becomes an arm of the law, a department of the district attorney's office, or an adjunct of the police force, and fills a quasi-public position. (p. 4)

Cushings believed that the society needed to develop "along somewhat new lines," noting that "the times are full of changes, and charitable methods are changing rapidly" (p. 4). Changes in the court system were a good illustration, he noted: "The theory of a stated punishment for a stated offence is gradually giving way to the theory that the offender should be given the chance to rehabilitate himself, and should be encouraged to mend his ways" (p. 5). Cushings proposed that the society change direction in its work in a manner similar to changes in the court system:

> Just as the courts have extended their jurisdiction to include remedial and preventive measures, so we cannot feel satisfied until we feel sure that every effort has been made, either by our own officers or though the action of some other organization, not only to see to it that the children who have been taken from parents through our intervention are permanently well cared for, but that the conditions which made our interference necessary are improved. (p. 5)

Cushings then made his famous statement, the one that has been repeated in various forms and venues by child welfare social workers with such frequency during the past century that it has become something of a mantra:

> It seems often futile to take from a man and a women one set of children, and in a few years time be called on again to take from them another set of children which they have been allowed to bring into the same surroundings of squalor and crime. (p. 5)

The final point Cushings made in that report to the society's board and members referred to the aloofness of child protection agencies. He stated that the Massachusetts society would cease this attitude: "We believe that by entering more closely into relations with other charitable organizations, rather than by standing apart on a different plain, we can best serve our generation" (p. 6).

The general agent of the Massachusetts society, Charles K. Morton, with the backing of the secretary of the influential New York society, vigorously opposed the change of direction that Cushings and the board proposed. Cushings (Massachusetts Society, 1907) summarized the situation by saying, "The difference of opinion as to methods between Mr. Morton and the Directors is radical" (p. 17). Because of the differences, Morton's contract was not renewed. The board hired a new general agent, C. Carl Carstens (mentioned earlier), who was a social worker with the progressive

New York Charity Organization Society. Carstens was an associate of Mary Richmond and Edward Devine, undoubtedly the two leading figures in the development of the new social work profession.

Carstens proved to be a tireless advocate of the new approach the board desired. Under his leadership, the Massachusetts society quickly developed a program of remedial and preventive social work and of environmental reform. Carstens defined a threefold task for the agency:

> It must rescue children from degrading conditions, it must avail itself of every reasonable opportunity to try to reconstruct such families as are moving on to inevitable shipwreck, and, while it is working with each individual instance, it must try to seek out the causes which bring about these bad conditions, so that it may do its part to prevent them. (Massachusetts Society, 1907, p. 17)

Carstens was a national figure in social work and had national plans and ambitions. No sooner did he establish the new approach to children's services, an approach that came to be known as *child protection*, than he began to advocate for other anticruelty societies to also adopt it. In doing this, he faced heavy opposition, mainly from the established child rescue societies. Elbridge Gerry, the founder of the New York Society for Prevention of Cruelty to Children, complained about Carstens's activities: "There is nothing today which scientific charity does not seek to appropriate to itself; and when it cannot absorb collateral work, it endeavors to obtain possession of the subject of that work and utilize it for its own ends." William Stillman, president of the American Humane Association from 1904 to 1924, also complained: "New social reforms are dividing, or seeking to divide, our humane patrimony."

When Carstens and his supporters, a group Stillman referred to as "cranks and bores," failed in a 1912 vote to gain control of the American Humane Society, Carstens disaffiliated the Massachusetts society from the national organization (Anderson, 1989, p. 225). In 1915, Carstens and other like-minded executives founded the Bureau for the Exchange of Information among Child-Helping Agencies, which in 1921 became the Child Welfare League of America (CWLA). From 1921 until his death in 1939, Carstens served as executive director of CWLA. From that platform, he not only presided over the spread of a social work approach to child welfare, but he also served as a staunch advocate for making child welfare a responsibility of the government.

The Development of Public Child Welfare Services

Until the twentieth century, child welfare services were generally provided by private agencies, although sometimes with public subsidization. In the early 1900s, progressive social work leaders began to agitate for the development of public child welfare. In 1914, the Secretary of the Pennsylvania Society for the Prevention of Cruelty to Children said in an address at a conference of the American Humane Association, "This thing we are doing is, after all, the job of the public authorities. The public ought to protect all citizens, including children, from cruelty and improper care. As speed-ily as conditions admit, we should turn over to the public the things we are at present doing" (Bremner, 1971, p. 217).

At the 1915 National Conference of Charities and Correction, Carstens presented "A Community Plan in Children's Work," which was basically a call for public child welfare services. He said, speaking of the welfare of children, "Subject to the limitations which the federal and state constitutions have for the time being established, there is no task which the community in its public capacity may not undertake and under certain circumstances should not undertake." (p. 94)

As the century progressed, the government, on all levels, showed an increasing willingness to become involved in providing social services, particularly those involving children. The 1909 White House Conference on Children resulted in the establishment in 1912 of the U.S. Children's Bureau, located in the Department of Commerce and Labor. It was charged with investigating and reporting on "matters pertaining to the welfare of children and child life among all classes of our people" (Bremner, 1971, pp. 761–762). In 1921, the Maternity and Infancy Protection Act was passed, which set up infant and maternal health centers administered by state health departments. In 1924, Carstens observed that in many areas of the country, "the children's protective and children's aid functions are being combined under one society" and that in some areas, "public departments have been given the power and to some extent the equipment to take over the whole of the children's protective services" (Bremner, 1971, p. 220). Finally, in 1935, child welfare services became a predominantly public function with passage of the Social Security Act, which under Title V (later Title IV) authorized the Children's Bureau to fund and assist states in providing child welfare services for dependent and neglected children.

Child Welfare Becomes a Dormant Issue

The basic structure of the child protective services system was put in place with passage and implementation of Title V of the Social Security Act of 1935. Following this landmark legislation, however, was a period of nearly three decades of apathy regarding child welfare. Although child protective services were now officially a responsibility of government, the services were spotty and poorly funded. Three states had no protective services at all. In the states that did have services, an American Humane Association survey (DeFrancis, 1973) found that "much of what was reported as child protective services was in reality nonspecific child welfare services or nonspecific family assistance services in the context of a financial assistance setting" (pp. 323–331). In addition, the survey found that services provided by private agencies had undergone a long-term decline.

This decline in interest in child protective services can be explained by a combination of factors. First, following World War I, the United States entered a series of historical epochs, in which interest in the internal affairs of families took a back seat to other issues perceived to be more pressing. The 1920s were an era of conservatism and resistance to social reforms in reaction to the major changes that had occurred during the prior progressive era. In the 1930s, the nation was fixated on the Great

Depression, and when the Social Security Act was passed in response to the economic situation, people naturally believed that social problems were under control. In the 1940s and early 1950s, World War II and the Korean conflict occupied the nation's interest. When the major social disruptions caused by the Depression and wars ended, the country focused on reestablishing an environment conducive to the formation and development of normal family life; consequently, any effort that smacked of government interference with the family did not receive support.

An additional explanation of the relative lack of interest in child welfare issues from the 1920s through the 1950s relates to the decline of the feminist movement, which in its early form, had perceived a close tie between women's issues and children's issues (Costin, 1982). In this atmosphere of complacency and denial, the rediscovery of child abuse in the late 1950s exploded like a bomb.

The Rediscovery of Child Welfare

Beginning in the late 1950s and continuing through the 1960s, Americans were in an introspective and self-critical mood and ready for change. During this period, a number of social problems were discovered and burst out of the headlines: poverty, juvenile justice, and civil rights, to name but a few. Probably the most significant development for the well-being of children was the recognition of poverty and subsequent liberalization of public welfare policy, such that the majority of poor children eligible for assistance actually received it. From the end of 1961 to 1969, Aid to Families with Dependent Children (AFDC) added 800,000 families to its rolls, more than doubling the number of recipients. The addition of programs such as food stamps, Medicaid, and expanded public housing meant that, for the first time in the nation's history, children no longer had to be separated from their parents simply for reasons of poverty.

Another problem area also began to receive close scrutiny by the press and the general public: child maltreatment. This attention resulted from the activities of two professions and highlighted two separate yet related aspects of the problem. First, and most dramatic, was the belated recognition by the medical profession of child abuse as a child health problem. Second, social work researchers identified a huge number of children drifting in foster care, with little hope of reunification with their families yet no alternative plan.

Medicine Identifies the Battered Child

Perhaps the major reason for the rediscovery of child maltreatment was recognition of the problem by the medical profession. As noted in Chapter 1, in the late 1940s and early 1950s, radiologists began to recognize injuries that we now know generally result from abuse and neglect—injuries that previously the medical profession had tended to view as accidental. In 1960, a social worker at Children's Hospital in Pittsburgh published an article that attributed this resistance to both a repugnance of the problem and a difficulty in assuming an objective attitude with abusive parents (Elmer, 1960).

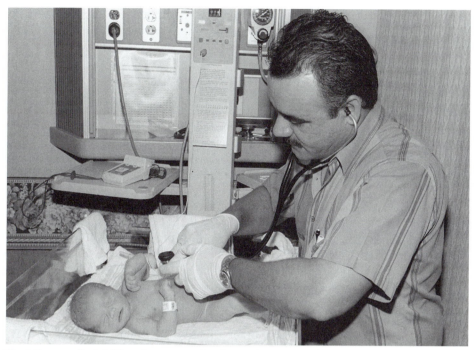

The "discovery" of child maltreatment by the medical profession resulted in a massive increase in public interest in child welfare.

C. Henry Kempe (1978), the physician instrumental in overcoming this resistance recalls, "When I saw child abuse between 1956 and 1958 in Denver, our house staff was unwilling to make this diagnosis [child abuse]. Initially I felt intellectual dismay at diagnoses such as 'obscure bruising,' 'osteogenesis imperfecta tarda,' 'spontaneous subdural hematoma'" (p. 257). In 1960, Kempe used his prerogative as program committee chair of the American Academy of Pediatrics to plan a plenary session on child abuse. The rest of the committee agreed, provided he could come up with a catchy title for the session. The title Kempe coined was "The Battered Child Syndrome." Shortly after the meeting, Kempe, with the assistance of a psychiatrist and a radiologist, published an article with the same title in the *Journal of the American Medical Association.*

As Williams (1980) notes, "The speed of public and professional response, enhanced by medical coverage, was incredible" (p. 86). In 1962, the U.S. Children's Bureau held a conference to draft model child welfare legislation. That same year, the Social Security Act was amended to require all states to develop a plan to provide child protective services in every political subdivision. In 1963, 18 bills were introduced in Congress dealing with child abuse, and 11 of them passed. By 1967, all states had passed laws requiring professionals to report child abuse. Increased public awareness of the problem of child maltreatment, combined with the reporting laws, resulted in a massive increase in the number of referrals and thus the sizes of caseloads of child welfare agencies. In 1967, there were only 9,563 child abuse reports nationally; by 1980, reports had increased to over 1 million. That number has continued to increase, such that the current number is more than 3 million (NCANDS, 2003).

Foster Care: From Solution to Problem

During the first half of the twentieth century, procedures for home study, child placement, and supervision were developed by social workers. As these procedures were developed, Title IV of the Social Security Act was passed in 1935 to publicly fund foster homes. As an anti-institutional ideology continued to grow, the number of children in orphanages declined and the number in foster care increased until foster care became the option of choice for dependent and neglected children. Foster care became a standard item in the child welfare worker's toolkit. It was a resource that existed with little examination until the late 1950s and early 1960s, when two things happened that shook the confidence of the policymakers. First, several studies cited serious deficiencies in the foster care system. And second, the discovery of child abuse (noted earlier) led to an explosion in the number of referrals, which led to a consequent explosion in the number of children placed in foster care and hence a huge cost increase.

The study that opened the floodgates for criticism of the foster care system was published in 1959 by social workers Henry Maas and Richard Engler. Maas and Engler (1959) sent researchers into nine communities thought to be representative, where they looked at a number of aspects of foster care. As there was no central data-reporting mechanism for foster care, the Maas and Engler study provided the first valid look into the overall picture of foster care in the United States. The facts they uncovered were disturbing. They found that the assumption that foster care was a temporary respite for children and families was untrue. The average length of placement was three years, many children were destined to grow up in foster care, and less than one-quarter of the children were likely to return home. Equally disturbing was the finding that the parents of foster children indicated, in most cases, that they either had no relationship or a negative relationship with the child placement agencies, and in only one-third of the cases did a parent ever visit the child in care. In an afterword to the study, Child Welfare League of America Executive Director Joseph Reid (1959) referred to foster children as "orphans of the living" (p. 380).

The Maas and Engler (1959) study was followed by several other studies of foster care done from scientific, journalistic, and legalistic perspectives: Jeter (1963); Goldstein, Freud, and Solnit, (1973); and Fanshel and Shinn (1978). These studies identified four major concerns with the foster care system:

1. The foster care system was not guided by any systematic scientific knowledge or principles.
2. Foster care was in many, if not most, cases definitely not a temporary but rather a long-term situation.
3. Many children were not placed in one stable foster home, but in a series of foster homes. (This concern came to be called *foster care drift.*)

4. Agencies placing children in foster care rarely had any kind of long-term plan for the children, other than to keep them in care until such time as they could be returned home—which in many cases would be never.

The Search for Answers

As a result of the discovery of child abuse and the passage of reporting laws, child welfare caseloads increased dramatically. The result of the studies by Maas and Engler (1959) and others was dissatisfaction with the favorite tool in the social worker's toolkit: foster care. This resulted in a situation with which we are still struggling: recognition of a problem, commitment to do something about it but no really good idea about what to do, plus a general unwillingness on the part of society to pay the massive cost of any solution. As Costin, Karger, and Stoez (1996) have noted, "Able to document abuse, health and human service professionals generated enough reports to indicate that non-accidental injury to children was epidemic. Remedying child abuse, however, was another matter" (p. 116).

In response to the rapidly emerging problem of child abuse, a section was included in Title XX of the Social Security Act, passed in 1972, which made protective services mandatory in all states and provided federal funding to pay for these services. Once funding was in place for services, however, it quickly became apparent that no one had much useful information on just how to design action programs. This problem led to the passage in 1974 of the Child Abuse Prevention and Treatment Act (CAPTA). This act had two major components. First, it established within the Department of Health and Human Services the National Center for Child Abuse and Neglect, a research and data clearinghouse designed to help remedy the huge gaps in knowledge that were becoming apparent as attempts were made to remedy child protection problems. The second component was a model statute for state child protection programs, which was eventually adopted by all 50 states. The model statute specified the following provisions:

> (1) a standard definition of child abuse and neglect, (2) standard methods of reporting and investigating child abuse and neglect, (3) guarantees of immunity for those reporting suspected injuries to children, and neglect, and (4) development of prevention and public education efforts to reduce the incidence of child abuse and neglect. (quoted in Costin et al., 1996, p. 116)

CAPTA provided only a limited amount of funding to support these activities by the states (initially, only $22 million), but in spite of this, all 50 states were in compliance with the provisions of the bill by 1980.

The uniform data collected under the provisions of this act have done little to calm the fears of children's advocates. The data revealed that the number of reports of abuse and neglect doubled between 1976 and 1986. Moreover, the number of children in foster care, following a brief decline in the 1970s, had increased to record levels by 1996 and continues to increase (Lindsay, 2004, p. 85).

The rapidly increasing size and cost of the foster care caseload led Congress to once again adopt a new approach, as provided by the Adoption Assistance and Child

Welfare Act of 1980. This act directed federal fiscal incentives toward permanency planning objectives—namely, the development of preventive and reunification services and adoption subsidies. For states to be eligible for increased federal funds, they were required to implement a service program designed either to reunite children with their families or to provide permanent substitute homes. They were also required to take steps, such as the establishment of foster placement review committees and procedures for regular case review, to ensure that children enter foster care only when necessary, are placed appropriately, and are returned home or else moved on to permanent families in a timely fashion. The act also created fiscal incentives for states to seek adoptive homes for hard-to-place children, including children who were older, disabled, or minority group members. Unfortunately, the funding promised to support the goals of the Adoption Assistance and Child Welfare Act never materialized, due to budget cuts during the Reagan administration. Consequently, the foster care population and child welfare caseloads have continued to climb.

During the 1980s, the idea that it made more sense to save the family for the child than to save the child from the family began a major resurgence. This resurgence was partly philosophical, but in reality, it was probably more a result of the continuing increase in the foster home population and the resultant increase in costs. In an effort to prevent children from being removed from their homes, states began to adopt a program first developed in Washington state known as *intensive family preservation*. This approach is discussed in detail in Chapter 7 and so will only be briefly described here.

The idea behind family preservation is that in many cases, when out-of-home placement appears imminent, it is possible to prevent placement by providing intensive services delivered in the child's home over a brief, time-limited period. Family preservation services in some form are now in place in every state. These services are provided by both public and private agencies, generally in some form of partnership. In 1993, family preservation officially became part of federal child welfare policy with the passage of the Family Preservation and Support Program as part of the Omnibus Budget Reconciliation Act. This act extended the provisions of Title IV-B of the Social Security Act by establishing Part 2, which provided $930 million over a five-year period for the support of family preservation services.

The initial evaluations of family preservation services were glowing in their praise and led to near universal acclaim of this method as the key to dealing with child welfare. More recent (and better-designed) studies have not been so positive, however. These, combined with powerful anecdotal accounts of child deaths and injuries during provision of family preservation services, have prompted some serious reevaluation. The most significant study to date was conducted in 1993 in Illinois by the University of Chicago's Chapin Hall Center for Children, under contract with the state's Department of Children and Family Services. The study ran for three years and collected data on several levels. It ultimately concluded that the family preservation program in Illinois, called Families First, had no effect on either the frequency or the duration of child placements (Lindsay, 2004, pp. 54–56).

Data from studies such as this, combined with his experience on child death review teams, has led influential family violence expert Richard Gelles to call for a return to a child protection, rather than a family preservation approach to child welfare. Gelles (1996) writes,

> Children must come first in the words and deeds of the agencies that are entrusted with protecting them. It is time to move beyond the lip service paid to children and to develop a social structure, from top to bottom, that guarantees their safety, both by supporting families so that abuse will not occur in the first place and by absolutely guaranteeing the future safety and developmental integrity of children who have been abused and neglected. (pp. 171–172)

A high level of publicity surrounded the child deaths and injuries that were generally attributed to the "reasonable efforts" doctrine of the 1980 Adoption Assistance and Child Welfare Act and to family preservation efforts funded under the 1993 Family Preservation and Support Program. Largely in reaction to this publicity, Congress passed the Adoption and Safe Families Act of 1997. Here is a breakdown of what this act did:

1. Altered the "reasonable efforts" that state agencies were required to make to preserve or reunite families (specifying some instances where no efforts at all are required)
2. Set deadlines for initiation of termination of parental rights hearings
3. Provided procedural protections and mandated criminal background checks for foster and adoptive applicants
4. Encouraged adoption by providing incentive payments to states
5. Required permanency hearings at 12 months, rather than 18 months
6. Encouraged establishment of an advisory panel to report on kinship care
7. Expanded foster children's access to independent-living services
8. Eliminated geographic and bureaucratic obstacles to adoption
9. Reauthorized and redefined family preservation and support services
10. Ensured postadoption health care for special-needs children
11. Required states to develop and implement foster care standards

Although many critics view the Adoption and Safe Families Act as primarily a reaction against the emphasis on family preservation in recent years, that is only partially the case. Under the new title Promising Safe and Stable Families, the act continues the federal family preservation and support services program. It actually authorized an increase in expenditures earmarked for family preservation of $20 million per year beginning in 1999, up to a maximum of $305 million in 2001. The president's 2004 budget request included $505 million for this program. While the act supports family preservation, Congress added several provisions emphasizing that "the safety of the children to be served shall be of paramount concern."

A significant aspect of the Adoption and Safe Families Act is its recognition of formal kinship foster care. Throughout history, relatives have cared for a large number of children through informal arrangements. In recent years, however, a formal concept of kinship care has developed: The state protective services agency places children in the homes of kin and provides financial and psychosocial support to the placement. This form of placement has increased, until now almost one-fifth of all children placed by state agencies (over 107,000) are living with relatives. The act has postponed specific legislative changes related to kinship care until completion of a comprehensive study by the U.S. Department of Health and Human Services of state utilization policies and practices.

As American society has searched for an answer to the problem of mistreated children, the conception of the problem and the solutions has gone from simple to complex. It has taken 100 years of intervening in families for us to recognize some very basic realities. We now know how complex the problem is, and we now know there are no simple solutions. We understand the overwhelming importance of the family to the well-being of a child. We have learned that the government is a crummy parent, and regardless of how well intentioned the effort, there is no real substitute for a child's own family. We keep fighting this reality because, as a society, we want to help children, but we also want to punish ineffective parents. The notion that in order to help children, we have to help parents is a bitter pill for many of us to swallow.

Even among those who accept the idea that it is necessary to help parents in order to help children, there is much disagreement about what to do and at what level to intervene. Most people working in child welfare still advocate the *micro approach,* which seeks to provide counseling and support to parents with the goal of improving their parenting skills. An increasing number of people in the field, however—notably, Duncan Lindsey and Leroy Pelton—argue for *macro approaches.* They view child maltreatment as merely one more manifestation of poverty and argue that to address the problem of child maltreatment, we need to deal with the problem of poverty. For those in our society who believe that people are poor due to their own misbehavior and bad choices, proposals to improve the lives of these people (and consequently their children's lives) through increased financial assistance are distasteful. Regardless of the validity of Lindsey and Pelton's arguments, it is apparent from recent welfare reform programs that we are becoming stingier, rather than more generous, in our attitude toward helping the poor.

To conclude this survey of the history of child welfare the United States, consider this quote from a summary of the Adoption and Safe Families Act:

> Despite all the uncertainty, one thing is clear: the job of reform is now handed over to those in the field—guardians ad litem, juvenile court judges, caseworkers, parents, foster parents, and others. . . . Any hope of improvement in the lives of children will depend, as it always has, on the commitment that these participants in the child welfare system bring to reform. (Grimm, 1997, p. 10)

REFERENCES

Anderson, P. G. (1989). The origin, emergence, and professional recognition of child protection. *Social Service Review, 63,* 222–244.

Ashby, L. (1997). *Endangered children: Dependency, neglect, and abuse in American history.* New York: Twayne.

Aries, P. (1962). *Centuries of childhood: A social history of family life.* New York: Vintage Books.

Axinn, J., & Levin, H. (1975). *Social welfare: A history of the American response to need*. New York: Dodd-Mead.

Bossard, J., & Boll, E. S. (1960). *The sociology of child development*. New York: Harper and Brothers.

Boston Children's Aid Society (BCAS). (1887). *Twenty-third report of the executive committee of the Boston children's aid society, from June, 1886 to June, 1887*. Brookline, MA: Chronicle Press/C. A. W. Spencer.

Brace, C. L. (1872). *The dangerous classes of New York and twenty years' work among them*. New York: Wynkoop & Hallenbeck.

Bremner, R. H. (Ed.). (1971). *Children and youth in America: A documentary history*. Cambridge, MA: Harvard University Press.

Bruno, F. J. (1946). *Trends in social work as reflected in the proceedings of the national conference of social work, 1874–1946*. New York: Columbia University Press.

Carstens, C. C. (1915). Report of the Committee: A community plan in children's work. (pp. 92–111) *Proceedings of the National Conference of Charities and Correction*, May 12–19, 1915. Chicago, IL: Hildmann Printing Company.

Clement, P. F. (1979). Families and foster care: Philadelphia in the late nineteenth century. *Social Service Review, 53*, 406–420.

Crenson, M. A. (1998). *Building the invisible orphanage: A prehistory of the American welfare system*. Cambridge, MA: Harvard University Press.

Costin, L. B. (1982). Cruelty to children: a dormant issue and its rediscovery, 1920–1960. *Social Service Review, 56*, 177–198.

Costin, L. B., Karger, H. J., & Stoesz, D. (1996). *The politics of child abuse in America*. New York: Oxford University Press.

DeFrancis, V. (1973). *Protecting the abused child*. Hearing before the Subcommittee on Children and Youth, 93rd Congress, on the Child Abuse Prevention and Treatment Act (S1191), 323–331.

deMause, L. (1975, April). Our forebears made childhood a nightmare. *Psychology Today*, 85–88.

Demos, J. (1986). *The family and the life course in American history*. New York: Oxford University Press.

Downs, S. W., & Sherraden, M. (1983). The orphan asylum in the nineteenth century. *Social Service Review, 57*, 272–290.

Dulberger, J. A. (1996). *Mother donit fore the best—Correspondence of a nineteenth century orphan asylum*. Syracuse, NY: Syracuse University Press.

Elmer, E. (1960). Abused young children seen in hospitals. *Social Work, 5*, 98–102.

Fanshel, D., & Shinn, E. B. (1978). *Children in foster care: A longitudinal investigation*. New York: Columbia University Press.

Fry, A. R. (1974). The children's migration. *American Heritage, 26*, 4–10, 79–81.

Gelles, R. (1996). *The book of David: How preserving families can cost children's lives*. New York: Basic Books.

Gerry, E. T. (1882). The relation of societies for the prevention of cruelty to children to child saving work. In *Proceedings of the national conference of charities and corrections, 1882*. (pp. 637–654). Madison, WI: Midland Publishing Company.

Goldstein, J., Freud, A., & Solnit, A. (1973). *Beyond the best interests of the child*. New York: Free Press.

Grimm, W. (1997). Adoption and safe families act brings big changes in child welfare. *Youth Law News, 28*, 10.

Hacsi, T. (1995). From indenture to foster care: A brief history of child placing. *Child Welfare, 74*, 162–181.

Handler, J., & Hasenfeld, Y. (1991). *The moral construction of poverty: Welfare reform in America*. Newbury Park, CA: Sage.

Hart, H. H. (1909). The care of the dependent child in the family. *Pedagogical Seminary, 14*, 464–472.

Jeter, H. (1963). *Children, problems, and services in child welfare programs*. Washington, DC: U.S. Children's Bureau.

Kempe, C. H. (1978). Child abuse: The pediatrician's role in advocacy and preventive pediatrics. *American Journal of Diseases in Children, 132*, 255–260.

Maas, H. S., & Engler, R. E., Jr. (1959). *Children in need of parents*. New York: Columbia University Press.

Massachusetts Society for the Prevention of Cruelty to Children. (1906). *Twenty-sixth annual report* (December 31, 1906). Boston: Griffith-Stillings Press.

Massachusetts Society for the Prevention of Cruelty to Children. (1907). *Twenty-seventh annual report* (December 31, 1907). Boston: Griffith-Stillings Press.

McOllough, V. (1988, Fall). The orphan train comes to Clarion. *Palimpsest, 145*.

Pleck, E. (1987). *Domestic tyranny: The making of American social policy against family violence from colonial times to the present*. New York: Oxford University Press.

Reid, J. H. (1959). Action called for—recommendations. In H. S. Maas & R. E. Engler (Eds.), *Children in need of parents* (pp. 379–386). New York: Columbia University Press.

Ross, C. J. (1980). The lessons of the past: Defining and controlling child abuse in the United States. In G. Gerber, C. Ross, & E. Zigler (Eds.), *Child abuse—An agenda for action* (pp. 63–81). New York: Oxford University Press.

Thomas, M. P., Jr. (1972). Child abuse and neglect—Part I: Historical overview, legal matrix, and social perspectives. *North Carolina Law Review, 50*, 293–349.

Vandepol, A. (1982). Dependent children, child custody, and the mothers' pensions: The transformation of state-family relations in the early 20th century. *Social Problems, 29*, 221–235.

Wiebe, R. H. (1967). *The search for order, 1877–1920*. New York: Hill and Wang.

Williams, G. J. (1980a). Child abuse and neglect: Problems in definition and incidence. In G. J. Williams & J. Money (Eds.), *Traumatic abuse and neglect of children at home* (pp. 1–8). Baltimore, MD: Johns Hopkins University Press.

Williams, G. J. (1980b). Cruelty and kindness to children: Documentary of a century, 1874–1974. In G. J. Williams & J. Money (Eds.), *Traumatic abuse and neglect of children at home* (pp. 63–83). Baltimore, MD: Johns Hopkins University Press.

Williams, G. J. (1980c). Introduction to Part II / Protection of children against abuse and neglect: Historical background. In G. J. Williams & J. Money (Eds.), *Traumatic abuse and neglect of children at home* (pp. 47–52). Baltimore, MD: Johns Hopkins University Press.

Zelizer, V. A. (1985). *Pricing the priceless child: The changing social value of children*. New York: Basic Books.

CHAPTER 3

Families and Children Served by Child Welfare Agencies

A. Suzanne Boyd, Carole A. Winston, and Marianne Berry

So far in this text, we have looked at child welfare as a specific field of social work and public policy and surveyed the history of child welfare. In this chapter, we take as our subject the many influences and stresses that bring children and families into the child welfare system. Why do some parents maltreat their children? Our discussion begins with a look at the political mood of the U.S. and how it relates to the rapid increase in child welfare caseloads.

The Political Environment for Families

Prior to repeal of the Aid to Families with Dependent Children (AFDC) entitlement program and subsequent passage of the Personal Responsibility and Work Opportunity Reconciliation Act of 1996, needy families with children could look to government welfare aid in the form of cash assistance, Medicaid, and food stamps. The 1996 law essentially transformed welfare programs into employment programs. The new law's focus was "to provide assistance to needy families with children so they can be cared for in their own home, and to reduce dependency by promoting job preparation, work and marriage" (National Conference of State Legislators, n.d.). Families receiving cash assistance from Temporary Aid to Needy Families (TANF) were given more stringent work requirements, sanctions for noncompliance, and a five-year lifetime limit for receiving benefits.

When the economy was strong, the new welfare reform programs successfully moved many poor, single-parent women from welfare to work but not out of poverty. Even before the economic downturn around 2000, some families were unable to overcome barriers to employment, and many families who found employment still needed additional support to meet their needs.

There are several fundamental differences between the TANF block grant program and its predecessor, the AFDC program. Implemented during the 1930s, Aid to Families with Dependent Children (AFDC) was designed to accommodate the needs of parents and be family friendly, supporting mothers who stayed at home to raise their children. AFDC set rates of financial assistance based on the number of children in the household and the financial assets owned by the family.

The economic, political, and social environment shifted greatly from the 1960s to the 1990s, however. Economically, more families were forced to have two incomes to meet the rising cost of living. Socially, it became more and more accepted that women could and would work outside the home. Politically, it became clear that for poor families, working mothers were essential to the survival of their families, particularly given the bleak employment landscape for African American and Hispanic American males.

By the 1990s, the social and political landscape had changed so much that individuals and families on welfare were demonized as cheaters and exploiters of the public goodwill. Due to this changed political climate, welfare reform efforts received almost universal support for limiting the time and amount of public financial assistance that an individual could receive. The reformers wanted to provide incentives to the recipients of aid—to make them search for employment and economic self-sufficiency and thereby reduce public expenditures on welfare. The TANF program, as welfare reform, was designed to provide parents with only temporary financial help. By placing time limits on assistance, the reformers reportedly thought they would help motivate parents to find employment in order to become self-sufficient and be able to provide care for their own children without economic assistance. The key element of TANF was these term limits on supports, such as financial assistance and child care.

Did TANF increase the economic viability of families? Given the mandate that they had to leave the welfare roll, many parents did. But the new federal requirement that parents had to work caused these low-income working parents to seek other ways to economically care for their children. (Moreover, child care and health insurance benefits are seldom a part of poverty-wage employment.) For example, in almost every state, the percentage of Black children represented in foster care is higher when compared to the state's general population (Pecora, Whittaker, Maluccio, & Barth, 2000).

In addition to setting time limits for assistance, welfare reform legislation gave the states increased flexibility in designing their own welfare and support programs for low-income families. For example, North Carolina's Work First program, begun in 1995 in anticipation of the passage of the federal welfare reform legislation, was "built upon the premise that all people have a responsibility to their families and community to work and provide for their children (Wake County Government, n.d.). Work First provided short-term job training, child care assistance, and other services designed to help families become self-sufficient. Designated counties were directed to develop local Work First grant plans that involved an amalgam of public, private, and for-profit groups. Proposed grants had to describe project strategies by businesses, community groups, nonprofits, and religious groups to develop measurable statewide outcome goals that reflected the concept of economic self-sufficiency for citizens of North Carolina.

The final TANF regulations, effective in October 1999, clarified the types of assistance that were subject to the federal time limit and work requirements. Many supports were noticeably excluded from these requirements, including child care, transportation, Individual Development Accounts (IDAs), refunded portions of state-earned income tax credits, crisis intervention services, and case management (Zedlewski, 2002). To their credit, some states have begun to use TANF monies, alone or in combination with other funds, to establish programs providing housing assistance to families who are ineligible for federal housing assistance and cannot afford to pay the full cost of housing in the private market. These supports, however, are provided on a state-by-state basis and are subject to changing social and political sentiment regarding poor families.

While poverty overall has declined under welfare reform, a significant segment of the population of poor families is worse off, in part because after leaving welfare, many families do not receive other government supports designed to help them. Many studies have confirmed that families who leave welfare also leave behind government assistance for food, health insurance, and child care (Isaacs & Lyon, 2000).

Social services providers across the country are attempting to respond to the needs of families nearing their time limits for assistance, families that are particularly difficult to serve. According to a spokesperson for Catholic Charities in the mid-Atlantic region, of all the families leaving welfare in Maryland, almost two-thirds had worked at least a few, but not all, months in the two years before coming onto the welfare roll, indicating that they were not able to sustain employment. The chair of a Maryland-area coalition on welfare notes, "These are families with multiple barriers, very

Under provisions of the 1996 welfare reform act, recipients, including parents of young children, must either be working or in job training.

little education, very little job experience, who are maybe on the fringe of mental illness. It is very hard to serve this population quickly, which is what providers are being asked to do" (Vallianatos, 2002, p. 3).

Former President Bill Clinton oversaw the overhaul of welfare during his administration. Partnered with an emphasis on economic self-sufficiency for families, his administration stressed the importance of education for the nation's workforce and for national well-being, assuring the public that his educational proposals would improve access to higher education and reward academic achievement by including tuition tax credits for students who maintained a "B" average. By stark contrast, the new welfare law drastically limits the number of recipients who can participate in education, since it specifically mandates a work-first policy. Higher education has been one of the most promising pathways out of poverty, but poor women on welfare are now required to take any jobs available, with extremely limited options provided for job training and no options provided for higher education.

Family Structure and Marriage Promotion

Two other key themes in the 1996 welfare reform law promoted marriage and a reduction in out-of-wedlock births. Provisions of the law that addressed these goals focused primarily on allowing more liberal welfare eligibility criteria for two-parent families and imposing more stringent requirements on unmarried minor teen parents. The rationale for the increases for two-parent families was to increase the potential for two incomes and thus the potential for one parent to stay home with young children, so the state would not have to subsidize child care. Many critics have charged that these financial incentives for two-parent households have put battered women in the difficult position of choosing between economic survival and physical survival (Correia, 2000).

The research literature has repeatedly shown that nearly 60 percent of all first marriages are expected to end in divorce and 60 percent of all divorces involve children. One-third of all births are out of wedlock, nearly 40 percent of children do not live with their biological fathers, and a large number of nonresident fathers neither support nor see their children on a regular basis. Children living with single mothers are five times as likely to be poor as those in two-parent families, and growing up in a single-parent family may double the risk that a child will drop out of school, have difficulty finding a job, or become a teen parent (Edin, 2000; Ooms, 2002).

The Bush administration's 2002 welfare reform reauthorization proposal included $300 million for federally sponsored demonstration grants to focus on promoting healthy marriages and reducing out-of-wedlock births. This initiative supports an overwhelming consensus of social science research findings that when parents are married, children tend to be better off emotionally and financially. It is not just the presence of two adults in the home that helps children, since children living with both married biological parents fare better than children living with cohabiting partners and in stepfamilies. The benefits of marriage also accrue to husbands and wives. According to sociologists Linda Waite and Mary Gallagher (2001), married adults are more productive on the job, earn more, save more, have better physical and mental health, and live longer.

Proponents of the logic that married people are more likely to create a healthy environment for their children because they are married tend to underplay the importance of economic and noneconomic factors in the equation. Their critics argue that it is not that single mothers are poor because they are unmarried; they are unmarried because they are poor. Researchers Kathryn Edin and Laura Lein (2000) conducted in-depth multiple interviews with single mothers, whether on welfare or in low-wage employment. They talked with over 130 black, white, and Puerto Rican mothers in nine neighborhoods across the Philadelphia metropolitan area. The interviews revealed four major motives for nonmarriage among the poor: affordability, respectability, trust, and control. Overall, the interviews showed that although mothers aspire to marriage, they feel it entails more risks than rewards, at least marriage to the kinds of men who fathered their children and live in their neighborhoods. They are willing and even eager to wed if the marriage represents substantial economic upward mobility and their husband does not beat them, abuse them, abuse their children, insist on making all the decisions, or " fool around" with other women. If they cannot enjoy economic stability and respectability from marriage, they see little reason to expose themselves and their children to a man's lack of trustworthiness and sometimes violent behavior or to risk the loss of independence they fear marriage might exact from them. Ironically, when asked why they do not marry the mothers of their children, low-skilled and unemployed men cite their inability to provide income to their families as the major reason (Ooms, 2002, p. 26).

Other researchers have suggested that replacing welfare with work might discourage marriage. Rigorous studies of welfare programs in two states have found that the chances that a single mother will wed are significantly reduced by the stricter work requirements of the current welfare policy. Like middle-class married women, whose divorce rates increased with jobs and with rising wages that made them more self-reliant, some women who move from welfare to work may have become less willing to settle for the wrong man. At the same time, strict work requirements and low wages may have left some mothers with less time, energy, and income to attract a partner or nourish a relationship. The results of a study of mothers and children randomly assigned to Connecticut's Jobs First program showed that after three years, only 7 percent of the mothers who had gone through Jobs First were married and living with a spouse, compared with 15 percent of those randomly assigned to receive traditional welfare benefits under the old program, Aid to Families with Dependent Children (AFDC). Among women in the two groups with stronger employment histories, the difference was even greater: 6 percent versus 18 percent.

Two of the study's respondents reported the following:

Janna, age 26, is the mother of two: Erin, now 6, and Sarah, 1. Janna explained that she would not push to marry the father of Sarah because she enjoyed her independence. Janna said she studied and worked and supported her older daughter partly through a welfare grant she collected under AFDC while earning a degree that tripled her wages to $15 an hour.

Nyla, age 30, wondered if the government also planned to offer help with divorces if the marriages of the poor did not work out. Nyla fled an abusive husband when their daughter was an infant and her son was about 5. She was stunned when the first divorce lawyer she called wanted a $2,500 retainer. Now she is in a relationship with a man who has a good job and is the father of her third child. He has other children from a previous marriage and has steep child support payments. They have not set a date to marry because they cannot afford to marry.

Poor two-parent families are twice as likely as nonpoor families to divorce. Successful marriages are more difficult to maintain when husbands and wives are poorly educated, lack access to jobs that pay a decent wage, and cannot afford decent child care. Economic hardship and other problems associated with poverty, including inadequate housing, domestic violence, substance abuse, and mental illness, can seriously undermine couples' relationships.

Ooms (2002) suggests several strategies for reducing the stress of poverty and unemployment on poor and working-poor parents so that they might enter into and remain in healthy marriages—marriages that promote appropriate parent–child and spousal interactions. First, she points to the Minnesota Family Investment Program (MFIP), which subsidized the earnings of employed parents receiving public assistance. The results of the demonstration program found that marriage rates increased for both single-parent, long-term recipients and two-parent families. Married two-parent families were significantly more likely to remain married. MFIP also reduced the reported incidence of domestic abuse. Second, when couples are employed, workplace stress spills over into the home. Employers are increasingly demanding nonstandard work schedules. A recent study found that married couples with children who work night and rotating shifts are at higher risk of separation and divorce. The absence of affordable and reliable child care forces many parents who would prefer a normal workday to work split shifts for the sole purpose of making sure that one parent is at home with the children (Ooms, 2002, p. 27).

Marriage is only a partial solution toward improved well-being for poor families. Just as marriage was never a guaranteed path to economic security, declines in marriage, high divorce rates, and stagnating earnings among low-skilled men and women mean that marriage is an increasingly incomplete path to economic security.

In addition to promoting marriage, the 1996 welfare reform law also called on the U.S. Department of Health and Human Services to establish a strategy for preventing out-of-wedlock teen pregnancies and provided new funding for abstinence education and bonuses for states with the highest reduction in out-of-wedlock births (Shields & Behrman, 2002). Educators and health care workers are not permitted to discuss abortion with teens, so their ability to influence a reduction in the teen birth rate is limited. Teens with children are, as noted earlier, given financial incentives to marry and raise their children, which diminishes their futures educationally and financially.

The Dual Role of Child Welfare

Taking a broad view, we must say that a child's welfare is supported by all aspects of the social environment necessary for healthy development, including medical care, day care, education, recreation, and public safety. The focus of child welfare as an aspect of social work practice is much more limited. Public child welfare is concerned with the special needs of children and families in two categories: (1) families in which the parents are unwilling or unable to provide safe and adequate parental care and (2) families in which the children are unable to remain in the home because of behavioral, emotional, or developmental impediments.

Child welfare legislation and practice target two concurrent responsibilities, which we can categorize as supporting the child's protection and the child's connections. Children must be protected against maltreatment and danger, and that protection must be monitored and ensured. Furthermore, a child's development is supported through consistent and primary relationships, most commonly with the biological parents or kin. Child welfare agencies are charged with the dual responsibility of protecting children while maintaining their primary relationships, even if or when those relationships have involved maltreatment.

Protection of Children

Although the philanthropic goal of protecting children from cruelty and harm was established for child welfare well before the beginning of the twentieth century, the main concern of the largely church-based programs of that time was the placement of abandoned and orphaned children. When public child welfare agencies came into being in the 1920s, child abuse was just one of many concerns of the public child welfare system; child labor and family poverty were the primary concerns of agencies at that time in U.S. history. Kadushin and Martin (1988) note a "decline of interest [in child protective services] between 1920 and the 1960s. Child maltreatment as a social concern dropped out of the public agenda" (pp. 222–223).

Lindsey (1994) argues that the decline of interest during that period was related to society's distaste for discussing the possibility of abuse within the sanctity of the family home and to the difficulty of proving that a child's injuries were the result of parental abuse. Social workers lacked the means of determining whether injuries were accidental or inflicted by a parent or another adult caregiver. As noted in earlier chapters, until the late 1940s and early 1950s, medical providers resisted diagnosing parental child abuse as the cause of children's injuries. By 1955, a report published in the *Journal of the American Medical Association* (JAMA) reviewed a number of reports of infants seen in medical facilities with serious physical injuries of unknown origin, including inflammation of bone tissue and subdural hematoma with multiple long-bone fractures. In 1960, pediatrician C. Henry Kempe published an article in *JAMA* that defined the *battered child syndrome*. He cited unusual injuries, broken bones, and cranial injuries to infants and children less than 3 years old that were inadequately or inconsistently explained by physicians (Lindsey, 1994, p. 92). By 1962, the findings of both articles had provided the impetus for the U.S. Children's Bureau to develop a model child abuse reporting law that directed physicians to report cases of suspected child battering. By 1967, all states had passed legislation requiring professionals, including social workers, to report incidents of child abuse to their state agencies.

Since then, a major task assigned to the child welfare system has been the investigation of allegations of abuse and neglect. An appropriate name—*child protective services*—was coined for the agencies and social workers charged with this task. Since 1974 and passage of the federal Child Abuse Prevention and Treatment Act, citizens and/or professionals are mandated report known or suspected incidents of child maltreatment, including physical abuse, neglect, sexual abuse, and abandonment (see Figure 3.1). Each state defines in its own family code of behaviors (i.e., commissions of abuse or omissions of care) that constitutes various types of maltreatment, and each state has its own system and policies for responding to the reports. Mandatory reporting has led to an overwhelming increase in the number of reports received by state child welfare agencies, with the result that the system has been hard pressed to adequately investigate and serve the children it is mandated to protect.

In recognition of the emergence of mandatory child abuse reporting, social policy analysts Kamerman and Kahn (1990) studied child welfare programs in a number of geographical locations throughout the United States. Their findings demonstrated that within the decade of the 1980s, child welfare agencies had been transformed from foster care agencies to child protective service agencies, with the primary function of investigating the ever-increasing numbers of child abuse reports.

Connections for Children

Historically, the method of protecting children from parents who were perceived as inadequate, neglectful, or harmful has been to place those children in foster care. Throughout the 1950s and 1960s, children were removed from their families and placed in foster care in increasing numbers, and the length of time they spent in foster care was allowed to be of any duration—namely, until child welfare professionals thought it was safe for them to go home. In many instances, a child placed in foster care benefited from the resources and supports provided, and thus it became difficult for the child welfare agency to decide to return the child to the parents—not because of the parents' behavior but because withdrawal of state services and supports might hinder the child's continuing growth.

Many child and family advocates began to lament the lack of attention to parental needs that resulted while child protection was so emphasized. Demonstration programs in the 1970s showed that when appropriate services were focused on the parents, rather than the children, more children were able to go home and be safe there. Since the safety of the child is a parental responsibility, it seemed logical and indeed effective to focus attention and services on parental abilities.

As a result of the model programs, sweeping federal legislation called the Adoption Assistance and Child Welfare Act was enacted in 1980. This law stated in legislation and funding formulas that states must make reasonable efforts to keep maltreated children (those so identified) with their families. According to this law, if a child had to be removed from the family, the state had to make reasonable efforts to return the child home in a timely fashion. This legislation was the beginning of what is called *family-centered,* rather than *child-centered,* child welfare services and policy.

As the focus of child welfare policy and practice has come to include both the child and the family, the child welfare system has become increasingly complex. No longer is it enough to care for neglected or abused children. The current mandate further directs that services be provided to children *and* families, so that family life will be strengthened and families will remain safely intact. Current wisdom acknowledges that the family plays a crucial role in the maintenance of an orderly society and is the best institution for providing nurturance, stability, and continuity for its members. This current emphasis on family-centered social work practices is paramount. Services offered in support of that belief include family preservation programs; abuse prevention education; child guidance centers; mental health clinics; day care programs; breakfast, lunch, and after-school programs; and in-home social services, to name a few.

The Complexity of Providing for the Welfare of Children

While the mandate to provide direct services to children and families is clear, the child and family welfare system has evolved into a system with two distinct roles: (1) to provide protective and supportive direct services to children and families where problems are identified and (2) to support public policy and programs designed to improve the lives of all children. Child welfare is now faced with the challenge of supporting policies and programs that affect traditionally underserved populations and families new to the system of child welfare services. As HIV/AIDS has created a population of orphans, and family violence, substance abuse, divorce, and incarceration have torn apart families from all socioeconomic strata, the child welfare system has had to forge new alliances with individuals, neighborhoods, communities, and organizations in the micro and macro service delivery systems to address the complex needs of families and children. In response to the growing number of children being cared for in kinship care families (i.e., households headed by grandparents, other relatives, and non-related adults), public and private agencies, along with grass-roots coalitions nationwide, have begun to expand services and supports for those children living inside or outside the confines of the foster care system. For example, in North Carolina, approximately 135,000 children, or 6.9 percent of all children under age 18, live in grandparent-headed households, another 39,000 live in homes headed by relatives other than grandparents, and an additional 36,000 live in homes headed by nonrelatives (North Carolina Division of Aging, 2002).

As the economic, social, and physical challenges of raising children have become more complex and reached across the social strata of families, public and private child-serving agencies have been forced to think creatively and economically about how to address general social problems and individual family crises. The economic and political landscape for families in the United States has been shown to be nonsupportive, so agencies are often expected to "solve major social problems, one family at a time" (Schuerman, Rzepnicki, & Littell, 1997, p. 241).

The Focus of Child Welfare

Under the broad definition, *child welfare* refers to all aspects of the social environment necessary for the well-being of children, including medical care, day care, education, recreation, and public safety. The focus of child welfare as a field of social work practice is, by comparison, very limited. Pubic child welfare is specifically concerned with two focuses: (1) the special needs of children and families when parents are unwilling or unable to provide parental care and (2) the special needs of the child who cannot remain in the family home because of behavioral, emotional, or developmental impediments.

Child Maltreatment Defined

The concept of *child maltreatment* has been variously defined and redefined in Western society. Although there is ample historical evidence that children have been abandoned, sexually exploited, beaten, murdered, indentured, and forced into labor by parents and caregivers, (Crosson-Tower, 2002; English, 1998; Popple & Leighninger, 2002), those actions were not formally defined as unacceptable treatment of children until the midtwentieth century. No universally applied child maltreatment definition exists.

In 1974, the U.S. Congress passed the Child Abuse Prevention and Treatment Act (CAPTA) to provide a national definition of child maltreatment. CAPTA, as amended by the Keeping Children and Families Safe Act of 2003, defines *child abuse and neglect* as, at minimum, "any recent act or failure to act on the part of a parent or caretaker which results in death, serious physical or emotional harm, sexual abuse or exploitation; or an act or failure to act which presents an imminent risk of serious harm" (NCCANI, 2004).

The federal CAPTA legislation sets minimum definitional standards for child abuse and neglect, but the states vary in their criteria of specific definitions of maltreatment. For example, some states include educational neglect (i.e., when a child consistently fails to attend school) in their definition of child maltreatment, while others do not. Because of the variability of standards and procedures for the determination of child maltreatment across the states, it is difficult to compare abuse and neglect statistics nationwide (English, 1998). Nonetheless, the following four types of child maltreatment are recognized in most states: (1) neglect, (2) physical abuse, (3) sexual abuse, and (4) emotional abuse. These often occur together (NCCANI, 2004). Figure 3.1 summarizes the major forms of child maltreatment, as defined by the National Clearinghouse for Child Abuse and Neglect Information (NCCANI). As previously mentioned, individual states may not include all of the examples listed in Figure 3.1, and they may also include additional forms of child maltreatment not in this list.

These definitions of abuse and neglect are not problem free. For example, poverty and cultural values may be contributing factors to the child neglect situation, indicating the family is in need of information or assistance. In addition, the acts defined as physical abuse do not consider whether the caregiver's acts were intentional; there

---

FIGURE 3.1   Major Types of Child Abuse and Neglect

Neglect is the failure to provide for a child's basic needs. It may involve any of the following:

- Physical (failure to provide necessary food or shelter or lack of appropriate supervision)
- Medical (failure to provide necessary medical or mental health treatment)
- Educational (failure to educate a child or attend to special education needs)
- Emotional (inattention to a child's emotional needs, failure to provide psychological care, or permitting the child to use alcohol or other drugs)

These situations do not always mean a child is neglected. Sometimes cultural values, the standards of care in the community, and poverty may be contributing factors, indicating the family is in need of information or assistance. When a family fails to use information and resources and the child's health or safety is at risk, then child welfare intervention may be required.

Physical abuse is physical injury (ranging from minor bruises to severe fractures or death) as a result of punching, beating, kicking, biting, shaking, throwing, stabbing, choking, hitting (with a hand, stick, strap, or other object), burning, or otherwise harming a child. Such injury is considered abuse regardless of whether the caretaker intended to hurt the child.

Emotional abuse is a pattern of behavior that impairs a child's emotional development or sense of self-worth. This may include constant criticism, threats, or rejection, as well as withholding love, support, or guidance. Emotional abuse is often difficult to prove, and therefore, Child protective services may not be able to intervene without evidence of harm to the child. Emotional abuse is almost always present when other forms are identified.

Sexual abuse includes activities by a parent or caretaker such as fondling a child's genitals, penetration, incest, rape, sodomy, indecent exposure, and exploitation through prostitution or the production of pornographic materials.

Source: National Clearinghouse for Child Abuse and Neglect Information, 2004.

are times when a child is harmed because parental discipline results in an unintended injury. Finally, emotional abuse can be very difficult to prove.

Numbers of Children Abused and Neglected

According to the National Child Abuse and Neglect Data System (NCANDS, 2004), *Summary of Key Findings* from calendar year 2002, approximately 896,000 U.S. children were found to be victims of child abuse and neglect. Just over half of child victims (60 percent) experienced neglect, about 20 percent were physically abused, 10 percent were sexually abused, and 7 percent were emotionally maltreated. The rate of child victims per 1,000 children in the population dropped from 13.4 children in 1990 to 12.3 children in 2002.

Despite extensive research into the causes of child maltreatment, the consensus is that the dynamics of child abuse and neglect are too complex to be explained by a single theoretical construct. It is now believed that child maltreatment, like other social welfare problems, may result from the interaction of individual parental personality characteristics and environmental stressors. Family, cultural and historical factors also contribute to child maltreatment and subsequent involvement in the social services system.

The Ecosystems Model of Social Work Practice

The *ecosystems model* of social work practice is an analytical tool we can use to examine, organize, and better understand the many different factors that contribute to the problem of child maltreatment. We use the ecosystems model (Morales & Sheafor, 2004) here as a framework to organize our discussion of the reasons some families and children become involved in the social services system. The ecosystems model organizes the contributing factors at five levels: individual, family, cultural, socio-environmental, and historical. As we examine the five levels, we will apply them to the following vignette:

Judy is a tall, thin, 24-year-old European American woman who is seeking help from a community mental health clinic because she is often tearful for no apparent reason, is having difficulty sleeping, and is often irritable and impatient with her two young children. She has never hit her children, but she is afraid she may lose her temper and hurt them.

Judy is the oldest of seven children, none of whom finished high school. Her youngest sister, age 17, is pregnant and does not plan to return to school after her baby is born. Judy's parents have been married for almost 25 years. Her father drinks heavily and was often physically abusive to his wife and his children. Despite his drinking, her father has managed to keep his job as a security guard at a small manufacturing plant in town. Judy would sometimes have to call her father's place of employment stating that he was sick or his car had broken down. Her mother has never worked outside the home, believing her role is that of wife and mother. Judy describes her mother as unhappy most of the time and very depressed when her father is drinking. Judy and her siblings have suggested to their mother that she leave their father, but none of them believe she will.

A single mother of two children, ages 4 and 2, Judy began receiving welfare in 2000. She lives in a small, rural community in New York's Catskill Mountains, an area hit hard by the economic recession. Judy dropped out of school in the ninth grade. She was pregnant at 18 and married at 19 to Mark, a man she said made all the decisions at home, from buying groceries to dressing the children.

Mark left when Judy was pregnant with their youngest child. At the time, Judy felt lost. At first, she did not know how to drive, nor did she know how to shop for herself and the children. She found the everyday activities of life overwhelming. She was fired from her first job as a beauty supply store clerk because her babysitter was unreliable. She was evicted from the $800-a-month apartment she lived in because she allowed her sister and her sister's boyfriend to move in to help with expenses. Judy says the small rural church she had attended rejected her and her children when Mark left her and she became a single parent.

Because there are no reliable bus lines in the Catskills, Judy has learned to drive and gained access to a clunker car. She now holds a part-time job ringing up groceries at a supermarket 25 miles from home. She is thankful for a babysitter who has agreed to match her erratic work schedule: a 10:00 A.M. shift one day, a 2:30 P.M. shift another.

Judy's paycheck varies from $80 on a bad week, when she is scheduled to work barely 14 hours, to $140 on a good one. The county still sends her $300 in food stamps every month, the same as before she found the part-time job, but only $128 a month in cash assistance, less than one-third of what she got before she began working. The county pays for the babysitter, and Judy is responsible for one-fourth of her rent, or $200 per month. She still cannot afford a telephone, and she pays $100 a month to a local furniture store to pay down the debt on a two-year-old bedroom suite that is already falling apart.

In sum, Judy does not make enough money to get off welfare. She also needs help with health care for her two children. If nothing changes, she will reach her five-year limit on cash benefits at the end of 2005.

After completing a detailed assessment, Judy's mental health clinic social worker focused on Judy's self-reported fear that she may lose control and hurt her children and what family support services may be beneficial for her and her children. Based on the assessment, the social worker has made a referral to child protective services (CPS). CPS will help Judy identify the needed family supports to address the individual, family, cultural, socioenvironmental, and historical factors that have influenced her current situation.

Individual Factors

As shown in Figure 3.2, the individual level is the nucleus of the ecosystems model. The parents being served by the child welfare system have experienced a variety of individual factors, factors that still work in tandem to affect their actions, including the neglect or abuse of their own children. The focus at the individual level is the biopsychosocial endowment of each person. This includes (1) communication and language skills, (2) habit formation, (3) problem-solving skills, (4) personality strengths, (5) level of psychosocial development, (6) cognition, (7) perception, (8) emotional maturity and temperament, (9) intelligence, and (10) confidence (Morales & Sheafor, 2004).

FIGURE 3.2	**Ecosystems Model for Social Work Practice**

V. Historical

Historical roots and heritage and
positive/negative experiences in both
country of origin and in the United States. Include
duration of these experiences and age experiences, and
how impacted by these experiences. Include landmark events
(war, ethnic cleansing, deportations, etc.)

**IV.
Environmental–Structural**

Elements of political, economic, and social
structural forces in social environment which
enhances or causes psychosocial problems for the
individual, family, group or communication; especially the
educational, medical, welfare, religious, correctional, police, health
and mental health, and other social systems.

III. Culture

Cultural values, belief systems,
ethnicity, lifestyle, and societal norms of
both the original culture and U.S. culture.
Especially language, food, ethnic/cultural identification,
sex roles, kinship styles, religion, customs, and
communication networks.

II. Family

Unique family lifestyle and
specific cultural way of intrafamily
interaction, family values, beliefs, authority
levels, affective style, emotional/economic,
vulnerabilities, and coping patterns

I. Individual

Biopsychosocial endowment
and parental nurturing experiences
and subsequent psychological
development. Cognitive, verbal, and problem-
solving skills, communication and language,
emotional maturity and temperament, personality
strengths/limitations, intelligence, social skills
and interaction, attitudes, beliefs, confidence,
maturity, lifestyle appropriate to
developmental stage, stress coping
skills, and ability to learn from life
experiences.

Source: From Armando T. Morales & Bradford W. Sheafor, *Social Work: A Profession of Many Faces,* 10th.ed. Published by
Allyn & Bacon, Boston, MA. Copyright © 2004 by Pearson Education. Reprinted by permission of the publisher.

Faller and Ziefert (1981) and Downs, Costin, and McFadden (1996) have identified the individual personality characteristics frequently found in maltreating parents. The most common include these:

1. *Low self-esteem:* These parents often think they are unworthy, incompetent, or bad. They often neglect themselves as well as their children, thereby reinforcing their feelings of worthlessness and incompetence.
2. *Excessive dependency:* Overly dependent parents are immature and have not sufficiently differentiated from their own parents. Because of their unmet dependency needs, they are unable to respond appropriately to the needs of their children.
3. *Serious difficulty coping with the demands of parenting:* These parents may have children in order to feel loved and nurtured, rather than to love and nurture their children.
4. *Poor impulse control:* These parents are unable to control their aggressive impulses. Feelings of anger and frustration can lead to physical or sexual assault on the child.
5. *Rigid superego structures:* Parents with rigid superegos have fixed ideas about how things should be. They are often unable to tolerate unruly behavior or disobedience. As a result, when things do not go their way, they are likely to lash out at their children.
6. *Deficient superego development:* These parents appear to lack appropriate empathy toward their children and feel little remorse when they abuse them.
7. *Lack of parenting skills and knowledge of child development:* Many parents who abuse and neglect their children have unreasonably high expectations of young children. Immaturity and the absence of parenting preparation and skills—coupled with a lack of knowledge about children's normal developmental milestones and how to determine reasonable, age-appropriate expectations for children's physical and emotional growth—can contribute to the incidence of abuse. Appropriate care may be withheld due to lack of knowledge, rather than purposeful neglect. The overall pressure of raising children can be particularly overwhelming for young, adolescent mothers. Studies have shown that children of single parents are at higher risk of physical abuse and of all types of neglect.
8. *Social isolation:* Maltreating parents often feel emotionally distant from their social environment. They do not join churches and other community groups, and they may be cut off from family and shun neighbors who might offer social support.

Research conducted during the last 30 or so years suggests that parental emotional or psychiatric disorders are contributing factors to child abuse and neglect (Taylor et al., 1991). However, not all parents diagnosed with psychiatric disorders maltreat their children. Walsh, MacMillan, and Jamieson (2002) studied the relationship between parental psychiatric disorder and the increased risk of child physical and sexual abuse among a representative community sample of 8,548 participants in the Ontario Mental Health Supplement. The participants completed a self-report measure of childhood sexual and physical abuse and were also interviewed about parental psychiatric history. Twenty-five percent of the respondents were exposed to physical abuse, 8 percent to sexual abuse, and 28.7 percent to any abuse (physical or sexual abuse, or both). One-fifth of the participants (19 percent) reported either a father or a mother or both with at least one psychiatric disorder. A diagnosis of depression in either parent was the most frequently reported psychiatric disorder (15.8 percent), followed by mania (3.7 percent), schizophrenia (2.4 percent), and antisocial behavior (2.4 percent). Prevalence estimates suggest two major findings:

1. Parental psychiatric disorder has a direct association with both physical and sexual abuse; the risk for both physical and sexual abuse is increased.
2. The relationship to depression, mania, and schizophrenia is similar for physical, sexual, and any abuse.

In sum, the results from this research study (Walsh et al., 2002) suggest a correlation between parental history of psychiatric disorder and an increased risk of child sexual and physical abuse.

Taylor et al. (1991) examined the court records of 206 seriously neglected or abused children and their families in a large urban area. The authors found that 84 percent showed evidence of parental psychiatric disorder and 51 percent revealed an intellectual (low-IQ) or *DSM-III* diagnosis (see Chapter 1 for an explanation of the *DSM*). The findings further revealed that 23 fathers were diagnosed with an intellectual or emotional disorder. Five fathers (21.7 percent) were diagnosed with schizophrenia, four (17 percent) with personality/character disorders, and three (13 percent) with severe depression. Of the mothers who were diagnosed with a specific mental or emotional disorder, 24 were diagnosed with severe depression and 15 with schizophrenia. The findings of the study (Taylor et al., 1991) do not mean we can conclude that parental psychiatric disorder causes child maltreatment.

Maltreating parents who are substance abusers are most likely to neglect their children because they are intoxicated and cannot attend to the daily responsibilities of providing care. According to Drug Strategies' *Keeping Score 1998,* as many as 80 percent of child abuse cases are associated with alcohol and other drug use. The number of child abuse and neglect cases nationwide climbed from 1.4 million in 1986, the beginning of the crack cocaine epidemic, to 2.8 million in 1993. Overall, few studies have been conducted that directly studied the relationship between parental substance abuse and child maltreatment, with the exception of child sexual abuse (Dore, Doris, & Wright, 1995). Research suggests that compared to other parents, parents who have a documented history of substance abuse are more likely to lose custody of their children, repeat the child maltreatment, and ignore court-ordered services (Murphy et al., 1991). A longitudinal study examining parental substance abuse as a predictor of child maltreatment re-reports found that parental substance abuse does increase the chance of poorer family functioning and higher re-report rates to child protective service agencies (Wolock & Magura, 1996). Magura and Laudet (1996) provide an excellent review of parental substance abuse and child maltreatment.

Dore and colleagues (1995) have studied the relationship between parental substance abuse and child mental health problems. The authors provide an overview of the documented empirical research literature dealing with the psychological risks for children whose parents abuse substances. Effects of parental substance abuse on their children include impaired intellectual and academic functioning, increased incidence of conduct and hyperactivity disorder, and lowered self-esteem and perceived lack of control over their environment.

Even though we do not fully understand how individual factors contribute to child maltreatment (and the preceding examples are certainly not comprehensive), we do know that individual factors contribute to child maltreatment. Thus, these individual factors must also be addressed by child welfare social workers during the risk assessment and safety assessment process.

Let's look now at Judy, from our earlier example. Numerous individual factors have influenced her situation. Early in life, Judy did not develop good problem-solving skills, as evidenced by the fact that she would call her father's place of employment stating that he was sick or his car had broken down. In addition, Judy perceived that education would not be helpful to her future, for her mother and most of the women in her small community had limited education. Judy herself completed only the ninth grade. Most important, Judy sought help because she had difficulty sleeping and was often tearful for no apparent reason. These symptoms suggest that Judy was likely experiencing clinical depression and therefore at an increased risk of harming her children.

Family Level

The second level in the ecosystems model of social work practice is the family level (see Figure 3.2). It focuses on "the nature of family lifestyle, culture, organization, family, division of labor, sex role structure and intergenerational dynamics" (Morales & Sheafor, 2004, p. 235). Given that each family unit is unique in its cultural context, the following factors are also reviewed at this level: (1) how a family unit manages stress (internal/external), (2) values, (3) beliefs, (4) affective style, (5) emotional support capacity, and (6) family strengths and vulnerabilities. The family level also stresses examining the relationship between spouses or partners and the parent's connection to the child and extended family members.

Family factors often contribute to child maltreatment. How family dynamics contribute to child neglect and abuse is not yet clear, but Faller and Ziefert (1981) have identified some of the important dynamics:

1. *Parental collusion:* In two-parent families, when abuse or neglect occurs, both parents are thought to play a role in the dynamics of the maltreatment. One or both parents may be the active abusers, but in most instances, there is a passive parent who gives covert permission for the other parent to neglect or abuse the child.
2. *Scapegoating:* When there is marital discord and the parents are in conflict, the antagonism between them may be displaced on the child as abuse or neglect. Frequently, the scapegoat child reminds the abuser of the other parent or is defined as bad and said to invite the maltreatment.
3. *Reorganized families:* A reorganized family is one in which one or more parent has remarried and brings children from a prior marriage with them to a new marriage, thus forming a reorganized family. Research and clinical data suggest that children in reorganized families are more likely to suffer maltreatment than children who live with biological parents. In the reorganized family, the incest taboo is not as strong, and resentment between members of the reconstituted household may result in the physical and sexual abuse of the children.
4. *Single-parent status:* Single-parenting, in and of itself, does not place children at risk for abuse or neglect, but poor single parents are overrepresented among

Understanding a family's cultural background is essential in assessing allegations of child maltreatment.

parents reported to child protective services. It is unclear how much this is a consequence of reporting bias or an indicator of single parents' difficulty in parenting.

5. *Adolescent parents:* Single adolescent parents are at greater risk for both abuse and neglect of their children. Because adolescence is a period characterized by physical, emotional, and intellectual upheaval, adolescent parents may not be psychologically equipped to meet the demands made by young children. If and when parenthood does not measure up to the young parent's expectations, frustration mounts and the child may be neglected or abused.

6. *Lack of extended family:* Parents who mistreat their children often lack the social and economic support of an extended family.

Several family factors affected Judy. Her family valued loyalty to its members, despite their differences. Judy received little emotional support from her mother, who was sad most of the time, but she received support from her siblings—a family strength. Judy was 18 years old when she had her first child and 20 years old when her second child. In addition, she was poor and a single parent—both factors that increase a family's risk of becoming involved in social service delivery systems.

Cultural Factors

The third level of the ecosystems model focuses on culture (see Figure 3.2). It puts the focus "on understanding the cultural values, belief systems, and societal norms of the host culture and, in the case of [people of color], their original culture" (Morales

& Sheafor, 2004, p. 235). Individual cultures "develop behavioral responses influenced by the environmental, historical or societal processes incorporating specific structures" (p. 235). Cultural influences include (1) food, (2) kinship styles, (3) language, (4) norms, (5) beliefs, and (6) religion.

The contribution of cultural factors to child maltreatment is one of the more difficult to pinpoint and understand, for it involves cultural values, belief systems, and societal norms. Family units have their own kinship styles, and cultural groups use language differently. The vernacular speech of a family under investigation by child protective services can be a hindrance to understanding. For example, a child in a rural area may say "My mom beat me last night," but investigation may indicate that the child received a spanking and was not bloodied or even bruised.

Cultural factors greatly influenced Judy's situation. Judy perceived that her role as a woman, based on community norms and beliefs, was to be a wife and a mother. In addition, she saw in her mother role model the belief of the importance of commitment to a marriage, even if alcohol or abuse was present in the relationship.

Environmental–Structural Factors

Environmental–structural factors comprise the fourth level of the ecosystems model (see Figure 3.2). Theories at this level hypothesize that both the economic and social structure of our Westernized society cause problems and struggles for oppressed populations (Morales & Sheafor, 2004). When the social environment is unsupportive, the ability of individuals and families to cope with difficulties in constructive ways is compromised.

Environmental–structural stressors may be acute or chronic. Acute stressors are commonly identified in cases of abuse, and taken together, these stressors may lead to abandonment of children or withdrawal from parenting responsibilities. The most common acute stressor is actual or perceived child misbehavior. Chronic stressors, on the other hand, occur consistently over longer periods of time. The most persistent chronic stressor that reflects both society's economic and social structure is poverty. For that reason, an extensive overview of poverty and maltreatment is warranted. Studies have found that with all other factors held equal, poor children are more likely than nonpoor children to be reported to child protective services (Ards, 1989; Drake & Pandey, 1996; Garbarino & Knostelny, 1992), and children from low-income families are more likely to be placed in foster care (Waldfogel, 1998).

No one fully understands the links between poverty and child maltreatment. The stress and frustrations of living in poverty may combine with attitudes toward the use of corporal punishment to increase the risk of physical violence. When a family lacks the basic resources needed to provide for a child, neglect is likely, as the family is in a state of distress; however, other external factors, such as social isolation and lack of a support system, may also contribute to child maltreatment. Most poor people do *not* abuse or neglect their children. The effects of poverty appear to interact with other risk factors—such as unrealistic expectations, depression, isolation, substance abuse, and domestic violence—to increase the likelihood of maltreatment.

While the United States continues to rank as the wealthiest country in the world, its poverty continues to worsen. Poverty among the elderly has essentially been

TABLE 3.1	Health and Human Services Poverty Guidelines: 1991–2004		
Year	First Person	Each Additional Person	Four-Person Family
2004	$9,310	$3,180	$18,850
2003	8,980	3,140	18,400
2002	8,860	3,080	18,100
2001	8,590	3,020	17,650
2000	8,350	2,900	17,050
1999	8,240	2,820	16,700
1998	8,050	2,800	16,450
1997	7,890	2,720	16,050
1996	7,740	2,620	15,600
1995	7,470	2,560	15,150
1994	7,360	2,480	14,800
1993	6,970	2,460	14,350
1992	6,810	2,380	13,950
1991	6,620	2,260	13,400

Note: 1999 and 2000 poverty figures should not be used in connection with determining poverty population figures from 2000 Decennial Census data. Poverty population figures are calculated using the U.S. Census Bureau poverty thresholds, not the poverty guidelines.

Source: U.S. Department of Health and Human Services, 2004. Available online: http://aspe.hhs.gov/poverty/figures-fed-reg.shtml

eliminated with establishment of social programs such as Medicaid, Medicare, and Meals-on-Wheels, but the nation's children are as likely to live in poverty today as they were two decades ago. Several studies have found that the United States continues to have the highest child poverty rate among major industrialized nations (UNICEF, 2000). The poverty rate for children has fluctuated since the 1980s and reached a peak of 22 percent in 1993. The rate dropped to 16 percent in 2000 (Federal Interagency Forum on Child and Family Statistics, 2005) and has remained steady since that time. With the recent economic downturn that forced mass layoffs, the United States may see again the levels of poverty associated with the recessions of the early 1980s and 1990s. In the United States today, almost 12 million children live in poverty and 5 million children live in extreme poverty, meaning their parents make only half of the income of the official federal poverty level (Hsien-Hen, 2003).

As reflected in Table 3.1, the 2004 poverty rate for a four-person family was $18,850. Since 1994, this rate has increased by only about 21 percent, which means it has not kept up with the cost of inflation and the additional needs of families and children during an economic recession. The poverty rates are somewhat higher for Alaska and Hawaii.

Sixty percent of African American children (6 million) live in low-income families and 62 percent of Latino children (8.2 million) live in low-income families, compared to 26 percent of white children (10.9 million) (National Center for Children in Poverty, 2005a). The figures for children younger than six in low-income families are almost identical to these numbers (National Center for Children in Poverty, 2005b). These figures remain consistent for children age three and under: the percentage of African American and Latino children who live in low-income families is about twice that of white families (National Center for Children in Poverty, 2005c).

Factors that contribute to childhood poverty include declining wages, unemployment, single-parent families, educational level of parents, pay inequity, sexism, and racism. Even in the robust economy of the late 1990s, the number of low-wage workers continued to grow, suggesting that work alone will not necessarily keep a family out of poverty (Crosson-Tower, 2002). In the recent recession, the unemployment rate edged up to 5.8 percent, an increase of 1.8 percentage points in one year. The loss of jobs was felt most acutely by the poor and so-called near poor, as they are usually the least skilled and the most expendable. As individuals and families struggle with the effects of a recession, the federal government is less prepared to assist them than it was 50 years ago. For example, the unemployment insurance system covers less than 40 percent of the people who are currently out of work. Also, the food stamp program, which once served 90 percent of eligible families, now serves just 60 percent of those who qualify for assistance (Herbert, 2001).

The concept of *family* continues to evolve. The prototypical nuclear family now takes its place alongside an increasing number of family models, including blended families, homosexual families, multigenerational families, and single-parent families. Single parents raising children are usually women. When they enter the workforce, they are often relegated to the secondary labor market, where work is sporadic, salaries are low, and fringe benefits are nonexistent. Characteristics that distinguish the primary labor market are steady employment, higher salaries, unemployment compensation, health insurance, pensions, and paid vacations. Parents who have less than a high school education are more likely to be poor than parents with more education. In today's job market, those who are unskilled or semiskilled will be relegated to low-level positions paying low wages.

Judy's economic struggles were strongly affected by the traditional economic structure of Westernized society. The slow economy and geographic isolation of her small town contributed greatly to her inability to find a job close to her home. She had to drive 25 miles to work. Even with the in-kind supports of housing assistance, child care, and food stamps, Judy still did not make enough money to get off welfare. Judy was very willing to work, but the fact that she had only a ninth-grade education further contributed to poverty for her and her children.

Historical Factors

The final level of factors in the ecosystems model (see Figure 3.2) notes the historical experience of individuals in oppressed populations and how their experiences influence the nature and quality of their interactions with the social environment (Morales & Sheafor, 2004). This historical set of influences can further help us understand the experience of families that become involved in the child welfare system. For example, African American and Hispanic American youth tend to be overrepresented in cases of child abuse and neglect and therefore in investigations by child protective services. A historical examination of the oppression experienced by such populations can explain the high levels of mistrust of the social service system in general and social workers in particular. Similarly, women as a group have experienced discrimination in terms of career opportunities, higher education, and the perceived stereotypical role of the mother as the homemaker. Wage inequality is one historical factor that still continues today; a woman generally earns 73 cents for every dollar earned by a man (Morales & Sheafor, 2004).

The deep historical roots of Judy's family in her town have greatly influenced how Judy interacts with the social institutions that are a part of her life: church, work, and family. Judy's mother fulfilled the historical stereotype of a mother's role: She never worked outside the home and believed that her role was that of wife and mother. When Judy's husband left while she was pregnant with her second child, she was forced to challenge the traditional mother role and find a way to support her children, which she managed by finding a job and getting public assistance. The history within Judy's marriage, such that Mark made all decisions (including buying groceries), meant she had to learn how to do even elementary tasks. Judy also experienced rejection from her church congregation because her living situation violated their historical stance that women with children should be married.

This brings to a close our review of Judy's situation. We can only hope the best for her and her two children when she has exhausted the limit (five years) of eligibility for cash assistance.

We have presented the ecosystems model as an analytical tool that can help us recognize the multiple influences that contribute to child maltreatment on an individual family basis. As we have seen, families in our society—especially poor families—are increasingly vulnerable. To meet the growing needs of these families, social service agencies need to provide preventive services, including intensive family support, to help families address the contributing factors that prevent them from fulfilling their parental obligations. Additionally, the families in crisis that are currently served by the child welfare system require more intensive support services provided over longer periods of time. The provision of such services can decrease the chance of a family's repeat involvement in the child welfare system.

REFERENCES

Ards, S. (1989). Estimating local child abuse. *Evaluation Review, 13*, 484–515.

Correia, A. (2000). *Strategies to expand battered women's economic opportunities.* Washington, DC: National Resource Center on Domestic Violence.

Crosson-Tower, C. (2002). *Understanding child abuse and neglect* (5th ed.). Boston: Allyn & Bacon.

Dore, M. M., Doris, J. M., & Wright, P. (1995). Identifying substance abuse in maltreating families: A child welfare challenge. *Child Abuse & Neglect, 19*(5), 531–543.

Downs, S. W., Costin, L. B., & McFadden, E. J. (1996). *Child welfare and family services: Policies and practices.* White Plains, NY: Longman.

Drake, B., & Pandey, S. (1996). Understanding the relationship between neighborhood poverty and specific types of child maltreatment. *Child Abuse & Neglect, 20*(11), 1003–1018.

Drug Strategies. (1998). *Keeping Score 1998.* Retrieved September 7, 2005, from www.drugstrategies.org/ks1998/use.html

Edin, K. (2000, January 3). Few good men. *American Prospect, 11*(4), 26–31.

English, D. (1998). The extent and consequences of child maltreatment. *Future of Children, 8.* Retrieved June 30, 2001, from www.futureofchildren.org/use_doc/vol8no1ART3.pdf

Faller, K. C., & Ziefert, M. (1981). Causes of child abuse and neglect. In K. C. Faller (Ed.), *Social work with abused and neglected children: A manual of interdisciplinary practice* (pp. 32–54). New York: Free Press.

Federal Interagency Forum on Child and Family Statistics. (2005). *America's children: Key national indicators of well-being 2005.* Retrieved September 7, 2005, from www.childstats.gov/americaschildren/index.asp

Garbarino, J., & Knostelny, K. (1992). Child maltreatment as a community problem. *Child Abuse & Neglect, 16*(4), 455–464.

Herbert, B. (2001, November 19). The vanishing act. *New York Times.* Retrieved November 19, 2001, from www.nytimes.com

Hsien-Hen, L. (2003, July). *Low-income children in the United States.* Retrieved August 5, 2003, from the National Center for Children in Poverty website, www.nccp.org/pub_cpf03.html

Isaacs, J. B., & Lyon, M. R. (2000). A cross-state examination of families leaving welfare: Findings from the ASPE-funded leavers studies. Washington, DC: Assistant Secretary for Planning and Evaluation.

Kadushin, A., & Martin, J. (1988). *Child welfare services* (4th ed.). New York: Macmillan.

Kamerman, S. B., & Kahn, A. J. (1990). Social services for children, youth, and families in the United States. *Children and Youth Services Review, 12,* 1–184.

Lindsey, D. (1994). *The welfare of children.* New York: Oxford University Press.

Magura, S., & Laudet, A. B. (1996). Parental substance abuse and child maltreatment: Review and implications for interventions. *Children & Youth Services Review, 18*(3), 193–220.

Morales, A. T., & Sheafor, B. (2004). *Social work: A profession of many faces* (10th ed.). Boston, MA: Allyn & Bacon.

Murphy, M., Jellinek, M., Quinn, D., Smith, G., Poitrast, F., & Goshko, M. (1991). Substance abuse and serious child maltreatment: Prevalence, risk, and outcome in a court sample. *Child Abuse & Neglect, 15*(3), 197–211.

National Center for Children in Poverty (NCCP). (2002, March). *Early childhood poverty: A statistical profile (March 2002).* Retrieved August 5, 2003, from http://cpmcnet.columbia.edu/dept/nccp/ycpt:html

National Center for Children in Poverty (NCCP). (2005a). *Basic facts about low-income children: Birth to age 18.* Retrieved September 7, 2005, from www.nccp.org/pub_lic05.html

National Center for Children in Poverty (NCCP). (2005b). *Basic facts about low-income children: Birth to age 6.* Retrieved September 7, 2005, from www.nccp.org/pub_lic05.html

National Center for Children in Poverty (NCCP). (2005c). *Basic facts about low-income children: Birth to age 3.* Retrieved September 7, 2005, from www.nccp.org/pub_lic05.html

National Clearinghouse for Child Abuse and Neglect Information (NCCANI), National Adoption Information Center. (2004, January). *What is child abuse and neglect?* Retrieved January 27, 2005, from http://nccanch.acf.hhs.gov/pubs/factsheets/whatiscan.cfm

National Conference of State Legislatures. (n.d.). *Analysis of the personal responsibility and work opportunity reconciliation act of 1996: Conference agreement for H. R. 3734.* Retrieved September 7, 2005, from www.ncsl.org/statefed/hr3734.htm #TEMPORARYASSISTANCE

North Carolina Division of Aging. (2002, May). *Grandparents and other relatives raising grandchildren: A state fact sheet (May 2002).* Retrieved from www.dhhs.state.nc.us/aging/grandp.html

Ooms, T. (2002, April 8). Marriage plus. *American Prospect, 13*(7), 24.

Pecora, P. J., Whittaker, J. K., Maluccio, A. N., & Barth, R. P. (Eds.). (2000). *The child welfare challenge: Policy, practice and research* (2nd ed.). New York: Aldine de Gruyter.

Popple, P. R., & Leighninger, L. (2002). *Social work, social welfare, and American society* (5th ed.). Boston: Allyn & Bacon.

Schuerman, J., Rzepnicki, T., & Littell, J. (1997). *Putting families first.* Hawthorne, NY: Aldine de Gruyter.

Shields, M. K., & Behrman, R. E. (2002). Children and welfare reform: Analysis and recommendations. *Children and Welfare Reform, 12*(1), 5–25.

Taylor, C. G., Norman, D. K., Murphy, J. M., Jellinek, M., Quinn, D., Poitrast, F. G., et al. (1991). Diagnosed intellectual and emotional impairment among parents who seriously mistreat their children: Prevalence, type, and outcome in a court sample. *Child Abuse & Neglect, 15*(4), 389–401.

UNICEF. (2000). *Innocenti Report Card One: A league table of child poverty in rich nations.* Florence, Italy: Innocenti Research Centre.

U.S. Department of Health and Human Services. (2004, April). *Child maltreatment 2002: Summary of key findings.* Retrieved January 27, 2005, from http://nccanch.acf.hhs.gov/pubs/factsheet/canstats.cfm

Vallianatos, C. (2002, February). Welfare limits: Disaster in the making. *NASW News,* 3.

Waite, L., & Gallagher, M. (2001). *The case for marriage: Why people are happier, healthier, and better off financially.* New York: Broadway Books.

Wake County Government. (n.d.). *Work first program.* Retrieved September 7, 2005, from www.wakegov.com/general/employment/jobresources/workfirst.htm

Waldfogel, J. (1998). *The future of child protection: How to break the cycle of abuse and neglect.* Cambridge, MA: Harvard University.

Walsh, C., MacMillan, H., & Jamieson, E. (2002). The relationship between parental psychiatric disorder and child physical and sexual abuse: Findings from the Ontario Health Supplement. *Child Abuse & Neglect, 26*(1), 11–22.

Wolock, I., & Magura, S. (1996). Parental substance abuse as a predictor of child maltreatment re-reports. *Child Abuse & Neglect, 20*(12), 1183–1193.

Zedlewski, S. R. (2002). Family economic resources in the post-reform era. *Children and Welfare, 12*(1), 121–145.

CHAPTER 4

Risk Factors and Risk Assessment in Child Welfare

Diane DePanfilis

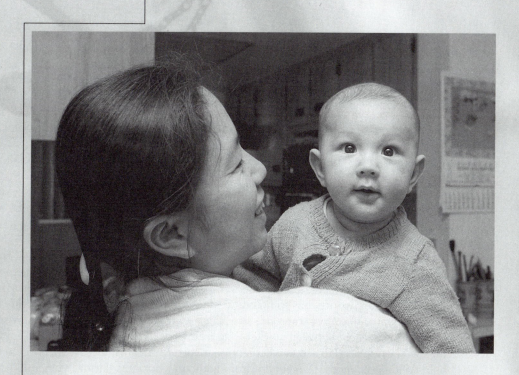

Jacqueline K., age 20, and her three children live in a one-bedroom apartment. Ms. K. has struggled with three unsuccessful attempts to recover from an addiction to crack cocaine. Her children—4-year-old Mitchell, 2-year-old Stephanie, and 2-month-old Lindsay—were identified as "drug exposed" at birth. Relatives have at some points cared for Mitchell and

Stephanie. The fathers of the children are unknown. Ms. K. has periodically turned to prostitution to support her addiction. When Ms. K. was five months pregnant with Lindsay, she was badly beaten and ended up in the hospital. This brief hospitalization for her physical problems and a 28-day in-patient treatment helped her stay clean from cocaine for the rest of her pregnancy up through the first two months of Lindsay's life.

Ms. K. was discharged from the hospital with few people to support her and her children. The family members who had helped after the birth of her first two children were frustrated with having been taken advantage of in the past and told Ms. K. that this time, she was on her own. After seeing Lindsay at a well-child visit in the pediatric clinic, the pediatrician called child protective services (CPS) with concerns that Lindsay was not gaining weight. The CPS worker visited the household and found the conditions sparse, with few furnishings and little food. The worker also discovered that Ms. K. had been watering down her baby's formula because she couldn't afford the cost.

The CPS worker has indicated neglect in the report. The CPS worker now has to assess the likelihood of future maltreatment (risk) and assess whether or not the children are unsafe (with immediate risk of serious harm) before deciding whether and how the child welfare agency will stay involved with this family.

The K. family is typical of families referred to child protective service agencies because of suspicion of child maltreatment. *Child protective services (CPS)*, in state and local social services departments, is at the center of every community's child protection efforts. In most jurisdictions, CPS is the agency mandated by law to conduct an initial assessment or investigation of a report of child abuse or neglect. CPS also offers services to families and children in cases in which maltreatment has occurred or is likely to occur (DePanfilis & Salus, 2003).

Agencies use different approaches in making decisions about whether children are safe or at risk of future maltreatment. Fifteen years of effort have gone into developing and validating risk assessment approaches, but it is unlikely that any assessment instrument will ever be devised that can accurately predict future maltreatment in all cases (Cicchinelli & Keller, 1990). Assessment of the risk of maltreatment and safety of children is as much an art as a science (Cash, 2001).

Since the primary purpose of CPS is to ensure that children are protected from future maltreatment, assessment of risk and safety are crucial. Deciding whether a child is safe from immediate risk of serious harm is one of the most difficult decisions the child welfare worker has to make. While specific methods of assessment vary between jurisdictions, most states use structured approaches to help ensure that assessments are consistent between workers and from one case to the next. In the K. family, the social worker has to assess whether or not current circumstances (e.g., poor household conditions, mother's recovery from addiction, social isolation, vulnerability of a 2-month-old infant, etc.) can be addressed such that the children may safely remain in the family.

The purpose of this chapter is to synthesize (1) what the field knows about assessing risk and safety of maltreated children and their families and (2) how these assessments are integrated in the child welfare practice process. The chapter begins by identifying risk factors and defining terms and then illustrates how core concepts are applied at each stage of the case process. Finally, models for assessing risk and safety and relevant research findings are reviewed.

The Concept of Risk in Child Welfare

Risk Factors

Social workers assess *risk*. In child welfare, *risk* means "probability of an undesirable outcome." Two types of risk are assessed: ① risk of future maltreatment if the child stays with the family and ② risk of placement in out-of-home care (Masten & Wright, 1998). According to the National Association of Public Child Welfare Administrators (NAPCWA, 1999), the mission of the child protective service agency is to (1) assess the safety of the children; (2) intervene to protect the children from harm; (3) strengthen the ability of the family to protect their children; or (4) provide an alternative safe family for the children. The Child Welfare League of America (1999) affirms this mission: The CPS agency assesses the risk to and safety of children and provides or arranges for services to achieve safe permanent families for children who have been abused or neglected or who are at risk of abuse or neglect. To achieve these outcomes, CPS agencies facilitate community collaborations and engage formal and informal community partners to support families and protect children from abuse and neglect (CWLA, 1999).

The core mandate of assessing risk and ensuring safety is accomplished when the agency has appropriate procedures for (1) gathering relevant information about risk and protective factors; (2) analyzing information; and (3) making decisions that will provide interventions that increase safety, reduce the risk of maltreatment, and address any effects of child maltreatment. Decisions regarding the risk of future maltreatment and the safety of children, made at various points in the child welfare process, constitute the critical professional function of the child welfare system. In order to ensure quality services to families, child welfare agencies continually seek to improve assessment technology and the skills of the social workers charged with responsibility for making valid and reliable risk and safety assessments.

Before risk and safety can be assessed, the concept of risk factors must be understood. Thomlison (2004) defines *risk factors* as "those characteristics or conditions that, if present for a given child, make it more likely that this child, rather than another child selected from the general population, will experience child maltreatment" (pp. 94–95). Reflect for a moment on the situation of 2-month-old Lindsay K. What factors in her current situation cause concern that, without intervention, she may experience child maltreatment in the future?

In your reflection, did you notice that you were concerned about factors related to the mother, the family system, Lindsay herself, as well as the environment? It is commonly recognized that child maltreatment is the result of factors related to the (1) environment, (2) caregivers, (3) the family system, and (4) the individual child. Therefore, as was illustrated in the K. family situation, an *ecological developmental framework* (Belsky, 1980; Bronfenbrenner, 1979) helps social workers identify risk factors at all levels of the social ecology. An understanding of the specific circumstances that place children at risk helps the social worker tailor interventions to address the risk factors apparent in an individual family.

In child welfare agencies, social workers usually work with families in which maltreatment has already occurred. The risk assessment therefore focuses on factors that will increase the likelihood of a new incidence of maltreatment in the future. A comprehensive risk assessment considers risk factors at all levels of the social ecology and, most important, the interrelationships among individual, family, and social support factors to the presenting problems in the family (Belsky, 1993).

The problem that prompted the referral of the K. family to CPS was that Lindsay was failing to gain weight due to nutritional neglect. What could contribute to future abuse or neglect for Lindsay and her siblings? To answer this question, the social worker must make an assessment that focuses on risk factors specific to this family: the children's ages and developmental stages and the mother's capacity to adequately meet her children's needs, given her history of drug addiction, her current physical and mental health, and her parenting knowledge and skills. The assessment must also consider the family system, sources of stress or support in the home and neighborhood, and the quality of child welfare intervention available to respond to the needs of this specific family.

Variables Associated with Child Maltreatment Recurrence

The research on risk factors associated with repeat maltreatment is extensive (English & Pecora, 1994). In the discussion that follows, some of this literature is summarized. Research results provide information about the precursors and correlates of child maltreatment and child maltreatment recurrence. An important point to keep in mind is that risk factors are related to *probabilities,* not *causes.* The presence of a behavior or condition only increases the likelihood that a future incidence of child maltreatment will occur. The presence of a risk factor does not always mean a specific child will be maltreated.

To identify risk factors, researchers use information about families with known child maltreatment compared to families without known child maltreatment (Black, Heyman, & Slep 2001a, 2001b; Black, Slep, & Heyman, 2001) to build statistical models and predict the occurrence or recurrence of child maltreatment. Researchers always strive to increase the precision of their predictions. However, because of the variations in human beings and their environments, researchers usually misestimate the risks or odds of future maltreatment. Predicting that specific families with certain characteristics will be in the maltreatment group when they really have not maltreated their children is called a *false positive.* In contrast, predicting that specific families with other characteristics will not experience maltreatment in the future when maltreatment, in fact, does occur is called a *false negative.* When using an ecological developmental framework, we must remember that the meanings of specific risk factors for individual families will always vary. In particular, variation across and within cultures must always be considered. Both vulnerability and adaptation are deeply embedded in cultural systems (Fraser, Kirby, & Smokowski, 2004).

Differences in types of research samples, definitions of recurrence of child maltreatment, follow-up study intervals, and methods of analysis make the results of studies of the recurrence of maltreatment difficult to compare (DePanfilis & Zuravin, 1998). Therefore, in the sections that follow, you will see examples of variables that have been identified as risk factors in some child maltreatment recurrence studies. Keep in mind the points made earlier, as the presence of any one or more of these factors will not always mean that an individual child will be maltreated in the future.

We now turn our attention to these variables, which fall into six categories by domain: (1) nature and type of maltreatment; (2) child vulnerability factors; (3) parent or other caregiver characteristics; (4) family characteristics; (5) socioeconomic and environmental characteristics; and (6) service-related characteristics.

NATURE AND TYPE OF MALTREATMENT   Most risk assessment instruments identify characteristics of the initially reported child maltreatment as risk factors for repeated maltreatment. In fact, characteristics of the child maltreatment—such as type, severity, nature, and extent—have proven the most reliable predictors of maltreatment recurrence (Baird, 1988; Baird, Wagner, & Neuenfeldt, 1993; DePanfilis, 1993; Schuerman, Rzepnicki, & Littell, 1994; Wagner, 1994; Wood, 1995).

Here is a list of some of the risk factors associated with the initially reported incidence of child maltreatment:

1. Neglect as the type of initially reported maltreatment (Berkeley Planning Associates, 1983; DePanfilis, 1995; DePanfilis & Zuravin, 1999a; Marks & McDonald, 1989; McDonald & Johnson, 1992; Wagner, 1994; Wood, 1995)
2. Number of abuse/neglect types (more indicate increased risk) (Baird, 1988)
3. Severe consequences at the first reported maltreatment incident (Berkeley Planning Associates, 1983; Browne, 1986; Cohn, 1979; Marks & McDonald, 1989; Weedon, Torti, & Zunder, 1988)
4. Number of children or caregivers involved in the abuse/neglect incident (more equals increased risk) (Wagner, 1994; Wood, 1995)
5. Biological mother present (decreased risk) (Marks & McDonald, 1989)
6. Access to the child by the perpetrator (increased risk) (English, Aubin, Fine, & Pecora, 1993; Marks & McDonald, 1989)
7. Amount of time the abused child spends with the abusing adult (increased risk) (Johnson & L'Esperance, 1984)
8. View of abuse by nonperpetrator caregiver (Baird, 1988)
9. Child's fear of a caregiver (English et al., 1993)

An understanding of the factors in the social ecology that may have led to the initial incident or could lead to future incidents is extremely helpful in developing plans for ensuring safety and reducing risk. Social ecology factors, however, are not a primary help when choosing the appropriate intervention.

CHILD VULNERABILITY FACTORS   In their review of the literature on the etiology of child maltreatment, the National Research Council (1993) suggests that child characteristics may play only a minor role in the initiation of child maltreatment but may be more important in the maintenance or persistence of abusive relationships or the escalation of at-risk relationships. For example, some children are more difficult to care for due to their special needs. A child with attention-deficit hyperactive disorder (ADHD) is especially vulnerable if the parent is single and has no one to turn to for respite or support. Theoretically, the relationship between child characteristics and the recurrence of child maltreatment is partly due to the effects of child maltreatment on children. Maltreated children may exhibit negative behaviors or conditions as a consequence of their maltreatment experiences. As a result, they may be more difficult to care for, which in turn increases the risk for continued maltreatment.

Examples of behaviors or conditions that have been associated with child maltreatment recurrences in at least one study include the following:

1. Abnormalities at birth, length of stay in the hospital after birth (Herrenkohl, Herrenkohl, Egolf, & Seech, 1978), and low birthweight (DePanfilis, 1993)
2. Age or ability of the child (younger children are at greater risk) (Berkeley Planning Associates, 1983; Fuller, Wells, & Cotton, 2001; Weedon et al., 1988)
3. Socioemotional problems and behavior problems in school (Herrenkohl et al., 1978); number of child problems (e.g., physical, emotional, behavioral) (Fuller et al., 2001)
4. Number of developmental problems, number of socioemotional problems, and number of health problems all increased risk of recurrence for different age groups (Berkeley Planning Associates, 1983)
5. A three-item child vulnerability index representing families with young children, a child with a developmental disability, or a child with mental health problems (DePanfilis, 1995; DePanfilis & Zuravin, 1999a).

Variables related to all of these vulnerability factors have been identified in a number of studies related to the etiology of child maltreatment (Belsky, 1992). Except for age, child vulnerability factors are usually enduring factors, rather than situational factors. Thus, they can present ongoing stress and conflict, particularly if children have not received treatment.

PARENT OR OTHER CAREGIVER CHARACTERISTICS   Various parent and other caregiver characteristics have been associated with child maltreatment recurrence in multiple studies. For example, in the case of Ms. K, even with the limited information we have, we would identify the history of cocaine addiction and her apparent insufficient knowledge about the nutritional needs of infants as factors that could increase the risk of future maltreatment of Lindsay. Conducting a social history may identify even more risk factors.

Examples of caregiver history and personal characteristics that have been associated with the recurrence of child maltreatment are as follow:

1. Caregiver abused as a child (Baird, 1988; Baird et al., 1993; Wood, 1995); caregiver neglected as a child (Baird, 1988); perpetrator neglected as a child (McDonald & Johnson, 1992, 1993)
2. Amount of time the maternal caregiver lived with the biological father during the first six years of life (less time means increased risk) (Herrenkohl et al., 1978)

Various caregiver characteristics, such as depression, are associated with maltreatment recurrence.

3. Quality of the maternal caregiver's relationship with her own childhood caregivers (poorer quality means increased risk) (Herrenkohl et al., 1978)
4. Low self-esteem and feelings of apathy and hopelessness (Baird et al., 1993; Johnson, 1994)
5. History of depression (Baird, 1988; Baird, Wagner, & Neuenfeldt, 1993); emotional stability, ability to control impulses, and intellectual/reasoning capacity (Baird et al., 1993; Wagner, 1994; Wood, 1995)
6. Cocaine problems (Schuerman et al., 1994); a drug or alcohol abuse problem (Baird, 1988; Baird et al., 1993; Wagner, 1994); parental substance abuse (Wolock, Sherman, Feldman, & Metzger, 2001)
7. History of domestic violence (Baird et al., 1993)
8. Criminal history (Baird, 1988)

9. Multiple caregiver problems (Fuller et al., 2001)
10. Personality factors such as problem-solving ability, being outgoing, and reactions to emotional stimuli (Pianta, Egeland, & Erickson, 1989)

There is considerable evidence that the personal resources of the caregiver play a determining role in child maltreatment (Belsky, 1992); thus, their strength as predictors of recurrence should not be a surprise. Conceptually, it is likely that parental risk factors interact with stress factors to accentuate these problems, which in turn contribute to continued maltreatment.

Another set of parent-related variables related to maltreatment recurrences are categorized as *parenting attitude and skill factors:*

1. Maternal expectations of the child (unrealistic expectations increase risk) (Herrenkohl et al., 1978; Johnson & L'Esperance, 1984)
2. Problems of parenting factor score (Herrenkohl et al., 1978) and a parent–child interaction factor score (Zunder, 1990)
3. Problems with parenting skill (Baird et al., 1993; Johnson & L'Esperance, 1984); child care skill deficits (Schuerman et al., 1994)
4. Caregiver is a domineering parent (Baird et al., 1993)
5. Inadequate physical or affective care and supervision (Johnson, 1994; Marks & McDonald, 1989; McDonald & Johnson, 1992; Wagner, 1994)

There has been considerable debate in the child maltreatment literature regarding whether parenting and parent–child interaction factors contribute to child maltreatment or whether parenting adequacy encompasses a continuum of behaviors, including those that are maltreating (Belsky,1993). With respect to the recurrence of maltreatment, it seems likely that maltreating parents who are evidencing more ongoing problems with parenting will be at greater risk for maltreating their children again than parents whose everyday parenting behaviors are adequate.

FAMILY CHARACTERISTICS   Research reports regarding the influence of family structure on child maltreatment have been inconsistent. However, the literature review completed by the National Research Council (1993) identified studies that have found correlations between child maltreatment and the following variables: (1) young maternal age, (2) single parenting, (3) large numbers of closely spaced children, and (4) large family size. Most of these have been tested in recurrence research, as well. The relationship between these variables and child maltreatment is theoretically expected because of the additional stress or burden that these conditions place on the caregiving capacity of parents. Here are some examples of family factors that have been found to be associated with child maltreatment recurrence:

1. Number of children in the home (more increase risk) (Baird, 1988; Baird et al., 1993; Johnson & L'Esperance, 1984; Wolock et al., 2001)
2. Number of adults in the home (more means increased risk) (Baird, 1988; Baird et al., 1993)
3. Single-parent home (Baird, 1988) or family structure (i.e., two parents, single parent, and other family structures) (Coleman, 1995; Fuller et al., 2001)

Single-parenting is a family factor that is associated with maltreatment recurrence.

4. Age of youngest or primary caregiver (younger parents at increased risk) (Baird, 1988; Berkeley Planning Associates, 1983; Wagner, 1992)
5. Female caregiver (Berkeley Planning Associates, 1983)
6. Biological father present (Johnson, 1994)
7. Domestic violence (DePanfilis, 1995; DePanfilis & Zuravin, 1999b)

The child maltreatment literature at large has also reported a higher risk of maltreatment when parents and children have communication and interaction problems (Ammerman, 1991; Wolfe, 1985).

SOCIOECONOMIC AND ENVIRONMENTAL FACTORS   Ecological models of maltreatment suggest that when the stressors outweigh the supports (or said another way, if there are fewer protective factors than risk factors in the family's social ecology), the probability of child maltreatment increases (Belsky, 1993). Stress-related risk factors that have been associated with child maltreatment recurrence include these:

1. Stress due to economic problems, such as bill collectors, household income fluctuation, unemployment, and adequacy of income (Herrenkohl et al., 1978); amount of income (Baird et al., 1993; Herrenkohl et al., 1978); job change (Browne, 1986); receipt of welfare (Wolock et al., 2001)
2. Stress due to pregnancy (Herrenkohl et al., 1978)
3. Stress due to breakup of the family (Herrenkohl et al., 1978)

4. Stress due to environmental problems such as housing problems (Herrenkohl et al., 1978) and number of working utilities (more decreased risk) (Marks & McDonald, 1989)
5. Neighborhood problems factor score, crowding in the neighborhood, frequency of family moves (Herrenkohl et al., 1978)
6. Stress factor score (Zunder, 1990) and stress index score (DePanfilis, 1995; DePanfilis & Zuravin, 1999b)
7. Number of stressful events (Browne, 1986)
8. Number of presenting problems (Berkeley Planning Associates, 1983)

To offset these stress-related variables, it is important to understand whether a deficit in social support also increases the risk for child maltreatment or whether having social support reduces the risk of future maltreatment. Examples of social support–related factors associated with child maltreatment recurrence are as follow:

1. Current social relationships factor score; current conflict with others factor score; conflict with relatives; marital relationship factor scale; and lack of friends (Herrenkohl et al., 1978)
2. Negative social relationships and socially isolated/withdrawn (Baird, 1988; Baird et al., 1993; DePanfilis, 1995; DePanfilis & Zuravin, 1999b; Wood, 1995)
3. Frequency of seeing a confidante (someone to turn to for emotional support) (DePanfilis, 1993) and frequency of participating in church activities (DePanfilis, 1993) or frequency of participating in church or social organizations (Johnson, 1994)

Further exploration of the impact of social support, in particular, seems important because of the implications for intervention. Social isolation and the availability of social support have been found to be especially important in cases of child neglect (DePanfilis, 1996b).

SERVICE-RELATED FACTORS Once the CPS agency gets involved, it is important to understand whether the availability and quality of services and the degree to which a family actively participates in services will reduce the risk of future maltreatment. Prior reviews of child maltreatment recurrence studies (DePanfilis, 1995; Miller, Williams, English, & Olmstead, 1987) have identified a small set of service-related risk factors. Similarly, a rather small set of intervention or service-related risk factors are included in risk and safety assessment models (DePanfilis & Scannapieco, 1994; Doueck, English, DePanfilis, and Moote, 1993; Marks, McDonald, & Bessey, 1989; McDonald & Marks, 1991).

Intervention or service variables that have predicted recurrence (or nonrecurrence) are of two types: (1) variables that describe the intervention that was provided previously or in relation to the current incident and (2) variables that describe the level of motivation and cooperation by the family to use services as intended (DePanfilis & Zuravin, 2002). Here are some examples of intervention characteristics that predicted recurrence of child maltreatment:

1. Prior CPS case for the family (increased risk) (Johnson, 1994; Marks & McDonald, 1989); new to child welfare (decreased risk) (Schuerman et al., 1994); prior

placements (increased risk) (Baird, 1988); prior inpatient treatment for a family member (increased risk) (Coleman, 1995)

2. Child placed out of the home (increased risk) (Browne, 1986)
3. Level of training of workers (less training increases risk) (Cohn, 1979)
4. Length of CPS services (longer services decreases risk) (Berkeley Planning Associates, 1983; Johnson & L'Esperance, 1984); however, no relationship between length of services and recurrence of child maltreatment was also found (Johnson & Clancy, 1990)
5. Number of in-person casework visits (more means decreased risk) (Johnson, 1998)
6. Number of concrete services provided in the first 90 days (positive relationship with recurrence) (Schuerman, Rzepnicki, & Littell, 1994)
7. Use of risk assessment procedures (decreases risk) (Fluke, 1991; Fluke, Edwards, Bussey, Wells, & Johnson, 2001).

It is important to remember that some service-related variables may statistically show the opposite effect than what one would expect—for example, the effect of the length of service is a complex case. It may not be possible to determine the net effect of the length of service, since such a case usually gets more and longer service from the outset. As emphasized at the beginning of this section, identifying a risk factor does not indicate with certainty that the risk factor will *cause* recurrence of child maltreatment. The identification of the risk factor merely shows a correlation between the factor and the possibility of recurrence.

Most risk assessment instruments include information about the degree to which a family cooperates with the CPS agency. The following list provides examples of factors that have been found to be associated with a reduced recurrence of child maltreatment:

1. Motivation of perpetrator or caregiver (Baird, 1988; Baird et al., 1993; Wagner, 1994)
2. The caregiver viewed the current incident as seriously as or more seriously than the investigating worker (Wagner, 1994)
3. Cooperation with the agency by the nonperpetrator caregiver (Baird, 1988; Baird et al., 1993)
4. Attendance at referred services (DePanfilis & Zuravin, 2002)

Some variables predicted a higher likelihood of recurrence of child maltreatment:

1. Negative attitude toward the agency (McDonald & Johnson, 1992)
2. Family's ability to use agency resources (Johnson & L'Esperance, 1984; Marks & McDonald, 1989)
3. Willingness to use agency resources (Johnson, 1994)

We have now completed our survey of the six categories of variables of risk factors associated with child maltreatment recurrence. By studying the family's social ecology, we can identify individual risk factors, but doing so is merely the first step. The primary task is to compile a comprehensive assessment that examines the complex interplay between risk and protective factors. When making the comprehensive assessment, we must always remember the following points.

1. Different types of child maltreatment often occur at the same time or occur over time in the life of a child.
2. The risk of maltreatment recurrence is better predicted by multiple and interacting variables, rather than by single risk factors.
3. Protective and compensatory factors, as well as risk factors, must be assessed.
4. Child maltreatment is related to many other social problems, and each of these problems affects the child and family in different ways.

Working Definitions for Assessing Risks

Critical to accurately assessing the risk and safety of maltreated children is the need to consistently understand and use a common set of definitions. For example, when considering the concept of *risk* (i.e., the probability of a future event or outcome), we must clarify whether we are concerned with the risk of any maltreatment, the risk of one or more specific subtypes of maltreatment, the risk of harm, or the risk of placement in out-of-home care. These concepts are not the same. We are usually concerned with predicting the likelihood of maltreatment in the future, but we may also be concerned about the risk of harm or consequences if maltreatment should occur. In child welfare, we are often faced with assessing the risk of repeated maltreatment after a determination is made that some type of maltreatment has already occurred. If the risk of maltreatment is likely, we must also assess whether a child is safe or whether safety services are needed to protect the child in or outside the home. Here are some key points to remember:

1. *Risk of maltreatment* and *safety* are not the same concepts. Risk of maltreatment relates to the probability of maltreatment in the future, whereas safety is concerned about the likelihood of future maltreatment that may result in imminent and serious harm.
2. Risk is dynamic, not static. The probability of maltreatment changes as the conditions and circumstances within a family change.
3. Risk of maltreatment is the consequence of interactions between behaviors and conditions that may be present (i.e., multiple pathways).
4. Factors that may increase the probability of maltreatment may be offset by protective factors. Relevant risk-related definitions are presented in Table 4.1.

Along with the concepts of risk and risk assessment, we must understand the corollary concepts of compensatory and protective factors. *Compensatory factors* are assets or resources that generally predict good outcomes. With families that have compensatory factors to offset and balance high-risk conditions, we would expect better outcomes (Masten & Wright, 1998). For example, a 20-year-old single parent may feel stressed by taking care of her infant who has difficulty sleeping. A compensatory factor could be the fact that this mother knows she can depend on the infant's grandmother to come to the house every day so she can get out of the house for a couple of hours of respite. Or consider a grandmother caring for five grandchildren, all of whom have mental health or developmental disabilities. In spite of the daily stress that this grandmother endures, she is a spiritual person and turns daily to a higher power for support. She also reaches out to a faith community as a source of strength and support.

TABLE 4.1	Glossary of Risk Terminology
Concept	**Definition**
Risk	An elevated probability of an undesirable outcome (Masten & Wright, 1998, p. 10). The likelihood of a future event usually varies over time, either increasing or decreasing, depending on other factors that influence it. Risk implies uncertainty, either about whether a hazard will occur or about outcome once a hazard has occurred (Masten & Wright, 1998, p. 9).
Risk of maltreatment	The probability or likelihood of maltreatment in the future. This suggests that some type of physical abuse, neglect, sexual abuse, or emotional maltreatment may occur in the future. It is likely that the risks of some subtypes of maltreatment are higher than others. Risk of the recurrence of maltreatment or repeated maltreatment is the likelihood that maltreatment will occur more than once.
Risk of harm	When assessed in the context of maltreatment, it is the likelihood of future maltreatment that may have serious consequences. Risk of harm is often used in the context of evaluating the safety of maltreated children, suggesting that children are unsafe when there is an immediate danger of moderate or serious risk of harm (NAPCWA, 1999).
Risk of placement	The probability that threatening family conditions are present and that without intervention, the child will likely need to be placed to ensure the child's safety (Holder, Costello, Lund, & Holder, 2000).
Imminent risk	Conditions are present and interacting in a manner that leads a reasonable person to conclude a high likelihood that a child will be maltreated in the immediate future (Holder et al., 2000).
Cumulative risk	Risk status that is compounded by (1) the presence of multiple risk factors, (2) multiple occurrences of the same risk factor, or (3) the accumulating effects of ongoing risk or adversity (Masten & Wright, 1998, p. 10). While the concept of cumulative risk is relevant for all types of maltreatment, it is particularly relevant for child neglect.
Cumulative harm	The harm that a child may experience as a consequence of repeated episodes of negative events. Repeated stressors and chronic or repeated maltreatment are associated with more damaging consequences and worse outcomes (Garmezy & Masten, 1994; National Research Council, 1993). Child neglect, because of its chronic nature, may contribute to cumulative harm for children.
Risk factor	A measurable characteristic of individuals that heightens the probability of a worse outcome in the future for groups of individuals who share the risk factor or who have more of the risk factor than a comparison group (Masten & Wright, 1998, p. 10).
Enduring risk factor	Psychological, environmental, cultural, or biological factors that decrease or increase the odds for maltreatment (Thomlison, 2004, p. 95). These factors are more likely to need change-oriented interventions in order to reduce the risk of maltreatment.
Transient risk factor	Situations such as illness, injury, marital discord, and other life stressors—both perceived and actual—that may impair a vulnerable parent and lead to abuse or neglect of a child (Thomlison, 2004, p. 95). These factors may be controlled through safety-oriented or short-term interventions or through change-oriented interventions to prevent recurring transient risk factors (e.g., frequent household evictions).

(continued)

TABLE 4.1	*Continued*

Concept	Definition
Risk mechanism	The process whereby a risk factor contributes over time to heightened vulnerability. No single event produces a negative outcome. Rather, interactional processes shape behaviors and problems over time (Fraser et al., 2004, p. 21).
Risk trait	An individual predisposition toward developing a specific problem condition (Pellegrini, 1990).
Vulnerability	Individual susceptibility to undesirable outcomes related to traits or conditions (Masten & Wright, 1998, p. 10). For example, certain characteristics may make a child more vulnerable to the consequences of neglect or abuse.
Child safety	The absence of risk factors or threatening family conditions that could lead to imminent risk of harm or imminent risk of severe harm (DePanfilis, 1997).
Risk assessment	The systematic collection of information to determine the degree to which a child is likely to be abused or neglected in the future (English & Pecora, 1994, p. 452).
Safety assessment	The identification and evaluation of threats of harm (Holder et al., 2000, p. 5). Concepts of imminent risk of harm regarding the specific vulnerability of a child are relevant for assessing safety.
Risk management	The implementation of interventions or change strategies that are targeted to achieve outcomes that will reduce the risk of maltreatment.
Safety plan	An in-home or out-of-home service strategy usually created after initial assessment/investigation that specifically addresses and manages threats of harm (Holder et al., 2000, p. 5).

In contrast, *protective factors* may function to prevent risks or ameliorate their effects. For example, families who spend time together and support one another through thick or thin may avoid negative consequences when times become difficult, as when family income is reduced or lost. The concept of *cumulative protective factors* is also important to consider. Defined as the "presence of multiple protective factors in an individual's life, whether within or across time" (Masten & Wright, 1998), such factors may explain why some families manage stress or negative conditions better than others.

At the level of the individual, some children are resilient to the negative forces in their lives. *Resilience* is defined as the "successful adaptation or development during or following adverse conditions that challenge or threaten adaptive functioning or healthy development" (Masten & Wright, 1998). There are generally believed to be three explanations for resilience (Fraser et al., 2004). The first is that some children seem to overcome the odds of difficult circumstances. An example might be a preterm infant at risk for negative outcomes due to low birthweight who overcomes the odds and grows and develops normally.

The second explanation of resilience, grounded in the literature on stress and coping, refers to sustained competence under stress (Fraser et al., 2004). The notion behind this explanation is that some children's thoughts and actions help them cope with adverse events and circumstances. This could be true, for example, for the oldest child in a family who believes she can manage her world in ways that look out for her younger siblings. When her parents start fighting, she might take her younger siblings out for a walk or to a neighbor's house for safety. The third explanation of resilience relates to children who are able to recover from traumatic experiences such as sexual abuse.

While the process for each of these explanations differs, the end result is that some children are able to successfully adapt to their circumstances and not experience the intensity of the harmful effects that may be associated with the negative condition or situation. In summary, many influences operate simultaneously in a child's life that will either increase or decrease the risk of maltreatment. When risk is present, the focus for the social worker is to work with the family to increase the protective or compensatory factors and thereby reduce the risk of maltreatment.

Assessing Risk and Safety throughout the Child Welfare Case Process

If the primary purposes of CPS are to address the consequences of child maltreatment and reduce the risk of repeated maltreatment, then agencies must have in place good methods of gathering and analyzing information regarding risk factors and protective factors. Furthermore, instruments and tools should guide the assessment process and help social workers arrive at consistent decisions at different stages of the case process. Not every stage of the assessment process is labeled *risk assessment,* but at every stage, the processes for gathering and analyzing information hopefully lead to appropriate decisions about risk and safety.

There are seven stages of the CPS case process (DePanfilis & Salus, 2003), and assessing and managing risks are tasks at each stage. "The goal for all assessments in CPS is to gather and analyze information that will support sound decision-making regarding the safety, permanency, and well-being of the child"(U.S. DHHS, 2000).

Intake

The primary purpose of the intake process is to screen reports of child abuse and neglect and determine the urgency of the CPS response to the referral. Social workers are assigned to answer the phone and gather information from someone in the community who believes a child has been abused or neglected. At intake, the hotline or intake worker must assess whether referral information meets the state definition of an appropriate referral, and the agency must have a protocol for assessing whether the threat of harm suggests the need to respond immediately.

In states with differential response systems, a decision may also need to be made about who should respond to the referral. Agencies often have screening checklists, sometimes called *risk assessment intake instruments,* to help social workers gather sufficient information that will increase the likelihood that the correct decision is

TABLE 4.2	Child Welfare Decisions and Assessments at Intake

Decisions	Assessments Needed to Guide Decision Making
Does the referral information suggest that a child may be abused or neglected?	A protocol for asking questions of referral sources that would help determine whether the referral is appropriate for an initial assessment.[1]
Does the referral information suggest that the child may be at imminent risk of serious harm?	A protocol that identifies threats of harm that could indicate imminent risk of serious harm.
What is the urgency of the response needed by the child welfare agency or another community agency?	A framework for analysis of referral information to determine the appropriate response time and for determining the best person/agency to respond.[2]
Should the referral be screened out from initial assessment by the child welfare agency? If so, does this family need referrals to other agency or community services?	Screening criteria for determining when a referral is not appropriate for CPS response. Resource databases and interagency agreements to assure that families are offered appropriate services that may prevent child maltreatment.

[1]In states that require a substantiation decision, the intake worker is assessing whether the information being reported, if true, meets the definition of child abuse or neglect according to state law and therefore should result in an initial assessment with face-to-face contact with the child, family members, and others who have information. In states with differential response systems, the intake worker is determining whether the referral information suggests the need for a response by the child welfare agency or another community agency.

[2]Depending on the state, the first contact could be made by the CPS worker alone, law enforcement alone, CPS and law enforcement as a team, a community-based agency alone, or the CPS worker in conjunction with a community service provider (e.g., public health nurse, family support worker).

made. Failing to accept a referral when a child is really at risk of child maltreatment can have serious consequences, especially for young children. Similarly, deciding that a case is a low priority and doesn't need someone to go out for five days can also lead to negative consequences if the situation actually warranted an immediate response. See Table 4.2 for a review of the decisions made at intake and the types of assessment protocols that may assist with these decisions.

Initial Assessment

The primary purposes of the initial assessment are to investigate the report of child abuse or neglect, to assess risk and safety, to determine whether a safety plan is needed, and to decide whether continuing services should be offered to the family. The social worker is involved in conducting a series of interviews and gathering other relevant information to achieve these purposes of the initial assessment. An initial assessment may be completed by the CPS worker alone, the CPS worker and law enforcement as a team, a community service provider, or the CPS worker in conjunction with another service provider. It is this stage of the process that has traditionally been associated with risk and safety assessment.

| TABLE 4.3 | Child Welfare Decisions and Assessments at Initial Assessment |

Decisions	Assessments Needed to Guide Decision Making
Is the child safe from imminent risk of serious harm?	An initial safety assessment approach that evaluates threats of harm that could indicate a child is likely to be harmed with serious consequences in the near future.
Is child abuse or neglect substantiated, as defined by state statute?	Procedures for gathering and analyzing the facts of any maltreatment that has already occurred.[1]
Is the child at risk of future maltreatment, and if so, what is the level of risk?	A risk assessment protocol that identifies the probability of future maltreatment.
Is the child safe? If not, what safety services are needed to increase safety?	Safety assessment protocol and planning process including decision-making criteria for determining when out-of-home placement is necessary.
Is the family experiencing other crises that are not jeopardizing the child's immediate safety but could affect the child's safety in the future?	A process for identifying and responding to other emergency needs of families (e.g., nonworking utilities).
Does the family need continuing services to address the effects of maltreatment and/or to reduce the likelihood of maltreatment in the future?	Depending on the policies of the state, this decision could be made on the basis of the substantiation decision, the risk assessment, the safety assessment, or some combination of these processes.

[1]As noted in Table 4.2, not all states require a substantiation decision regarding child abuse or neglect.

In some agencies, the decision to offer continuing services is made based on a determination or substantiation of a report of child abuse or neglect. However, nationally, as few as 50 percent of the cases substantiated for abuse or neglect actually receive continuing services designed to address the effects of child maltreatment or to reduce the likelihood of future maltreatment (U.S. DHHS, 2004). Because most child welfare agencies do not have sufficient resources to serve all families, they prioritize as they decide which families will receive continuing services. In most agencies, regardless of whether substantiation is a decision made by the agency, CPS agencies use risk assessment and/or safety assessment to determine which families they will serve. An outline of the key decisions made at the initial assessment stage of the child welfare process and the assessment protocols that may assist with these decisions is provided in Table 4.3.

Family Assessment

The primary purpose of the family assessment is to understand which of the risk or protective factors identified during the initial assessment should be the focus of continuing services provided both by the child welfare agency and other community service systems. If continuing services are provided, the child welfare agency and other service providers need methods for gathering and analyzing information that will identify risk and protective factors relevant for guiding the intervention process. The family assessment is a comprehensive process of identifying, considering, and weighing relevant factors for developing, in partnership with the family, the plans and services needed to assure the child's safety, permanency, and well-being (U.S. DHHS, 2000). This process should target specific case outcomes that, if achieved, will indicate a reduction in the effects of maltreatment and risk of maltreatment.

A family assessment, in order to be most effective, should be strengths based, culturally sensitive, and developed with maximum involvement of the family. It should be designed to help the parents recognize and remedy conditions so their children can safely remain in their own home (National Association of Public Child Welfare Administrators, 1999). Given the new emphasis on timeliness built into the Adoption and Safe Families Act (1997), the assessment of the family's strengths and needs should be considered in the context of the length of time it will take for the family to provide a safe, stable home environment (U.S. HDDS, 2000).

It is at this stage of the process that protective and compensatory factors are particularly relevant. A strengths-based assessment recognizes that people in most cases, regardless of their difficulties, can change and grow; that healing occurs when a family's strengths (not its weaknesses) are engaged; and that the family is the agent of its own change (Child Welfare League of America, 1999, p. 41). Family members should be engaged as active participants while outcomes and interventions are designed to match the results of the assessment process. Outcomes should be selected that, if achieved, will indicate that risks are reduced and protective factors are increased (DePanfilis, 2000; Holder & Lund, 1995). Finally, interventions should be designed to assist family members to achieve outcomes and also to give them choices about the service providers they perceive to be the most helpful to their situation. Services should be geared to empower families to change conditions and behaviors that may increase the risk of future maltreatment. Key decisions and assessment processes that will assist service providers with these decisions are outlined in Table 4.4.

Planning

The primary purpose of the planning stage is to collaborate with the family about the goals and services that will help reduce the risk of future maltreatment. Intervention with abused and neglected children and their families must be planned and purposeful. The success of the outcomes is more easily measured at the client level, where the individual family member is directed toward the achievement of outcomes.

There is a consensus among scholars regarding the effectiveness of client-level outcomes in targeting global change. Many scholars believe that societal improvement begins with successful client-level outcomes, for all CPS intervention is geared toward child safety, child permanence, child well-being, and family well-being (Courtney, 2000). Client-level outcomes and overall programmatic outcomes are accomplished in each individual case through the specification of precise case outcomes and goals. Plans for achieving the goals involve the development and implementation of three types of plans: (1) a *safety plan,* (2) a *case plan* (also called a *treatment plan, service plan,* or *service agreement*), and (3) a *concurrent permanency plan* (DePanfilis & Salus, 2003).

TABLE 4.4	Child Welfare Decisions and Assessments at Family Assessment

Decisions	Assessments Needed to Guide Decision Making
What are the risk factors that affect the safety, well-being, or permanency of the child and/or family?	A family assessment protocol and clinical assessment measures
What are the protective and compensatory factors that may increase the safety, well-being, or permanency of the child and/or family?	A family assessment protocol and clinical assessment measures
What are the effects of maltreatment that affect the safety, well-being, or permanency of the child and/or family?	A family assessment protocol and clinical assessment measures
Is the child safe? If not, is the family actively participating in safety services designed to increase the child's safety?	A safety assessment protocol[1]
What is the caregiver's level of readiness to change and motivation and capacity to assure safety, well-being, and permanency?	A family assessment protocol and clinical assessment measures
What client-level outcomes match the risk factors and will increase the likelihood of achieving safety, well-being, and permanency program-level outcomes?	A family assessment protocol and clinical assessment measures

[1]Safety-focused services should be in place, if needed, prior to the initiation of change-oriented services.

SAFETY PLAN   At any point in the CPS process or whenever it is determined that the child is in imminent risk of harm, a safety plan is developed. Safety is assessed at all stages of the CPS process: receipt of referral, first contact with the family, initial investigation and assessment, development of the case plan, case review, and case closure. If it is determined that a child is not safe, a plan is developed to control the factors that are contributing to the risk of imminent serious harm to the child. In the safety plan, the child welfare worker or other service provider targets the factors affecting the safety of the child and, with the family, identifies the interventions that will control the safety factors and assure the child's protection. If the plan cannot assure the child's safety in the home or placement setting, then another placement is needed.

Consider the situation of Mr. and Mrs. Simpson:

The family has been referred because of physical abuse. The assessment indicates that Mr. Simpson has difficulty with impulse control, especially when he is tired. He works from 11:00 P.M.. to 7:00 A.M. in a local factory. His wife works at the local grocery store and needs to be at work by 8:00 A.M. She works eight-hour days, six days a week. Their two boys, ages 7 and 8, are very active and usually up by 6:30 or 7:00 A.M. The family functions well during the school year, but in the summer, when the boys are at home, they frequently make so much noise that Mr. Simpson gets no more than a few hours of sleep a day. By the time his wife arrives home, he has "had it" with the boys and is usually drinking his third or fourth beer. Mr. Simpson blames his wife for being "too easy" on the boys. She thinks their behavior is normal for their age.

This pattern of sleep deprivation, excessive alcohol consumption, marital stress, and family communication problems led to the most recent abuse incident. After an initial assessment and safety evaluation, the CPS worker met with the family to develop a safety plan. Here's a snapshot of the first part of the safety plan:

- *Outcome:* Stress management and impulse control (Mr. Simpson)
- *Goal:* Mr. Simpson will recognize emotional triggers and manage his emotions.
- *Task:* Mr. Simpson will sleep at least eight hours per day.
- *Task:* The boys will be provided age-appropriate activities away from the house for eight hours, five days a week.
- *Service:* The family will be provided with a list of summer day camps with age-appropriate activities for the boys.

CASE PLAN A case plan targets measurable change that (1) increases protective and compensatory factors, (2) decreases risk factors, and (3) helps family members achieve outcomes and goals that will eventually increase safety, well-being, and permanency. The child welfare worker and family members identify what needs to change to increase protective factors and reduce risk factors, then determine the actions necessary for change, and finally implement the strategies and interventions to facilitate change. The case plan is developed when a child welfare case is opened. It may incorporate a safety plan.

Here are sample additional components that could be added to the safety plan for the Simpson family:

- *Outcome:* Family functioning
- *Goal:* Each family member will communicate clearly with the others about his or her wants, needs, and wishes.
- *Task:* The family will hold daily family meetings, possibly in conjunction with dinner, to check in with each other about their day. Each family member will contribute something to the daily discussion.
- *Service:* A continuing protective service worker or family preservation worker will meet with the family weekly to help them work out the format for family meetings and to help them solve any problems with implementation of their discussion times.

CONCURRENT PERMANENCY PLAN This plan identifies alternative forms of permanency. It addresses both how reunification can be achieved and how legal permanency with a new parent can be achieved if efforts to reunify fail (U.S. DHHS, 2000). This plan may be part of the case plan. The format for the concurrent permanency plan is similar to the format for the safety plan and case plan, with specified outcomes, goals, tasks, and services.

Simultaneously with planning for reunification, the social worker may be exploring other permanency options, on the chance that reunification will not be successful. The example that follows is a snapshot of one small element of a permanency plan focused on reunification. Note that the first parts of a reunification plan are similar to those of a safety plan. The focus is on controlling the behaviors or conditions that suggest that the children will be unsafe if returned home.

The Gordon children, ages 3 and 4, were placed in foster care when their mother abandoned them at a neighbor's house. She asked the neighbor to provide child care for two hours but did not return. When it was time for the babysitter to put her own children to bed and the mother had still not returned, she called the police. Soon, the police were knocking on the mother's door. No one answered. The police broke into the home and found the mother unconscious beside an empty bottle of sleeping pills. Emergency medical procedures were followed, and the mother was rushed to the hospital. She was admitted to the mental health unit, where a CPS worker interviewed her.

Ms. Gordon related that she decided to end her life because she could no longer provide for her children. She had been trying to work two part-time jobs but still could not earn enough to pay for rent and child care. When she was late getting to one of her jobs that week because the 3-year-old was sick, she was fired. She does not have friends or family in the area. The children's father abandoned them six months earlier, saying he was going to go work out west. He also said he would send money, but only one small check had arrived. There was no return address on the envelope, and the postmark was too difficult to read.

Here is the first part of the safety plan for the Gordon family:

- *Outcome:* Control of emotions
- *Goal:* Ms. Gordon will adjust to her current circumstances and manage the negative effect of her emotions on the care of her children.
- *Task:* Ms. Gordon will take time to do something relaxing for herself on a daily basis.
- *Services:* The reunification worker will collaborate with a team at the mental health center to assure that Ms. Gordon receives appropriate treatment for her depression and counseling to help her manage the stress in her life.
- *Outcome:* Daily supervision and care of the children
- *Goal:* The children will be provided with supervised activities daily while Ms. Gordon is working.
- *Task:* Ms. Gordon will take the children to the Head Start program on a daily basis and participate in parent activities at the center.
- *Services:* The reunification worker will arrange for the children to get two emergency slots in the neighborhood Head Start program. The children will be returned home at the end of the Head Start day when the mother's psychiatrist advises that she has the capacity to manage her situation. This is a special collaboration between the child welfare agency and the Head Start program.

The primary focus of this chapter is to identify the key decisions necessary for implementing approaches that will enhance protective factors and decrease risk factors.

TABLE 4.5	Child Welfare Decisions and Assessments during the Planning Stage

Decisions	Assessments Needed to Guide Decision Making
What goals must be accomplished to achieve case outcomes that will indicate that the risk of maltreatment has been reduced and the effects of maltreatment have been successfully addressed?	A family assessment protocol, clinical assessment measures, and case planning formats
What safety and change-focused interventions and services are necessary to assist family members to achieve case-level outcomes, goals, and tasks?	Protocols to assist with matching interventions to case outcomes and goals
How and when will progress toward achievement of outcomes and goals be achieved?	Clinical assessment measures (self-report and/or observational measures designed to document change over time)

Specific decisions and processes for assessment will vary, depending on the type of planning. Decisions and assessment processes that may be helpful for facilitating good decision making in case planning are outlined in Table 4.5.

Intervention and Services

Once the case plan has been developed, the child welfare social worker must provide or arrange for the services identified in the plan to help family members achieve family-level outcomes, case plan goals, and tasks. Selecting and matching interventions that will support the family in achieving desired outcomes and goals is a critical step in the casework process. To the extent possible, interventions should be selected that have demonstrated some level of success in addressing the issues that bring families to CPS agencies.

Other chapters in this text address methods for delivering treatment, intervention, and services. In this chapter, we consider how types and levels of interventions relate to the level of risk to the child. A conceptual framework developed by the National Association of Public Child Welfare Administrators (NAPCWA, 1999) is helpful in thinking about the levels of services appropriate to the level of risk presented by the family (see Figure 4.1).

The top one-third of the pyramid represents those reports of child abuse and neglect that present the highest risk for children, are concerned primarily with child safety, and often involve child removal and court-ordered services. The primary role for the social worker with these families is to help them understand and accept the nature of the risk factors that contributed to or could lead to serious maltreatment and engage them in developing safety, case, and concurrent permanency plans that will lead to achievement of child safety and permanency. Services are often court ordered. The

FIGURE 4.1   Child Protection Service Pyramid

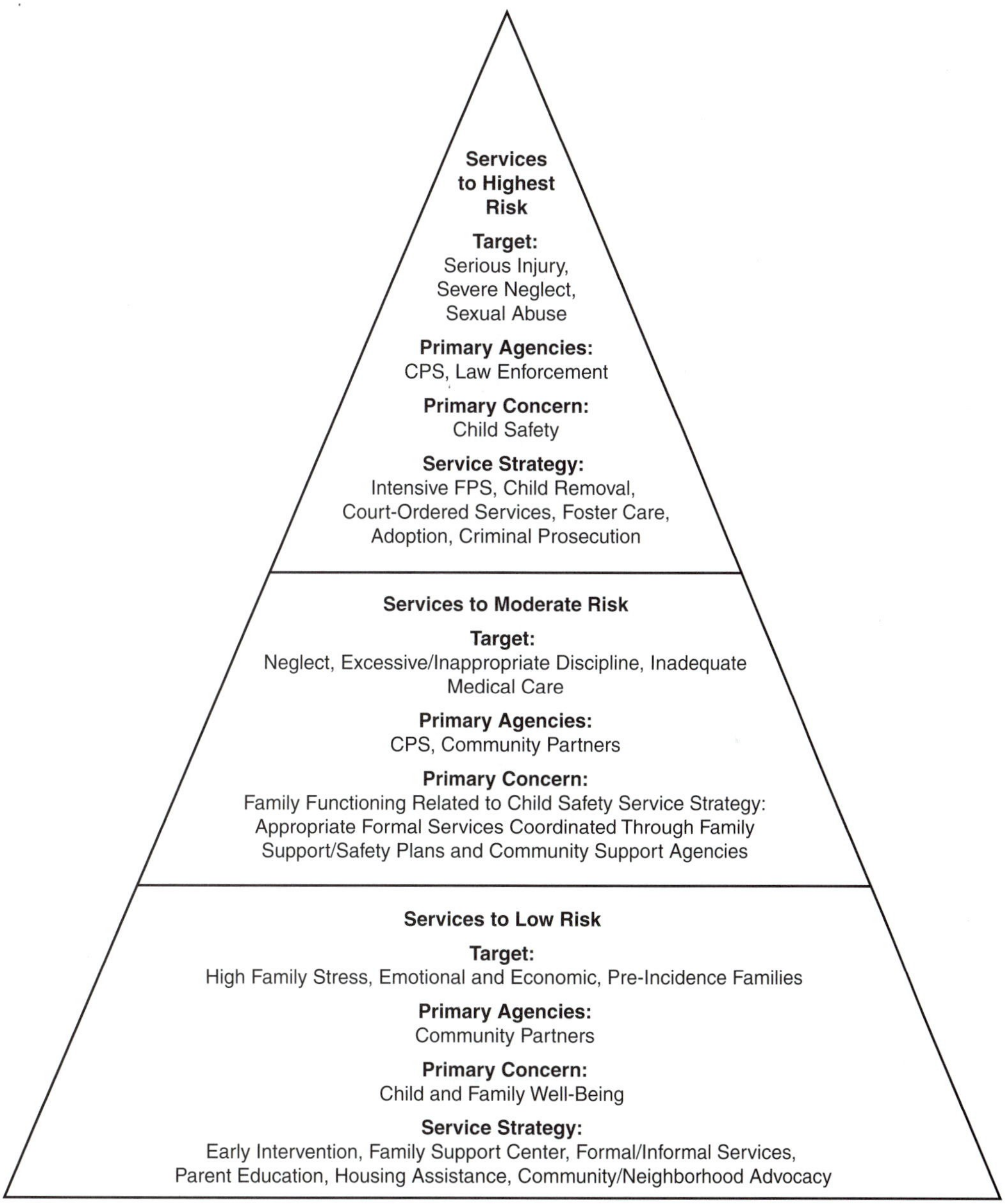

**Services
to Highest
Risk**

Target:
Serious Injury,
Severe Neglect,
Sexual Abuse

Primary Agencies:
CPS, Law Enforcement

Primary Concern:
Child Safety

Service Strategy:
Intensive FPS, Child Removal,
Court-Ordered Services, Foster Care,
Adoption, Criminal Prosecution

Services to Moderate Risk

Target:
Neglect, Excessive/Inappropriate Discipline, Inadequate
Medical Care

Primary Agencies:
CPS, Community Partners

Primary Concern:
Family Functioning Related to Child Safety Service Strategy:
Appropriate Formal Services Coordinated Through Family
Support/Safety Plans and Community Support Agencies

Services to Low Risk

Target:
High Family Stress, Emotional and Economic, Pre-Incidence Families

Primary Agencies:
Community Partners

Primary Concern:
Child and Family Well-Being

Service Strategy:
Early Intervention, Family Support Center, Formal/Informal Services,
Parent Education, Housing Assistance, Community/Neighborhood Advocacy

Source: National Association of Public Child Welfare Administrators (NAPCWA), *Guidelines for a model system of protective services for abused and neglected children and their families* (Washington, DC: American Public Human Services Association, 1999). Reprinted with permission.

likelihood of success may depend on two points: (1) how effectively the child welfare worker communicates the potential benefits of the intervention strategies and (2) how the family responds. A case example follows:

Esther Watkins was arrested for prostitution and drug charges. During the arrest, the officers found out that she had a 3-month-old infant at home. Ms. Watkins has two other children, ages 1 and 2, who have already been placed in foster care. The social worker met with Ms. Watkins in jail to discuss her circumstances. Ms. Watkins was uncommunicative at first but gradually broke down and begged the worker for help. She said she was at the end of her rope and really wanted to change her life around. The CPS worker developed a concurrent permanency plan for all three children. The primary risk factors she chose to address were the mother's drug addiction, depression, and social isolation. Since all three children were born with some effect of substances, they all have received specialized medical assessments and ongoing follow-up. The foster parents, the Carters, expressed an interest in working with Ms. Watkins to help her get her life back together. They are also interested in being considered as adoptive parents for the children, if Ms. Watkins is unable to make the necessary changes in her life over the next 12 months.

The middle one-third of the pyramid (see Figure 4.1) represents family conditions that present moderate risks to children, warrant services by CPS, are focused on child safety and family well-being, and often involve collaboration with other service providers. The success of intervention with this type of family will be directly related to the capacity of the child welfare worker to develop a partnership with the family. The role of the child welfare worker with such a family is to help family members prepare for change and to collaborate on safety and case plans that will lead to improvements in family well-being and child safety. The following example describes a family that may be served in this middle section of the pyramid:

Sarah and Ralph Collins met while they were both in-patients at the local mental health center. They both have struggled with life-long mental health problems that have periodically impaired their capacity to manage on their own. They have been married one year, and three months ago, Mrs. Collins gave birth to a healthy baby girl. Mr. Collins works as a custodian at the local community college. Mrs. Collins has experience working in a nursing home but is not currently working. A public health nurse made the referral to CPS because the infant was not gaining weight and had been left in the crib for hours without her diaper changed. This resulted in a diaper rash on the infant's buttocks and legs. After an initial assessment, the CPS worker was concerned that Mrs. Collins was suffering from postpartum depression and sleeping most of the day while Mr. Collins was working. The worker developed a safety and case plan with services in collaboration with the public health nurse, the mental health center, and the infant's pediatric clinic. The risk factors that were the primary target of these plans included the mother's depression, the history of mental health problems of both parents, the social isolation of the family, and the age and vulnerability of the infant.

The bottom one-third of the pyramid (see Figure 4.1) represents families who experience high family stress but are identified as being at low risk for immediate maltreatment. These families can often be served by early intervention, family support centers, and other informal helping systems. Primary program outcomes for these families are enhanced child and family well- being. Here is an example of a family who may be served in this manner:

Mrs. James is caring for her two grandsons, ages 5 and 7, because their mother and father are unable to care for them. Both parents have addictions to heroin and cocaine. The father has not been involved in the children's lives for at least the last three years, as he has been incarcerated for grand theft and assault of a police officer. He is not expected to be out of jail for at least the next three years. The mother has not made contact with the children in the last 18 months. The school has reported that the boys, in the first and second grades, seem to have difficulty concentrating in school. The younger boy has been in several fights during recess. The older boy keeps to himself and does not get involved in play activities with his peers. Mrs. James admits that she is overwhelmed with the boys' behavior at home and says she thinks their "hearts are broken." After being screened at intake, the family was referred to the local family resource center, which provides family strengthening services for families who are at risk for neglect or abuse. The social worker developed a family assessment in collaboration with the school psychologist and targeted the following risk factors for attention: child behavior and mental health problems, child management skills for Mrs. James, and attachment difficulties of the boys. Ongoing services were provided by the family resource center social worker in collaboration with the mental health center and a mentoring program.

Evaluation of Family Progress and Case Closure

The primary purpose of the evaluation-of-family-progress stage is to assess the achievement of outcomes, goals, and tasks and to examine the degree to which risk factors have decreased and protective factors have increased. The primary purpose of case closure is to determine whether risk has been sufficiently reduced such that services are no longer necessary.

Determining the extent and nature of client improvement is central to intervention implementation. Monitoring change should begin as soon as intervention is implemented and continue throughout the life of a case, until the client-level and programmatic outcomes have been achieved (Ivanoff, Blythe, & Tripodi, 1994). If assessment measures have been used as part of the family assessment, they can be used again to specifically document the changes in behaviors and conditions that indicate an increase in protective factors, decrease in risk factors, and achievement of client-level outcomes. A specific assessment of safety should also occur at this stage. Key decisions and assessment processes that may facilitate these decisions are outlined in Table 4.6.

We have seen that concern for the child's risk and safety are always at the heart of the change process in child welfare. At CPS intake and initial assessment, risk assessment protocols guide our decisions. As we choose appropriate interventions, we focus on child welfare outcomes. In the later stages of the child welfare case process, protective and compensatory factors are particularly relevant. Family assessment protocols and

TABLE 4.6	Child Welfare Decisions and Assessments during the Family Evaluation Stage

Decisions	Assessments Needed to Guide Decision Making
Is the child safe? Have the threats of harm been reduced or eliminated?	A safety assessment protocol
What protective and compensatory factors exist in this family?	Clinical assessment measures
What changes have occurred in the previously identified risk factors? Are other risks present that may not have been previously identified?	Clinical assessment measures (self-report and/or observational measures designed to document change over time)
What case outcomes have been achieved? What is the level of change in these outcomes?	Clinical assessment measures (self-report and/or observational measures designed to document change over time)
Has sufficient change occurred to demonstrate that the risk of future maltreatment is reduced?	Clinical assessment measures (self-report and/or observational measures designed to document change over time)

clinical assessment measures are helpful for assessing, over time, the degree to which the family succeeds at decreasing risk factors, increasing protective and compensatory factors, and achieving case-level outcomes that lead toward safety, well-being, and permanency.

Risk and Safety Assessment Approaches

English and Pecora (1994) suggest that risk assessment approaches have at least four goals: (1) to help CPS workers better identify situations where children are vulnerable to abuse or neglect; (2) to improve the consistency of CPS decisions; (3) to help child welfare administrators determine which of the families at highest risk should receive continuing CPS intervention; and (4) to help CPS staff design outcome-oriented case plans and effectively target services. Hollingshead and Fluke (2000) state the goals this way: (1) to guide and structure decision making; (2) to predict future harm and classify cases; (3) to aid in resource management by identifying service needs; and (4) to facilitate communication within the agency and with community stakeholders.

Safety assessment systems are designed to assess the imminent risk of serious harm and guide the development of a safety plan, if a safety threat is identified. The different definitions and purposes of risk and safety assessment, as identified in the first section of this chapter, may explain the differences in the stating of goals for these systems (Starr, DePanfilis, & Hyde, 1994). The multiple goals are accomplished at different stages of the CPS case process.

Types of Risk Assessment Approaches

Multiple types of assessment approaches are needed in CPS to guide decision-making throughout the child welfare service delivery process. Not all the approaches are designed with the primary goal of predicting future maltreatment. Some are combinations of risk and family assessment formats, for the primary purpose of targeting outcomes and services. For example, the Family Assessment Form (FAF) is a practice-based instrument to help child welfare practitioners standardize the assessment of family functioning and service planning for families receiving home-based services (Children's Bureau of Southern California, 1997).

Risk assessment instruments are usually used to help guide data collection and analysis during the initial assessment of a new CPS report. When they are designed to predict the risk of future maltreatment, they may also be used to assess changes in risk over time. At least four categories of assessment approaches are used today in child welfare agencies.

THE MATRIX APPROACH   Beginning with the first risk assessment approach developed in the state of Illinois in the 1980s, the matrix approach has traditionally used a table comprised of between 16 and 35 factors that are rated in terms of their severity of risk to the child. Each item includes anchors indicating the level of risk related to the individual risk factor. While most of the risk factors in these models were initially included because of some empirical support of their association with child maltreatment, most of these models have not been subjected to rigorous empirical testing.

ACTUARIAL MODELS   These models are constructed from case record data and are specific to the local and state jurisdictions that served to guide their development. Risk factors are selected after an analysis of the variables shown to be associated with new reports of child abuse or neglect or new substantiated reports of child abuse or neglect in the specific state or jurisdiction. These models are often the most concise, as they are specifically designed to predict the risk of maltreatment in the future. Some of the risk factors in these models may predict future maltreatment but may not be helpful for determining how to work with a family to reduce the risk of maltreatment. For example, a criminal record might predict future maltreatment but is not something that can be changed in the future.

FAMILY ASSESSMENT SCALES   Approaches such as the Child Well-Being Scales (Magura & Moses, 1986), Family Risk Scales (Magura, Moses, & Jones, 1987), Family Assessment Form (Children's Bureau of Southern California, 1997), and North Carolina Family Assessment Scale (Reed-Ashcraft, Kirk, & Fraser, 2001) use behaviorally anchored scales to assess the levels of parent, child, family, and household functioning in order to identify areas of concern that should be the targets of child welfare interventions. The purpose of these scales is not to predict the risk of maltreatment but to help families achieve child welfare outcomes such as safety and well-being.

CHILD-AT-RISK FIELD The fourth approach to risk assessment is an ecological approach developed by ACTION for Child Protection (Holder & Corey, 1986) that was designed to organize the collection and analysis of information around five areas: child, parent, family, maltreatment, and intervention. Similar to the matrix approach in design, individual areas are included in the assessment outline because they have been empirically correlated to child maltreatment. The approach to assessment was designed as a social work approach to understanding the family so that interventions could be targeted to control or change the identified risk factors, rather than to predict child maltreatment recurrence.

Safety Assessment Approaches

One of the first approaches to safety assessment was developed and tested by ACTION for Child Protection as a component of the Child-at-Risk Field in the late 1980s (DePanfilis, 1988; DePanfilis & Scannapieco, 1994). Designed to identify safety threats that could result in immediate and severe harm, most states are now adopting or creating safety assessment approaches in response to mandates of the Adoption and Safe Families Act.

The safety assessment model developed by the Illinois Department of Children and Family Services in 1995 has had the most rigorous testing of any safety assessment model to date. The Illinois model, called the Child Endangerment Risk Assessment Protocol (CERAP), guides workers to assess 14 factors associated with immediate danger to children, and if concerns are identified, workers are directed to develop safety plans to protect the child (Fluke et al., 2001). Results of a time series design suggest that the recurrence of indicated maltreatment for at-risk children in Illinois was significantly reduced by 28.6 percent by the second year following implementation of the CERAP (Fluke et al, 2001). The implication of these findings is that if social workers use an instrument to identify elements that present danger to children, they will develop safety plans to address the safety concerns and thereby decrease the recurrence of child maltreatment.

Other research results on the model have suggested that predictors of maltreatment recurrence vary, depending on the point in the case process (Fuller et al., 2001). Age of the youngest child, single-parent household, number of child problems, type of maltreatment, and case disposition were all predictors of short-term recurrence for investigation cases. Five days after the case had been opened for in-home services, the absence of a completed CERAP form and lack of service provision were the milestone predictors. At both points in time, the number of previous indicated reports on the perpetrator and the presence of multiple caregiver problems (e.g., alcohol/drug dependency, domestic violence) were predictive of short-term maltreatment recurrence.

Implementation Challenges

Whether risk and safety assessment approaches can be successful in achieving their goals is directly related to the degree that they are used for the purposes for which they were intended and in the manner in which they were designed. A number of authors have noted the challenges with motivating child welfare workers to use these models to guide decision making (Berkowitz, 1991; DePanfilis, 1996a; Doueck, Bronson, & Levine, 1992; English & Pecora, 1994; Hornby, 1989; Pecora, 1991). The results of two national studies suggest that agencies that turn to risk assessment as a quick fix for major system problems are less likely to be successful in implementation than agencies that strategically plan the implementation process (Cicchinelli & Keller, 1990; Hornby, 1989).

Risk assessment implementation will be more successful if the model selected is credible and has the potential to improve practice, the process for implementation is well planned, there is motivation to change based on realistic expectations about what the model will and won't do, and the reasons for resistance are identified and addressed rather than ignored (DePanfilis, 1996a). Other ingredients for successful implementation include engaging the commitment of supervisors and managers, integrating changes in practice by amending laws and policies to support the innovation, providing ongoing training to increase the competency of staff, and adjusting the workload to accommodate differences in practice expectations.

Further study is needed on the degree to which risk assessment approaches can be used over time to measure risk reduction and the positive achievement of outcomes. One study has suggested that the differences between risk scores at beginning and end of services were largely due to the artificial inflation of initial risk scores by caseworkers in order to ensure children's acceptance for ongoing child protective services (Lyle & Graham, 2000). Since more attention is now given to measuring outcomes through the Adoption and Safe Families Act and child and family service reviews (U.S. DHHS, 2000), child welfare managers need a different level of quality assurance to minimize the measurement error that can occur when social workers face conflicting demands to obtain services for families.

As we seek to improve the effectiveness of risk and safety assessment approaches, we must remember the complex interplay between risk and protective factors and make sure the systems take this interplay into account. Instruments should consider the strengths within a family as they may be maximized to minimize the effect of risk on the child (Berry, 1997; Fraser, 2004). Risk assessment instruments should also operate from an ecological perspective and take into account contextual effects with a family's system (Cash, 2001).

Since risk assessment instruments are constantly evolving and textbooks tend to be static, copies of risk and safety assessments are not provided in this text. Readers are encouraged to search the Internet for risk assessment and safety evaluation models in child welfare and child protective services. Many agencies now publish copies of their instruments on their webpages. As these instruments are located, try to identify the type of model and the purposes and decisions that the instrument is designed to address.

REFERENCES

Ammerman, R. T. (1991). The role of the child in physical abuse: A reappraisal. *Violence and Victims, 6*(2), 87–100.

Baird, S. C. (1988). Development of risk assessment indices for the Alaska Department of Health and Social Services. In T. Tatara (Ed.), *Validation research in CPS risk assessment: Three recent studies* (Occasional Monograph Series no. 2, pp. 84–142). Washington, DC: American Public Welfare Association.

Baird, S. C., Wagner, D., & Neuenfeldt, D. (1993). Actuarial risk assessment and case management in child protective services. In T. Tatara (Ed.), *Sixth National Roundtable on CPS Risk Assessment Summary of Highlights* (pp. 152–168). Washington, DC: American Public Welfare Association.

Belsky, J. (1980). Child maltreatment: An ecological integration. *American Psychologist, 35,* 320–335.

Belsky, J. (1992). *The etiology of child maltreatment: An ecological–contextual analysis.* Paper commissioned by the National Academy of Science, Commission on Behavioral and Social Sciences and Education, Panel on Research on Child Abuse and Neglect.

Belsky, J. (1993). Etiology of child maltreatment: A developmental–ecological analysis. *Psychological Bulletin, 114,* 413–434.

Berkeley Planning Associates. (1983). *Evaluation of the clinical demonstrations of the treatment of child abuse and neglect, Volume 2, The exploration of client characteristics, services, and outcomes: Final report and summary of findings* (HEW 105-78-1108). Washington, DC: National Center on Child Abuse and Neglect, Office of Human Development Services, U.S. Department of Health and Human Services.

Berkowitz, S. (1991). *Key findings on definitions of risk to children and uses of risk assessment by state CPS agencies from the state survey component of the study of high risk child abuse and neglect groups.* Paper prepared by Westat, Inc., and presented to the National Center on Child Abuse and Neglect Symposium on Risk Assessment in Child Protective Services, Washington, DC.

Berry, M. (1997). *The family at risk: Issues and trends in family preservation services.* Columbia, SC: University of South Carolina Press.

Black, D. A., Heyman, R. E., &, Slep, A. M. S. (2001a). Risk factors for child physical abuse. *Aggression and Violent Behavior, 6,* 121–188.

Black, D. A., Heyman, R. E., &, Slep, A. M. S. (2001b). Risk factors for child sexual abuse. *Aggression and Violent Behavior, 6,* 203–229.

Black, D. A., Slep, A. M. S., & Heyman, R. E. (2001). Risk factors for child psychological abuse. *Aggression and Violent Behavior, 6,* 189–201.

Bronfenbrenner, U. (1979). *The ecology of human development: Experiments by design and nature.* Cambridge, MA: Harvard University Press.

Browne, D. (1986). The role of stress in the commission of subsequent acts of child abuse and neglect. *Journal of Family Violence, 1*(4), 289–297.

Cash, S. J. (2001). Risk assessment in child welfare: The art and science. *Children and Youth Services Review, 23,* 811–830.

Child Welfare League of America. (1999). *CWLA standards of excellence for services for abused or neglected children and their families* (Rev. ed.). Washington, DC: Author.

Children's Bureau of Southern California. (1997). *Family assessment form, A practice-based approach to assessing family functioning.* Washington, DC: Child Welfare League of America.

Cicchinelli, L. F., & Keller, R. (1990). *A comparative analysis of risk assessment models and systems.* Final report prepared for the National Center on Child Abuse and Neglect (Grant no. 90-CA-1302). Lakewood, CO: Applied Research Associates.

Cohn, A. H. (1979). Effective treatment of child abuse and neglect. *Social Work, 24,* 513–519.

Coleman, H. D. J. (1995). *A longitudinal study of a family preservation program.* Doctoral dissertation, University of Utah, School of Social Work.

Courtney, M. (2000). What outcomes are relevant for intervention. In H. Dubowitz & D. DePanfilis (Eds.), *Handbook for child protection practice* (pp. 373–383). Thousand Oaks, CA: Sage.

DePanfilis, D. (1988). *Final report: Determining safety in child protective services and child placement decisions.* Submitted to the Edna McConnell Clark Foundation. Charlotte, NC: ACTION for Child Protection.

DePanfilis, D. (1993). *A proximate test of the construct and predictive validity of the Child At Risk Field decision-making system.* Unpublished manuscript. University of Maryland at Baltimore, School of Social Work, Baltimore.

DePanfilis, D. (1995). The epidemiology of child maltreatment recurrences. *Dissertation Abstracts International, 56*(12), 1996.

DePanfilis, D. (1996a). Implementing child mistreatment risk assessment systems: Lessons from theory. *Administration in Social Work, 20*(2), 41–59.

DePanfilis, D. (1996b). Social isolation of neglectful families: A review of social support assessment and intervention models. *Child Maltreatment, 1,* 37–52.

DePanfilis, D. (1997). Is the child safe? How do we respond to safety concerns? In T. Morton & W. Holder (Eds.), *Decision making in children's protective services* (pp. 121–142). Atlanta, Georgia: National Resource Center on Child Maltreatment.

DePanfilis, D. (2000). How do I match risks to client intervention outcomes? In H. Dubowitz, & D. DePanfilis (Eds.), *Handbook for child protection practice* (pp. 365–370). Thousand Oaks, CA: Sage.

DePanfilis, D., & Salus, M. (2003). *Child protective services: A guide for caseworkers.* Washington, DC: U.S. Department of Health and Human Services, Administration on Children and Families, Administration for Children, Youth, and Families, Children's Bureau, Office on Child Abuse and Neglect.

DePanfilis, D., & Scannapieco, M. (1994). Assessing the safety of children at risk for maltreatment: Decision-making models. *Child Welfare, 73,* 229–245.

DePanfilis, D., & Zuravin, S. J. (1998). Rates, patterns, and frequency of child maltreatment recurrences among public CPS families. *Child Maltreatment, 3,* 27–42.

DePanfilis, D., & Zuravin, S. J. (1999a). Epidemiology of child maltreatment recurrences. *Social Services Review, 73,* 218–239.

DePanfilis, D., & Zuravin, S. J. (1999b). Predicting child maltreatment recurrences during treatment. *Child Abuse and Neglect, 23*(8), 729–743.

DePanfilis, D., & Zuravin, S. J. (2002). The effect of services on the recurrence of child maltreatment. *Child Abuse and Neglect, 26,* 187–205.

Doueck, H. J., Bronson, D. E., & Levine, M. (1992). Evaluating risk assessment implementation in child protection: Issues for consideration. *Child Abuse and Neglect, 16,* 637–646.

Doueck, H. J., English, D. J., DePanfilis, D., & Moote, G. T. (1993). Decision-making in child protective services: A comparison of selected risk-assessment systems. *Child Welfare, 72,* 441–452.

English, D. J., Aubin, S. W., Fine, D., & Pecora, P. J. (1993). *Improving the accuracy and cultural sensitivity of risk assessment in child abuse and neglect cases.* Seattle, WA: University of Washington, School of Social Work.

English, D. J., & Pecora, P. J. (1994). Risk assessment as a practice method in child protective services. *Child Welfare, 73,* 451–475.

Fluke, J. (1991). Risk assessment and workload characteristics. In T. Tatara (Ed.), *Fourth National Roundtable on CPS Risk Assessment: Summary of Highlights* (pp. 121–143). Washington, DC: American Public Welfare Association.

Fluke, J., Edwards, M., Bussey, M., Wells, S., & Johnson, W. (2001). Reducing recurrence in child protective services: Impact of a targeted safety protocol. *Child Maltreatment, 6,* 207–218.

Fraser, M. W. (2004). The ecology of childhood: A multisystems perspective. In M. W. Fraser (Ed.), *Risk and resilience in childhood: An ecological perspective* (2nd ed.) (pp. 1–9). Washington, DC: NASW Press.

Fraser, M. W., Kirby, L. D., & Smokowski, P. R. (2004). Risk and resilience in childhood. In M. W. Fraser (Ed.), *Risk and resilience in childhood: An ecological perspective* (2nd ed.) (pp. 13–66). Washington, DC: NASW Press.

Fryer, G. E., & Miyoshi, T. J. (1994). A survival analysis of the revictimization of children: The case of Colorado. *Child Maltreatment, 18,* 1063–1071.

Fuller, T. L., Wells, S. J., & Cotton, E. E. (2001). Predictors of maltreatment recurrence at two milestones in the life of a case. *Children and Youth Services Review, 23,* 49–78.

Garmezy, N., & Masten, A. S. (1994). Chronic adversities. In M. Rutter, L. Herzov, & E. Taylor (Eds.), *Child and adolescent psychiatry* (3rd ed.). Oxford, England: Blackwell.

Herrenkohl, R. C., Herrenkohl, E. C., Egolf, B., & Seech, M. (1978). *Final report from the project: An investigation of the effects of a multidimensional service program on recidivism/discontinuation of child abuse and neglect* (prepared for the National Center on Child Abuse and Neglect, Grant no. 90-C-428). Bethlehem, PA: Lehigh University.

Holder, W., & Corey, M. (1986). *Child protective services risk management: A decision-making handbook.* Charlotte, NC: ACTION for Child Protection.

Holder, W., Costello, T., Lund, T. R., & Holder, T. (2000). *Safety assessment and family evaluation.* Charlotte, NC: ACTION for Child Protection.

Holder, W., & Lund, T. R. (1995). Translating risks to positive outcomes. In D. DePanfilis, D. Daro, & S. Wells (Eds.), *APSAC Advisor, 8*(4), 20–24.

Hollinshead, D., & Fluke, J. (2000). What works in safety and risk assessment for child protective services. In M. P. Kluger, G. Alexander, & P. A. Curtis (Eds.), *What works in child welfare* (pp. 67–74). Washington, DC: Child Welfare League of America.

Hornby, H. (1989). *Risk assessment in child protective services: Issues in field implementation.* Portland, ME: National Child Welfare Resource Center for Management and Administration.

Ivanoff, A., Blythe, B., & Tripodi, T. (1994). *Involuntary clients in social work practice.* New York: Aldine de Gruyter.

Johnson, W. (1994). Maltreatment recurrence as a criterion for validating risk assessment instruments. In T. Tatara (Ed.), *Seventh National Roundtable on CPS Risk Assessment: Summary of highlights* (pp. 175–182). Washington, DC: American Public Welfare Association.

Johnson, W. B. (1988). Child-abusing parents: Factors associated with successful completion of treatment. *Psychological Reports, 63,* 434.

Johnson, W., & Clancy, T. (1990). Preliminary findings from a study of risk assessment accuracy and service effectiveness in home-based services physical abuse cases. In T. Tatara (Ed.), *Third National Roundtable on CPS Risk Assessment: Summary of highlights* (pp. 161–171). Washington, DC: American Public Welfare Association.

Johnson, W., & L'Esperance, J. (1984). Predicting the recurrence of child abuse. *Social Work Research and Abstracts, 20*(2), 21–26.

Littell, J. H. (1997). Effects of the duration, intensity, and breadth of family preservation services: A new analysis of data from the Illinois Family First experiment. *Children and Youth Services Review, 19*(½), 17–39.

Lyle, C. G., & Graham, E. (2000). Looks can be deceiving: Using a risk assessment instrument to evaluate the outcomes of child protection services. *Children and Youth Services Review, 22,* 935–949.

Magura, S., & Moses, B. (1986). *Outcome measures for child welfare services.* New York: Child Welfare League of America.

Magura, S., Moses, B. S., & Jones, M. A. (1987). *Assessing risk and measuring change in families the family risk scales.* Washington, DC: Child Welfare League of America.

Marks, J., & McDonald, T. (1989). *Risk assessment in child protective services: Predicting the recurrence of child maltreatment.* Portland, ME: University of Southern Maine, National Child Welfare Resource Center for Management and Administration.

Marks, J., McDonald, T., & Bessey, W. (1989). *Risk factors assessed by instrument-based models.* Portland, ME: National Child Welfare Resource Center for Management and Administration.

Masten, A. S., & Wright, M. O. (1998). Cumulative risk and protection models of child maltreatment. In B. B. R. Rossman & M. S. Rosenberg (Eds.), *Multiple victimization of children* (pp. 7–30). New York: Haworth Press.

McDonald, T., & Johnson, W. (1992). Predicting recurrence of maltreatment for child sexual abuse cases. In T. Tatara (Ed.), *Fifth National Roundtable on CPS Risk Assessment: Summary of highlights* (pp. 72–89). Washington, DC: American Public Welfare Association.

McDonald, T., & Johnson, W. (1993). Tracking reported sexual abuse cases. *Journal of Child Sexual Abuse, 2*(2), 1–11.

Miller, J. S., Williams, K. M., English, D. J., & Olmstead, J. (1987). *Risk assessment child protection: A review of the literature.* Washington, DC: American Public Welfare Association.

National Association of Public Child Welfare Administrators (NAPCWA). (1999). *Guidelines for a model system of protective services for abused and neglected children and their families.* Washington, DC: American Public Human Services Association.

National Research Council, Panel on Research on Child Abuse and Neglect, Commission on Behavioral and Social Sciences and Education. (1993). *Understanding child abuse and neglect* (p. 125).Washington, DC: National Academy Press.

Pecora, P. (1991). Investigating allegations of child maltreatment: The strengths and limitations of current risk assessment systems. In M. Robin (Ed.), *Assessing child maltreatment reports: The problem of false allegations* (pp. 73–92). New York: Haworth Press.

Pellegrini, D. S. (1990). Psychosocial risk and protective factors in childhood. *Developmental and Behavioral Pediatrics, 11,* 201–209.

Pianta, R., Egeland, B., & Erickson, M. (1989). Results of the mother–child interaction research project. In D. Cicchetti & V. Carlson (Eds.), *Child maltreatment: Theory and research on the causes and consequences of child abuse and neglect* (pp. 203–253). New York: Cambridge University Press.

Reed-Ashcraft, K., Kirk, R. S., & Fraser, M. S. (2001). The reliability and validity of the North Carolina Family Assessment Scale. *Research on Social Work Practice, 11,* 503–520.

Schumaker, J. A., Slep, A. M. S., & Heyman, R. E. (2001). Risk factors for child neglect. *Aggression and Violent Behavior, 6,* 231–254.

Schuerman, J. R., Rzepnicki, T. L., & Littell, J. H. (1994). *Putting families first: An experiment in family preservation.* New York: Aldine de Gruyter.

Starr, R. H., DePanfilis, D., & Hyde, M. (1994). Current issues in risk assessment. *Seventh National Roundtable on CPS Risk Assessment: Summary of highlights* (pp. 183–198). Washington, DC: American Public Welfare Association.

Thomlison, B. (2004). Child maltreatment: A risk and protective factor perspective in child maltreatment. In M. W. Fraser (Ed.), *Risk and resilience in childhood* (2nd ed.) (pp. 89–131). Washington, DC: NASW Press.

U.S. Department of Health and Human Services (DHHS), Administration on Children and Families, Children's Bureau. (2000). *Rethinking child welfare practice under the Adoption and Safe Families Act of 1997.* Washington, DC: Government Printing Office.

U.S. Department of Health and Human Services (DHHS), Administration on Children, Youth, and Families. (2004). *Child maltreatment 2002.* Washington, DC: Government Printing Office. Retrieved May 30, 2004, at www.acf.hhd.gov/programs/cb/publications/cmreports.htm

Wagner, D. (1994). The use of actuarial risk assessment in criminal justice: What can we learn from the experience? In T. Tatara (Ed.), *Seventh National Roundtable on CPS Risk Assessment: Summary of highlights* (pp. 211–223). Washington, DC: American Public Welfare Association.

Weedon, J., Torti, T., & Zunder, P. (1988). Vermont Division of Social Services Family Risk Assessment Matrix: Research and evaluation. In T. Tatara (Ed.), *Validation research in CPS risk assessment: Three recent studies* (Occasional Monograph Series no. 2, pp. 2–43). Washington, DC: American Public Welfare Association.

Wolock, I., Sherman, P., Feldman, L. H., & Metzger, B. (2001). Child abuse and neglect referral patterns: A longitudinal study. *Children and Youth Services Review, 23,* 21–47.

Wolfe, D. A. (1985). Child-abusive parents: An empirical review and analysis. *Psychological Bulletin, 97,* 467–482.

Wood, J. M. (1995, June). *NCCD predictors of re-abuse and re-neglect in a predominantly Hispanic population.* Paper presented at the Ninth National Roundtable on CPS Risk Assessment, San Francisco, CA.

Zunder, P. (1990). Recent empirical findings of the Vermont family risk assessment instrument. *National Conference on CPS Risk Assessment from Research to Practice: Designing the future of child protective services, summaries of highlights* (pp. 1–16). Washington, DC: Vermont Division of Social Services, American Public Welfare Association, and American Association for Protecting Children.

CHAPTER **5**

Assessing and Intervening with Families

Ineke Way and Marlys Staudt

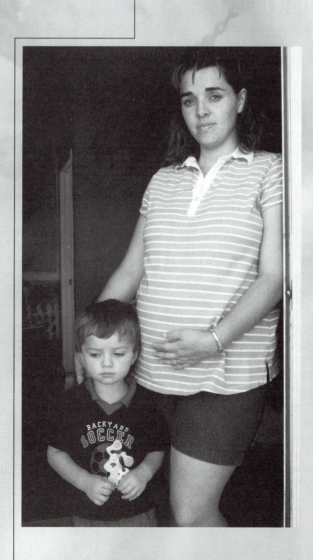

ne hallmark of child welfare services is that *families,* rather than individual family members, are often referred for services. This focus on family systems fits social work's emphasis on the person in the context of environment and on the transactional approach (Shulman, 1999). As the previous chapters have pointed out, child welfare issues are frequently problems of interactions within families; therefore, family-focused interventions are often the most meaningful. Even when providing services to an individual family member, the social worker should consider the absent family members and their strengths, needs, issues, relationships, and dynamics. In this chapter, we examine how the child protective services (CPS) social worker can understand a family's needs, prioritize those needs, make an assessment, and effectively intervene to meet the unique needs of the family.

Understanding Family Needs

Mr. and Mrs. Sanchez* have brought their nephew Mario (age 2) to the emergency room with burns over much of his body. They state that all the children were together downstairs in the house and that Mr. Sanchez was outside working. Mr. Sanchez states that he came inside and saw his son Pedro (age 7) with a curling iron, standing by Mario; Mario was crying. Mr. Sanchez states that when he asked Pedro what happened, Pedro began crying. He said that he didn't know but Mario would not stop crying and he tried to make him stop crying. The hospital emergency room staff was concerned about the extent of burns Mario had suffered and referred the case to CPS for suspected child abuse.

Six months earlier, the Sanchez family had moved to a Midwestern midsized U.S. city from another state to join their extended family after hearing about job opportunities. Two months ago, Mr. and Mrs. Sanchez had traveled to Mexico and brought back Mario, Mrs. Sanchez's nephew, to stay with the family. Mrs. Sanchez explains that she missed having a baby in the home because "my babies are growing up." She acknowledges that Mr. Sanchez "never liked Mario" and that he often yelled at him. Mr. Sanchez works the third shift for a textile company. Mrs. Sanchez stays home to care for the children. Mr. and Mrs. Sanchez speak broken English. Their first language is Spanish, and Mrs. Sanchez explains that when she is frightened, her English "leaves" her.

During the CPS investigation, Pedro and his sister Anna (age 6) refuse to talk with the social worker. When asked direct questions about what happened to Mario, they begin to cry and ask to go home. After two weeks, Mr. Sanchez loses his job due to the many interviews needed to investigate the CPS complaint. When Mr. and Mrs. Sanchez are unable to pay their rent, the landlord threatens to evict them, stating, "They don't pay, and I don't want people in my apartments who abuse their kids."

The first step in providing child welfare services is to learn what brings a family to the attention of the child welfare system and understand their unique situation. While child maltreatment may be categorized by type (e.g., sexual abuse, physical abuse,

---

*Identifying information has been changed to protect client confidentiality.

physical neglect, emotional abuse, emotional neglect), families bring their unique circumstances and histories.

Consider the social worker assigned to the Sanchez family. That social worker needs a roadmap that shows where to focus in gathering information about the family and their crisis situation. The following section looks at theories about how parents may come to maltreat their children. These explanations can guide the social worker in knowing which questions to ask family members.

Theories of Etiology of Maltreatment

When working with a family entering the child welfare system, the social worker must consider all the family members, the history they bring to the current crisis, and the societal context in which they live. A number of theorists—all with the goal of preventing harm for children and effectively focusing intervention—have proposed explanations for child maltreatment. Belsky (1993) outlines three possible explanations for why parents maltreat their children: (1) *intergenerational theory*, (2) *interactional context theory*, and (3) *sociocultural context theory*. In the next few sections, we look at these three theories plus one other that is known as an *integrated model*.

INTERGENERATIONAL THEORY   The intergenerational explanation takes an individual focus and suggests that parents who maltreat their children were themselves maltreated when they were young (Belsky, 1993; Zuravin et al., 1996). This etiologic theory argues that maltreated children are affected in multiple ways. First, these children have poor role models for parenting and therefore do not learn appropriate parenting skills. Second, these children develop problems as a result of being maltreated, including inadequate empathy for others (Straker & Jacobson, 1981), poor anger management skills, and insufficient coping skills. If adults have not worked through their childhood experiences, they may be at risk of using the same abusive parenting styles their parents used with them (Zuravin et al., 1996).

Based on the intergenerational theory, it would be important to ask Mr. and Mrs. Sanchez about their early life experiences and how their parents treated them. The social worker would ask about how their parents disciplined them and how anger was expressed in the family.

INTERACTIONAL CONTEXT THEORY   A closely related theory is the interactional context theory, which focuses on negative patterns of interaction between parent and child. This etiologic theory suggests that parents who abuse their children also have a lot of other negative interaction patterns with them (Belsky, 1993). For example, studies have found that maltreating parents have more negative interactions and more harsh disciplinary styles than nonmaltreating parents (Belsky, 1993; Whipple & Webster-Stratton, 1991). Here is an explanation from Belsky (1993):

> Abuse appears to emerge in the immediate context of parent–child interaction when a parent with a predisposition toward anxiety, depression, and hostility becomes irritated with a child, attempts to physically and instrumentally control the child, but

becomes so aroused as to lose control of him or herself and overdoes what was initially intended to be an act of discipline. (p. 421)

This theory would guide the social worker to ask Mr. and Mrs. Sanchez and their children about how the family members relate and communicate and about the typical patterns of solving problems. The social worker might choose to bring the family in to the office and observe their interactions as they are working on a group project, such as building a tower with Legos or Tinker Toys.

SOCIOCULTURAL CONTEXT THEORY   This theory focuses on the societal level and argues that American society has grown to accept a high level of interpersonal violence as normal. The United States is criticized as "a country that practices and approves violence" (Straus, 1974, as quoted in Belsky, 1993). This theory suggests that over the years, movies, television, song lyrics, and computer games have contained increasingly more violence, such that violence has become normalized. Children and adolescents learn to accept violence as a normal and expected part of interpersonal relationships (Staub, 1996).

Guided by this theory, the social worker would ask Mr. and Mrs. Sanchez about their cultural beliefs and values and learn about their involvement in American popular culture. The social worker would also assess their knowledge of parenting practices.

INTEGRATED MODEL   Azar, Povilaitis, Lauretti, and Pouquette (1998) have proposed an integrated model for explaining child maltreatment (physical abuse, neglect, emotional abuse) that includes five factors. First, a parent may misinterpret the child's behavior. For example, the parent with a 2-year-old that yells "No!" may label the child adversarial or malicious, instead of recognizing that this is developmentally appropriate behavior. Second, parents may not be able to change their parenting style as the child grows older and experiences different developmental needs. Third, parents may react to a child's behavior impatiently and angrily. Fourth, parents may have poor stress management skills and move from crisis to crisis, such that the ability to focus on the child's needs is compromised (Whipple & Webster-Stratton, 1991). Fifth, parents may have poor social skills that lead to increased isolation, lack of social support, and inability to develop constructive relationships with their children.

Based on this theory, the social worker would ask questions about Mr. and Mrs. Sanchez's beliefs and attitudes toward their children's behavior and about what they see as appropriate behavior for their children's ages. The social worker would also inquire about coping skills and how the parents manage stress. Last, the social worker would want to learn about the Sanchez family's social support network.

As this section demonstrates, there are several different theories and each one suggests a different way to work with maltreating parents. The social worker's task is complicated by the fact that families are usually dealing with many problems by the time they come to the attention of the child welfare agency, and they may not even want services or may feel angry that they have been referred for the suspected abuse/neglect of their children. This means that the social worker assesses and helps resolve issues at a number of different levels, while keeping in mind that all assessments and interventions aim at keeping the child safe.

Prioritizing a Family's Needs

Children and families who enter the child welfare system may need assistance in dealing with a variety of issues; therefore, the social worker must assess and prioritize a family's needs in order to plan the work and address first things first. Maslow's (1970) hierarchy of human needs suggests that basic needs such as food and housing must be met before family members can focus energy and effort toward issues such as self-esteem and self-actualization (see Figure 5.1). Maslow's framework helps us categorize the types of issues families may have as they enter the child welfare system: (1) physiological needs, (2) safety needs, (3) belongingness needs, (4) esteem needs, and (5) self-actualization needs. These needs are discussed in the following sections and applied to the Sanchez family.

Physiological Needs

All people need to have their basic needs met in order to survive and thrive. Families that struggle with chronic poverty need help first in resolving such concrete issues as hunger and adequate nutrition, lead poisoning from inadequate water supplies or peeling paint, lack of heat, and homelessness (Eamon, 2001). The children's health and welfare often depends on skilled social work intervention at this most basic level.

The Sanchez family initially presented with their concrete needs being met. They had an apartment with heat and running water and also had adequate food and clothing. Then they learned about the threat of losing their apartment, and their needs changed. While these problems may be partially assessed in the office, their resolution requires contacting community resources, working through complex bureaucratic application processes, and effectively advocating for action. Practice wisdom suggests that one way to develop a relationship with a family that is distrustful of services is to help them meet a concrete need. With the Sanchez family, this might include contacting the landlord to ask what needs to be done to help the family avoid eviction. Another way the social worker can help meet a concrete need is to help the family apply for food stamps and register for TANF (Temporary Assistance for Needy Families).

FIGURE 5.1   **Pyramid of Maslow's**
Hierarchy

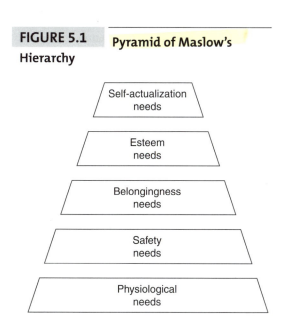

Safety Needs

The second level of need for children is to be safe from harm or the threat of harm. Unsafe home environments include situations where a child is being sexually or physically abused or where a child is being neglected in ways that deprive him or her of necessary food, supervision, or medical care. Unsafe community conditions may include neighborhood violence, neighborhood crime, and racism. These environments introduce risks for physical and emotional harm. Wyatt (1990) suggests that minority group children may experience a range of potentially traumatizing situations, including societal racism and discrimination, media stereotypes of sexuality, neighborhood violence, and police abuse of authority.

In the Sanchez family, Mario had been severely burned over a large portion of his body. Safety needs must take priority over higher-level needs, such as belongingness and keeping the family together.

Belongingness and Love Needs

The third level of need, to belong within a family and community and be loved, comes into play as the child welfare social worker assesses the extent to which the children in the Sanchez home have experienced nurturing support. This assessment extends to the parents, as well, and includes the extent to which they have friends and other social support (Whipple & Webster-Stratton, 1991). For instance, the Sanchez family stopped attending church as their family problems escalated, which resulted in further isolation.

Esteem Needs

The fourth level of Maslow's (1970) hierarchy refers to the sense of personal pride that children feel about themselves and their family. As a result of their early life experiences, children may feel shame or guilt. *Shame* refers to feelings about who we are at our core; *guilt* refers to feelings about behaviors or things we have done (Bradshaw, 1988; Feiring, Taska, & Lewis, 1996; Ferguson, 1991; Harder, 1995). Shame may develop as the result of secrets the child has kept about the family—for example, a parent's use of alcohol or domestic violence between the parents. Shame may also result from secrets about what has happened to the child, such as sexual abuse by a parent. Even when children have been abused and neglected, they may want to protect their parents due to loyalty and in an effort to maintain a sense of esteem. The Sanchez children may not be able to tell the full story about what happened in the home as long as they feel a need to protect their parents.

Self-Actualization Needs

Maslow's (1970) highest level is the need for self-actualization. This refers to a person's deepening sense of self-awareness and living life intentionally. This level of need is not directly related to children's safety, so the child welfare system generally does not help families meet their needs at this highest level. Because the Sanchez family has many pressing needs at lower levels, it would be inappropriate to focus services at this highest level of need.

The Sanchez family will probably need help at many levels. Maslow's (1970) hierarchy of human needs provides a framework for understanding where to begin and lays out a roadmap for the work that can be done after the initial crisis has been resolved.

TABLE 5.1	Domains for Initial Assessment

Domain	Focus
Presenting issues/precipitant	What brings the family in, why now, what previous efforts have been made to resolve issues
Current functioning	Parents' relationship, relationship of each parent to each child, emotional and physical safety
Psychosocial history	Significant historical events, moves, beginnings, endings, changes
Extended family	Relationships, level of support, unresolved conflicts
Cultural	Values, traditions, practices
Health/mental health	Medication, counseling, surgery, hospitalization, substance use
Financial	Income, debts
Legal status	Current and past contact with child protective services, police, attorney; immigration status
Social support network	Friends, church, school
Service network	Connections with other agencies and services in the community

Assessing the Family System

Chapter 4 in this text focuses on investigating the maltreatment referral. In this chapter, we focus on the process of assessing the family system. In order to provide quality child welfare services, we must first thoroughly assess the family's circumstances and needs. We must understand what is going on with the family at this particular time and also learn how things have gone for the family in the past.

Table 5.1 outlines these areas, based on the integrative theory of child maltreatment and Maslow's hierarchy of human needs. The first step in child welfare services is to assess the presenting problem and make a plan to ensure the children's safety.

Assessment Procedure

A child welfare assessment generally involves multiple interviews with family members; contact with *collateral sources*, such as other social workers that have had contact with the family, extended family members, and school and court staffs; and a study of previous reports that summarize the family's social service history. The interviews may take place in the social worker's office, in the family's home, or by telephone.

For each collateral contact that a social worker wants to make in completing the assessment, a signed release of information must be obtained from the parents. Ethical practice requires explaining to the parents what information the social worker is seeking, where the information will be sought, how the information will be used, how long the release of information will be in effect, and how the family can reverse their permission to have information released. The parents should voluntarily sign permission only after they have had the opportunity to ask questions, and they should

The genogram portrays the extended family and is intergenerational.

receive a copy of the signed release. Children are not able to give this permission for themselves; parents sign a separate release and on behalf of each of their children.

Assessment Tools

A thorough assessment of a family's social support resources and social network characteristics helps the social worker understand the context within which the child was maltreated (DePanfilis, 1996). Once this understanding has been gained, interventions can be designed to meet the unique needs of the family. The *genogram* (Hartman, 1978), *ecomap* (Hartman, 1978), and *culturagram* (Congress, 1994) are paper-and-pencil tools that can be used to help assess a family's linkages with outside systems and to learn about the characteristics of a family's social networks. Figures 5.2, 5.3, and 5.4 show a genogram, ecomap, and culturagram (respectively) for the Sanchez family.

GENOGRAM A genogram shows the primary family members and describes their relationships (see Figure 5.2). It portrays the extended family so that multigenerational patterns may be examined.

It is evident that Mrs. Sanchez has strong emotional connections to each of the children, her sister, and her parents. In contrast, Mr. Sanchez has conflictual relationships with his father-in-law and Mario, and his relationships with his wife and his

FIGURE 5.2 Genogram of the Sanchez Family

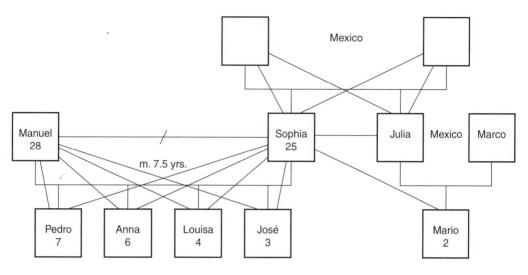

children are distant. In developing the genogram for the Sanchez family, the social worker learns that Mrs. Sanchez's parents strongly urged her not to marry her husband. The genogram thus provides direction for further assessment about relationships, sources of conflict and tension, and potential for support.

ECOMAP In contrast to a genogram, an ecomap portrays the family as a whole and details relationships with resources in the community (see Figure 5.3). An ecomap assessment quickly identifies strengths and needs for connections with resources.

For the Sanchez family, the primary support linkages are with Mr. Sanchez's employer and Mrs. Sanchez's one friend. There are a number of conflictual linkages, including those with CPS and with Mrs. Sanchez's extended family. The link with the church, a potential source of emotional and social support, has been broken. This finding indicates an area for further assessment.

CULTURAGRAM A culturagram may be used with immigrant families to help understand their worldview, their strengths, and the challenges they face (see Figure 5.4). It may also be used with families whose ethnicity or culture differs from that of the worker or even when the worker shares the same ethnicity as the family but there are variations in acculturation and beliefs within ethnicities and cultures.

The culturagram for the Sanchez family portrays the family's values and traditions and identifies some of the conflicts they are facing in relation to their cultural identity. Mr. and Mrs. The Sanchez are hardworking, and they have strong religious beliefs. Yet, but they may be experiencing isolation, as they are not connected with a church and have not connected with any cultural institutions.

FIGURE 5.3   **Ecomap of the Sanchez Family**

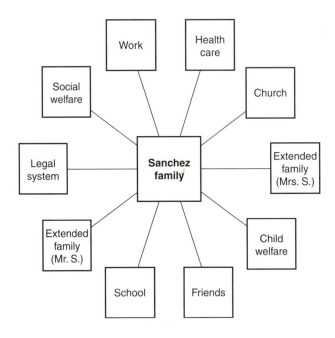

To summarize, the presenting problem provides a narrow window on the family's experiences and needs. The child welfare social worker first ensures the children's safety and proceeds to assessing the family system in order to understand how to intervene. With a completed assessment, the social worker makes an informed referral for services.

Referring the Family to Appropriate Services

Child welfare social workers do not usually provide ongoing services to families. More and more, child welfare services are *investigative only,* which means the CPS worker assesses to determine whether abuse or neglect has occurred and whether services are needed (Salovitz & Keys, 1988) and then refers the family to the appropriate services. Social workers employed by community agencies do provide services to families.

The child welfare worker must have skills in making good referrals and communicating with other agencies. A complicating factor in making referrals is that sometimes services are not available in the community, or if they are available, families may not want or may be unable to effectively use them (Pecora, Whittaker, Maluc-

FIGURE 5.4   **Culturagram of the Sanchez Family**

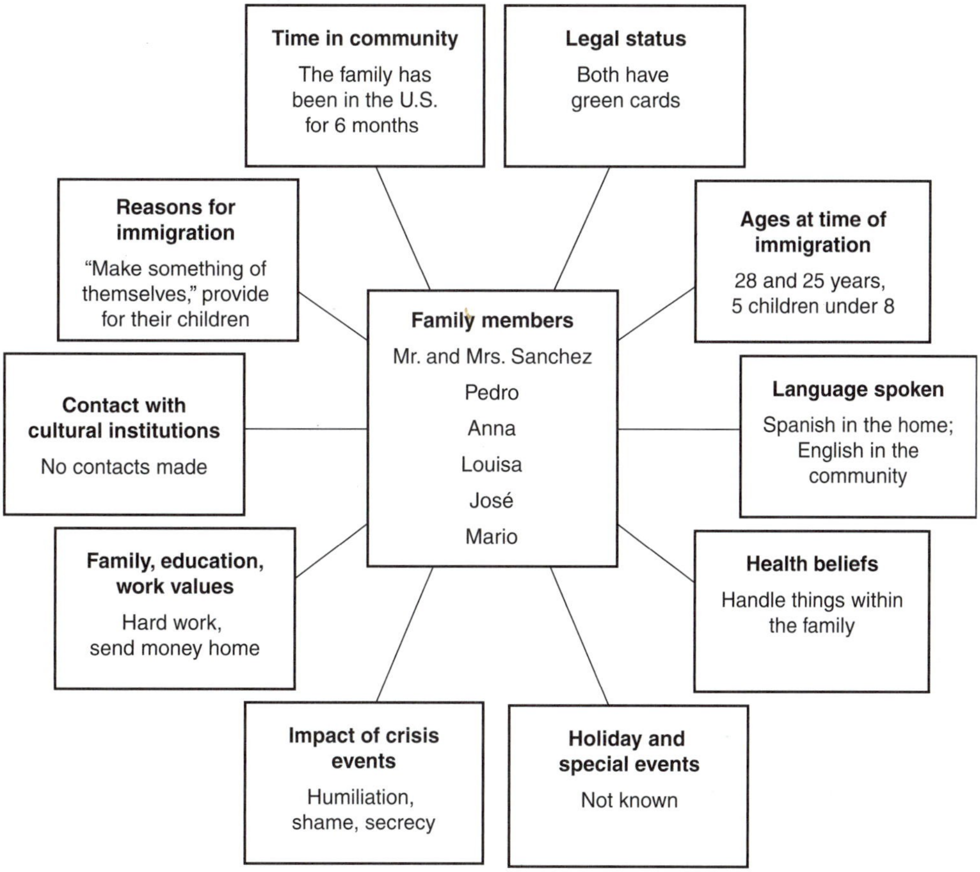

Time in community

The family has been in the U.S. for 6 months

Legal status

Both have green cards

Reasons for immigration

"Make something of themselves," provide for their children

Ages at time of immigration

28 and 25 years, 5 children under 8

Family members

Mr. and Mrs. Sanchez

Pedro

Anna

Louisa

José

Mario

Contact with cultural institutions

No contacts made

Language spoken

Spanish in the home; English in the community

Family, education, work values

Hard work, send money home

Health beliefs

Handle things within the family

Impact of crisis events

Humiliation, shame, secrecy

Holiday and special events

Not known

Source: Based on Congress (1994).

cio, & Barth, 2000). In any community, services may be available from emergency assistance agencies (such as food pantries and emergency financial assistance programs), child welfare programs (such as family service agencies), community mental health centers, and social workers in individual or group private practice.

Once the CPS social worker has completed a thorough assessment of the family's needs, the next step is to link the family with the appropriate services. To make effective referrals, the worker must (1) know the services in the community, (2) discuss the service possibilities with the family, (3) prepare the referral information, (4) send the referral information or participate in a referral meeting, and (5) follow up to ensure that the referral was successful.

The caseworker needs to know not only which service agencies are in the community but also what each agency does and how. The worker should know the following:

1. The specialty or focus of the agency: utility/rent payments, emergency food, individual or group therapy for sexually abused children, parenting groups, mental health evaluation, psychological evaluations, psychotropic medication?
2. The ethnic and racial diversity of the agency's staff: Will the family see staff members who look like them when they go to the agency?
3. The agency's criteria for eligibility.
4. How program costs are handled: a fee, sliding scale for the fee, mandatory Medicaid eligibility, contract with the department of social services?
5. The agency's referral process: phone call, sending of referral reports, attending screening meeting?

Once the caseworker has researched agencies in the community, he or she should discuss them with the family whenever possible. This gives the family an opportunity to ask questions, discuss their ideas and preferences, and begin to prepare to connect with the new services. In some agencies, referrals are routed through a central screening by an individual or team. Other agencies hold regular meetings to discuss and accept referrals. Still other agencies request that referrals be made directly to the individual worker, by phone or mail, or both.

An effective referral provides the information that has already been collected, so that families do not need to repeat their stories again. The referral information should be objective and respectful to family members and specific about the concerns and issues the family is currently facing. Sometimes, scheduling a joint contact with the new worker and the family helps to bridge the two services.

Once the referral has been made and necessary reports have been sent, the next step is to follow up with the family and the new worker to make sure that (1) appointments have been kept by the family, (2) the worker and family have begun to connect and work together, and (3) there are no remaining questions for the referring caseworker.

To make an effective referral, we must know not only which types of interventions are available and effective but also how to link specific needs to appropriate services. The remainder of this chapter discusses effective interventions for physically abused and neglected children and their families.

Intervening with Families

The two primary ways to intervene with a family who has been referred because of child maltreatment are (1) out-of-home placement of children and (2) services to prevent children being placed out of the home. Often both types of services are provided to the same family with two goals: to ensure child safety (always the primary concern throughout the case process) and to provide permanency.

The basic premise underlying permanency planning is that children have the right to a permanent home, where life-long relationships can be maintained. If at all possible, this home should be with the child's birth family. When it is necessary for children to be placed out of the home, steps should be taken to return them to their own homes if at all possible. If not, plans should be made to ensure that they have a permanent home, which may mean arranging for adoption or placement in long-term foster care.

Children are not usually placed in foster care without first providing services to try and alleviate the problems that brought them to the attention of the child welfare agency. In some cases, it is necessary to use foster care or another placement outside the home to keep the children safe while a more thorough assessment is being completed or while services are being provided. A family is often provided services to help them prepare for the child's return home, and once the child is back in the home, services may be provided to help the family adjust to being together again. These supports are called *reunification services.*

Because child safety is the first aim and primary function of child welfare services, it is sometimes necessary to place children in foster care or even terminate the parental rights and custody of the parents. In the last 25 years, however, there has been an emphasis on preventing placements by providing services to parents and families to enhance their functioning so children can remain safely at home. Some early studies found that many children in foster care experienced multiple placements and were not provided a plan for helping them return home (Fanshel & Shinn, 1978; Maas & Engler, 1959; Shyne & Schroeder, 1978). To overcome these and other shortcomings of the foster care system, policy and legislation were implemented that stress permanency planning for children. The services developed to prevent placement are usually called *family preservation services* or *prevention services.* They reflect the goal of keeping families together by preventing unnecessary and inappropriate out-of-home placements.

The dual missions of ensuring child safety and preserving families has led to much debate in the child welfare field about whether efforts to preserve families and prevent placements have gone too far and resulted in children being at risk of harm in their own homes. Some contend that family preservation is emphasized over child safety (see Chapter 1). Too often, child protection and family preservation are viewed separately, with little recognition of how both can be accomplished (Maluccio, Pine, & Warsh, 1994).

Many experts believe that child safety and family support can and should be stressed simultaneously (Pecora, Whittaker, Maluccio, & Barth, 2000). One way to ensure child safety is to help families (Pecora et al., 2000). Most parents care deeply about their children and want to do whatever is best for them. Parents who are referred for alleged physical abuse or neglect in most cases are not bad, mean, evil, morally corrupt, lazy, or mentally ill, although some do have depression and other disorders. Usually, such parents are unable to adequately care for their children because of financial hardships, interpersonal and relationship problems, lack of support, and personal stresses. Social workers and other helping professionals can often help parents overcome their problems so they can provide better care for their children, thus preventing foster care placements.

The Child Welfare League of America (CWLA, 1989) has categorized three types of family services: (1) family resource, support, and education; (2) family-centered casework; and (3) intensive family-centered crisis services. The first category, *family support services*, cites prevention services available to all families, regardless of whether they are experiencing problems. Emphasis is placed on community and parent involvement in the development of these services. Family support programs focus on "enhancing the capacity of parents in their child-rearing roles; creating settings in which parents are empowered to act on their own behalf and become advocates for change; and providing a community resource for parents" (Weissbourd & Kagan, 1989, p. 21). Such services are not our focus here, but it is important to note the potential of prevention programs to reduce the risk factors related to child maltreatment (Guterman, 2001; Nelson, Laurendeau, & Chamberland, 2001; Wekerle & Wolfe, 1993).

We now turn our attention to interventions currently available for families that have come under the aegis of child welfare agencies. Foster care is not discussed here, but it is important to remember that foster care placement may be appropriate and necessary for some children.

Family-Centered Casework Services

Family-centered casework services provide support to families already experiencing problems, including inability to meet basic needs, family violence, drug and alcohol abuse, parent–child conflict, child behavior problems, child maltreatment, and physical or mental impairment of family members (CWLA, 1989). The child welfare casework process incorporates a variety of services, including counseling, case management, advocacy, and education, with the overall goal to "promote the protection and well-being of children by helping their parents to increase their parenting abilities, and by furthering a nurturing and stable family environment to enable the children's healthy growth and development" (CWLA, 1989, pp. 29–30). Some specific interventions in family-centered casework are multifamily group therapy (MFGT), parent training, and social support groups.

MULTIFAMILY GROUP THERAPY *Multifamily group therapy (MFGT)* is a family intervention for treating the effects of physical abuse and neglect. Here is one definition:

> An intervention with two or more families present in the same room with a trained therapist for all or most of the sessions. Each participating family should have two or more members that represent at least two generations in the family and are present for all or most of the sessions. Sessions should have an explicit focus on problems or concerns shared by all families in attendance. These focal problems should pertain directly or indirectly to cross-generational family interaction. Sessions should implicitly or explicitly emphasize patterns of interfamilial interaction, as well as utilize actual or potential alliances among members of different families based on similarities of age, sex, focal problem or family role. (O'Shea & Phelps, 1985, p. 573)

MFGT has been implemented with different populations of children and adults, but only one group of researchers has reported on its implementation and evaluation for physically abused and neglected children and their families (Meezan & O'Keefe, 1998a, 1998b; Meezan, O'Keefe, & Zariani, 1997). These researchers described the

MFGT intervention as it was implemented in a California agency. Weekly group sessions, with six to eight families and four counselors, were held for eight months. The treatments incorporated included providing of information, interactive teaching, modeling, role-playing, problem solving, and reinforcement of appropriate behaviors.

Sessions were organized this way: informal gathering time (15 minutes); opening/coming together (10 minutes); structured activity (20 minutes); regrouping and feedback (10 minutes); living skills (20 minutes); regrouping and feedback (10 minutes); informal break (10 minutes); separate parents' and children's groups (40 minutes); regrouping and closing (15 minutes) (Meezan et al., 1997, p. 76).

Meezan and his colleagues compared MFGT to the traditional family therapy offered by the agency, in which families are seen individually by a therapist. The outcomes measured were social support, problem solving, attitudes toward childrearing, knowledge of child development, family functioning, and appropriate discipline. There were no significant differences between the families who received MFGT and the families who received traditional family therapy on some of the outcome measures (Meezan & O'Keefe, 1998). Families in both groups improved on most outcomes. However, families who received MFGT showed significantly more improvement on two important outcomes: social support and appropriate discipline. Moreover, families in MFGT were significantly more likely to stay in treatment than families who received the usual services (Meezan & O'Keefe, 1998). This finding is of particular importance because dropout rates in mental health and social services range from 11 percent to 47 percent (Armbruster & Fallon, 1994; Danoff, Kemper, & Sherry , 1994; Kazdin & Mazurick, 1994; McKay, McCadam, & Gonzales, 1996), and, rates are even higher for some parents and families referred for maltreatment (Famularo, Kinscherff, Bunschaft, & Spivak, 1989; Meezan & O'Keefe, 1998). Even treatments and services known to be effective cannot help if the families do not participate or drop out prematurely.

Families in both groups (MFGT and traditional family therapy) also received case management (Meezan & O'Keefe, 1998), for as they had presented with many and complex problems. Many of the families were poor and thus at risk for all the problems associated with poverty. This study sample is an example of how interventions in child welfare often need to be multifaceted to take into account the numerous personal, interpersonal, and environmental problems experienced by families.

PARENT TRAINING   Reducing anger and stress and improving discipline and interactive skills: these are usually the desired outcomes of parent training, whether with individuals or groups of parents. Acton and During (1992) described a group for which training consisted of teaching anger management, communication skills, problem-solving skills, and how to respond with empathy. The group met once a week for 90 minutes across 13 weeks. Each group session began by discussing the results of the prior week's homework assignment. Homework consisted of performing some task outside the session to help achieve stated goals. For example, the parents might be asked to practice ignoring their child's whining instead of reacting to it by scolding and to keep track of how many times they were able to ignore and how many times they reverted to scolding. The group leader then taught a specific skill—for example, how to make clear requests of children and how to respond when they do not

Parent training has been found to be effective in reducing anger and stress and in improving discipline and interactive skills.

comply. Group members practiced the skill with one another and talked about how they could apply the skill in their own homes. Finally, the group leader gave a homework assignment. Although there was no comparison group, testing of the parents before and after the 13-week series (using the same measures) suggested that the group was successful in reducing the risk of child abuse.

Schinke and colleagues (1986) described a similar type of group that focused on stress management. The group met once a week for a two-hour session for 10 weeks. Topics included how to improve self-control, interpersonal communication, positive discipline, and social support. When the topic of the session was interpersonal communication, the group began with the parents talking about how their families communicated. The group leaders then talked about the negative and positive consequences of communicating in these ways and role-played how the parents could communicate with their children without being abusive. The parents practiced the communication skills and received feedback from the leaders and other group members. The parents in the groups showed significantly more improvement in behaviors related to interacting with their children than did a comparison group of parents who did not receive the training. Schinke et al. (1986) suggested that the group may be most successful with parents who still have custody of their children and before serious problems have occurred that require court action. Services are likely to be more effective before problems are so longstanding and serious that parents and families have lost hope of being able to change. This speaks to the importance of prevention services and family support services.

Parent training with individual parents is similar to that for parent training within groups. Both methods of training focus on teaching, modeling, and practicing new skills to enhance parent–child interaction. Wolfe and his colleagues (1988) provided individual parent training consisting of two components. The first was training the parent in basic child-management skills, which consisted of teaching, modeling, and rehearsal. The second component consisted of activities with mother and child to improve the child's adaptive skills and social interaction. The mother observed how the therapist worked with the child and so learned firsthand how to interact with and teach her child.

A benefit of individual parent training is that it is easier to have the children present (especially when the training is provided in the home), allowing the parents to practice interacting with their children in the presence of the social worker, who can provide feedback and model appropriate ways to interact. On the other hand, in parent-training groups, the parents have the opportunity to meet other parents and learn they are not alone in their struggles. Studies are needed to determine whether individual or group parent training is more effective and which parents benefit most from each modality.

A word of caution is in order about parent training: Parents referred because of possible abuse or neglect usually need much more than training in how to parent. Many of them must cope with a myriad of personal and environmental stresses that interfere with parenting duties. Therefore, interventions for parents will be most effective when they are multifaceted and move beyond focusing solely on parenting behaviors to address other concerns, such as stress, money and job worries, child care, transportation, and personal as well as interpersonal concerns (Dore & Lee, 1999). Remember Maslow's (1970) hierarchy of human needs. It is difficult for parents to engage in changing parenting behaviors when they are concerned with their families' basic needs for food, shelter, and medical care.

SOCIAL SUPPORT GROUPS   Some families who come to the attention of child welfare because of alleged abuse/neglect are socially isolated. Researchers have studied the effectiveness of interventions aimed to increase social support and improve interactions in the parents' social network. Most of these interventions have consisted of group training in prosocial and interpersonal skills (Lovell & Richey, 1995, 1997; Richey, Lovell, & Reid, 1991).

Lovell and Richey (1991) describe a social support training group. The group met for 16 sessions, the first 12 of which focused on helping group members develop and improve adult friendships and relationships. As in the parenting groups described earlier, the group leaders demonstrated skills that are important to all relationships—for example, initiating a conversation with a stranger and changing the topic of a conversation. The leaders then asked the group members to role-play the skills and provided feedback on the performances. Tasks were also assigned for group members to work on between sessions. The last four sessions were used to help the members transfer their new skills to their own environments, so they could maintain their skills when the sessions stopped. Case management to assist the members in maintaining and using their new social skills was provided after the group sessions ended.

The primary finding from research on the effectiveness of social support groups was that parents who participated in social skills training had a significantly higher number of professional contacts in their social networks and a smaller percentage of other friends at the conclusion of treatment than did parents in a comparison group (Lovell & Hawkins, 1988; Lovell & Richey, 1995, 1997). Richey and colleagues (1991) found that women who participated in interpersonal skill training had increases in network size, improved quality of daily contacts, and more satisfaction with the support they received from friends, but participants also reported decreased satisfaction with family supports.

At first glance, the findings of an increased proportion of professionals and a decreased proportion of friends in the social network and decreased satisfaction with family supports seemed to be negative. Lovell and Richey (1995) explained, however, that one of the intervention's goals was to link parents with community resources and that those linkages may have supported positive parenting; other friends and family, however, may have condoned or supported negative parenting practices. The lack of normative guidelines on the social networks of nonmaltreating parents and gaps in knowledge about the underlying mechanisms of how social support and networks lead to maltreatment make it difficult to interpret the clinical significance and practical meaning of the findings (Lovell & Richey, 1997).

OTHER FAMILY-CENTERED CASEWORK SERVICES   The literature provides examples of other types of interventions for families referred for maltreatment or its risk, and some of these could be considered family-centered casework. For example, Kolko (1996) compared three interventions to ascertain which was more effective in alleviating the risk of child maltreatment. Family therapy was provided to one group of parents. Families (parents and children) met in the therapist's office for one hour for at least 12 sessions. The purpose of family therapy was to improve family relationships. The therapists taught positive communication skills and how to work together to solve family difficulties. The negative consequences of physical punishment were also discussed. It was hoped that families would learn better ways to solve problems and not resort to physical force and domineering and threatening behaviors. In a second treatment group, children and parents were seen separately and similar types of treatment were provided. The focus with the children and parents was to teach skills for coping and interpersonal relationships. The children were taught how to relax and how to be assertive. The parents were taught how to control their anger, how to reinforce their children, and how to use time-out. Just as in family therapy, the children and parents were seen for one hour for 12 sessions. Yet a third group received the services that would usually be provided in the community, including homemaker services, support groups, and information on child management.

Many different outcomes were studied (Kolko, 1996). Families in all three groups showed improvement on some of the outcomes. Families varied on some of the outcomes, depending on the type of intervention they received. The families that received the individual child and parent therapy or the family therapy showed significantly more improvement on some outcomes than did the families who received the usual community services. Improvements included decreased child abuse potential, reduced externalizing behaviors in children (e.g., acting out, antisocial and aggressive behaviors), lower parent distress, and improved family functioning. As reported by the children, the families that received family therapy had a greater reduction of parent-to-child violence than did the families who received the usual service or the individual therapy. Community services seemed the most effective in decreasing general family dysfunction than the other types of therapy.

Intensive Family-Centered Crisis Services

There are a number of similarities between family-centered casework services and intensive family-centered crisis services. Sometimes it is difficult to distinguish between them in practice.

DEFINITION   Services in both programs are family focused and individualized to meet the unique needs of the family. Intensive family-centered crisis services may be called *family preservation, intensive family preservation,* or *intensive home-based services.*

All intensive family-centered crisis services have one point in common: They are services for families who are in crisis and have children at imminent risk for out-of-home placement (CWLA, 1989). Therapists carry small caseloads (two to six families), services are short term (four to twelve weeks), and they are provided in the home.

Another distinguishing feature of family-centered crisis services is that they are intensive. For example, the therapist may go to a family's home every day for the first week and spend several hours at each visit. The therapist may also accompany the family on shopping and recreational outings, if these are settings where the parents have difficulties interacting with their children. The therapist may also accompany the parents to school conferences to support them and advocate for the child's needs.

Homebuilders, which began in 1974 in Tacoma, Washington, is the prototype for intensive family-centered crisis services (Forsythe, 1992; Kinney, Madsen, Fleming, & Haapala, 1977). A primary criticism of intensive family-centered crisis services is that crisis theory is not applicable to many of the families served by the programs (Barth, 1990; Corcoran, 2000). That is, the chronic and multiple problems experienced by many families referred because of maltreatment are unlikely to be resolved by short-term crisis services.

EXAMPLE   A promising intensive family-centered crisis intervention called *multisystemic therapy (MST)* was developed by Henggeler and his colleagues (Henggeler, Schoenwald, Borduin, Rowland, & Cunningham, 1998). MST services are based on systems and ecological theories that recognize that behaviors are multidetermined.

Intervention targets the systems that are contributing to or maintaining the problem and is individualized to the unique needs of each family. MST is home based. Therapists work flexible hours, as determined by the needs of the family. Nine principles guide multisystemic therapy:

1. The purpose of assessment is to understand the fit between the problems and the environmental context.
2. Strengths are emphasized and used to facilitate change.
3. Interventions are aimed to promote responsible behavior and decrease irresponsible behavior among family members.
4. Interventions are focused in the present, and well-defined problems are targeted for change.
5. Interventions target sequences of behavior within and between all the systems (e.g., family, school, child protective agency).
6. Interventions are appropriate to the developmental level of the child.
7. Interventions are designed to require daily or weekly effort by the family.
8. The effectiveness of the intervention is continually evaluated.
9. Interventions are designed to enhance the maintenance of change after services are terminated. (Henggeler et al., 1998)

Much research evidence supports the efficacy of MST with antisocial adolescents (Henggeler, Melton, & Smith, 1992; Henggeler, Melton, Smith, Schoenwald, & Hanley, 1993). Brunk, Henggeler, and Whelan (1987) studied the effectiveness of MST compared to that of parent group training for physical abuse and neglect. MST treatment lasted for eight weeks. For the sake of measuring outcomes, the duration and intensity of services for each type of intervention were kept the same. The families in each type of intervention showed decreased parent psychiatric symptoms, reduced stress, and improvement in individual and family problems (Brunk et al., 1987). Comparison of figures for the MST program and the parent group training suggested that MST was better than parent group training in restructuring parent–child relationships, while parent group training was better than MST in decreasing social problems (Brunk et al., 1987). Researchers are continuing to test the efficacy and effectiveness of MST.

In some ways, MST is similar to other family preservation programs that have been widely implemented in child welfare. They are home based, services are individualized for each family, and therapists work flexible hours. However, rigorous research has not been conducted on the widely implemented family preservation programs (Heneghan, Horwitz, & Leventhal, 1996). Many of the program evaluations have used out-of-home placement as the primary outcome, and placement has been criticized as an indicator of program success on several counts. Sometimes children need out-of-home placements, and therefore placement is not a negative outcome. Also, factors other than intervention influence whether or not children are placed out of home. Overall, little is known about the effectiveness of family preservation services for changing family interactions, increasing parenting skills, and ensuring child safety.

Much more research is needed to increase knowledge about effective family interventions for physical abuse and neglect. Although there is some support for the interventions described in this section, the small number of studies and their limitations (e.g., small sample sizes, no follow-up) make it difficult to draw firm conclusions about the effectiveness of family interventions for physical abuse and neglect. It is unlikely that child welfare workers will directly provide these interventions, but they must be aware of available interventions so they can make appropriate referrals.

REFERENCES

Abney, V. D., & Gunn, K. (1993). A rationale for cultural competency. *APSAC Advisor, 6,* 19–22.

Acton, R. G., & During, S. M. (1992). Preliminary results of aggression management training for aggressive parents. *Journal of Interpersonal Violence, 7,* 410–417.

Allen, D. M., & Tarnowski, K. J. (1989). Depressive characteristics of physically abused children. *Journal of Abnormal Child Psychology, 17,* 1–11.

Armbruster, P. & Fallon, T. (1994). Clinical. Sociodemographic, and systems risk factors for attrition in a children's mental health clinic. *American Journal of Orthopsychiatry, 64,* 577–585.

Azar, S. T., Povilatitis, T. Y., Lauretti, A. F., & Pouquette, C. L. (1998). The current status of etiological theories in intrafamilial child maltreatment. In J. R. Lutzker (Ed.), *Handbook of child abuse research and treatment: Issues in clinical child psychology* (pp. 3–30). New York: Plenum Press.

Azar, S. T., & Siegel, B. R. (1990). Behavioral treatment of child abuse: A developmental perspective. *Behavior Modification, 14,* 279–300.

Azzi-Lessing, L., & Olsen, L. J. (1996). Substance abuse-affected families in the child welfare system: New challenges, new alliances. *Social Work, 41,* 15–23.

Barth, R. P. (1990). Theories guiding home-based intensive family preservation services. In J. K. Whittaker, J. Kinney, E. M. Tracy, & C. Booth (Eds.), *Reaching high-risk families: Intensive family preservation in human services* (pp. 89–112). New York: Aldine de Gruyter.

Barth, R. P., Blythe, B. J., Schinke, S. P., & Schilling, R. F. (1983). Self-control training with maltreating parents. *Child Welfare, 62,* 313–324.

Belsky, J. (1993). Etiology of child maltreatment: A developmental-ecological analysis. *Psychological Bulletin, 114,* 413–434.

Bradshaw, J. (1988). *Healing the shame that binds you.* Deerfield Beach, FL: Health Communications.

Brunk, M., Henggeler, S. W., & Whelan, J. P. (1987). Comparison of multisystemic therapy and parent training in the brief treatment of child abuse and neglect. *Journal of Consulting and Clinical Psychology, 55,* 171–178.

Burns, B. J., Hoagwood, K., & Mrazek, P. J. (1999). Effective treatment for mental disorders in children and adolescents. *Clinical Child and Family Psychology Review, 2,* 199–254.

Camras, L. A., & Rappaport, S. (1993). Conflict behaviors of maltreated and nonmaltreated children. *Child Abuse & Neglect, 17,* 455–464.

Cerezo, M. A., & Frias, D. (1994). Emotional and cognitive adjustment in abused children. *Child Abuse & Neglect, 18,* 923–932.

Child Welfare League of America (CWLA). (1989). *Standards for services to strengthen and preserve families with children.* Washington, DC: Author.

Congress, E. P. (1994). The use of culturagrams to assess and empower culturally diverse families. *Families in Society: The Journal of Contemporary Human Services, 75,* 531–539.

Corcoran, J.(2000). Family interventions with child physical abuse and neglect: A critical review. *Children and Youth Services Review, 22,* 563–591.

Crimmins, D. B., Bradlyn, A. S., St. Lawrence, J. S., & Kelly, J. A. (1984). A training technique for improving the parent-child interaction skills of an abusive-neglectful mother. *Child Abuse & Neglect, 8,* 533–539.

Culp, R. E., Heide, J., & Richardson, M. T. (1987). Maltreated children's developmental scores: Treatment versus nontreatment. *Child Abuse & Neglect, 11,* 29–34.

Culp, R. E., Little, V., Letts, D., & Lawrence, H. (1991). Maltreated children's self-concept: Effects of a comprehensive treatment program. *American Journal of Orthopsychiatry, 61,* 114–121.

Dachman, R. S., Halasz, M. M., Bickett, A. D., & Lutzker, J. R. (1984). A home-based ecobehavioral parent-training and generalization package with a neglectful mother. *Education and Treatment of Children, 7,* 183–202.

Danoff, N. L., Kemper, K. J., & Sherry, B. (1994). Risk factors for dropping out of a parenting education program. *Child Abuse & Neglect, 18,* 599–606.

Davis, S. P., & Fantuzzo, J. W. (1989). The effects of adult and peer social initiations on the social behavior of withdrawn and aggressive maltreated preschool children. *Journal of Family Violence, 4,* 227–248.

Dawson, B., deArmas, A., McGrath, M. L., & Kelly, J. A. (1986). Cognitive problem-solving training to improve the child-care judgment of child neglectful parents. *Journal of Family Violence, 1,* 209–221.

Denicola, J., & Sandler, J. (1980). Training abusive parents in child management and self-control skills. *Behavior Therapy, 11,* 263–270.

DePanfilis, D. (1996). Social isolation of neglectful families: A review of social support assessment and intervention models. *Child Maltreatment, 1,* 37–52.

Dore, M. M., & Lee, J. M. (1999). The role of parent training with abusive and neglectful parents. *Family Relations, 48,* 313–325.

Eamon, M. K. (2001). The effects of poverty on children's socioemotional development: An ecological systems analysis. *Social Work, 46,* 256–266.

Eckenrode, J., Laird, M., & Doris, J. (1993). School performance and disciplinary problems among abused and neglected children. *Developmental Psychology, 29,* 53–62.

Eckenrode, J., Rowe, E., Laird, M., & Brathwaite, J. (1995). Mobility as a mediator of the effects of child maltreatment on academic performance. *Child Development, 66,* 1130–1142.

Egan, K. J. (1983). Stress management and child management with abusive parents. *Clinical Child Psychology, 12,* 292–299.

Famularo, R., Kinscherff, R., Bunschaft, D., & Spivak, G. (1989). Parental compliance to court-ordered treatment interventions in cases of child maltreatment. *Child Abuse and Neglect, 13,* 507–514.

Fanshel, D., & Shinn, E. B. (1978). *Children in foster care: A longitudinal investigation.* New York: Columbia University Press.

Fantuzzo, J. W., Jurecic, L., Stovall, A., Hightower, A. D., Goins, C., & Schachtel, D. (1988). Effects of adult and peer social initiations on the social behavior of withdrawn, maltreated preschool children. *Journal of Consulting and Clinical Psychology, 56,* 34–39.

Fantuzzo, J. W., Stovall, A., Schachtel, D., Goins, C., & Hall, R. (1987). The effects of peer social initiations on the social behavior of withdrawn maltreated preschool children. *Behavior Therapy and Experimental Psychiatry, 18,* 357–363.

Fantuzzo, J., Sutton-Smith, B., Atkins, M., Meyers, R., Stevenson, H. Coolahan, K., Weiss, A., & Manz, P. (1996). Community-based resilient peer treatment of withdrawn maltreated preschool children. *Journal of Consulting and Clinical Psychology, 64,* 1377–1386.

Fantuzzo, J., Weiss, A. D., & Coolahan, K. C. (1998). Community-based partnership-directed research: Actualizing community strengths to treat child victims of physical abuse and neglect. In J. R. Lutzker (Ed.), *Handbook of child abuse and treatment* (pp. 213–237). New York: Plenum Press.

Feiring, C., Taska, L., & Lewis, M. (1996). A process model for understanding adaptation to sexual abuse: The role of shame in defining stigmatization. *Child Abuse & Neglect, 20,* 767–782.

Ferguson, T. J. (1991). Children's understanding of guilt and shame. *Child Development, 62,* 827–839.

Feshbach, N. D. (1989). The construct of empathy and the phenomenon of physical maltreatment of children. In D. Cicchetti & V. Carlson (Eds.), *Child maltreatment: Theory and research on the causes and consequences of child abuse and neglect* (pp. 349–373). Cambridge, MA: Cambridge University Press.

Forsythe, P. (1992). Homebuilders and family preservation. *Children and Youth Services Review, 14,* 37–47.

Gaudin, J. M., Wodarski, J. S., Arkinson, M. K., & Avery, L. S. (1990–1991). Remedying child neglect: Effectiveness of social network interventions. Journal of Applied Social Sciences, 15, 97–123.

Greene, B. F., Norman, K. R., Searle, M. S., Daniels, M., & Lubeck, R. C. (1995). Child abuse and neglect by parents with disabilities: A tale of two families. *Journal of Applied Behavior Analysis, 28,* 417–434.

Guterman, N. B. (2001). *Stopping child maltreatment before it starts: Emerging horizons in early home visitation services.* Thousand Oaks, CA: Sage.

Harder, D. W. (1995). Shame and guilt assessment and relationships of shame- and guilt-pronenesss to psychopathology. In J. P. Tangney & K. W. Fischer (Eds.), *Self-conscious emotions: The psychology of shame, guilt, embarrassment, and pride* (pp. 368–392). New York: Guilford Press.

Hartman, A. (1978). Diagrammatic assessments of family relationships. *Social Casework, 59,* 465–476.

Haskett, M. E., & Kistner, J. A. (1991). Social interactions and peer perceptions of young physically abused children. *Child Development, 62,* 979–990.

Heneghan, A. M., Horwitz, S. M., & Leventhal, J. M. (1996). Evaluating intensive family preservation programs: A methodological review. *Pediatrics, 97,* 535–542.

Henggeler, S. W., Melton, G. B., & Smith, L. A. (1992). Family preservation using multisystemic therapy: An effective alternative to incarcerating serious juvenile offenders. *Journal of Consulting and Clinical Psychology, 60,* 953–961.

Henggeler, S. W., Melton, G. B., Smith, L. A., Schoenwald, S. K., & Hanley, J. H. (1993). Family preservation using multisystemic treatment: Long-term follow-up to a clinical trial with serious juvenile offenders. *Journal of Child and Family Studies, 2,* 283–293.

Henggeler, S. W., Schoenwald, S. K., Borduin, C. M., Rowland, M. D., & Cunningham, P. B. (1998). *Multisystemic treatment of antisocial behavior in children and adolescents.* New York: Guilford Press.

Hohman, M. M. (1998). Motivational interviewing: An intervention tool for child welfare case workers working with substance-abusing parents. *Child Welfare, 77,* 275–289.

Kaufman, J. (1991). Depressive disorders in maltreated children. *Journal of the American Academy Child and Adolescent Psychiatry, 30,* 257–265.

Kaufman, J., & Cicchetti, D. (1989). Effects of maltreatment on school-age children's socioemotional development: Assessments in a day-camp setting. *Developmental Psychology, 25,* 516–524.

Kazdin, A. E. & Mazurick, J. L. (1994). Dropping out of child psychotherapy: Distinguishing early and late dropouts over the course of treatment. *Journal of Consulting and Clinical Psychology, 62,* 1069–1074.

Kinney, J. M., Madsen, B., Fleming, T., & Haapala, D. A. (1977). Homebuilders: Keeping families together. *Journal of Consulting and Clinical Psychology, 45,* 667–673.

Kolko, D. J. (1996). Individual cognitive behavioral treatment and family therapy for physically abused children and their offending parents: A comparison of clinical outcomes. *Child Maltreatment, 1,* 322–342.

Kurtz, P. D., Gaudin, J. M., Wodarski, J. S., & Howing, P. T. (1993). Maltreatment and the school-aged child: School performance consequences. *Child Abuse & Neglect, 17,* 581–589.

Lovell, M. L., & Hawkins, J. D. (1988). An evaluation of a group intervention to increase the personal social networks of abusive mothers. *Children and Youth Services Review, 10,* 175–188.

Lovell, M. L., & Richey, C. A. (1991). Implementing agency-based social-support skill training. *Families in Society, 72,* 563–572.

Lovell, M. L., & Richey, C. A. (1995). The effectiveness of social-support skill training with multiproblem families at risk for child maltreatment. *Canadian Journal of Community Mental Health, 14,* 29–48.

Lovell, M. L., & Richey, C. A. (1997). The impact of social support skill training on daily interactions among parents at risk for child maltreatment. *Children and Youth Services Review, 19,* 221–251.

Maas, H. S., & Engler, R. E. (1959). *Children in need of parents.* New York: Columbia University Press.

Maluccio, A. N., Pine, B. A., & Warsh, R. (1994). Protecting children by preserving their families. *Children and Youth Services Review, 16,* 295–307.

Maslow, A. H. (1970). *Motivation and personality.* New York: Harper & Row.

McKay, M. M., McCadam, K., & Gonzales, J. J. (1995). A comprehensive training model for inner-city social workers. *Arete, 20,* 56–64.

Meezan, W., & O'Keefe M. (1998a). Evaluating the effectiveness of multifamily group therapy in child abuse and neglect. *Research on Social Work Practice, 8,* 330–353.

Meezan, W., & O'Keefe, M. (1998b). Multifamily group therapy: Impact on family functioning and child behavior. *Families in Society, 79,* 32–44.

Meezan, W., O'Keefe, M., & Zariani, M. (1997). A model of multi-family group therapy for abusive and neglectful parents and their children. *Social Work with Groups, 20,* 71–88.

Moore, E., Armsden, G., & Gogerty, P. L. (1998). A twelve-year follow-up study of maltreated and at-risk children who received early therapeutic child care. *Child Maltreatment, 3,* 3–16.

Nelson, G., Laurendeau, M-C., & Chamberland, C. (2001). A review of programs to promote family wellness and prevent the maltreatment of children. *Canadian Journal of Behavioural Science, 33,* 1–13.

Nicol, A. R., Smith, J., Kay, B., Hall, D., Barlow, J., & Williams, B. (1988). A focused casework approach to the treatment of child abuse: A controlled comparison. *Journal of Child Psychology and Psychiatry, 29,* 703–711.

O'Hare, T. (1996). Court-ordered versus voluntary clients: Problem differences and readiness for change. *Social Work, 41,* 417–422.

O'Shea, M., & Phelps, R. (1985). Multiple family therapy: Current status and critical appraisal. *Family Process, 24,* 555–582.

Pecora, P. J., Whittaker, J. K., Maluccio, A. N., & Barth, R. P. (2000). *The child welfare challenge: Policy, practice, and research.* New York: Aldine De Gruyter.

Pinderhughes, E. E. (1991). The delivery of child welfare services to African American clients. *American Journal of Orthopsychiatry, 61,* 599–605.

Powell, M. B., & Ilett, M. J. (1992). Assessing the incestuous family's readiness for reconstitution. *Families in Society: The Journal of Contemporary Human Services, 73,* 417–423.

Richey, C. A., Lovell, M. A., & Reid, K. (1991). Interpersonal skill training to enhance social support among women at risk for child maltreatment. *Children and Youth Services Review, 13,* 41–59.

Rogeness, G. A., Amrung, S. A., Macedo, C. A., Harris, W. R., & Fisher, C. (1986). Psychopathology in abused or neglected children. *Journal of the American Academy of Child Psychiatry, 25,* 659–665.

Salovitz, B., & Keys, D. (1988). Is child protective services still a service? *Protecting Children, 5,* 17–23.

Salzinger, S., Feldman, R. S., Hammer, M., & Rosario, M. (1993). The effects of physical abuse on children's social relationships. *Child Development, 64,* 169–187.

Sarber, R. E., Halasz, M. M., Messmer, M. C., Bickett, A. D., & Lutzker, J. R. (1983). Teaching menu planning and grocery shopping skills to a mentally retarded mother. *Mental Retardation, 21,* 101–106.

Schinke, S. P., Schilling, R. F., Kirkham, M. A., Gilchrist, L. D., Barth, R. P., & Blythe, B. J. (1986). Stress management for parents. *Journal of Child and Adolescent Psychotherapy, 3,* 293–298.

Scott, W. O., Baer, G., Christoff, K. A., & Jelly, J. A. (1984). The use of skills training procedures in the treatment of a child-abusive parent. *Journal of Behavior Therapy and Experimental Psychology, 15,* 329–336.

Shulman, L. (1999). *The skills of helping individuals, families, groups, and communities* (4th ed.). Itasca, IL: F. E. Peacock.

Shyne, A. W., & Schroeder, A. G. (1978). *National study of social services to children and their families.* Washington DC: Department of Health and Human Services, U.S. Children's Bureau.

Spurlock, J. (1985). Assessment and therapeutic intervention of Black children. *Journal of the American Academy of Child Psychiatry, 24,* 168–174.

Starr, R. H., Dubowitz, H., & Bush, B. A. (1990). The epidemiology of child maltreatment. In R. T. Ammerman & M. Hersen (Eds.), *Children at risk: An evaluation of factors contributing to child abuse and neglect* (pp. 23–53). New York: Plenum Press.

Staub, E. (1996). Cultural-societal roots of violence: The examples of genocidal violence and contemporary youth violence in the United States. *American Psychologist, 51,* 117–132.

Straker, G., & Jacobson, R. S. (1981). Aggression, emotional maladjustment, and empathy in the abused child. *Developmental Psychology, 17,* 762–765.

Tracy, E. M., & Abell, N. (1994). Social network map: Some further refinements on administration. *Social Work Research, 18,* 56–60.

Tracy, E. M., & Whittaker, J. K. (1990). The social network map: Assessing social support in clinical practice. *Families in Society, 7,* 461–470.

Watson-Perczel, M., Lutzker, J. R., Greene, B. F., & McGimpsey, B. J. (1988). Assessment and modification of home cleanliness among families adjudicated for child neglect. *Behavior Modification, 12,* 57–81.

Weissbourd, B., & Kagan, S. L. (1989). Family support programs: Catalysts for change. *American Journal of Orthopsychiatry, 59,* 20–31.

Wekerle, C., & Wolfe, D. A. (1993). Prevention of child physical abuse and neglect: Promising new directions. *Clinical Psychology Review, 13,* 501–540.

Whipple, E. E., & Webster-Stratton, C. (1991). The role of parental stress in physically abusive families. *Child Abuse & Neglect, 15,* 279–291.

Whiteman, M., Fanshel, D., & Grundy, J. F. (1987). Cognitive-behavioral interventions aimed at anger of parents at risk of child abuse. *Social Work, 32,* 469–474.

Wiehe, V. R. (1986). Empathy and locus of control in child abusers. *Journal of Social Service Research, 9,* 17–30.

Wolfe, D. A., Edwards, B., Manion, I., & Koverla, C. (1988). Early intervention for parents at risk of child abuse and neglect: A preliminary investigation. *Journal of Consulting and Clinical Psychology, 56,* 40–47.

Wolfe, D. A., & Sandler, J. (1981). Training abusive parents in effective child management. *Behavior Modification, 5,* 320–335.

Wolfe, D. A., Sandler, J., & Kaufman, K. (1981). A competency-based training program for child abusers. *Journal of Consulting and Clinical Psychology, 49,* 633–640.

Wolfe, D. A. & Wekerle, C. (1993). Treatment strategies for child physical abuse and neglect: A critical progress report. *Clinical Psychology Review, 13,* 473–500.

Wyatt, G. E. (1990). Sexual abuse of ethnic minority children: Identifying dimensions of victimization. *Professional Psychology, 21,* 338–343.

Zuravin, S., McMillen, C., DePanfilis, D., & Risley-Curtis, C. (1996). The intergenerational cycle of child maltreatment: Continuity versus discontinuity. *Journal of Interpersonal Violence, 11,* 315–334.

CHAPTER **6**

Universal Services for Children and Families

with Joseph Gianesin

In our previous discussion of institutional versus residual services (Chapter 1), we explained that the United States has been unable to develop a national family policy to establish a comprehensive continuum of services for all children and families. In the absence of a national family policy, the United States has created an uneven collection of services that stress volunteerism, pluralism, and minimal government intervention. The assumption is that most families do not need help.

Given this, services are generally available to some families based on their ability to meet specific income eligibility requirements. Other services are available to selected families based on a specific problem-oriented category of service. In some sections of the United States, families are unable to get help meeting even basic needs for health, nutrition, and housing. Child welfare scholars believe that many of the problems addressed by child protective services (CPS) would not exist if a wider array of services—especially early intervention services—were readily available to all families.

As noted in Chapter 2, our history of caring about children's welfare has been long and eventful. The United States has been concerned about the relationship of poverty to child welfare for nearly 100 years, but not much progress has been made. Over 90 years have passed since the first White House Conference on Children declared that poverty was an insufficient reason for removing children from the care of their parents. Many of the children in orphanages were not orphans. They were children whose mothers were too poor to feed, clothe, and house them. The 1909 White House Conference on Children led to the convening of a White House Conference on Children and Youth every decade through 1970.

In 1987, Congress established the National Commission on Children to serve as a forum on behalf of the children of the nation, yet today, over 20 percent of American children still live in poverty. This statistic suggests that although the United States is aware of the relationship of poverty to child welfare, the nation has not been successful in translating this knowledge into a cohesive system of preventive and supportive services—not even for the poorest families.

Government programs that support families have undergone significant philosophical and policy changes in the area of public assistance, specifically with Temporary Assistance to Needy Families (TANF). These alterations reflect society's changed attitudes and values regarding the parenting of young children.

In the United States, programs that serve children and families tend to be piecemeal and residual in nature. (See Chapter 1 for a discussion of residual services.) The programs are *means tested*, requiring participants to meet specific economic eligibility requirements. In addition, they are controlled regionally, which makes service delivery inconsistent. The services are dependent on matching funds from local and state levels, so they compete with one another for funds that are in short supply.

Some services duplicate one another, a fact that may result in service gaps. A community, for example, may have several day care providers for the 4- to 12-year-old age group but none for infant care. Day care providers may choose not to meet the strict government requirements of low adult-to-infant ratios. Few incentives are provided, either by the government or the free market, to make providers want to fill the gap. These and similar frustrating problems exemplify how the nation's social welfare programs suffer from the lack of a coordinated and comprehensive social policy.

The United States provides far fewer services than most Western industrial societies (Kamerman & Kahn, 1995). The technologically advanced health system in the United States has reduced infant mortality and increased the number of children who in many other countries would not survive premature births or developmental abnormalities. Despite these advancements, a great number of children in the United

States are likely to experience low birthweight, physical and functional developmental defects, childhood illnesses, accidental deaths, poor learning, drug and alcohol dependency, cognitive and environmental deprivation, and a multitude of other childhood social ills.

"America's children are in trouble, and Americans know it" is the cry from Kamerman and Kahn (1995, p. 3), who advocate support for families and children right from the start. Early intervention services provide support to families from the prenatal period through early childhood to support child development and strengthen healthy family life. According to the Carnegie Task Force on Meeting the Needs of Young Children (1994), early childhood is one of the most crucial periods of development. Children under 3 years of age are vulnerable to more physical damage and social and emotional deprivation than children at other stages of childhood (Kamerman & Kahn, 1995).

The importance of starting children out under the best possible circumstances makes common sense, but that knowledge has not yet translated to a comprehensive social policy strategy in the United States. Our country is still far behind its European counterparts in aiding children and families toward healthy beginnings.

A comparison of statistics for the United States and other industrialized countries points dramatically to the failure of the United States to effectively support families and children. Researchers have looked at figures for such specifics as the number of infant deaths occurring during the first year of life, the percentage of children living in poverty, and the number of young children who are never immunized. Kamerman and Kahn (1995), Zigler and Styfco (1993), and Schorr (1988) are some of the major researchers who have made compelling arguments in favor of greatly increasing early childhood programming in the United States. Similarly, a report by the National Commission on Children (1991), compiled by a bipartisan committee with consultation from experts throughout the United States, made widespread recommendations to increase significantly the current continuum of resources and supports available to families and children. The Carnegie Task Force on Meeting the Needs of Young Children (1994), which focused on birth to 3 years, reached similar conclusions regarding the importance of greatly strengthening voluntary supports for all families with young children.

In sharp contrast to the United States, many European countries employ an institutional social policy approach that makes services available to all families. The comprehensive programs focus on early childhood programs: (1) income support and economic security for families with children, (2) access to services that provide early identification and treatment of physical and mental health problems, (3) early childhood care and education services, and (4) parenting supports that include training and social supports for child care leave in the labor force. Such comprehensive programs are already in place in many industrialized countries, where the populace recognizes the importance of the first 3 years of life as a critical and crucial developmental period.

In Denmark, Finland, France, Germany, Great Britain, Ireland, Italy, the Netherlands, Norway, and Sweden, home health visitation programs are part of *universal health care*. Professionally trained health providers with experience in pediatrics visit

Early identification programs identify children and families
who need support.

families at their homes. All services are free, voluntary, and not income tested (Kamerman & Kahn, 1995, p. 102). All the programs employ professionals, usually registered nurses, who provide health education, preventive care, and social support to children under 3 years of age and their parents. The home health visitor connects the family with other needed services and is helpful, for example, in identifying child abuse and postpartum depression.

Because the United States has failed to reach agreement on the value of and need for a system of universally available preventive services for all children and their families, the services that are available are scattered, inconsistent, and not always accessible by those most at risk. This chapter provides an overview of the services currently available. As we look at what is available, we will also note some problems and inadequacies. The knowledge gained in this chapter can equip the child welfare worker to participate in the ongoing debate concerning gaps in the current system and funding for a universal system of voluntary services available to all children and families.

Early Identification and Intervention Programs

Early identification programs identify children and families that need support; *early intervention programs* provide services to children from the prenatal period through birth and early childhood. Children and families with risk factors that impede the healthy development of physical, social, educational, and cognitive functioning must first be identified; then appropriate support and services must be provided. Programs are designed to intervene early and reduce the impact of risk factors that include low birthweight, environmental hazards, developmental delays, childhood illnesses, drug and alcohol dependency, learning problems, and cognitive delays.

Hawaii's Healthy Start

We now turn our attention to the Hawaii Family Support Center Healthy Start Program, an example of a state-initiated program that focuses on early identification and early intervention (see References for source information). It is a nationally recognized program model supporting the healthy development of at-risk first-time parents through regularly scheduled home visitations by a trained paraprofessional. Started in 1985, the program has been implemented statewide to strengthen families and promote healthy child development and as an effective approach to preventing child abuse and neglect among children from birth to age 5. This program is generally viewed as a successful model of an institutional preventative approach to promoting healthy child development and preventing child abuse and neglect.

The program determines eligibility for service through a process that reviews hospital records and assesses all first-time parents for risk factors that potentially increase stress and result in poor, negligent, or abusive parenting behaviors. The record review and maternal interview are conducted, with family approval, either during the prenatal period or at the birth of a new infant. All families receive information about community resources. Additionally, overburdened families are given the opportunity to receive a home visitor on a voluntary basis. A typical case example follows:

Tom is a single father with twin daughters. With the assistance of a Healthy Start family support worker, he grew from a shy, insecure, and overwhelmed parent into a much more outgoing person with confidence in his parenting ability. He was able to move out of very unsafe living conditions and away from his children's drug-addicted mother. The twins have blossomed under his care and guidance. They are no longer fearful, clingy, and distrustful. After three years in the Healthy Start program, Tom proudly states, "I now know I am a good parent." He attributes the change to "the home visitor who was there for me and my girls, week after week, and never stopped believing in me."

A family that chooses to participate in Healthy Start is assigned a home visitor and works together with the home visitor to develop a plan. This plan specifies the time and frequency of home visits. Typically, the home visitor visits the family on a regular basis. The goals of the visits include (1) parent education, (2) monitoring the health and development of the infant, (3) supporting the parents in maintaining appropriate and timely pediatric or well-baby clinic check-up and immunization schedules, and (4) identifying needs for community services, such as financial assistance. A family may continue to receive services from the home visitor until the child is 5 years old. The philosophy of offering long-term support is based on the belief that a highly stressed family benefits from ongoing support until the child is in school, at which point the education system takes over as the monitor and support of healthy development.

Hawaii's Healthy Start Program is administered by the Hawaii State Department of Health and funded by the state legislature. The program began as a result of advocacy efforts of the Hawaii Academy of Pediatrics in the interest of reducing child maltreatment. Following the 1988 successful evaluation of the pilot program, the Maternal and Child Health Department worked with eight private providers to extend services across the state. In 1994–1995, 12 Healthy Start programs were in operation, supported by state funding of $8.3 million. Private funding from foundations, the United Way, and local governments contributes to the support of local programs.

Internal and external evaluations continue to assess whether the Healthy Start program is meeting its goals to prevent child abuse, to increase childhood immunizations, to identify a medical care provider, and to administer prenatal care. The National Committee to Prevent Child Abuse conducted a study that identified specific outcomes: 99 percent of families enrolled for 12 months had no confirmed reports of abuse; 94 percent of Healthy Start children were fully immunized by age 2; 99 percent of Healthy Start children had an identified medical care provider; 99 percent of all births in West Hawaii were screened in hospitals; and 100 percent of enrolled women received prenatal care within 30 days after the pregnancy was made known.

A more recent three-year study conducted by Johns Hopkins University School of Medicine had mixed findings, as reported in *Pediatrics* (Willis, Malloy, & Kliegman, 2000) and *The Future of Children* ("Home visiting," 1999). The National Institute of Health has committed funding to conduct the next phase of study.

As evaluation continues, replication of the program in other states has been made possible through the Healthy Families America initiative, a program of the Hawaii Family Support Center with the National Committee to Prevent Child Abuse (now Prevent Child Abuse America). Family Support Center conducts training plus consultation to sites and states and has helped establish a training institute to prepare trainers to introduce the program across the United States and internationally.

Research has documented program effectiveness in determining infant maltreatment risk status, linking families with a primary care provider, and improving family wellness. Healthy Start programs exist in selected communities in the United States; they are not universally available. Given the many stresses that families in the United States are experiencing, it is clear that many families could benefit from early intervention programs like Healthy Start.

Early childhood education helps overcome the negative academic odds for poor children.

Head Start

In an effort to overcome the negative academic odds for poor children, early childhood education has been provided in several model programs at state and national levels. Such endeavors are generally based on the theory that providing early intellectual stimulation will enhance cognitive development, thereby allowing children to enter school better prepared to learn. This should, in turn, increase the probability of early school success, lead to later scholastic success, and eventually result in vocational achievement and successful social adaptation in adulthood. Poverty in early childhood has long-lasting negative consequences for cognitive development and academic outcomes, as shown by numerous studies. Poor children tend to begin lagging behind in the earliest school years, suggesting that they enter school inadequately prepared for success (Abecedarian Experiment, 1991). This observation is behind the inception of programs like Head Start.

Head Start is a federally funded preschool program for disadvantaged children. It aims to improve the children's skills so they can begin schooling on an equal footing with their more advantaged peers. Head Start serves almost 800,000 children in predominantly part-day programs (U.S. Administration on Children, Youth, and Families, 1999). Although the program is large, enrollment represents only about 35 percent of eligible 3- and 4-year-old children. The program is not an entitlement but is funded by an appropriation, which means that when funds run out, eligible children cannot be served. Head Start is a popular program. Federal appropriations for it have grown during recent administrations.

Head Start is run at the local level, but local operators are subject to federal quality guidelines. These guidelines specify that Head Start is to provide a wide range of services in addition to providing a nurturing learning environment. For example, Head Start is required to facilitate and monitor utilization of preventive medical care by participants, as well as to provide nutritious meals and snacks.

Launched in 1965 under the general authority of the Economic Opportunity Act (1964) and President Lyndon B. Johnson's war on poverty, Head Start is one of the most highly touted programs to survive Johnson's social experiment. Head Start and Early Head Start are comprehensive child development programs that serve children from birth to age 5 as well as pregnant women and their families. They are child-focused programs and have the overall goal of increasing the school readiness of young children in low-income families. The children receive daily nutritious meals and many opportunities for social, emotional, and intellectual growth. The national Head Start Bureau has determined that the ultimate goal of the program is "to enhance the social competence of children from low income families" (U.S. Administration for Children, Youth, and Families, 2003, p. 1).

After years of study, Head Start researchers have provided educators and other human service providers with the knowledge and skills necessary to help children be successful in school. They have demonstrated that prereading, language, and social skills are requisite to a preschooler's later success in school. Reading scores in the tenth grade can be predicted with surprising accuracy based on a child's knowledge of the alphabet in kindergarten.

According to the U.S. Administration for Children, Youth, and Families (2003), more than 40 states have initiatives aimed at helping preschool children prepare for kindergarten. This is the case because educators know that the academic skills of children entering school from poor families are not as developed as the skills of children entering from more privileged families.

The No Child Left Behind Act of 2001 holds states accountable for ensuring that all children are proficient in reading and math, a mandate that gives states an additional reason to develop high-quality preschool programs. Since 1965, Head Start has provided a comprehensive program for children in poverty, including activities that aim to promote social, emotional, and cognitive development as well as health services. In light of what we know about the preschool years, early education must be a priority. Head Start sites that have implemented carefully designed programs that focus on school readiness have shown significant gains for children.

Head Start is one of many federal and state programs that together provide approximately $23 billion in funding for child care and preschool education. In programs other than Head Start, states have the responsibility and the authority through planning, training, and regulation to have a substantial impact on the type and quality of services provided, and they are held accountable for the delivery of high-quality programs. Head Start funding, however, goes directly from the federal level to local organizations, which means states do not have the authority to integrate or align Head Start programs with their own state-provided early childhood programs.

Head Start is an important element in child welfare. It provides parenting supports, early childhood intervention opportunities, and developmental guidance for the low-income families that have difficulty providing or obtaining the services and supports needed for rearing healthy children. Head Start is often touted as the most successful program for children from low-income households. Despite such accolades, Head Start suffers from funding shortages and legislators who are not fully committed to it.

According to Janet Currie (2000) of the Brookings Roundtable on Children,

> Early intervention programs are once again in the public eye. Questions being debated include these: Whether government should fund a universal pre-school program; whether Head Start should be fully funded so that all poor 3 to 5 year old children can attend; and whether to create a Head Start-like program for younger children. Are there policies the government can pursue to improve the quality of early interventions? (p. 3)

Parenting Support and Education Programs

As parents face the challenges of understanding their children's emerging needs, they benefit from parent education and parent support programs. As parents gain new knowledge and confidence, they strengthen emotional bonds with their children and gain interpersonal skills to build strong social networks and connections in the community. Researchers attribute deficits in parenting skills to child maltreatment, which is exacerbated by lack of support and social isolation (Iwaniec, 1997).

Parenting education and support programs generally focus on (1) child development (what behaviors are normal at various ages), (2) ways for parents to set goals and establish clear communication, (3) methods of managing behaviors, and (4) discipline techniques. Parent education and support is available to families in their own homes, in classes, or in small discussion groups, depending on location and funding. If the family's risks are deemed severe, individual service planning, case management, case advocacy, or crisis intervention may accompany parent education.

Hawaii Family Support Center's Classes for Child Protection

Hawaii Family Support Center offers many parenting classes, but one set requires a referral from the state child protective services agency responsible for investigating and treating allegations of abuse and neglect. A case manager from the Family Support Center works with each of the families who attend one of the specialized parenting education programs:

- The *SOS* program offers an eight-week parenting class that covers the basic topics of discipline, stress management, and setting goals.
- *HEAL* (Helping, Empowering, Advocating, and Learning) discusses separation and reunification, substance abuse, communication, and discipline.
- *Boundaries* is a four-week class on techniques for setting and keeping the healthy boundaries that are essential to maintaining a solid relationship between parent and child.

Waterbury, Connecticut's Family Ties Program

Deputy Commissioner Joyce Lee Taylor (personal communication, April 15, 2004) identifies the Family Ties Program at the Waterbury Youth Service System, Inc. as an example of a parenting support and education program where most classes are open to all parents. The public is invited and charged no fee for classes such as

- The Nurturing Parent, eight sessions to discuss raising children in a nonviolent environment
- Parenting with Care, six sessions to discuss discipline, stress management, and communication
- Learning at Play, eight weeks of interactive time for parents to join in on structured craft activities, stories, music, and puzzles
- Lifestyle Makeovers, eight sessions that focus on developing positive and mutual supports to motivate self-improvement
- Anger Management, four sessions that cover techniques for curtailing destructive behavior
- For Dads Only, two sessions that focus on what children need from fathers and ways to be a nurturing father

Parent education and support programs are also designed along a variety of specializations. These classes target specific problems, such as mental health disorders. One of the most frequently offered special classes deals with the social problem of divorce.

Connecticut's Divorce Classes

Connecticut has designed a specific parent education program for parents going through the divorce process. Programs such as this are especially significant to child welfare because of the large number of families disrupted by divorce and the potentially detrimental effects of divorce on children.

According to the National Center for Health Statistics (2000), there were 957,200 divorces in the United States in 1999. Over 40 percent of first marriages end in divorce within 10 years. Divorce often has a serious impact that contributes to a number of societal issues, including the financial, health, mental health, and social welfare of children.

In addition to having to adjust to custody and visitation arrangements, the child of a divorce grieves the loss of friends, pets, and teachers if financial pressures require the family to move. Inevitably, the child experiences a variety of emotions—fear, anxiety, anger, rejection, loneliness, and guilt. The child may harbor hope of reconciliation, a hope that can be complicated by feelings of relief. The emotional impact for the child is tremendous, especially if the parents do not understand and respond constructively to the child's needs.

In an effort to reduce the negative effects of divorce, Connecticut joined other states in passing legislation to enact mandatory parent education programs. The state requires both parents to attend a six-hour instruction called *Putting Children First:*

Skills for Parents in Transition. The curriculum helps parents understand the emotional effects of divorce on children and encourages them to provide assurance, support, and stability. Most important, parents are guided to remove their children from the middle of their own hostility and disagreements surrounding the divorce. In keeping with the theme of keeping the child's interest at the forefront, parents are encouraged to explore their own anger control and learn techniques to resolve conflicts together. The prevailing philosophy is that children need both parents' love, acceptance, and attention.

Parenting education courses for divorced parents are an important resource, according to Deputy Commissioner Joyce Lee Taylor (personal communication, April 15, 2004). Such programs emphasize consistency, flexibility, and tolerance of the other parent on special occasions for the child, such as school events and birthday parties. Parents are encouraged to provide unrestricted telephone contact and predictable visitation arrangements, but they are strongly advised to remove the child from parent-to-parent communication regarding such topics as changing visitation schedules and finances. The following case illustration explains how the program improved communication.

Mr. and Mrs. Carter are both in their early thirties and enjoy a middle-class lifestyle. They have a 3-year-old son and a 5-year-old daughter. They were married for six years. Mrs. Carter enjoys her job at a company that distributes resources to libraries and schools. Her husband is a successful pharmaceutical sales representative. Before either of them attended the parenting course, they struggled through the parenting issues of breaking up. Their daughter began experiencing behavioral problems and sleep disruptions.

Mr. and Mrs. Carter attended classes at different times, but through class exercises, they each practiced communication and negotiation skills and learned to focus on their children. Before the class, they could not agree on parenting styles. The class helped them understand the importance of compromising. The therapist that worked with them reported that Mr. and Mrs. Carter were able to create a healthier setting for the children once they were armed with better tools and awareness. The divorce is now finalized, and their daughter no longer experiences behavioral and sleep problems.

Parents involved in the divorce process can expect to encounter a myriad of obstacles as they seek good outcomes for themselves and their children. Heatherington (1999) has studied the effects of divorce through three longitudinal studies over a span of 25 years. She emphasizes that parents and children are more resilient and capable of countering the ill effects of divorce than previous research indicates yet confirms that the challenges are all too real. According to Heatherington, "Twenty-five percent of youths from divorced families in comparison to 10 percent from non-divorced families [have] serious social, emotional, or psychological problems" (p. 7).

Upon the family breakup, the family's income also diminishes. Heatherington (1999) estimates that a woman's postdivorce economic resources decline by 30 percent in comparison with a man's postdivorce economic resources, which are estimated to decline by 10 percent. Research has widely documented that single-parent families are more likely to be poor. The Children's Defense Fund (2002) found that almost 40 percent of children in households headed by single mothers were poor in fiscal year 2000, compared to only 8.2 percent of children in traditional nuclear families with two parents. Of all the families receiving Temporary Assistance to Needy Families in 2002, 64 percent were families headed by single adults (Children's Defense Fund, 2002).

Public Aid

Temporary Assistance to Needy Families (TANF) provides financial assistance to families whose income falls below the poverty level. The financial assistance is distributed to families on a monthly basis.

Temporary Assistance to Needy Families was formerly named *Aid to Families with Dependent Children (AFDC)*, which originated in 1935 with the Social Security Act. In 1996, welfare reform introduced federal lifetime benefit limits of five years and work requirements through the Personal Responsibility and Work Opportunities Reconciliation Act. States receive block grants and exercise flexibility in administering their TANF programs. The amounts granted to recipients vary, with decisions generally based on family size, other sources of income available to the family, the state's cost of living, and the poverty level. Each state legislature considers its own budget when designating amounts, for TANF block grants cover only a portion of program costs. Nationally, the average TANF amount in January 2000 was $379 per month for a family of three persons (Children's Defense Fund, 2004). State TANF programs emphasize self-sufficiency through job searches, minimum work requirements, family caps, child support enforcement, and welfare time limits as short as 24 months. The state of Massachusetts also applied a school attendance requirement.

Many families receiving TANF also receive food stamps, housing assistance, or medical insurance coverage. (See the following sections for individual discussions of these supplements.) The policy reform of 1996 also made supplemental child care and transportation available to TANF adults who enter the workforce. (See the Child Care section later in this chapter.)

Some states, such as Connecticut, offer creative programs to help families make the transition from welfare to work. One such program, Family-to-Family Mentor Support Program, trains volunteer mentors who help adults problem solve regarding their frustrations of job interview nervousness, child care dilemmas, dressing for new jobs, and parenting or discipline problems.

Food Assistance

Food stamps are distributed in monthly amounts either in the original form of paper stamps or coupons or through electronic bank transfer cards similar to debit cards. Food stamps provide the freedom of making personal food choices but may not be used for nonfood necessities, such as laundry detergent, toilet paper, postage stamps, and diapers. The food stamp program is federally funded as an antihunger program that also supports the United States' agricultural economy. The national average in January 2000 amounted to only $262 per month for a family of three persons (Children's Defense Fund, 2004). Given three meals a day for three persons for 30 days in the month, a family could only afford to spend an average of 97 cents per person per meal. A family may also be eligible for a the Supplemental Nutrition Program for Women, Infants, and Children (WIC) if their income is low and the mother is pregnant or has children under the age of 6. WIC assistance is different from food stamps in that it provides coupons that can be redeemed specifically for items such as milk, cheese, cereal, juice, and infant formula.

Another nutritional program for poor families is the federally subsidized program that provides school meals. Children can receive breakfast and lunch at their own schools at no cost or at a reduced price, based on their family's income eligibility. Generally, schools send applications home with children in the first week of school. This subsidy also benefits infants and preschool children at day care programs, whether the day care center is a large one or an in-home family day care center. Providers can apply for subsidies if they provide nutritious meals in a licensed child care setting and the families qualify as low income. At-home day care centers must submit income information about their enrolled families, as well as menus and documentation of the meals they serve.

Housing Assistance

The cost of housing tends to be the greatest expense for families. Inadequate, crowded, or costly housing can pose serious problems to children's physical, psychological, or material well-being (Kaufman, 1996). A large percentage of poor children report living in inadequate housing.

Problems with housing include the lack of complete plumbing for exclusive use; unvented room heaters used as primary heat sources; and multiple upkeep problems, such as water leakage, open cracks or holes, broken plaster, and signs of rats. In 1995, 36 percent of U.S. households with children, both owners and renters, had one or more of three housing problems: physically inadequate housing, crowded housing, or housing that cost more than 30 percent of household income (Kaufman, 1996). Poor families often cope with unsafe or substandard housing conditions, live with other families, accept overcrowded conditions, or pay more than half their income for rent. Without the ability to afford decent housing, a family may accept a rundown apartment with a roach infestation. Lead poisoning in old apartments can cause a child to become seriously ill or suffer long-term learning disabilities. Research studies have demonstrated a correlation between roaches and a higher rate of asthma cases for exposed children.

The U.S. Department of Housing and Urban Development provides a limited number of housing vouchers for low-income families. Local housing departments administer the vouchers. The waiting lists are long, as the number of applicants far exceeds the number of available vouchers.

Even if a family receives a voucher, they may have difficulty locating suitable housing with a landlord who is willing to accept the voucher for the amount of the subsidy. At least three reasons are behind this fact:

1. The market for affordable housing is limited.
2. Many landlords are unwilling to meet the inspection and building requirements associated with Section 8 vouchers.
3. Some landlords are wary of renting to tenants who receive public assistance.

According to O'Hare and Mather (2003), from the Annie E. Casey Foundation, between 1990 and 2000, there was a decrease in the number of children living in high-poverty neighborhoods. This fact is potentially misleading, however, as it provides an incomplete picture. Using a more comprehensive measure of neighborhood quality, researchers found that the number of children living in severely distressed neighborhoods increased significantly between 1990 and 2000. *Severely distressed neighborhoods* are defined here as census tracts with at least three of these four characteristics: (1) high poverty rate (27.4 percent or more); (2) high percentage of female-headed families (37.1 percent or more); (3) high percentage of high school dropouts (23.0 percent or more); and (4) high percentage of working-age males unattached to the labor force (34.0 percent or more) (O'Hare & Mather, 2003).

Despite the booming economy of the 1990s, the number of children living in severely distressed neighborhoods increased from 4.7 million in 1990 to 5.6 million in 2000 (an 18 percent change). The number of adults living in such neighborhoods also increased, from 10.4 million to 12.5 million (20 percent) during the 1990s. Of the 5.6 million children growing up in severely distressed neighborhoods, 55 percent were black and 29 percent were Hispanic. Over one-quarter of all black children (28 percent) lived in severely distressed neighborhoods, and more than 1 in 10 Hispanic children (13 percent) lived in these neighborhoods, compared with 1 percent of non-Hispanic white children (O'Hare & Mather, 2003).

The increase in children living in severely distressed neighborhoods during the 1990s is a cause for concern because neighborhoods influence many important outcomes for children. The high concentration of black and Hispanic children in disadvantaged neighborhoods indicates that a significant segment of our most vulnerable children are not likely to get the kinds of supports they need. These neighborhoods present serious risk factors. Children in such neighborhoods experience (1) a high rate of dropping out of high school; (2) a high rate of males not in the labor force (Population Reference Bureau, 2000); and (3) a high rate of violent crime and drug abuse exposure. The future for the children in these distressed communities looks very bleak compared to that for children in neighborhoods without such health and social risks.

Medical Assistance

Access to medical treatment is essential to children's optimal healthy development. Families can apply for medical coverage at state welfare offices. All families who are eligible for TANF are automatically eligible for federally supported medical coverage under Title IVA, called *Medicaid*. The income eligibility is extended in the Medicaid program, so that children of working-poor families may be eligible for medical coverage even if their incomes are a bit higher than TANF eligibility levels. When families come off TANF because they have transitioned into jobs, they may continue to receive Medicaid for a longer period of time.

This is important because the trends of welfare reform since 1997 are just becoming documented: Minimum-wage, entry-level jobs offer low prospects for long-term job retention, and employers rarely pay for medical insurance coverage. Access is an issue beyond the ability to pay. In some areas of the country, poor families have difficulty finding medical providers who accept the Medicaid level of reimbursement, especially in medical specializations such as neurology and pediatric ophthalmology.

Child Care

For many families, including those currently receiving TANF, having adequate child care is a critical component for entry into the workforce. Child care options range from day care arrangements to more sophisticated early childhood education alternatives. Parents, whether employed or in training for employment, must have child care that is available, affordable, and convenient.

As more and more mothers have joined the ranks of the employed, child care has become one of today's most widely debated social and political issues. Many families are confronted with the financial reality that they cannot afford child care. This results in many young children being left at home alone. Even those parents who can afford to pay for child care cannot always find providers that are reputable. News stories recount the horrors of providers who neglect, abuse, or exploit the children in their care. Parents from all economic levels not only worry about the safety of their children but are also demanding that child care programs offer curriculums that (1) increase academic readiness, (2) provide environments of acceptance and nurturance, and (3) are affordable.

In the remainder of this section, we provide definitions for child care and discuss trends in child care. For examples of government-funded programs designed to provide care and training for children at an early age, see the coverage of Healthy Start and Head Start earlier in this chapter.

Child Care Defined

Child care refers to those services that provide care and training for a child or children who may or may not be related to the caretaker on a regular basis. The term *child care* entails a wide scope of arrangements that parents make for their children's care and development. In the United States, child care services come in many configurations. *In-home day care* consists of relatives or nonrelatives staying in the home to care for the child. The in-home caregiver may be a trained nanny or au pair. *Out-of-home care* means parents leave their children at a relative's home or in the home of a day care provider.

Most parents choose day care centers, referred to as *nursery schools* or *day schools*. The day care center may be a public or private agency and may be a for-profit or nonprofit organization. The day care center's primary focus is to provide child care in lieu of the parent, including full-day and part-time care of children from infancy to early adolescence. Many school-age children require care before and after school, often requiring that transportation be provided by the day care center. In most cases, day care services must meet particular standards and must be licensed by the governing state agency. Minimum standards for day care providers usually include specific standards for (1) facilities, (2) the staff-to-child ratio, (3) group size, and (4) staff screening and training.

Child Care Trends

Employers recognize that mothers have become an integral part of the workforce and that the difficulties employees face in arranging care for their children result in absenteeism, tardiness, low morale, and productivity problems. To counteract or prevent these negative consequences, some employers are looking at steps they can take to help employees who are parents. The critical connection between available child care and an employee's job effectiveness has resulted in employer-sponsored on-site daycare programs across the country.

Despite these efforts by employers, there are significant problems with our current system of child care. According to the report *Working for Children and Families: Safe and Smart Afterschool Programs* (2000), published by the U.S. Departments of Education and Justice, 69 percent of all married-couple families with children ages 6 to 17 years old have both parents working outside the home. In 71 percent of single-mother families and 85 percent of single-father families with children ages 6 to 17, the custodial parent is working. The gap between parents' work schedules and children's school schedules can amount to 20 to 25 hours per week.

Statistics from the U.S. General Accounting Office (GAO) (1997) of the National Institute on Out-of-School Time and other surveys show that the lack of affordable, accessible after-school opportunities for school-age children means that on any given day, an estimated 8 million and up to as many as 15 million children go home to an empty house after school—a fact that has given us the term *latchkey children*. Forty-four percent of third-graders spend at least a portion of their out-of-school time unsupervised, and about 35 percent of 12-year-olds are regularly left alone while their parents are at work.

According to data from the 1999 and 2000 Mott/J. C. Penney Nationwide survey on Afterschool programs (2005), more than 8 out of 10 of those polled agreed that access to after-school programming in the community is important and should be available to all children. Fewer than 4 out of 10 said their community provides after-school programs. According to the U.S. General Accounting Office (1997), the supply of after-school programs for school-age children in some urban areas meets as little as 20 percent of demand. In a study done by the David and Lucille Packard Foundation (1999), experts assert that the availability of school-age care in rural areas can cover only about one-third of the population of children with employed parents. As a result, millions of parents worry each day about where their children will go and what they will do.

Child care in general became more available during the 1990s, as the number of available slots grew faster than the population of young children. Most of the increase was in child care centers, with some increase in slots in family homes. School-age care also gained in number, as public and private agencies recognized the importance of keeping children safe and sound before and after school. Significant improvements have also been made in making culturally and linguistically appropriate care available for families of color.

Although these increases have been welcomed, significant gaps still remain. Infant care is at least as difficult to find as it was 10 years ago. Child care available during nonstandard hours is scarce. And parents of children with special needs face a real challenge as they seek quality care.

A survey by Sonenstein, Gates, Schmidt, and Boshun (2002) found that child care arrangements for children younger than 5 differ based on the income level of the working mother. Children in higher-income families, particularly 3- and 4-year-olds, are more likely to be placed in center-based arrangements, while low-income children are more likely to be left in the care of relatives. These differences may have implications for the school readiness of low-income children, for child care centers generally provide more environmental and cognitive stimulation. These types of findings also have policy implications for child welfare advocates.

After the public aid reform of 1996, supplemental child care and transportation became available to adult recipients of TANF who entered the workforce. The states also now receive federal assistance to maintain child care subsidies. A state can offer child care subsidies to TANF families meeting work requirements and to families at risk of becoming welfare recipients. The quality of service has been affected by the slow rate of federal reimbursement. For example, once a capable child care provider becomes available for an infant or preschool child, the delay in government payment may cause the loss of the child's slot or the child's discharge from a licensed child care program. Likewise, a relative staying at home to care for the child may become frustrated and financially overwhelmed by state reimbursement issues.

Services for Children with Disabilities

Child Find

In child welfare, early identification of the developmentally disadvantaged child is a crucial preventive strategy. Thirty years have passed since the federal government enacted the Education for All Handicapped Children Act, now known as the *Individuals with Disabilities Education Act (IDEA)*. Child Find is a program instituted under the IDEA to ensure that "all children with disabilities residing in the State, including children with disabilities attending private schools, regardless of the severity of their disability, and who are in need of special education and related services, are identified, located, and evaluated" (U.S. Office of Special Education Programs, 2005).

Child Find can be enacted as early as birth through age 2. Each state has its own plan, approved by the federal government, to intervene with the child early in life. Almost any professionals who deal with children, including physicians, nurses, and physical therapists, can refer children for evaluation. Child care providers, preschool personnel, and parents also may request evaluation to identify developmental problems that may infer a disability.

As used in this section, the term *child with a disability* means a child evaluated as having mental retardation, a hearing impairment including deafness, a speech or language impairment, a visual impairment including blindness, serious emotional disturbance, an orthopedic impairment, autism, traumatic brain injury, other health impairment, a specific learning disability, deaf–blindness, or multiple disabilities and who, by reason thereof, needs special education and related services. The earlier the disability is identified, the greater the likelihood that the interventions will be effective, for it is important to capitalize on the critical early learning years.

Many children benefit from early identification programs like Child Find. The assessments and evaluations are provided at no cost to the parent or child. The extent of the disability and gravity of the impairment usually become more obvious as the child matures. Childhood is characterized by periods of transition and reorganization. Assessments of the development of children and adolescents must be made in the context of familial, social, and cultural expectations of age-appropriate thoughts, emotions, and behaviors. Even though the range of what is considered normal is wide, some children and adolescents do have disabilities that fall outside the usual course of development.

According to the U.S. Surgeon General's (2000) report on childhood mental health, the period of development in children and adolescents is the focus of much research. Studies focus on normal and abnormal development, as researchers try to understand and predict the forces that will keep children and adolescents mentally healthy and maintain them on course toward becoming mentally healthy adults. These studies seek to understand the factors that place children at risk for mental illness and why other children exposed to the same risks remain healthy.

In addition to studies of normal development and risk factors, research focuses on what can be done to prevent and treat mental illness in childhood and adolescence. The science is challenging because of the ongoing process of development. The normally developing child hardly stays the same long enough for stable measurements to be made.

Special Education

A child that does not follow the normal rate of developmental progress may be identified as a child with a disability. School social workers and special education teachers stay on the alert to identify children who are not meeting their potential—not because they lack motivation but because something is interfering with their ability to function effectively. The most common of the disabilities are learning disabilities and emotional and behavioral disabilities. The latter two often manifest themselves simultaneously. Without appropriate intervention, the child may become frustrated, quit school, and never get to take advantage of the special education services available in public schools.

Special education is a term used to describe the multitude of services available to children in a school setting. Special educators and legal advisors refer to *FAPE (free appropriate public education),* an individualized educational program that is designed to meet the child's unique needs such that he or she does benefit from education.

The process that identifies a child with a disability starts with an initial referral, which is followed by a series of evaluations done by a team of professionals. A special education teacher tests for achievement or grade levels in math, written language, and reading. The school social worker conducts a behavioral assessment and psychosocial assessment. The school psychologist makes behavioral, emotional, and cognitive assessments. The school nurse makes a health assessment, with vision and hearing tests, and makes a medication assessment. The speech pathologist tests for speech impairments. Other specialized professionals, such as physical therapists, occupational therapists, vision specialists, and audiologists, may also be asked to perform assessments, depending on the extent of the disability.

After the testing and evaluation stage, the parents are asked to attend an initial *IEP (individualized education plan)* meeting, at which the professionals disclose their findings. The team, of which the parents are considered integral members, draws a conclusion based on testing results as to whether the child does have a disability.

If the team concludes that the child has a disability, a list of short-term and long-term goals are developed to assist the child in school. Services to implement these goals are discussed, using a guidepost set forth in IDEA and known as the *least-restrictive environment*. This means the child will be placed in an environment that will meet his or her current needs without restricting areas in which he or she does function appropriately. Most schools offer a continuum of services that utilize the least-restrictive environment concept. This continuum may range from consultation with a specialist for the classroom teacher to the extreme of an out-of-home residential setting for the child. This wide range of approaches is designed to ensure that the child will, if at all possible, stay with appropriate peers.

For child welfare professionals, knowledge of the special education process is important. Consider, for instance, a child in temporary custody who is placed in foster care. Without the parent to advocate for the child, the child welfare professional is required to assume that role and assist in finding the most appropriate placement for the child.

Adolescent Family Life Programs

Early sexual activity, adolescent pregnancy, childbearing, and childrearing are matters of serious national concern because of their pervasive health, economic, and social consequences. The teen pregnancy rate in 1999 was 86.7 per 1,000 females between the ages of 15 and 19 years old (Martin et al., 2003).

Current adolescent family life programs focus on a wide range of program goals and services. Some focus on pregnancy prevention by providing educational programs that promote abstinence from sexual activity among adolescents. Others provide comprehensive health care, counseling, and social services to pregnant and parenting adolescents and their infants. Many programs provide services to male partners and family members, while some make distinct efforts to design culturally responsive adolescent family life programs. Some communities recognize the need to provide housing for teen mothers who have been abused or neglected or cannot live at home for other reasons. Another key service frequently offered is support to teen mothers in the completion of their high school education and preparation for employment.

In addition to wide variations in the services provided, there are widespread differences in program locations, eligibility requirements, clients served, and duration of services. Programs may be based in hospitals, clinics, schools, or homes; others are set residential facilities. Programs may serve male and female adolescents under the age of 18 or females between the ages of 13 and 18 and males between the ages of 16 and 26. The duration of services varies considerably, it may begin during pregnancy and end soon after delivery or extend for several years. Professionals and paraprofessionals deliver these services. Many programs, particularly abstinence education programs, use peer mentors. Programs with a home-based service component may utilize paraprofessionals or trained volunteers. The more holistic programs—ones that offer a continuum of services—make use of many professional disciplines and multidisciplinary teams.

Although the network of community-based services is to be lauded, too few communities offer a full menu of pregnancy prevention and adolescent parenting services. Adolescents throughout the United States would benefit from a systematic national program of comprehensive adolescent family life services. Development of a national program would represent an understanding of the importance of adolescent pregnancy prevention and teen parenting services. A national network of programs with shared objectives would be more effective in achieving these important goals: (1) prevention of teen sexual activity and sexually transmitted diseases; (2) more healthy mothers and healthy babies; (3) increased selection of adoption as a positive alternative to adolescent parenting; (4) reduction in the incidence of repeat pregnancy; (5) enhancement of teen parenting skills; and (6) an increased rate of school completion and employability.

Three major national efforts support pregnant and parenting adolescents: Adolescent and Family Life Programs, administered by the Office of Adolescent Pregnancy of the Office of Population Affairs of the Department of Health and Human Services; Second Chance Homes, which resulted from legislation introduced in 1999; and the Florence Crittenton Division of the Child Welfare League of America. Each of these national programs makes an important contribution to the network of services that are currently engaged in adolescent pregnancy prevention and care services for pregnant and parenting adolescents.

Adolescent and Family Life Program

The Adolescent Family Life Demonstration and Research Program was created in 1981 to award research and demonstration grants for developing, implementing, and evaluating programs that promote abstinence education or care services for pregnant and parenting adolescents. In 2002, the program was funded at $28.9 million. In 2001, grants were made to 110 demonstration projects in 36 states. Of the total, 73 were prevention (abstinence) education programs and 37 were programs for pregnant and parenting adolescents and their infants, male partners, and families.

Second Chance Homes

Second Chance Homes, a program of the U.S. Department of Health and Human Services, Office of the Assistant Secretary for Planning and Evaluation, provide support and supervision and a safe place to live for teen mothers and their children who cannot live at home because of abuse, neglect, or other circumstances (U.S. Department of Health and Human Services, 2000). The Second Chance Home may be a group home, a cluster of apartments, or a network of homes that integrates housing and social services. Some homes provide short-term stays, while others provide services over a longer period of time.

Second Chance Homes are able to tailor the services they provide to the needs of the individual. This is an important benefit of the program and makes it possible for teens that need more than housing, education, or employment to receive services. For example, services specific to the needs of teens with histories of physical or sexual abuse or domestic violence are available. The two largest sources of funding for this program come from federal funds within the U.S. Department of Health and Human Services: the TANF block grant to states and the social services block grant.

Florence Crittenton

The Florence Crittenton Division of the Child Welfare League of America (CWLA) serves as a resource to the 31 Florence Crittenton Agencies in the United States (CWLA, 1998). The Crittenton Agencies were originally founded to provide assistance to pregnant adolescents who had no place to live. Today, they provide a range of services that include pregnancy prevention, pregnancy care, adoption, and counseling. Some programs have residential facilities, and at least one program has a school. The Child Welfare League of America (1998) publishes the *CWLA Standards of Excellence for Services for Adolescent Pregnancy Prevention, Pregnant Adolescents and Young Parents.*

Here is a case example from the Florence Crittenton Agency in Tennessee. Notice the network of support provided for this teen.

Latricia was 13 years old when she took a home pregnancy test that showed a positive result. A trip to the health department confirmed the results of the test. She says, "It was very depressing . . . very overwhelming. My boyfriend said he was okay with me being pregnant, but as it went on, he didn't want the responsibility. He isn't a part of our lives now. Most of my 'friends' turned their backs on me. Two of my very best friends stood by me."

Latricia became a mother when she was 13. "My mom and dad were very supportive when they found out I was pregnant, and they wanted me to finish school. Mom was going to keep Trent. During my freshman year, we found out that my mom had heart trouble. I missed a lot of school when she was in the hospital, and it was hard to keep up. By my junior year, her heart was only functioning 15 percent and I was planning to drop out and get my GED. That is when my older sister and grandmother stepped in. They said that after working so hard, they weren't going to let me fail. In my senior year, Trent was old enough for the Head Start program, and it made a really big difference to all of us."

Latricia graduated from high school. "It wasn't easy, and without my family, it would have never happened. And without CAPS [Child and Parenting Skills, a program offered by the Florence Crittenton Agency to high school students with babies], I wouldn't have had the energy to keep fighting all those problems and graduate. CAPS gave me people to talk to and let me know that I wasn't the only one. I learned a lot about parenting from my CAPS counselor. It was so important to have friends that were in the same situation that I was in, people who understood exactly what I was feeling."

Latricia's case manager was aware of the Crittenton program that goes into high schools and meets with pregnant or parenting teens to provide a support group. She was the one who recommended that Latricia get involved with the program.

Latricia credits the CAPS program coordinator with much of her success. "She just kept asking me, 'What are you going to do after high school, Latricia?—what are your plans after high school, Latricia?'" With a high school diploma and a 4-year-old son, Latricia decided on a plan. "I want to work to be a registered nurse. I am going to try to get a job in a nursing home to start with, and then I am going to take CNA classes and I want to be a nurse eventually."

This case example is one of many with clear implications of the need for a comprehensive child welfare policy. Without such a policy, thousands of children who could profit from interventions become statistics of poverty and despair.

In this chapter, we have seen how children and families in the United States are supported through the administration of a number of services. Much of the support, however, is residual in nature and thus available to only a segment of the population. We have provided comparisons between the United States and other Western industrialized nations to demonstrate the efficacy of universal policies in child welfare.

According to the study *America's Children: Key National Indicators of Well-Being*, childhood poverty has both immediate and lasting negative effects (Federal Interagency Forum on Child and Family Statistics, 2003). Children in low-income families fare far less well than children in more affluent families for many of the indicators presented in this chapter, including health and education. Children living in families who are poor are more likely than children in other families to have difficulty in school, to become teen parents, and to earn less and be unemployed more frequently as adults. A comprehensive social policy, with support and services available to all children and families, would yield valuable benefits for our society.

REFERENCES

Abecedarian Experiment. (1991). *Early learning, later success: The Abecedarian study* (Early Childhood Educational Intervention for Poor Children, Executive Summary). Retrieved January 5, 2004, from www.fpg.unc.edu/%7Eabc/summary.cfm

Carnegie Task Force on Meeting the Needs of Young Children. (1994). *Starting points: Meeting the needs of our youngest children.* New York: Carnegie Corporation.

Child Welfare League of America (CWLA). (1998). *CWLA standards of excellence for services for adolescent pregnancy prevention, pregnant adolescents and young parents.* (Rev. ed.) Washington, DC: Child Welfare League of America.

Children's Defense Fund. (2002). Support for both parents and single-parent families. Retrieved January 27, 2005, from www.childrensdefense.org

Children's Defense Fund. (2004). *Family income: Income support and welfare* (Basic facts on welfare, February 2004). Retrieved January 27, 2005, from www.childrensdefense.org/familyincome/welfare/basicfacts.asp

Currie, J. (2000). *Early childhood intervention programs: What do we know?* (Brookings Roundtable on Children). Retrieved October 24, 2004, from www.brookings.edu/dybdocroot/es/research/projects/cr/doc/currie20000401.htm

David and Lucile Packard Foundation. (1999). When school is out. *The Future of Children, 9*(2).

Federal Interagency Forum on Child and Family Statistics. (2003). *America's children: Key national indicators of well-being.* Washington, DC: U.S. Government Printing Office.

Florence Crittenton Agencies. (2000). CAPS participant graduates from high school. Retrieved September 9, 2005, from www.discoveret.org/fca/success1.html

Grason, H., Aliza, B., Hutchins, V. L., Guyer, B., & Minkovitz, C. (1999, June). Pediatrician-led community child health initiatives: Case summaries from the evaluation of the community access to child health program. *Pediatrics, 103*(6), 1394–1419.

Hawaii's Healthy Start:
   Descriptive and empirical information: www.kapiolani.org/facilities/programs-hfsc.html
   Evaluation of Hawaii's Healthy Start program: www.rwjf.org/app/rw_grant_results_reports/rw_grr/018303.htm
   Good description of Healthy Start: www.casanet.org/library/abuse/hawaii-hsp.htm
   Describes Healthy Start and other early childhood programs, including Early Head Start: www.fsswh.org/annual/7.htm
   Describes nationwide Healthy Start Initiative, with state-by-state links: www.healthystart.net/hsinitiative/in00.htm

Heatherington, E. (1999). *Coping with divorce, single parenting and remarriage: A risk and resiliency perspective.* Hillsdale, NJ: Erlbaum.

Home visiting: Recent program evaluations (Executive summary). (1999, Spring–Summer). *The Future of Children, 9*(1).

Iwaniec, D. (1997). Evaluating parent training for emotionally abusive and neglectful parents: Comparing individual versus individual and group intervention. *Research on Social Work Practice, 7*(3), 329–349.

Kamerman, Sheila B., & Kahn, Alfred J. (1995). *Starting right: How America neglects its youngest children and what we can do about it.* New York: Oxford University Press.

Kaufman, T. (1996). *Housing America's future: Children at risk.* Washington, DC: National Low-Income Housing Coalition.

Life Sciences Research Office and American Institute of Nutrition. (1990). *Core indicators of nutritional state for difficult to sample populations.* Bethesda, MD: Life Sciences Research Office and American Institute of Nutrition.

Martin, J. A., Hamilton, B. E., Sutton, P. D., Ventura, S. J., Menacker, F., & Munson, M. L. (2003). Births: Final data for 2002. *National Vital Statistics Reports 52*(10).

Miller, B. (2000, June). *Update of the National Childcare Survey of 1990.* Wellesley, MA: National Institute on Out-of-School Time.

Mott Foundation/J. C. Penney. (2000). Nationwide survey on after-school programs. Retrieved September 9, 2005, from www.afterschoolalliance.org

National Center for Health Statistics. (2000). *Advance data from vital and health statistics* (no. 323). Hyattsville, MD: Public Health Services.

National Commission on Children. (1991). *Beyond rhetoric: A new American agenda for children and families.* Washington, DC: U.S. Government Printing Office.

O'Hare, W., & Mather, M. (2003). *The growing number of kids in severely distressed neighborhoods: Evidence from the 2000 census.* Baltimore, MD: Annie E. Casey Foundation and Population Reference Bureau. Available online: www.aecf.org

Ramey, C. T., & Campbell, F. A. (1991). Poverty, early childhood education, and academic competence: The Abecedarian experiment. In A. Huston (Ed.), *Children reared in poverty* (pp. 190–221). New York: Cambridge University Press.

Schorr, L. (1988). *Within our reach.* New York: Doubleday.

Seppanen, S., Kaplan de Vries, D., & Seligson, M. (1993). *National study of before- and after-school programs.* Washington, DC: U.S. Department of Education, Office of Policy and Planning.

Sonenstein, F., Gates, G., Schmidt, S., & Boshun, N. (2002). Primary childcare arrangements of employed parents: Finds from the National Survey of America's Families (*Assessing the New Federalism,* Occasional Paper no. 59). Washington, DC: Urban Institute.

U.S. Administration for Children, Youth, and Families. (1999). *Head Start fact sheet 1998.* Washington, DC: Head Start Bureau. Retrieved January 27, 2005, from www.acf.hhs.gov/programs/hsb/research/hsreac/1999report/index.htm

U.S. Administration for Children, Youth, and Families. (2003). *Early childhood intervention programs: What do we know?* Retrieved October 10, 2004, from www.acf.hhs.gov/programs/hsb/about/generalinformation/index.htm

U.S. Department of Health and Human Services. (1999). *Evaluating Head Start: A recommended framework for studying the impact of the Head Start Program.* Washington, DC: Head Start Bureau. Retrieved January 27, 2005, from www.acf.hhs.gov/programs/hsb/research/hsreac/1999report/index.htm

U.S. Department of Health and Human Services. (2000). *Second chance homes: Providing services for teenage parents and their children.* Retrieved October 6, 2005, from http://aspe.hhs.gov/hsp/2ndchancehomes00

U.S. General Accounting Office. (1997, May). *Welfare reform: Implications of increased work participation for childcare* (GAO/HEHS-97-75). Washington, DC: U.S. Government Printing Office.

U.S. Office of Special Education Programs, Child Find. (2005). *What is child find?* Retrieved September 9, 2005, from www.childfindIDEA.org/overview.htm

U.S. Surgeon General. (2000). *Mental health: A report of the Surgeon General—Executive summary.* Rockville, MD: U.S. Department of Health and Human Services, Substance Abuse and Mental Health Services Administration, Center for Mental Health Services, National Institutes of Health, National Institute of Mental Health.

Willis, E., Malloy, M., & Kliegman, R. M. (2000, December). Welfare reform consequences for children: The Wisconsin experience. *Pediatrics, 106*(6), e83. Retrieved April 10, 1999, from http://pediatrics.aappublications.org

Working for children and families: Safe and smart afterschool programs. (2000). Washington, DC: U.S. Departments of Education and Justice.

Zigler, E., & Styfco, Sally J. (1993, October–November). An earlier Head Start: Planning an intervention program for economically disadvantaged families and children ages zero to three. *Zero to Three, 14*(1), 25.

CHAPTER **7**

Services to Families and Children at Home

with Joseph Gianesin and Joyce Lee Taylor

S ervices to families and children at home are one part of the continuum of child welfare services. The child protective investigation process often identifies families that are at risk but in which the safety of the child is not threatened to the extent that he or she needs to be removed from the care of the parents. In this chapter, we explore some of the typical services offered to these families. They are offered on a voluntary basis but also, in some instances, court ordered. We will look at four kinds of services to families at risk whose children remain in the home: (1) ongoing child protective services; (2) wraparound services; (3) home-based services; and (4) family preservation services.

First, though, let's examine how current legislation stipulates competing mandates—mandates that child welfare social workers must understand and keep in mind. We will see that the expectations of current national social policy are sometimes contradictory and thus complicate the social worker's role.

The Challenge Presented by Competing Mandates

A national policy debate has complicated the work of child welfare. Current legislation regarding child welfare has resulted in twin mandates: to protect children and to preserve families. Although everyone agrees on the importance of both mandates, how best to carry out these two goals is complicated by the very fact that the interventions that would accomplish the goal of keeping the child safe may make it impossible to preserve the family. Similarly, interventions directed toward preserving the family may not be successful in keeping the child safe. The challenge in child welfare practice is to understand the complexities that result from these twin demands and develop interventions to achieve the two goals of protecting children and preserving families. In this chapter, we examine the methods and resources a child welfare agency uses to improve the level of care a child receives without breaking up the family.

As noted in Chapter 2, four major federal laws reflect societal beliefs regarding the importance of child safety and family preservation:

- The Child Abuse Prevention and Treatment Act (CAPTA) of 1974 (Public Law 100-294) provided a mandate that states enact legislation to require the reporting of known or suspected instances of child abuse and neglect.
- The Adoption Assistance and Child Welfare Act of 1980 (Public Law 96-272) promoted permanency planning by encouraging the return of children from foster care to their biological families or other permanent placement through adoption.
- The Family Preservation and Support Program was passed in 1993 as part of the Omnibus Budget Reconciliation Act to support, through fiscal incentives, family preservation programs.
- The Adoption and Safe Families Act was enacted in 1997 to reemphasize the importance of keeping children safe.

An analysis of these four laws suggests that the legislative pendulum swings back and forth between emphasizing the safety of the child and the preservation of the family. The Child Abuse Prevention and Treatment Act focused on the need to identify abused and neglected children, but one of the unintended consequences of this legislation was the large and continually increasing numbers of reports to public child welfare agencies. Workers responded by employing the traditional child welfare services, such as foster care, day treatment, and residential placement. As more children were placed in foster care and studies documented that many children languished in the foster care system, new legislation was necessary to redirect the practice focus from out-of-home placement to permanency planning.

That new legislation was the Adoption Assistance and Child Welfare Act of 1980. This child welfare reform law uses funding incentives and procedural requirements to promote placement prevention and permanency planning. This law emphasizes the importance of placing children in foster care only when necessary and specifies goals of either returning the child home or seeking permanent placement in permanent foster care or adoptive families.

The widespread enthusiasm for family preservation services was the result of an awareness that child welfare services needed to be broadened considerably if abused and neglected children and their families were to be served in their own homes whenever possible and served in a meaningful, comprehensive, and coordinated fashion. The family preservation movement gained considerable momentum during the 1980s, with the promise of offering real options to out-of-home placement.

The Family Preservation and Support Program was passed in 1993. Empirical evidence found that outcomes for home-based programs varied, with some children experiencing continuous injury and even death. Examples were common in newspaper reports about children who were abused or suffered maltreatment while under the care and service delivery of a family support program. This resulted in a refinement in policy through the enactment of the Adoption and Safe Families Act of 1997, renamed the Promoting Safe and Stable Families Act. This law provides funding for family preservation programs yet also emphasizes that the safety of children is of paramount importance and must be considered in planning interventions. Another aspect of the 1997 legislation is concurrent planning: At the same time that reunification services are implemented, the child welfare agencies should be developing an alternative backup plan to provide the child with stability and permanence, should reunification fail.

The conundrum of keeping children safe and preserving families whenever possible requires the development of a comprehensive continuum of services appropriate to the needs of each child and family. When a risk assessment profile (as discussed in Chapter 4) indicates that home-based services are the most appropriate to improve the care of the child and strengthen the parents' capacity to care for the child effectively, the continuum of home-based services should include ongoing child protective supervision, family-centered services, family support, and intensive family preservation services. The assessment of risk and the appropriateness of the services for the specific child and family must guide the intervention. Too often, however, the most appropriate services are not available. In many communities, funding shortages translate to limited services for families. As a result, children and families are often referred to services that are a less-than-ideal match for their needs.

Ongoing Child Protective Supervision

Continuing or ongoing child protective supervision is designed to prevent future instances of child abuse and neglect in families that have been investigated by child protective services and deemed at risk. According to the *Children's Bureau Fact Sheet*, from the U.S. Department of Health and Human Services (2002), approximately 58 percent, or an estimated 528,000 child victims, received postinvestigation services in 2001. Of the children who were not found to be victims of maltreatment, 28.8 percent, or an estimated 629,000 children, received postinvestigation services. This compares to 2000 figures of 55.4 percent and 18.7 percent, respectively. The increased figure for nonvictims who received postinvestigation services was due in part to increased accuracy in reporting. Nineteen percent of the victims were removed from their homes (U.S. DHHS, 2001).

In most child protective service agencies, a continuum of services is offered to families identified as having risk factors for abuse and neglect. In many of the agencies, when a report of abuse is received, the child welfare worker is assigned the task of making an assessment of risk factors. For those cases in which child maltreatment is substantiated, caseworkers are assigned to monitor cases and provide ongoing protective supervision. For example, a review of Maryland's Carroll County Social Services reveals that a total of 181 families received in-home family services in 2002. The greatest percentage of services provided—to 78 of 181 families—were continuing or ongoing child protective services (Carroll County Department of Social Services, 2003).

We can best illustrate how ongoing and continuing child protective supervision functions by providing a case example from the Department of Children and Families in the Northeast. Let's call the child William Anderson.

William is 7 years old, the child of Greg and Allison Anderson. William's teacher notices bruises and red marks on his arms and legs and refers him to the school social worker. When questioned, William discloses that his mother was upset with him and punished him by striking him. The school social worker is familiar with William, for he has been referred before for pushing his classmates to the ground and punching and clawing them. These severe attacks are unpredictable and occur even if the teacher or another staff person is nearby. William has caused visible injuries (bruises and scratches) to several children and hits his teacher when she intervenes. The school has suspended William twice, and other parents have demanded his removal from school.

William's parents reported in a recent meeting that William is physically aggressive toward his 2-year-old sister and excessively argumentative and destructive at home. The parents reported that they use corporal punishment and that they are frustrated over the lack of responsiveness by William to their parenting techniques. William's pediatrician recently diagnosed him with attention-deficit hyperactivity disorder (ADHD).

Based on mandated reporting legislation, the school social worker reports the suspected abuse of William to the state Department of Children and Families (DCF). When the DCF social worker, Kathy Simpson, arrives at the home, Mrs. Anderson says her husband, Greg, isn't at home— that he's a painter and works all the time. Mrs. Anderson adds that

Greg has a hard time with outsiders interfering with his family. She sobs as she describes the events from the night before, saying that she and her husband love their child but are very frustrated with his recent aggressive behavior. According to his mother, William has no history of mental health hospitalizations or outpatient treatment but receives medication from his pediatrician. She digs the bottle of Ritalin out of her purse as she admits that she and her husband are having great difficulty in managing William's behavior. Again, she breaks down and cries as she admits that she and her husband are sometimes too forceful in their punishment of William.

Kathy Simpson describes the process of child protective services to Mrs. Anderson. She informs the mother that corporal punishment is not against the law but that if any marks are left on the child, it constitutes child abuse. Ms. Simpson asks the mother if she is interested in learning different parenting techniques that might be more effective with her son. The social worker recommends that she visit the Anderson family on a weekly basis to provide ongoing child protective supervision. The specific services she recommends are parenting classes in managing children diagnosed with ADHD, a home-based parent aide to model child management techniques, and her ongoing weekly visits to monitor the family's progress. Mrs. Anderson agrees to accept the services and promises that her husband will be available at the next meeting.

Not long after the services begin, Kathy Simpson receives a call from Mrs. Anderson. She can barely hear the words as Mrs. Anderson sobs into the phone: "Forget about the services; he can't live here. Take William to go to a boarding school . . . or hospital . . . or wherever he'll get the help he needs. We thought we could handle it ourselves, but we can't."

Without hesitation, Kathy Simpson tells Mrs. Anderson that she will be right over and that a team (Emergency Mobile Psychiatric Services, or EMPS) will also be dispatched to her home. Mrs. Anderson agrees. The EMPS team arrives shortly after Kathy Simpson. William is somewhat active but polite and agreeable to sitting and talking quietly with the EMPS clinician. Ms. Simpson and the clinician know from experience that one moment of orderly behavior does not discount violent behavior ten days ago or aggression a few hours later. William's history of behavior portrays a pattern of escalating aggression and violence, and his mental health needs have not been addressed.

The EMPS clinician assesses the child and consults with the program's psychiatrist. They determine that William is not currently at risk of harming himself or others—that he does not need immediate placement in a crisis stabilization bed or ambulance transport to the emergency room. The EMPS arranges for a behavioral health appointment the next day and will continue short-term clinical intervention, medication assessment, and medication management (meaning they will stay abreast of William's progress and adjust dosages accordingly). Intensive in-home therapeutic services are also implemented.

Ms. Simpson consults with her supervisor and child welfare colleagues about strengthening the services to William and his family. The team comes up with a plan:

1. Behavior management will be addressed via intensive in-home services and respite services (through a private agency that has a contract with DCF).
2. An educational evaluation will be requested from William's school.
3. A supervised therapeutic after-school program will be provided for William.

Mr. and Mrs. Anderson agree to accept the revised plan. During the course of the next few weeks, they feel that they lose their privacy because so many people come to their home. On the other hand, they look forward to the respite worker's twice-a-week visits and to the ongoing weekly contacts with Ms. Simpson. William is no longer physically violent and has made small gains toward self-control, but he also experiences periods of intense tantrums. Mr. Anderson cut back his working hours so he can spend more time with William. Over a period of focusing on meeting daily behavioral goals, Mr. and Mrs. Anderson present William with rewards and praise. Occasionally, as a treat, Mr. Anderson plays ball with William and even takes him to a couple of professional games.

By the end of July, William is doing so well that the behaviorist and respite workers worked toward terminating services. William continues with the therapeutic after-school program. The caseworker recommends that William's parents send him to baseball camp, which is coordinated by the local town parks and recreation department. He does well meeting new peers, without even one tantrum during the week of camp, so his parents become confident that he will handle school in a more positive manner.

Once school resumes, the teacher and school social worker rejoin the child-specific team. By late September, William is doing so well that the care coordinator releases the case. In October, William is discharged from the extended-day treatment program because he has accomplished his clinical goals. He is subsequently connected with an ongoing psychiatrist and therapist. When Kathy Simpson suggests that it is time to close the voluntary services case, Mr. Anderson exclaims, "He's not perfect, but he's doing so much better!" Mrs. Anderson says, "And we can always call you if we need you, right?" Kathy Simpson nods and smiles, for she has seen a change in William's parents—a good sign that William will continue to do better.

William Anderson's mental health needs were addressed by child protective services in a well-coordinated way. His parents came to have more confidence in their ability to parent William and to navigate the mental health care network. The initial child abuse report was addressed without removing the child from his family. The ongoing child protective supervision was necessary to reduce William's risk of being abused again. Although the outlook was at first grim, ongoing child protective services helped William and his family learn healthier ways to interact.

Wraparound Services

Wraparound services for children gained attention in the 1990s as a means of addressing a problem. Many children were receiving services from mental health, child welfare, schools, and perhaps other community service providers, but there was little or no coordination between the different services. Parents and children were confused by multiple conflicting goals and demands. Service providers struggled with their lack of agreement on target populations, financial challenges, liability, and coordination of resources. Families that were not system savvy became frustrated and angry and perhaps withdrew from services.

Collaboration between service providers results in wraparound services, a key trend in child protective services. According to the U.S. Department of Health and Human Services (2000) National Survey of Children and Adolescent Well-Being, child welfare providers identified increased collaboration among child service agencies as one of the

The wraparound service approach seeks to coordinate the activities and goals of child protective services with those of other providers, including the children's schools.

most promising developments in child welfare. Approximately 90 percent of state administrators reported formal collaboration with at least one other service provider.

In contrast to the traditional child welfare practice of removing the abused child from the family and offering structured services within the limits of narrow, categorical funding strategies, wraparound services promote the concept of a coordinated community team that keeps the needs of the child at the forefront of the discussion. The team consists of key community stakeholders engaged in providing services and supports for children and families.

According to VanDenBerg and Grealish (1996), the wraparound process has emerged as a viable option to a categorical services approach. With the current policy focus on keeping the child with the family whenever possible, the wraparound approach is especially beneficial. It employs a new philosophical attitude. Service providers coordinate services around the needs of the child, thus enabling him or her to remain in the care of the parents.

The wraparound philosophy requires agencies and organizations to change the way in which they have conducted service delivery for decades. Instead of offering services independently, agencies have begun to implement variations that include changes in the organization of service. Clark and Clarke (1996) describe the principles of the wraparound process: a least-restrictive, community-based service delivery environment; interagency coordination and integration of services; family- and child-centered care; flexible, unconditional service delivery; and highly individualized needs-based services.

These authors advocate child-based services that are well coordinated, rather than duplicative.

VanDenBerg and Grealish (1996) also describe the essential components of the wraparound approach. The primary component is the establishment of a community team that comprises all major public and private agencies in the schools and the social services, juvenile justice, mental health, and health care systems. A team perspective can best garner the resources and services for the child. The parents are viewed as active members of the team and as a resource, rather than hostile or resistant clients.

Optimal implementation of the wraparound process requires linkages between agencies. A continuum of care and flexibility in funding sources serves both the community and the individual child and family more effectively. Turf issues within an agency need to be overcome. The children and families in need of wraparound services generally have very complex needs and problems that can best be addressed via coordinated solutions. We saw this in our case example. William Anderson's aggressive behavior escalated and required many services: from the mental health system, the educational system, and child welfare's ongoing child protective services. When we implement interagency care, we create flexibility in the delivery of services.

Rosenblatt (1996) reports that many state social service agencies now contract out services to private agencies. The services are targeted to youth with multisystem needs, many of whom have had damaging experiences with prior service systems. Conscientious child welfare advocates see the potential and promise in providing a well-coordinated approach in conjunction with parents. Effective implementation requires all of the members of the community team to work cooperatively. This is often hard when public and private agencies compete for funding and a limited number of resources in the community.

Effective services require interagency collaboration at the child-specific level—agencies working together to meet one child's service needs. Whether there are 3 or 23 entities working with the child, each of them should be willing to adjust its involvement to help the child reach his or her fullest potential. At the macro level, agencies need to work together to create a helping network. Doing so is the best way to assure that all children in the community have access to quality services.

Home-Based Services

The Children's Bureau of the U.S. Department of Health and Human Services (2002) groups home-based services in two categories: preventive and postinvestigative. *Preventive services* are designed to increase the understanding of parents and other caregivers of the developmental stages of childhood and improve childrearing competencies. *Postinvestigative services* are offered on a voluntary basis by child welfare agencies or ordered by the court to ensure the safety of the child.

Throughout the text of this book, we note many instances of when and why a child welfare social worker makes home visits. In this section, we turn our focus to the home-based components in the continuum of services to families.

Homemaker Services

Homemakers (or *home health aides*) have been important constituents of child protective services for decades. Typically, they are used in times of crisis. Homemakers are trained to provide child care and a wide variety of homemaking and home management services. The concept behind these services is the belief that whenever possible, it is desirable and preferable to care for children in their own homes.

Homemakers provide (1) preventive care (child care, cooking, and cleaning), (2) educational assistance (including teaching and coaching), and (3) protective or therapeutic assistance. Some programs define the homemaker service differently—namely, as being closely related to the parent aide function.

Homemaker services are cost effective when compared with the costs of out-of-home placement alternatives, which in the absence of homemaker services may be the only option. Although homemaker services continue to be regarded as an important service on the continuum of home-based services, they are not available in all communities. Homemaker services are more often available in urban areas. They may be provided by public or private agencies.

Before we move on to coverage of parent aide programs, we want to emphasize again that the names of the home-based service providers differ in different programs. The efficacy of the programs, however, whatever their names, is unquestioned. As an example, let's look at child protection in one state to see how home-based services are used.

Our example comes from Arizona's Child Protective Services (2001). In cases in which child abuse was substantiated in 2001, more than half of the families received home-based services. Parent aides provided coaching on parenting techniques and education on such topics as preparing meals and family budgeting. In cases that were closed after an investigation because the children were not found to be at imminent risk for abuse, families were assigned a parent aide for short-term support services. The homemaker services included caring for the children when a parent was incapacitated (due to physical or mental illness) or for some other reason was unable to provide care and assisting a family in which a child had a long-term illness. The home-based service providers made it possible for children to be cared for in their own homes.

Parent Aide Programs

During the 1970s, *parent aide programs* were developed throughout the U.S. Parent aides nurture abusing and neglecting parents and serve as role models to maximize the possibility that abusive parents can continue to care for their children in their own homes. Some programs use volunteers; others employ paid paraprofessionals. All programs provide services to families in their own homes and by telephone. Generally, parent aide programs are operated by the private sector. Public child welfare agencies may have established contractual arrangements with these private providers.

According to the National Parent Aide Network (2002), *parent aides* are professionally trained individuals who become friends and role models to parents who need help in dealing with life's daily challenges. "Parent aides provide support and encouragement and demonstrate the normal ways of parenting, serve as an outside social control to stop abuse immediately, and address special needs of the family by referring them to community resources" (National Parent Aide Network, 2000).

Helfer, Kempe, and Krugman (1997) used parent aide programs with abusing and neglectful families in 1969 at Colorado Hospital. The primary focus was to have the parent aide serve as a nonjudgmental friend to abusing and neglecting parents.

Parent aide programs are utilized extensively by child protection agencies because they can provide a valuable service at an economical cost. Paraprofessionals who staff these positions assist with parenting, household management, social support, and linkage to community resources such as employment, education, and transportation. Maryland's Carroll County Department of Social Services (2003) indicates that of the total number of 181 families who received in-home family services in 2002, 42 families received parent aide services.

We conclude our discussion of home-based services with the following case illustration. It shows how parent aide programs work and how effective they can be.

The local school system reported Susan Cox to child protective services (CPS) for reasons of educational neglect. The investigator assigned to the case, Sheri Trivane, BSW, received only basic information—the family's address and a list of family members: Susan Cox (mother), Peter Cox (15-year-old son), and Rachel Cox (12-year-old daughter). The school reported that Peter had missed 15 days in the first semester of the eighth grade. Rachel missed 10 days in October. Ms. Trivane, with eight years of job experience, knew that reports of educational neglect were at the lower end of the risk continuum. She also knew that helping a family meant beginning with a thorough investigation of circumstances—circumstances that often led far beyond the initial reasons for referral.

During an unannounced visit to the Cox home, Sheri Trivane gathered information to assess the family's strengths and difficulties. Susan Cox was aware of the school's report but surprised that the state had sent a social worker to her home. She explained that she struggled with Peter every morning and was at her wit's end. She tried to reward him for going to school, offering to make his favorite dinner on Friday if he had a perfect week. Rachel's absences were due, she said, to a case of mononucleosis in October. "If the school wanted a doctor's note, why didn't they ask? Now, I find out like this, two weeks before Christmas? Everything goes from bad to worse." Mrs. Cox's anger at the school prompted Ms. Trivane to explain mandated reporting laws.

Ms. Trivane complimented Mrs. Cox on her home and asked for a tour. The fairly large three-bedroom house was adequately heated yet furnished with barely more than necessities: a bed and dresser in each of the bedrooms, a table and chairs in the kitchen, a television on the floor in the larger bedroom, and a couch in the living room before a small television on top of a milk crate. Boxes were stacked on the kitchen countertop. Ms. Trivane spotted kitchen utensils, paper towels, dry goods, and canned goods in some of the open boxes.

Mrs. Cox seemed embarrassed. With tears in her eyes, she said, "I am packing. We have lived here for almost 10 years, but I just got separated. My husband told us we had to be out in three weeks. Perfect timing! We're being evicted the week between Christmas and New Year."

Ms. Trivane, sensing Mrs. Cox's desire to talk about her problems, said, "You mentioned earlier that your family has come into some hard times."

Mrs. Cox said she had no idea where they'd move. "I'm really stressed out. Where will I get a security deposit in three weeks? How will I even afford a U-Haul? Where will I find an apartment in town so that the kids won't have to change schools? I only make minimum wage. Even if I can't count on getting child support on a regular basis, thank heaven the kids are covered by their father's health insurance. You know, he owns his own company."

The social worker reassured Mrs. Cox: If she would be receptive to service providers, together they could help the family regain some stability. Ms. Trivane explained the types of services available and recommended a parent aide to provide emotional support and concrete assistance in the home three times a week. She recommended a mental health assessment for Peter, counseling for Mrs. Cox, and ongoing protective services supervision, which would mean she would visit every two weeks.

Over the next several weeks, the parent aide helped Mrs. Cox establish a daily behavioral chart system. Peter was seen by a therapist, and a psychiatrist prescribed Zoloft for his depression. Mrs. Cox called Rachel's doctor for documentation of the child's illness in October. The parent aide accompanied Mrs. Cox to meetings with the school. This was the first time that Mrs. Cox had met the children's teachers in person, although she had spoken with them via notes and phone calls. With the parent aide, Mrs. Cox requested a special education evaluation for Peter.

Mrs. Trivane noted that Peter's treatment needs were being met and that Mrs. Cox was gaining skills in addressing his behaviors. She advised the parent aide to connect Mrs. Cox with legal aide services. Although there was a waiting list at legal aide for an attorney to work specifically with the divorce case, the legal clinic made Mrs. Cox aware of her rights and advised her about filing papers, which resulted in immediate relief from the courts concerning her pending "eviction." She received a hearing date in January regarding *pendente lite* orders. Mrs. Cox went back to the legal clinic the following week to ask questions about the upcoming court hearing.

While Mrs. Cox spoke with her counselor about coping with stress, she revealed a past history of emotional and physical abuse by her ex-husband. Then she admitted severe guilt because she could no longer afford the luxuries the children had once enjoyed, such as brand-name clothing, vacations, and outings to restaurants. She also felt guilty that the children experienced rejection from their father, who regularly canceled visits. Rachel and Peter had not seen their father in two months.

Mrs. Cox told the parent aide that she liked going to see the counselor but subsequently made excuses to cancel. The first time she used the excuse that she didn't like leaving her teenaged children at home alone for an hour. The second time she canceled due to bad weather, as it was raining and there was a forecast of a 10 percent chance of flurries.

Fortunately, Ms. Trivane is a skillful social worker. She suggested, "Let's list all the pros and cons of going to counseling." Mrs. Cox articulated several aspects of her personal life that she would like to discuss with the counselor as the "pros". On the list of "cons", Mrs. Cox listed issues of time, cost, and difficulty trusting the counselor. Regarding time, Ms.

Trivane stressed the importance of emotional strength by pointing out that Mrs. Cox must first take care of herself in order to take good care of the children. Regarding cost, she explained that the community mental health center determined the amount a client would pay based on wages—a sliding scale fee. Lastly, Ms. Trivane addressed the trust issue: "It takes quite a while to develop a trusting relationship with a counselor, but what in particular are you afraid of happening?"

Mrs. Cox replied, "The counselor explained that she's a mandated reporter, and I'm not worried about that. I'm certainly not going to hurt the kids or myself. I know that she said everything else would be completely confidential, but . . . what if he finds out? I also feel bad saying bad things about him. He is still my husband until we get divorced."

Ms. Trivane reassured her about the counselor's professional confidentiality and encouraged her to talk openly with the counselor about her fears. Mrs. Cox went back to see her counselor the next Tuesday and continued weekly sessions long after Ms. Trivane closed the child protective services case.

The parent aide's work spanned over the next six months. The parent aide maintained close contact with the Cox family and kept the child welfare office informed through an ongoing dialogue that included consultations, updates, and recommendations. Case goals and plans were synchronized, with consistent communication between the providers and the family. Mrs. Cox and her home aide developed a trusting relationship. Their talks eased Mrs. Cox's stress and helped her gain the strength she needed to deal with Peter and Rachel's needs, make decisions about housing, and manage the variety of daily challenges she faced as head of her household.

The parent aide also helped Mrs. Cox learn to utilize community resources. The legal aid attorney was eventually assigned. It was too late to prevent foreclosure, due to Mr. Cox's default on the mortgage, so Mrs. Cox did eventually have to leave her house. She moved into a small, affordable apartment. The attorney had Mr. Cox's wages garnished for weekly child support. The parent aide helped Mrs. Cox develop a reasonable budget that made every penny count. At the parent aide's case closing meeting, Mrs. Cox volunteered her self-assessment: She could now cope on her own because she had gained better problem-solving skills.

Family Preservation Services

When a child is deemed at high risk for placement in foster care, family preservation services go into effect. The family receives intensive professional services and greater frequency of home visits either by the child protective agency or a contracted agency. *Family preservation services* are family-centered placement prevention services designed to prevent unnecessary out-of-home placement. According to a report from Westat, the University of Chicago, and Bell Associates (2001), since the early 1970s the term "family preservation" has been used to describe a variety of programs that are intended to provide services to children and families who are experiencing serious problems that may eventually lead to the placement of children in foster care or otherwise result in the dissolution of the family unit.

The family preservation approach recognizes that a child's own family usually offers the best chance for a happy, stable future.

The concept of family preservation services was endorsed and encouraged at the federal level due to the Adoption Assistance and Child Welfare Act of 1980, which requires states to make reasonable efforts to prevent children from entering foster care and to reunify children who were placed out of the home with their families. The development of family preservation programs became a major focus of policy and planning in state child welfare systems. In 1993, the Family Preservation and Family Support budgeting provision further encouraged states to develop such programs. In 1997, the enactment of the Adoption and Safe Families Act renewed emphasis on safety, permanency, and adoption.

Family Preservation Models

Three primary models of family preservation programs have been developed, and many child welfare experts have categorized the models. Nelson, Landsman, and Deutelbaum (1990) describe three primary family preservation program models: (1) the crisis intervention model, (2) the home-based model, and (3) the family treatment model.

Homebuilders, a crisis intervention model, was started in the state of Washington in 1974 as an alternative to foster care. It rests on the assumption that families are more likely to be open to change during a crisis. The FAMILIES program also began in 1974 in Iowa. It provides home-based support and is based on family systems theory. Oregon's Intensive Family Services Program is based on a family treatment model. It relies less on the provision of concrete and supportive services and more on family therapy (Westat et al., 2001). These national program models contributed to a shift in child welfare policy and resulted in the development of a National Clearinghouse for Home-Based Services that began in 1977 at the University of Iowa and later became the National Resource Center on Family Based Services (Nelson & Landsman, 1992).

The distinctions among the three models may seem relatively minor. Each one, however, was a new intervention at the time it was established and made important contributions to preventing out-of-home placements. The collective contributions of these models helped advance thinking and resources in the child welfare field. Many programs have since been modeled on these early ones.

CRISIS INTERVENTION MODEL   The *crisis intervention model* operates on the assumption that families are more likely to be open to change during a crisis—when they are experiencing extreme discomfort and discovering that family coping mechanisms can no longer maintain family stability and independence. According to the National Coalition for Child Protection Reform (1997), these types of programs go into operation when a family is in crisis. They are designed for intervention with families whose children face imminent removal to foster care. The intervention is short (usually six weeks) but extremely intense.

A team of professionals that includes a social worker, psychologist, and parent aide is assigned to the case. Workers usually have caseloads of only three families and spend several hours every day with a family. Services are delivered primarily in the home, allowing the social worker to model behavior in a realistic setting (Kinney, Haapala, Booth, & Leavitt, 1988). The social worker is usually trained at the bachelor's level and supervised by a worker with a master's degree in social work (MSW). The social worker is available by phone 24 hours a day until the crisis subsides.

Family preservation workers, such as those in the Homebuilders program, help families find day care and job training and help them get the special education services their children may require. They teach practical skills and help with financial problems. Family preservation workers will even roll up their sleeves and help with the cleaning. These short-term, home-based interventions are designed to improve parenting skills, improve family living conditions, and create new coping skills that foster family independence. When the intensive intervention ends, the local child welfare agency continues to provide less intensive support to help the family maintain the gains they have made.

HOME-BASED MODEL　The founders of FAMILIES believe that families experiencing difficulty can only improve when all members of the family are engaged in the change process. FAMILIES serves as an alternative to out-of-home placement for adolescents. It is based on *family systems theory*, which emphasizes the family as the locus for change. This emphasis translates to a different strategy than the usual identification of one person as the major focus of intervention (often, an acting-out adolescent).

Family preservation workers in FAMILIES and home-based programs like it pay attention to (1) the family as a whole, (2) subsystems within the family, and (3) the family's interaction with its community. Staff members use a variety of approaches from family systems theory. For example, in making the comprehensive family assessment, the social worker employs genograms to clarify intergenerational patterns and interactions. Families often participate in setting their own treatment goals and provide their own perspectives on the family's strengths and weaknesses. The service providers in these programs include bachelor's-level and MSW-level social workers. Caseloads are kept small—usually, 5 to 11 cases per worker. According to a U.S. Department of Health and Human Services (2001) study, the Iowa Family Preservation Program provides services to an average of 3.5 families per worker for a maximum of eight weeks.

FAMILY TREATMENT MODEL　Family preservation programs built on this model rely on a theoretical view that says problems occurring with an individual family member, such as a runaway adolescent, are an indication of problems in the whole family. Emphasis is on providing therapy for the family. Professional family therapists work with the family in the home and in clinical settings. Sessions may last several hours, with several therapists participating in the intervention process. Such programs are modeled after Oregon's Intensive Family Services.

Case managers, parent coaches, homemakers, and other support services staff supplement the interventions of the therapists. There have been promising outcome studies with families who were treated with this approach. Outcomes have indicated that 73 percent of the families remained together 12 months after treatment and that this approach was more successful with disrupted adoption and sexual abuse cases than with neglectful families (Nelson, Landsman, & Deutelbaum, 1990).

Evaluating Family Preservation Services

The pieces of legislation mentioned early in this section made child safety and permanency planning the paramount concerns for child welfare, and this resulted, as we have seen, in family preservation programs. The U.S. Department of Health and Human Services (2001) authorized funds to evaluate family preservation and family support programs developed by the states. The 2001 report from this agency used three separate studies on family preservation in states across the country to evaluate the services. The three studies were designed to be complementary, with each one focusing on a different aspect of the 1993 legislation. But taken together, they represent a comprehensive examination of the programs authorized.

The growth in family preservation programs across the United States was due partly to early reports of positive evaluations and successes, as reported by those implementing the programs. Bath and Haapala (1994) reported unequivocally positive and high placement prevention successes. The more recent Department of Health and Human Services (2001) studies show mixed results. Although many nonexperimental studies have suggested that high percentages of families remain intact after intensive family preservation services, the results of randomized experiments are mixed. Seven of eleven studies reviewed by Littell and Schuerman (2002) found that the programs did not produce significant overall reductions in placement.

Despite these findings, family preservation and family reunification services continue as major policy initiatives across the United States. In many instances, services are provided through contracts with private agencies. Over the years, various states have adopted family preservation models, which are sometimes hybrids of the three we have described. The many differences among programs make outcome measures and the efficacy of services difficult to quantify.

Providing family preservation services has been shown to be a viable alternative to out-of-home placement. Doing so is much more cost effective than the alternative of removing the child from the home. At a time when child welfare caseloads continue to be high, family preservation interventions provide an opportunity to monitor high-risk cases in the home.

The child welfare field, like other specializations in social work, adapts to changing times and emerging research findings. Policy shifts dramatically change the climate of the work. Veteran workers with 20 years of experience speak of the swinging pendulum of policy changes: foster care drift, family preservation, permanency planning, and now concurrent planning. Putting new policies into effect can be confusing and frustrating for social workers—especially so before the corresponding shift to new resources and programs takes shape.

The child welfare community continues to work toward establishing home-based and family-centered services that match assessment with intervention, rather than merely slipping children and families into whatever services happen to be available. Although progress toward this goal continues, progress is uneven. In many communities across the country, availability and access are still major problems because of funding limitations and delays in allocating funds and adjusting budgets.

New programs cannot become the norm until we address these and other issues. Agency competition and vendor funding distribution issues must be navigated. Conflicting professional orientations and values must be addressed. The necessity for coordination must be considered in the planning and delivery of interventions. And multiple providers must find ways to clarify accountability and outcomes assessment. Chapter 11 details the importance of collaboration and collateral contacts.

REFERENCES

Arizona Child Protective Services. (March 2001). *Semi-annual report: Executive summary* (S. B. 1229) Retrieved April 15, 2004, from www.ahsc.arizona.edu/acainfo/statistics/cps01a/exec01.htm

Barth, R. P. (1990). Theories guiding home-based intensive family preservation services. In J. K. Whittaker, J. Kinney, E. M. Tracy, & C. Booth (Eds.), *Reaching high-risk families*. New York: Aldine de Gruyter.

Bath, H., & Haapala, D. (1994). Family preservation: What does the outcome research really tell us. *Social Service Review, 68*(3), 386–404.

Berry, M. (1994). Keeping families together. In S. Bruchey (Ed.), *Children of poverty: Studies of the effects of single parenthood, the feminization of poverty and homelessness*. New York: Garland.

Carroll County Department of Social Services. (2003, April 25). In-home family services. Retrieved April 27, 2004, from www.dhr.state.md.us/county/carroll/ihfs.htm

Clark, H. B., & Clarke, R. T. (1996). Research on the wraparound process and individualized services for children with multi-system needs. *Journal of Child and Family Studies, 5*(1), 1–5.

Helfer, M., Kempe, R., & Krugman, R. (1997). *The battered child* (5th ed.).Chicago: University of Chicago Press.

Kinney, J., Haapala, D., Booth, C., & Leavitt, S. (1988). The homebuilders model. In J. K. Whittaker, J. Kinney, E. M. Tracey, & C. Booth (Eds.), *Improving practice technology for work with high risk families: Lessons from the Homebuilders social work education project*. Seattle: Center for Social Welfare Research, University of Washington School of Social Work.

Littell, J. H., & Schuerman, J. R. (2002). What works best for whom? A closer look at intensive family preservation services. *Children and Services Review, 24*(9–10), 673–699.

National Coalition for Child Protection Reform. (1997, September 30). *Family preservation: What it is—and what it isn't*. Retrieved April 24, 2002, from www.joinhands.com/fostercare/family_preservation

National Parent Aide Network. (2000). Home page. Retrieved May 27, 2004, from www.preventchildabuse.com/parent.htm

Nelson, K. E., & Landsman, M. J. (1992). *Exploring child welfare: Community support—Family preservation*. Ann Arbor, MI: University of Michigan Press.

Nelson, K. E., Landsman, M. J., & Deutelbaum, W. (1990). Three models of family-centered placement prevention services. *Child Welfare, 69*(1), 3–21.

Rosenblatt, A. (1996). Bows and ribbons, tape and twine: Wrapping the wraparound process for children with multi-system needs. *Journal of Child and Family Studies, 5*(1), 101–116.

U.S. Department of Health and Human Services (U.S. DHHS), Administration for Children and Families. (2001). *Children's Bureau fact sheet* (Chapter 6, Services, Child Maltreatment). Retrieved April 27, 2004, from www.acf.dhhs.gov/programs/cb/publications/cm01/index.htm

U.S. Department of Health and Human Services (U.S. DHHS), Administration for Children and Families. (2002). *Children's Bureau fact sheet* (Chapter 6, Services, Child Maltreatment). Retrieved April 27, 2004, from www.acf.hhs.gov/programs/cb/publications/cm02/chaptersix.htm

U.S. Department of Health and Human Services (U.S. DHHS). (2000). *National survey of children and adolescent well-being.* Retrieved April 13, 2004, from www.acf. hhs.gov/programs/core/ongoingresearch/afc/wellbeingstatechild/wellbeing

VanDenBerg, J. E., & Grealish, E. M. (1996). Individualized services and supports through the wraparound process: Philosophy and procedures. *Journal of Child and Family Studies, 5*(1), 7–21.

Westat, University of Chicago Chapin Hall Center for Children, James Bell Associates. (2001, January 8). *Evaluation of family preservation and reunification programs* (An interim report submitted to the U.S. Department of Health and Human Services Assistant Secretary for Planning and Evaluation). Retrieved April 24, 2002, from www.aspe.hhs.gov/hsp/fampres94/index.htm

CHAPTER 8

Services to Families and Children with the Children in Substitute Care

Rebecca Turner

Nor, unfortunately, does there seem to be any reason for thinking that charities for caring for destitute, neglected, and delinquent children will soon become unnecessary. We learn to deal more and more wisely with those who are in distress, but the forces, which produce poverty, neglect, and crime, seem to be beyond our reach.

> The poor, the neglectful, and the vicious we shall have with us for a long time to come, and the hearts of the generous will continue to respond, both through individual and associate charity and governmental action. (Folks, 1911)

The number of children in out-of-home placements rose dramatically in a recent 15-year period: from 276,000 in 1985 to 581,000 in September 1999. Clearly, Homer Folks was correct in 1911 when he predicted that dependent children would continue to need substitute care. This chapter reviews social work services and processes in cases in which the child must be placed in substitute care, either because the risk to the child's safety is severe or the parent is unable to provide care for reasons such as death, illness, and imprisonment.

My mother's father died when she was 2, and when she was 11 years old, her mother died. Thus began for my mother and her two siblings a series of informal living arrangements with a number of relatives that lasted until she was 17, when she and her siblings emancipated themselves and lived independently, working, going to school, and taking care of one another. My mother was born in 1928, so not only was she orphaned at a young age, but she was also orphaned at an economically depressed time and long before the child welfare system had fully institutionalized substitute care for children. The practices of *placing out* and *boarding out* children—terms of the late nineteenth and early twentieth centuries to indicate ways of "caring for destitute children which differ from all the preceding, in that the children are, as a rule, boarded in private families until permanent free homes in families are found for them" (Folks, 1911, p. 150)—were new concepts in her day. For my mother and her siblings, the informal family system of caring for its dependent children was engaged. It was a system that was faulty and unstable. This was an early form of kinship care that grew out of a family's sense of responsibility for its own.

Definitions and Statistics

Foster care is generally considered to be a temporary substitute or out-of-home care for children who cannot live at home for reasons that range from abuse or neglect to parental inability to provide care and supervision due to illness or incapacity. *Foster family care* is foster care provided by individuals who are licensed by a state or county, meet minimum standards established for foster family care, and have received training in preparation for providing foster care service. *Kinship care* is foster care provided by relatives, a form of foster care that is on the increase. In some states, relatives are not required to meet licensing standards for foster family care; in others, they must meet those standards required of unrelated foster families.

Group home care is another form of foster care provided in a congregate setting. Generally, group home care is reserved for use with children of school age who cannot be served in a foster family setting. The use of group home care has declined over the years, in favor of a community-based, family-centered approach to providing services to children requiring substitute care.

A more specialized form of foster care is *therapeutic foster care (TFC)*, sometimes called *specialized foster care* or *treatment foster care*. The term refers to a foster fam-

TABLE 8.1	Placement Settings: 1998	
Setting	**Percentage of Children**	**Number of Children**
Preadoptive home	4%	22,484
Foster family home (relative)	26%	151,664
Family home (nonrelative)	47%	274,100
Group home	8%	46,279
Institution	10%	57,590
Supervised independent living	1%	4,979
Runaway	1%	7,886
Trial home visit	3%	15,818

Note: The 2003 AFCARS Report includes usable data from 49 jurisdictions, including the District of Columbia and Puerto Rico. Rounding figures results in numbers and percentages not adding up to reported totals or 100 percent.

Source: U.S. Department of Health and Human Services (2003). Available online: www.acf.hhs.gov.programs/ cb/publications/afcars/report10.htm.

ily care setting in which the providers have received training to care for children with special needs, such as a psychiatric diagnosis, an emotional or behavioral problem, or a medical condition requiring intensive and specialized care. Compared to regular foster family care, TFC homes are supported by wraparound services that support care to a limited number of foster children—usually one child, unless there is a sibling group.

Placement data can be found in the U.S. Department of Health and Human Services' (2003) AFCARS Report, the product of the Adoption and Foster Care Analysis Reporting System. Of the 542,000 children reported to be in foster care nationwide in 2001, the median age was 10.6 years. Thirty-seven percent of the children in foster care were white/non-hispanic, 33 percent were black/non-hispanic, 17 percent were Hispanic, and the remaining 8 percent were of other origins. The 2001 race and ethnicity percentages reflect increases in all categories except black/non-hispanic, which decreased by 11 percent from 44 percent in 1998. The placement settings for these children are shown in Table 8.1.

A review of these placement settings data reveals that most placement settings for children in need of substitute care were in family homes, related and unrelated. Sixty-seven percent of placement settings, or 363,140 children, were in foster family homes (U.S. DHHS, 2003). Smaller percentages reflect action toward more permanent placements for children in foster care. Four percent of the children were in preadoptive home placements, 1 percent were in supervised independent living, and another 3 percent were in trial home visits with their families, where reunification was the goal. Reported goals say almost half of the children in foster care (47 percent) have the goal of reunification with parents, relatives, or principal caregivers, 19 percent have the goal of adoption, and another 6 percent have the goal of emancipation. According to the AFCARS data, the length of stay for children in foster care was an average of 32 months, with most placements reported to be less that 24 months (47 percent).

With the average age of children entering foster care at 8.6 years and the average age of children exiting foster care at 10.3 years, it seems that most children in foster care are there for just under two years, consistent with the definition of foster care as a temporary substitute for family care. Of those children who exited foster care in 2001, most were reunited with parents (59 percent), some were placed with relatives (10 percent), some were adopted (16 percent), and others were emancipated (7 percent) (U.S. DHHS, 2003).

As positive as these outcomes are for the children who exited foster care, the number of children entering foster care continues to be higher than the number exiting foster care. For fiscal year 2001, the AFCARS data revealed that 290,000 children entered foster care while 263,000 children exited foster care, yielding a difference of 33,000 children remaining in substitute care (U.S. DHHS, 2003). Clearly, the challenge to provide temporary substitute care for children who cannot live with their families is significant.

A Brief History of Foster Care in the United States

In its early years, foster care was viewed as a permanent living arrangement for dependent children. Today, foster care is viewed, as well as defined, as a temporary form of substitute care for children. Throughout its history, foster care has experienced changes in emphasis, method, level of governmental involvement, outcome, and resources available that have influenced its practice as a way to serve children. A brief history of the development of foster care in the United States, from colonial times to the present, follows.

In colonial America, dependent children were indentured into other homes for the purpose of learning a trade. In addition, institutions called *asylums* were relied on to care for dependent children who were not indentured but were most assuredly poor. Television episodes of *Little House on the Prairie* offer an example in Albert, the young man who came to live with a family on the prairie to learn farming. Albert was one of many indentured youths who left their families in the city for greener pastures and work on the farms that were developing in the American heartland. As described in Chapter 2, the Children's Aid Society, beginning in the 1850s, devoted itself to caring for dependent children and sent impoverished urban children to western states to be placed in rural homes (Hacsi, 1995).

Child care institutions and group homes called *orphan asylums* were popular between 1830 and 1860 as appropriate settings for orphans and other dependent children, especially the impoverished. Had my mother been orphaned in 1839 instead of 1939, she and her two siblings would have most likely been placed in an orphan asylum. That is a troubling thought, considering the criticism leveled on orphan asylums—criticisms such as insufficient attention to young children and use of child labor.

Then, in 1853, a gentleman by the name of Charles Loring Brace founded the New York Children's Aid Society, an organization whose mission was to serve. An outspoken critic of orphan asylums, Brace's passion for his cause led to the practice

Foster care is defined as substitute care for children.

of *placing out* urban children to families in rural areas. Siblings were placed together, with the younger ones receiving care from the substitute family and the older children working on the farm. To reach their substitute family destination, dependent children were placed on trains headed west. Later called *orphan trains,* they transported thousands of children from urban to rural locations in the nineteenth century.

Not all placements were successful. Not all rural families were appropriate for placing out children, and not all children thrived in these placements. Criticisms of placing out focused on religion, especially the lack of placement resources for Catholic children, and inadequate screening of placement homes. Some saw the placing-out method of substitute care as an informal indenture strategy. As described by Cook (1995), between 1854 and 1930, approximately 150,000 children were placed by the Children's Aid Society or organizations based on their model. These children rode trains to California, Colorado, Illinois, Indiana, Iowa, Kansas, Michigan, Minnesota, Missouri, Nebraska, Ohio, Texas, and Wisconsin. A few children were also placed in southern states, and some were placed in rural areas of the Northeast.

In 1868, the Massachusetts Board of State Charities began paying families to raise orphaned children in its placing-out program. This form of substitute care, for which families were paid to care for children, replaced indenture as the method of substitute care for some children. Placing out was especially well suited to children with special needs, those with behavior problems, and those too young to be forced to work through indenture. In its earliest forms, placing out was the method of substitute care that most closely resembles today's foster care. Even then, the government's involvement in

The author's mother and aunt were orphaned at ages 11 and 9, shortly before this photo was taken in 1939, and then grew up in a series of informal foster homes because of the limited foster care system that existed at the time.

foster care can be seen through payments to families providing homes for dependent children. Placing out as a method of substitute care for dependent children peaked in 1875 and then experienced a decline until its demise in 1930 (Cook, 1995).

The end of placing out came, in part, due to debate over who should care for the children. Between 1880 and 1920, the question of whether to pay adults who took in other people's children complicated the debate on home placement versus institutional care. There was also debate over whether homes should offer free placements (*free homes*) or be entitled to a board fee (*boarding homes*) for the care of dependent children. Boarding homes for boarding out dependent children won that debate in the early part of the twentieth century, and boarding out to boarding homes became more common than placing out to free homes (Cook, 1995).

"The growing involvement of government in child welfare, first at the state and later at the federal level, was a central reason for the expansion of foster care in the twentieth century" (Hacsi, 1995, p. 167). The development of the juvenile court system from 1900 through the 1930s and the involvement of state government in both placing and boarding dependent children led to regulations guiding the *foster care process,* as it was soon to be known.

In 1935, passage of the Social Security Act through Title IV provided federal aid to poor families in an attempt to keep families together. It worked. No longer did families require the temporary service of an orphan asylum or indenture through placing out for their children when they hit on hard times. Families were now able to keep their children at home. When the occasion did rise—as in the case of my mother and her siblings, who were orphaned—children were more likely to be boarded in a family home.

According to Hasci (1995), "By 1950, more children were in foster homes than in institutions; by 1960, almost twice as many children were in foster care as were in institutions; and, in 1968, more than three times as many children were in foster care as in institutions" (p. 167). During the 1960s and 1970s, foster care reached a peak, when a combination of federal and state funding available to support foster care, plus the rediscovery of child abuse, led to a large number of children being placed in foster care. In fact, by 1976, over 100,000 children were in foster care, paid for with federal funds through Aid to Families with Dependent Children (AFDC) (U.S. General Accounting Office, 1977).

Again quoting Hacsi (1995), "The most important federal legislation of recent years regarding foster care is the Adoption Assistance and Child Welfare Act of 1980. This act targets money toward preventive services and efforts aimed at reuniting families, thus attempting to shift policy away from family breakup and toward family maintenance" (p. 168). Family preservation programs, however, have not been without their problems, and they are often criticized for keeping children with unfit parents in the interest of keeping a family together.

Kinship care, an important part of the foster care delivery system by 1990, became an alternative to foster care in unrelated homes and a way that families, through kin, could stay together. My mother's informal placement into her aunt's home was kinship care before it was formalized, before board payments could be made to relatives, and before family preservation was an identified priority when considering the needs of dependent children. Even in the 1990s, however, informal care by relatives was still far more common than formalized kinship care. The numbers are staggering: Between 1980 and 1992, the number of children being reared by their grandparents rose from 2 to 3 million, a number that dwarfs the foster care population (Tedford, 1992, p. 1).

The Adoption and Safe Families Act (ASFA) was enacted in November 1997 and amended the 1980 Adoption Assistance and Child Welfare Act by taking further steps to promote safety and permanence for children who are at risk for abuse or neglect in their own homes and are in need of substitute care. ASFA carried provisions for moving children who resided in foster care for long periods of time into permanent homes and established incentives for states to change policies and practices to improve services to children. This legislation provided guidelines that focused attention on both the protection of children and the planning of more permanent and long-term living arrangements for children in substitute care. The following quote from Senator John D. Rockefeller, IV, notes the importance of the legislation:

> The most significant overhaul of the American foster care system since 1980, the new law is the result of an unprecedented bipartisan effort on behalf of America's abused and neglected children. For the first time, this law makes it clear that the health and safety of a child are paramount. This simple but compelling statement will refocus our efforts to help abused and neglected children. In this landmark legislation, we have preserved and enhanced the range of choices available to promote the health and safety of children in foster care. Where appropriate, the law helps to speed a child's adoption into a loving family. At the same time, the Adoption and Safe Families Act preserves vital funding and service to reunify children with their families when it is safe to do so. (quoted in Curtis, Dale, & Kendall, 1999, p. 27)

At the time ASFA was passed, there was growing concern that young children were entering foster care and remaining in substitute care for too long. To address this concern, *concurrent planning* was introduced. This approach to permanency planning aimed at family reunification while establishing a backup permanency plan for the child who cannot safely return home to the biological parents. Concurrent planning was originally targeted especially toward the very young children who entered foster care, those under the age of 4. Previous practice in foster care applied a method that either prepared the child and family for reunification or for permanent placement in a resource other than the child's own family but did not incorporate simultaneous planning for both possible outcomes. Since its inception, the concept of concurrent planning has indeed changed the practice of child welfare.

In a 1998 summary of the components of the new law, the Administration for Children and Families (ACF), part of the U.S. Department of Health and Human Services, cited the following key principles found in the Adoption and Safe Families Act:

1. *Child welfare services are guided by a paramount concern for children's safety.* Recognizing that the reunification of families is important for children and families, the legislation places the safety of children above all else and provides support for the termination of parental rights when family reunification cannot ensure the safety of children.

2. *Foster care is temporary placement and not to be viewed as permanent.* In asserting the temporary nature of foster care, the law makes provisions that shorten the timeframe for making permanency decisions for children and for initiating proceedings to terminate parental rights. The law also emphasizes timely adoptions for children who cannot return safely to their own homes. For example, some circumstances—such as when a child is an abandoned infant or when a parent has committed murder, voluntary manslaughter, or felony assault of another of his or her children—lead to the termination in all but certain exceptions.

3. *A permanent plan should begin as soon as a child enters foster care and is enhanced by the provision of services to families.* The act requires the provision of quality services to families quickly and according to their specific needs. Through the delivery of intensive and timely services to families whose children are in foster care, the courts and child welfare agencies can make more informed decisions about a family's capacity to safely care for its children.

4. *The child welfare system must focus on both results and accountability.* The law expects results and requires annual reports on state performance, the creation of an adoption incentive payment for states (designed to support the president's goal of doubling the annual number of children who are adopted or permanently placed by the year 2002), and a study to make recommendation regarding incentives in child welfare.

5. *Innovative approaches are needed to achieve the goals of safety, permanency, and well-being.* Recognizing that the child welfare system of practice does not possess all the solutions needed to achieve the goals of ASFA, the legislation makes provisions for states to use greater flexibility in developing strategies to achieve improved services to families and children in accordance with the ASFA. In each fiscal year, states are given financial bonuses for each child adopted from foster care above the base year number assigned to them.

Termination of Parental Rights

The termination of one's parental rights is a serious step. In my early days as a social worker in public child welfare during the 1970s, the phrases "only as a last resort" and "when all efforts have failed" were used to describe the gravity with which we considered such an action. I had under my supervision one young social worker whose sense of family was so strong that he could not work with parents who faced the loss of their parental rights. I, too, had difficulty with the subject, but I had long ago learned that there are some parents who cannot safely parent their children. In such cases, we must recognize that fact and move forward with permanency planning for the children. The Adoption and Safe Families Act (1997) set forth provisions for the courts and agencies in shaping policies and procedures for the termination of parental rights.

Timelines to accomplish permanency planning have been imposed and required permanency hearings are to be held for children no later than 12 months after they enter foster care. The law also requires state agencies to track all children in the foster care system and initiate termination of parental rights proceedings and permanency planning in cases where children have been under the supervision of the state for 15 out of the last 22 months. As noted earlier, exceptions to the timelines apply in certain circumstances (e.g., when a child is an abandoned infant or when a parent commits a murder, voluntary manslaughter, or felony assault of another of his or her children). In individual cases, the law even allows for exceptions in these identified circumstances.

While timelines are meant to be observed and speed up the process for permanency planning, the termination of parental rights according to the timelines imposed is not automatic. ASFA requires that termination of parental rights be initiated according to the timelines, but it is the court that must determine if grounds for termination exist and if the child's best interest will be served by the termination of parental rights.

In ASFA, the termination of parental rights is associated with adoption. For the agency, that means that a permanent home for the child is sought, identified, and approved at the same time that a petition to terminate parental rights is filed. The following list notes exceptions to the mandatory timelines:

1. The child is in the care of a relative.
2. The state documents that the child's best interest would not be served.
3. The state agency has not provided to the child's family the services needed and identified in the case plan within the timeframe established.

Exceptions such as these are applied on a case-by-case basis and include an assessment of the individual needs of each child and family. After the first permanency hearing for each child, the court reviews the status and progress toward permanency every 6 months. A subsequent permanency hearing is required by ASFA every 12 months.

Concurrent Planning

The Adoption and Safe Families Act AFSA, (1997) mandated concurrent planning, which requires child welfare to work toward family reunification while establishing a permanency plan that can be implemented if children cannot return safely to their families (Lutz, 2001). Concurrent planning requires social workers to view permanency planning in conjunction with reunification efforts, rather than separately. Earlier child welfare policy organized these efforts sequentially: first foster care, then reunification efforts, and then permanency planning. Social workers are now expected to begin long-term planning for a child's permanence as soon as he or she enters foster care.

An earlier version of the emphasis on reunification occurred through the Adoption Assistance and Child Welfare Act of 1980. This act authorized appropriations for adoption and foster care assistance and required states to make reasonable efforts to prevent placement into foster care or to reunify children with their families. States followed the federal government with their iterations of the act, and in my state, Alabama, "reasonable efforts to place a child for adoption or with a legal guardian or custodian may be made concurrently with other reasonable efforts" (Ala. Code 12–15–65[n] Supp. 1998). The new method requires parallel thinking: a plan for the child's reunification with the family and a concurrent plan for the child's permanency, should the child be unable to safely return to the family home.

As mentioned earlier, concurrent planning was originally introduced due to concerns for young children, especially those younger than 4 years of age, who entered and remained in foster care for long periods of time. By 1998, however, a study conducted by the National Resource Center for Foster Care and Permanency Planning found that "the principles and best practices of concurrent planning were being used with children of all ages, to increase their likelihood of having lifetime family connections when they exit the foster care system" (Lutz, 2001, p. 4). The study suggested that successful implementation of concurrent planning requires these components (Lutz, 2001, p. 5):

1. Intensive casework with birth families
2. Frequent, meaningful visitation between the children and their birth families
3. Full disclosure with the birth families about the importance of permanence in the lives of children, the various options for permanency planning, and consequences of their actions or inactions; and consistent communication with birth families throughout the life of a case regarding feedback on positive case progress or the need to confront planning ambivalence
4. Diligent search efforts to find absent parents and address all paternity issues such as blood tests, child support, etc.
5. Aggressive diligent searches for and assessment of relatives who might have an interest in caring or planning for permanence for the child
6. Frequent and substantive case reviews that carefully assess the efficacy of services being provided to assist the family to achieve case plan goals and modification of the service plan as required
7. Use of permanency-planning resource families (foster families, relatives, guardians, or adoptive families) who can work towards and accept reunification and also be able to serve as permanency resources if needed

Concurrent planning offers a conceptual and practice framework for "expediting and intensifying efforts to achieve permanence for a child within one year—a timeframe that reflects a child's sense of the passage of time" (Lutz, 2001, p. 9). It provides structure for social workers to move children more quickly from the uncertainty of foster care to a more stable, permanent family. Concurrent planning operates within the principles of family-centered and community-based practice by implementing efforts to support family reunification concurrently with efforts to establish a permanent plan for children.

In addition, concurrent planning uses the same "respectful involvement of parents and family members early in the planning process, as well as identification of barriers to reunification or another permanency outcome" (Lutz, 2001, p. 9). Concurrent planning protects childhood attachments by building stronger bonds between the child and birth parents through reunification or by preserving the tie between the child and the permanency-planning parents through adoption or legal guardianship. In both reunification and permanency planning, intensive case-appropriate services are provided to meet the needs of children, parents, and potential parents. "Concurrent planning also supports finding alternate options to permanency such as relative care or legal guardianship" (Lutz, 2001, p. 10).

The implementation of concurrent planning in conjunction with the timelines established by ASFA requires that case reviews be conducted on schedule and modified as needed. The best efforts of social workers, supervisors, parents, family members, and other stakeholders involved in case planning may not produce the desired outcome (reunification) for families and children, in which case revision or modification of the case plan is necessary. An appropriate case plan (or service plan) for each child consists of a differential assessment of the child, the family situation, and the community resources available for meeting the needs. Such an assessment identifies the strengths of the family that are supportive of the goal of reunification and also identifies barriers to the accomplishment of that goal. In some agencies, team conferences that include staff, citizens, and quality assurance teams routinely review case plans, particularly those that present challenges or questions for foster care social workers. A foster child's family members are routinely included on the case planning team.

Although new to the concurrent planning model, states participating in a survey conducted by the National Resource Center for Foster Care and Permanency Planning in 1998 reported the following lessons learned in concurrent planning policy implementation and practice (Lutz, 2001, p. 30).

1. Visitation opportunities must be enhanced. The 60-minute pattern of visitations in cold sterile public agency offices must be changed and more creative visitation arranged in environments that present optimal chance for positive parent/child interaction. No longer is the social worker's office considered to be the optimal place for parent-child visits and no longer is just one hour enough time for such a visit to occur. Visits in the park or at the home of a relative, or in the foster home, are preferred.
2. Services must be flexible and service plans must be varied to reflect the variety of families for whom they are developed.
3. Supervision must include opportunities to ask questions about families and family systems and assist social workers in assessing case specific information pertinent to the case plan for reunification or permanency planning.
4. Agency staff and stakeholders in the legal system—such as attorneys, judges, and *guardians ad litem*—need ongoing training simultaneously so that the principles of concurrent planning are studied at the same time and in the same way.
5. Agency staff must be trained in conducting differential assessments and in using the information to establish service plans for reunification, while also searching for absent parents, other relatives, and addressing Indian Child Welfare Act requirements.

Therapeutic Foster Care

Therapeutic foster care (TFC), mentioned earlier in this chapter, is one of the most widely used forms of out-of-home placement for children with severe emotional and behavioral disorders. Developed as an alternative to residential placements for children, therapeutic foster care is family centered and community based. Therapeutic foster homes, unlike regular foster care, are supported by wraparound services and offer intensive clinical services to a limited number of children. By design, the care is less restrictive than institutional care and arranged as close as is safely possible to the child's family.

Chamberlain (1998) says, "When compared to residential and group care, outcomes for youngsters participating in TFC are favorable." Chamberlain cites these ways in which TFC differs from residential or group care:

1. Community families are recruited, trained, and supported to provide foster care services to children.
2. Children generally attend public schools.
3. No more than two youngsters are placed in a home.
4. Most TFC programs include a family therapy component with the biological parents or after-care resource.
5. TFC is significantly less costly than group care.

As an illustration of therapeutic foster care, a summary report of a 1998 quality assurance research project in an Alabama county is included in the following sections. Recent child welfare reform efforts have increased the number of children living in therapeutic foster homes. At the time of the study, only one child was usually assigned to a family, unless a sibling group, and just over 25 percent of all the children in out-of-home placements in the county were in therapeutic foster family homes. Senior social work students and members of the child welfare agency's quality assurance team assisted with data collection, data analysis, and report writing.

The first section that follows presents the result of interviews with social workers at the public child welfare agency. The second section presents the interviews with social workers at the private agency contracted by the county to provide services.

Findings at the Public Child Welfare Agency

Fifteen public child welfare workers were interviewed in face-to-face interviews (Turner, 2001), using the interview guide developed by the research team. Each interview lasted about 1.5 hours and was held in the worker's office. The social workers' combined years of experience in child welfare figured to a mean number of 4.28 years (a range of reported practice experience from 1.2 to 7 years). Four of the fifteen social workers had no prior experience working in foster care. The others reported an average of 3 years' practice experience in the foster care area.

At the time of the interviews, eight workers had no therapeutic foster care children in their caseloads. The remaining seven reported between one and four children (a total of twelve) currently in therapeutic foster care placements. Eight workers said they had children on waiting lists for therapeutic foster care. The numbers of respondents noted below do not always add up to 15 because scheduling conflicts and staff turnover prevented some interviews. The questions focused on the agency's procedures, policies, and protocols; the referral process; coordination of services; and outcomes. To fit coverage of the research report into this chapter, some questions have been ommitted and some answers have been summarized.

All the interviewed social workers seemed to know their cases well and were able to cite the specific disorders attributed to the children in their caseloads. The disorders cited were attention-deficit hyperactivity disorder, fetal alcohol syndrome, schizophrenia, posttraumatic stress disorder, physically handicapped, attention-deficit disorder, failure to thrive, excessively sexually reactive, oppositional defiance, depression, bipolar, and sexual abuse victim.

Q. How are you informed of a child who might need TFC?

A. Basically, if the child is not working out in the placements, if a therapist or doctor makes a recommendation, or if the child needs more stimulation than in regular foster care.

Q. What criteria lead to TFC referrals?

A. Being suicidal, making threats, sexually acting out, fire setting, hurting animals, not coping well in normal foster care placement.

Q. Does the agency require written protocols when making referrals to TFC, and what steps are taken once a determination is made that a child is a candidate for TFC?

A. Responses were unclear about the agency's protocol and steps taken to execute a referral. Most workers indicated that their supervisors and "staffing" determined if a child should be referred to TFC.

Q. Is a *DSM-IV* diagnosis [explained in Chapter 1] required before a referral to TFC is made?

A. Six said no diagnosis is needed; the other nine said yes.

Q. Who is responsible for such a diagnosis?

A. Clinician, physician, PhD.

Q. Do you avoid making the referral when you know no TFC resource is available, or do you make it anyway?

A. The social workers were split on the issue of making referrals anyway, despite no vacancies in therapeutic foster homes. Some referred children anyway, placing their names on the waiting list. Others did not. Six workers were aware of the waiting list, seven were unaware of the waiting list, and two said there was no waiting list. According to the social workers, if TFC had been available, 28 more children in their caseloads would have been referred.

Q. What is the length of time from referral to placement?

A. Answers varied: immediately, six to eight months, a few weeks.

Q. Have you made referrals that were declined or denied by the TFC provider?

A. Eight workers said their referrals were not usually declined; four said their referrals were denied due to no vacancies, and one responded that a denial could be due to race or ethnicity. The workers reported that when their referrals were denied, they continued providing the best care possible in other settings.

Q. Does TFC appear as a goal for children in your development of individualized service plans?

A. Twelve of the fifteen workers answered an emphatic "Yes." The other three answered "It should be," "It could be," and "No."

Q. How are the agency's individualized service plans for a child incorporated into the TFC program's goals and plans?

A. Thirteen indicated that their ISP [indiviualized service plan] goals were incorporated into the TFC treatment plans; one said "Not always, but they are supposed to be"; one had no children in a TFC program and declined to answer.

Q. How often are you in contact with a child after placement in TFC? [Policy requires a public child welfare worker assigned to a child's case to have regular contact with the child during TFC placement. The mandate is that visits with each child occur at least every three months.]

A. The workers prefaced their responses by saying that contacts depend on the situation and unique needs of a child. Four reported monthly contacts, five reported biweekly contacts, two said weekly contacts were necessary, one said visits occurred every three months, one did not know, one said contacts varied from child to child, and one reported only telephone contact with the child in placement.

Q. How often do you meet with the TFC program team members to review the status of your (shared) cases?

A. Most workers reported monthly meetings with the therapeutic foster care agency's staff, a few said meetings were held every couple of months, and one said meetings were held every six months to coordinate case planning and to evaluate interventions.

Q. How often do TFC personnel require the public child welfare agency's approval for a child's participation in events or activities?

A. Workers said the public child welfare agency's permission was seldom needed. Travel out of the state and medical procedures were cited as the two most frequent reasons for needing approval.

Q. Has the TFC program been effective for the children in your caseloads?

A. A majority (eight) of the fifteen public child welfare workers answered in the affirmative. They gave these examples of indicators used to evaluate success: reunification, improved grades, improved behavior at school, improved behavior overall, and foster parents wanting to adopt the child. Six workers answered the question negatively, with these reasons: placement was too restrictive for the child, the child did as well out of TFC, the child had to be removed from TFC.

Q. How many children in your caseloads have reached their goals through TFC?

A. Seven workers had a total of nineteen children reach their goals, six workers had no children reach their goals, one did not know the goals, and one had no experience with placing children in TFC.

Q. Are you involved with the child when the TFC placement ends?

A. All but one worker reported involvement in after care.

Q. Do the children in your caseloads ever re-enter therapeutic foster care?

A. Thirteen of the public child welfare workers responded positively to this question. The remaining two workers did not know if re-entry into therapeutic foster care was permissible.

Q. Is eventual placement to a less-restrictive environment a goal for the children? [Current legislation requires that children be placed in the least-restrictive environment.]

A. Twelve said "Yes"; one said "Maybe, maybe not"; one said "No, all my clients are still there and doing well"; and one said "In normal situations it would be, but it depends on the children's needs."

Findings at the Private Therapeutic Foster Care Agency

At the private agency contracted as the primary provider of TFC in the Alabama county, the research team (Turner, 2001) interviewed four social workers. They presented an employment history that included an average of 2.1 years in the agency and 3.75 years in child welfare. Caseloads ranged from three cases to seven cases per worker. The agency limited the number of children in a worker's caseload to eight.

The therapeutic foster care social workers reported that *DSM-IV* diagnoses (see Chapter 1) made within 90 days of admission were criteria for placement. The TFC staff indicated that decisions to accept a child for placement were based on referral information, observation of the child, and whether a resource home was available. At the time of the interviews, the TFC agency reported nine children on a waiting list for TFC. The twenty-six children served by the agency were ages 5 to 18 years old. Goals for the children were reported by TFC workers to be reunification and rehabilitation. While reported to be the responsibility of the TFC workers, the treatment plan for each child was developed in collaboration with the child, the child's family, the public child welfare worker, the public child welfare supervisor, the child's legal guardian, the child's school counselor, and the TFC parent. TFC workers reported that during the treatment plan's development, public child welfare agency ISP (individualized service plan) goals and objectives for each child and family were incorporated into the treatment plan.

We asked the TFC social workers how goals for an individual family and child were matched with appropriate TFC resources. The answers given were "Knowing what a family can tolerate," "We match strengths and needs of child and home," "During training, we have the parents fill out a matching form to see what they can handle or not handle. Preferences are listed on the matching sheets," and "If a bed is available and the TFC family agrees, the child is placed."

Since the court-ordered provision of services to children in public child welfare mandates permanency and reunification plans, the research team asked about the length of stay in care, specialized treatment, and training for TFC parents. Workers said treatment plans for each placement included discharge plans that projected the length of stay and that the projections varied by child according to the goals of the agency's ISP. The TFC guidelines that established policy for this private therapeutic foster care agency suggested a length of stay of six months. One social worker said,

"But it is usually a year." Another social worker reported lengths of stay as long as two years.

TFC children have specialized needs that require TFC parents and agency workers to be trained in the effects of medications. TFC parents are required to keep medication logs and consult with physicians and psychiatrists as needed. A minimum 40 hours of specified training is required of TFC parents before children are returned to their homes. This preliminary training was followed up with monthly training, usually in the form of selected content presented at support group meetings for TFC care providers.

TFC social workers at the private agency made weekly visits to children in placement and more frequent visits if necessary. They participated in treatment team meetings with public child welfare agency staff and counselors as needed but at least quarterly to discuss progress toward goals and to "assist in the continuum of care." Therapeutic foster care workers and supervisors held weekly staff meetings to evaluate cases.

The coordination of case planning efforts between the two responsible agencies presented challenges. TFC social workers said communication problems were an issue. The communication problems reportedly related to case coordination and included phone tag, scheduling conflicts, clarification of roles and responsibilities, and insufficient information on referrals.

The research team wanted to know about child safety and stability in therapeutic foster care. They inquired about abuse and neglect reports in placement. Workers indicated that such reports occur rarely. They reported that two reports had been filed in the previous two years. There was a protocol in place for handling such reports.

Crises and disruptions had occurred in the agency's placements, even though every effort had been made to prevent placement disruption. These reasons for disruption were cited by the social workers: care provider burnout; escalating behavior by the child that resulted in hospitalization; child behaviors such as manipulation, disrespect, and defiance; and inability of a child to form attachments with TFC care providers. Workers said interventions were used to prevent placement disruption. Interventions included support groups, crisis interventions, home visits, wraparound services, proper matching of child and home, care provider training, and respite care. The workers reported that backup plans for dealing with placement disruptions were in place.

A question regarding completion of the TFC program brought responses that could be placed into any of three categories. One category of TFC completion included children who age out of foster care—usually 18 to 19 years of age, depending on educational status. Another category included children who left TFC to be reunited with their families. The third category was children who left TFC because they needed more structure or specialized care than the agency's TFC homes could provide. Workers explained that in the case of reunification, children are gradually moved back into their families: first day visits, then overnight visits, and then weekend visits facilitate the transition for children and families.

Regarding follow-up with children after they leave TFC, the social workers reported that the agency provided after care for six months. The level of service provided depended on family needs, the public child welfare agency's requests, the plan for after care, and after-care decisions made at treatment team meetings.

Social workers in both the public child welfare agency and the private agency were asked what is needed in therapeutic foster care. Their answers included improved communication between the two agencies, completed paperwork, improved ISPs, more counselors, more licensed and qualified homes, more training for care providers and workers, better screening of resources, fair treatment for children, and more funding.

Before the quality assurance team completed the research project—and possibly as a result of quality assurance committee discussions—supervisors in the public child welfare agency made protocol changes to improve the referral process for TFC. More good news soon followed: Within a few months, the county approved a second TFC agency to meet the needs of the children on the waiting list.

In the Best Interest of the Child

Determining what is in each child's best interest is a fundamental challenge for those who work in foster care, in any capacity. It is as much a challenge to the social worker as it is to the judge who hears the petitions and acts on the merits of each case. The understanding of what is in the best interest of a child comes from careful collection of information pertinent to the case, careful assessment of that information, and wise planning on the basis of the assessments. This responsibility falls to the child welfare social worker. Since implementation of ASFA, social workers have been using the input of many experts and stakeholders when compiling assessments and case plans. Doing so has increased the likelihood of achieving recommendations and decisions in the child's best interest.

In his book *The Lost Boy,* Dave Pelzer (1997) shares his personal story of rescue from neglect and abuse, which started when he was placed, at the age of 12, in protective custody and foster care. It was, as he described it, very much in his best interest to leave the abusive home of his family and move to a home where he was treated with respect, given clean clothes to wear, and fed well. For him, these foster care experiences were a huge improvement over the life to which he had been subjected at the hands of an abusive mother and neglectful father. He needed foster care primarily for his safety and well-being, with permanence as a secondary consideration in the beginning. His placement into foster care was in his best interest, and if the placement had come years earlier, it would have been in his best interest.

Pelzer could advise those of us making decisions about children and foster care. He would likely have us look carefully and closely at safety issues, parental capacity and motivation to supervise their children, and the emotional health of children. What is in the best interest of a child depends on many factors, including these: safety now and later, mental and physical health, developmental needs and resources, stability and permanence, feelings of affection and emotional connections, family strengths and resources, and community resources.

As a means of improving outcomes for children in the foster care system, the Pew Commission on Children in Foster Care was launched in May 2003 as a nonpartisan group charged to develop recommendations. The desired outcomes were (and remain) to move children quickly from foster care into safe, permanent, nurturing families and to prevent unnecessary placements in foster care. In particular, the Pew Commission set out to develop a practical set of policy recommendations to reform federal child welfare financing and strengthen court oversight of child welfare cases. A year of work resulted in some interesting recommendations in May 2004. With regard to financing child welfare, the commission recommended the following:

1. That federal funds be provided for all children adopted from foster care and those who leave foster care to live with a permanent, legal guardian
2. That federal funds be provided to states to pay for foster care for every child who needs this protection
3. That states be allowed to reinvest federal dollars that would have been used on foster care to keep children out of foster care or leave foster care safely
4. That federal funds be combined and additional funding added to provide a broad range of direct services to children and their families, plus training for child welfare workers, court personnel, and allied professionals
5. That improvements to the federal child and family services reviews (CFSRs) be implemented to evaluate child well-being, conduct longitudinal studies, and convene a foster care expert panel to recommend the best outcomes and measures to use in data collection
6. That innovation and constant exploration continue toward finding the best ways to help children who have been abused and neglected.

Other recommendations from the Pew Commission (2004) focused on strengthening the courts involved in foster care. Whether the recommendations will be heeded remains to be seen.

An important step toward ensuring the safety of children proceeded from the implementation of the *child and family services review (CFSR)*, a collaborative effort between state and federal governments that provides a process for studying outcomes for children and families: what is happening to children and families, whether children are safe, whether children in foster care are moving toward permanent outcomes, and whether the well-being of children and families is promoted and ensured by the services provided (Milner, 2001, p. 1) Reviews are expected to give information that state, tribal, and other child welfare officials can use for making program improvements. The CFSR is a collaborative process that involves stakeholders from the local community to the federal level who bring insights and perspectives to the table. A planning process required by the Title IV-B of the Social Security Act, which provides flexible funds that can be used by states for a variety of child welfare services, involves nine categories of stakeholders in the process of reviewing children and family service plans:

1. All appropriate offices and agencies within the state child welfare agency
2. County social services or child welfare director or representatives
3. Other agencies and organizations with experience in administering any child welfare services
4. Parents (including birth, adoptive, foster) and consumers of services
5. Representatives of American Indian tribes

6. Representatives of professional and advocacy organizations
7. Representatives of state and local agencies administering federal funds
8. Administrators, supervisors, and frontline workers of the state and child family services agency
9. Other categories of organizations and individuals based on state and local circumstances

Involving representatives from these categories in the review process enriches the quality of the review process and contributes to a more productive consultation (Milner, (2000).

Are we wiser as a result of the process? Is our system of foster care improved as a result of this process of evaluation? Yes, foster care is better today than it was in the early days of indenture, placing out, and orphan asylums. Yet there remains much room for improvement.

Homer Folks (1911), whose quote began this chapter, would agree. He raised the following questions that are as fundamental now as they were in his day:

> Whenever the question arises of removing a child from its home, I wish that three questions might be asked and objectively answered: first, is there any real conclusive reason why the child should not stay where it is? Second, what is lacking in his present home, which we deem necessary for the child's care, and just how is that particular thing going to be provided under our proposed plan? Third, how much will our proposed plan cost and would that sum, if used to assist the child in his own home, secure better results? (p. 121)

Sound familiar? We ask these same questions today, every time we consider a child's safety at home or a child's protection in substitute care. Those of us who work in child welfare are charged with protecting children. Therefore, we continually remind ourselves of the most important point: the child's best interest.

REFERENCES

Chamberlain, P. (1998). *Multidimensional treatment foster care*. Boulder: University of Colorado.

Cook, J. F. (1995). A history of placing-out: The orphan trains. *Child Welfare, 74*(1) 181–208.

Curtis, G., Dale, G., & Kendall, J. (Eds) (1999). *The foster care crisis: Translating research into policy*. Lincoln, NE: The University of Nebraska Press/Washington, DC: Child Welfare League of America.

Folks, H. (1911). *The care of destitute, neglected, and delinquent children*. New York: Macmillan.

Hacsi, T. (1995). From indenture to family foster care: A brief history of child placing. *Child Welfare, 74*(1), 162–181.

Lutz, L. L. (2001). *Concurrent planning: Tool for permanency survey of selected sites*. New York: National Resource Center for Foster Care and Permanency Planning, Hunter College School of Social Work of the City University of New York.

Milner, J. L. (2001). CFSR: Just so darn close. *Best practice, next practice.* Washington, DC: National Child Welfare Resource Center for Family-Centered Practice, Children's Bureau, U.S. Department of Health and Human Services.

Pelzer, D. (1997). *The lost boy.* Deerfield Beach, FL: Health Communications.

Pew Commission on Children in Foster Care. (2004). *Fostering the future: Safety, permanence and well-being for children in foster care.* Washington, DC: The Pew Commission.

Tedford, D. (1992, June 22). A tough role for grandparents. *Houston Chronicle,* p. 1.

Turner, R. (2001). *Child welfare reform, quality assurance, and therapeutic foster care: A study of current practice in public child welfare.* Berkely, CA: U.S. Children's Bureau and the University of California at Berkley, California Social Welfare Education Center.

U.S. Department of Health and Human Services (U.S. DHHS), Administration of Children and Families. (1998).

U.S. Department of Health, Education, and Welfare (U.S. DHHS); Administration for Children and Families; Administration on Children, Youth, and Families; Children's Bureau. (2003). AFCARS Report. Online: www.acf.hhs.gov/programs/cb/publications/afcars/report10.htm

U.S. General Accounting Office. (1977). *Children in foster care institutions—Steps government can take to improve their care.* Washington, DC: Government Printing Office.

CHAPTER 9

Services for Children Who Cannot Go Home

Joan R. Rycraft

Many of the children who come into placement due to child maltreatment and other family issues will eventually be reunited with their parents or placed with relatives. Thousands of other children in placement cannot go home. Specific plans for their safety, permanence, and well-being must be made. The preferred option for most children is adoption. Adoption provides the child a legally recognized new family. Although the number of adoptions of children in the child welfare system is increasing, there are many children who will remain in foster care, unable to return home, and without the permanency of belonging to a new family. For those children, long-term placement with foster parents who make the commitment to provide a stable home for them until they reach adulthood appears to be the best alternative we have to offer. We have the additional responsibility of seeing that they get the training and support they need to make the transition to successful independent living. These responsibilities—to our children who cannot go home—are the subjects of this chapter. Our topics are adoption, long-term foster care, and independent living.

Since passage of the landmark Adoption Assistance and Child Welfare Act of 1980, the major emphasis in child welfare practice has been prevention of placement through family-based services, stability of placements, timely reunification of children with their parents, and permanency planning. More recent legislation, the Adoption and Safe Families Act of 1997 (ASFA), places stronger emphasis on safety, permanency, and well-being of children served by the child welfare system. The new legislation shortened permanency timelines to one calendar year and provided monetary incentives to increase the number of completed adoptions in each state. The Adoption and Safe Families Act, Indian Child Welfare Act, and Multiethnic Placement Act are the major laws currently guiding child welfare practices. They were crafted in response to escalating numbers of children in foster care who either were returned to unsafe homes only to enter the child welfare system again, or waited in foster care for lengthy periods of time before reunification with unstable parents or, in a few instances, adoption.

Our current child welfare policy not only guides our practices, it mandates specific services, timeframes, and outcomes. These policies reflect our growing recognition that, despite our sustained efforts, many children in out-of-home care will not be reunified with their parents or placed permanently with relatives. They also support the current philosophy of scholars and practitioners that these children need a stable family environment and preparation for becoming self-sufficient. For many years, the primary services for children who cannot go home have been adoption, long-term care, and independent living. These services will and must continue to be provided. Within the mandates of new policies and our expanded knowledge of best practices, these services have, however, undergone significant changes; it is hoped that they have been improved and are centered on the best interest of each child. With these mandates, it is expected that more children will be placed in adoptive homes to ensure their safety, permanency, and well-being. Adoption has become an accepted and honored social artifact of our society. People of all kinds and for various reasons make this lifetime commitment to children whose parents are unable or unwilling to care and provide for them.

Adoption: Creating a New Family

Adoption creates a permanent family for children whose birth parents are unable to care for them. It provides security, a sense of belonging, and the support system needed during a child's developmental phases. Adoption of a child is the cherished outcome, often long in coming, for families who cannot bear children but wish to expand their

Adoption creates a permanent family for children whose birth parents are unable to care for them.

families (Dukette, 1984). The bringing together of children in need of permanent families and families choosing to build a future with these children is an exemplary outcome of the public child welfare system. There are many children currently in the public child welfare foster home system eligible for adoption. Our challenge and goal is to find appropriate "forever" families for each waiting child.

Statistics and Demographics

Although there is no recognized national effort to collect data on all adoptions completed each year, there are sources that provide a general picture of the adoption arena. The Adoption and Foster Care Analysis and Reporting System (AFCARS) is a state by state reporting system that compiles information on adoptions and foster care in the public child welfare system. Another excellent depository of information on various facets of adoption is the National Adoption Information Clearinghouse. Adoption of children in the public child welfare system account for approximately 15 to 20 percent of finalized adoptions. Independent, international, and private adoptions are reported at 35 to 40 percent, 5 to 10 percent, and 40 to 45 percent respectively (National Adoption Information Clearinghouse, 2002b).

The most current data on adoption from AFCARS, released in January 2000 shows that of the approximately 520,000 children in foster care 117,000 (23%) were

TABLE 9.1	Demographic Characteristics of Children Adopted in Public Child Welfare

	Percentage
Age	
Under one year old	2
One to five years old	46
Six to ten years old	37
Eleven to fifteen years old	14
Sixteen to eighteen years	2
Gender	
Male	51
Female	48

Source: National Adoption Information Clearinghouse, 2002b.

eligible for adoption. This percentage of 20 to 25 percent of foster children eligible for adoption has remained stable for the past 25 years. It is estimated that approximately 30 percent of these children (35,000–37,000) will be adopted in any given year.

Younger children are much more likely to be adopted than older children. Almost one-half (48%) of children adopted through the public child welfare system are 5 years old or younger with 85 percent 10 years old or younger. Gender is not a significant factor in the adoption figures, with a fairly even split for boys (51%) and girls (48%). See Table 9.1.

The children in foster care awaiting adoption are predominately non-White (see Table 9.2). Approximately one half (51%) of these children are Black and 11 percent are Hispanic. White children in foster care awaiting adoption constitute approximately 32 percent. Why are Black children so highly overrepresented in the foster care system? There are several reasons being offered, including high levels of poverty among our black population, the impact of the drug epidemic, and institutional racism. Black families are being reported to child protective services with allegations of physical abuse and neglect at higher rates than other minority and white children. If the allegations are found to be true, and services to the family are unsuccessful, these children often enter foster care. The substantial increase of Black women being incarcerated and given lengthy sentences for drug-related crimes has brought an increase of Black children into the foster care system.

Currently, almost 80 percent of children awaiting adoption reside in foster care homes, 15 percent in preadoptive homes, 3 percent in group homes, and 5 percent in institutions. Their wait for an adoptive home is lengthy: almost half (47%) wait one to three years, and over half (53%) have been waiting from three to over five years. Although returning home is not a realistic option for these children, over 85 percent of them remain in foster care because the termination of their parents' rights has not been completed. Without this legal action, these children cannot be adopted (National

TABLE 9.2	Children in Foster Care Awaiting Adoption	
		Percentage
Race		
	Black	51
	Hispanic	11
	White	32
Current Placement		
	Foster care homes	80
	Preadopt homes	15
	Group Homes	3
	Institutions	5
Length of Wait		
	One year or less	10
	Two to three years	37
	Three to five years	26
	Five years or more	27

Source: National Adoption Information Clearinghouse, 2002b.

Adoption Information Clearinghouse, 2002a). This bleak picture of children living in foster care homes may improve over the next several years. Initiatives to increase adoptions have been legislated, and obstacles to transracial adoptions have diminished.

Current Adoption Policy

The former adoption policy required a permanent plan for a child within 18 months of placement but did not address the legal termination of parental rights required for adoption. In contrast, the Adoption and Safe Families Act (ASFA) requires that petitions for the termination of parental rights be filed for abandoned children, children who have been in foster care for 15 of the last 22 months, and children whose parent has been convicted of felony assault or murder of a child. Heeding the stated goal of former President Clinton to double the number of adoptions across the county by 2002, legislators added monetary incentives for the states to increase the number of adoptions of foster care children. A state begins with a base number denoting the average number of adoptions during a prior specified period; for each foster child adopted above that number the state gets $4,000. If the child is determined have special needs, another $2,000 is given the state, for a total of $6,000. The amount of funds appropriated for monetary adoption incentives was capped at $20 million (Gendell, 2001).

The ability of states to meet these and other mandates was assessed through child and family services reviews conducted in every state during 2001–2003. These reviews will continue every two years in those states that did not meet the established national standards on safety, permanency, and child well-being. For states that met the standards, the reviews will be held every five years. The data indicate that some progress is being made. Although the increases cannot be attributed solely to the mandates of ASFA, according to the North American Council on Adoptable Children (as cited in Gendell, 2001), the number of adoptions increased approximately 60 percent from 26,000 in 1995 to 44,000 in 1999. The report from the U.S. General Accounting Office (2002) indicates that the trend of increased finalized adoptions is continuing with 48,600 adoptions reported in 2000. If this legislation meets its goals, (1) parental rights will be terminated more quickly than in the past, (2) more children in foster care will have a permanency plan of adoption, and (3) more children in foster care will be adopted (hopefully within shorter waiting times).

In response to the large number of minority children eligible for adoption, in 1994 Congress passed and former President Clinton signed the Multiethnic Placement Act (MEPA) as an amendment to the Improving America's Schools Act (PL 103-382). This legislation and its subsequent amendments address the plight of minority children in the child welfare system. The specific goals of this legislation: (1) reduce the length of time that children wait for adoptive placement; (2) ensure that no individual is denied the opportunity to become an adoptive or foster parent solely on the basis of race, color, or national origin; (3) facilitate the identification and recruitment of foster and adoptive families that reflect the racial and ethnic diversity of waiting children (National Resource Center for Special Needs Adoption, 1995).

Prior to this legislation, a child's race was often the predominate factor considered in the selection of foster or adoptive parents. It became obvious that many children of color were unnecessarily languishing in foster care homes for lengthy periods of time waiting for a family of their race, ethnicity, or culture to adopt them.

This legislation diminishes obstacles for the adoption of children by families of a different racial, cultural, and ethnic background. The focus is now placed on the potential adoptive parents and their ability to meet the needs of a particular child. No longer is a child's race, culture, and ethnic background considered of first importance among the factors to be considered.

Child welfare agencies are required to make diligent efforts to recruit foster and adoptive parents that reflect the diversity of the child welfare population in the state. In trying to meet this goal, they face major challenges (Curtis & Alexander, 1996; National Resource Center for Special Needs Adoption, 1995). The agencies must develop a recruitment plan that includes but is not limited to the dissemination of information regarding the children waiting for adoption, instructions on how to adopt a child, cultural sensitivity training of staff, and the elimination of exclusionary standards (National Resource Center for Special Needs Adoption, 1995). The agencies must reach out to their various diverse communities and forge collaborations with necessary social support systems and political entities to encourage families within these communities to open their homes to children awaiting adoption.

The Adoptive Family

For the past six decades the number of potential adoptive parents has far exceeded the number of the most desired children: healthy infants (Freundlich, 1998). The

National Adoption Information Clearinghouse (2002c) reports some interesting facts regarding the people who are interested in adopting a child. Citing the 1988 National Survey of Family Growth, they report that 2 million women have sought at one time to adopt a child. Over one-half of these women did not adopt a child and are no longer pursuing adoption. However, over 600,000 have adopted one or more children, and over 200,000 are still pursuing adoption (Bachrach, London, & Maza, 1991, cited by National Adoption Information Clearinghouse, 2002c).

A study conducted in California by Barth, Brooks, and Iyer (1995, cited in National Adoption Information Clearinghouse, 2002c) indicated differences among parents adopting independently and those adopting children from the public child welfare system. In both instances the families are typically two-parent families between the ages of 31 and 40, with a growing number of 41- to 49-year-olds. Some parents adopting from the public child welfare system, however, were under 30 years old. The most significant difference is found in family income with parents who adopt independently having incomes of $50,000 or more, and parents adopting from the public welfare system earning $30,000 or less. They also found that parents adopting independently were more likely to have attended or graduated from college. In a 1994 study in Canada by Daley and Sobol, these differences were again supported. They also found that parents adopting from the public child welfare system were twice as likely to have children of their own and to have been foster parents.

The evidence reveals a two-tiered system in our society's approach to adoptions. Healthy infants are highly sought through independent adoptions. The couples seeking these children tend to have higher incomes, have higher levels of education, and are willing to wait several years for a child. Children in the foster care system are usually older, come in sibling groups, and have been subjected to difficult life experiences. Couples who adopt these children tend to have children of their own, have been foster parents, and have moderate incomes. The two-tiered system for adoption that has evolved seems to be based primarily on the financial means of the potential adoptive parents.

Daley and Sobol (1994) reported that the most important eligibility criteria in approving or selecting adoptive parents—by 90 percent of public and private agencies—were marriage stability, motivation to adopt, problem solving ability, adaptability, warmth and nurturance, and understanding of adoption. Health of the adoptive parents was considered important by almost 75 percent and sexual orientation by 50 percent. The major difference found was that private agencies placed the couple's skills in coping with infertility as of greater importance than public agencies. Criteria considered somewhat less important by both private and public agencies included the parents' education, income, religion, marital status, and having other children in the family.

Although most families are seeking healthy infants, there are few available—especially in the public child welfare system. Additionally, for adoptive parents who are willing to consider younger children, the children under 5 years of age in the public child welfare system often have older siblings, and due to their past home-life may have physical, emotional, or behavioral difficulties. There may also be the added obstacle of termination of parental rights. For families with substantial incomes, the avenues of adoption may not be less arduous but they are more varied. Media reports on adoptions by celebrities show that those who can afford to adopt by other means do not often adopt through public child welfare.

Of the children adopted through the public child welfare system, the majority are adopted by their foster care parents (65%), and a few are adopted by relatives (15%). The remainder of those adopted go to unrelated families (20%). Single parents adopt one-third of the children. A large majority of the families (86%) receive an adoption assistance subsidy to meet the special needs of the child (National Adoption Information Clearinghouse (2002a). With large numbers of children awaiting adoption in foster care and yet so few adopted by unrelated families, we can conclude that there are many other avenues open to families who want to adopt children.

Types of Adoption

The four most common types of adoption are public agency, private agency, independent, and intercountry. State laws vary, and prospective adoptive parents must choose carefully which avenue they will take to find a child. Adoption has become a lucrative business in the United States even though there are laws against the "selling" of babies and children. Gallagher (1998) advises potential adoptive parents in their pursuit of a child to "balance time, money, and emotional risk" (p. 1). The avenue chosen by the prospective adoptive parents often depends on the amount of money to be spent, the length of time to be taken, and the level of disappointment the family is willing to accept.

Public agency-sponsored adoptions are the least expensive, often less than $500 per child. These children, however, will most likely be older, of a minority group, come with siblings, and have special health and mental health needs. There are adoption subsidies available to help the adoptive family if the child has special needs. Very few "healthy white infants" are available through public agencies. Of approximately 15,000 white infants adopted in 1996 nationwide, less than 5 percent were from public child welfare agencies (National Council for Adoption, 1999). For families willing to adopt children in foster care whose parents' rights have been terminated, the process can be completed fairly quickly, usually within one year of the child being freed for adoption.

Private adoption agencies are secular or faith based. The cost for adopting a "healthy infant," preferably white, can range from $5,000 to $25,000 and even higher if the adoptive parents are expected to cover the medical and living costs of the expectant mother. These agencies often have long waiting lists, some up to five to seven years. Today, unlike in the past, the vast majority of single young women (98%) elect to keep and raise their children instead of giving them up for adoption; therefore, infants available for adoption are highly valued.

Independent adoptions are usually arranged through an attorney without the benefit of agency screening, evaluation, or oversight. This does cut the red tape considerably, thus the timeframe is usually much faster once a prospective child is located. Adoptive parents should be familiar with state adoption laws, especially the timeframe a birth parent is given to rescind the agreement to adoption. The media abound with stories of adoptive families having to give a child back to the birth parents after a few months. In some instances, typically due to questionable placement practices, a child is returned to the birth parents years after the child was placed. The more typical disappointment occurs when the family wanting to adopt has already provided living and medical costs to a young woman and she decides to keep the baby. It is essential that prospective adoptive families work closely with their attorneys to understand their legal rights, which are actually few, in these situations. Unfortunately there are disreputable attorneys and agencies that charge exorbitant fees, falsify documents, and even promise the same child to different families. Prospective adoptive families are advised to investigate fully the attorney or agency.

Many families turn to intercountry adoptions in search of infants, often in response to media campaigns on the plight of the many children in orphanages in foreign countries. Clark and Shute (2001) chronicle some of the pitfalls of intercountry adoption in their story of one couple's journey to adopt a young girl from Russia. Although intercountry adoptions are reportedly more costly than domestic adoptions, the number of foreign children adopted by U.S. families has more than doubled in the last decade. In the past five years most of these children have come from China, Russia, Guatemala, South Korea, Ukraine, Romania, and India. A listing of countries and numbers of children adopted can be found at a number of websites, including www.abolishadoption.com.

Intercountry adoptions require approval from both countries, and dealing with the U.S. Immigration and Naturalization Service can be especially time-consuming. The medical history of foreign-born children is of special concern. These children come from countries with underdeveloped medical care systems and have often been living in orphanages in desperate conditions. The children may be diseased or have significant developmental delays. Neuropsychologist Ronald Federici (cited in Clark & Shute, 2001) says these children are high risk and that the adoptive parents often take the ultimate risk of waiving their rights to recourse against the agency if the child is later found to have serious problems. An especially positive note regarding intercountry adoptions is the Childhood Citizen Act of 2000. Foreign children adopted by U.S. parents become citizens when they enter the United States. Additionally, the U.S. Congress has ratified the international treaty called the Hague Convention on Inter-Country Adoption. The purpose of the treaty is to encourage international adoption and eliminate the illegal trafficking of children (Clark & Shute, 2001).

The avid interest of prospective adoptive parents in procuring an infant to bring into their family is demonstrated by their ads in the personal sections of newspapers. Countless statements of a warm, loving environment, educational and social opportunities, pets, siblings, and all advantages of the good life are presented in hopes of connecting with a woman seeking to place her unborn child for adoption. Couples who are unable to have children or wish to expand their family appear almost desperate to find a child to adopt. For the many reasons stated these couples opt for independent, private agency, or intercountry adoptions. They are willing to wait years, meet the high financial costs, and take extraordinary risks to adopt an infant or very young child.

With so many thousands of children in the public child welfare system awaiting adoption, the public child welfare system has obviously lost the leadership position it once held in the adoption arena. Our children wait for families, languishing in supposed temporary foster care, while the private, independent, and international adoption sectors search for acceptable children. Adoption is of course the preferable permanency plan for our children who cannot return home; the sad truth is, however, that those of us who work in child protective services shoulder the responsibility for making other arrangements to ensure the safety, permanency, and well-being of the many children in this nation who will not be adopted.

Long-Term Care: Stability When Reunification or Adoption Are Not Appropriate Goals

In the United States, half a million children are placed in out-of-home care. Many are awaiting reunification or adoption and are in foster homes under the guise of temporary care. Many of those children will remain in foster care for lengthy periods of time in hopes of returning to their parental homes or being placed for adoption. The placement of children in foster care has always been intended as temporary placement until such time as the children can be safely returned to their parents. Unfortunately, for many children the return to the parental home is not possible and the

Long-term foster care provides stability when reunification or adoption are not appropriate goals.

prospect of being adopted is unlikely. These children are placed in long-term care and their living situation becomes "foster care with tenure."

For children who are unable to go home or for whom an adoptive home is not available or is not wanted, another living situation must be considered. A policy of reunification or adoption as the only acceptable permanency goal is far too limited. Is a permanent foster care placement with foster parents that have made a long-term commitment to providing care and support more advantageous for the child than waiting for the minimal possibility of reunification—a reunification that if forthcoming is apt to fail? Is such permanent foster care preferable to permanent placement with a relative that shows signs of not succeeding? Is it preferable to an adoption that is unwanted by the child? Many foster parents are willing to provide a home, nurturance, and guidance to children placed in their homes for several years. This commitment should be considered for those children who will not return to their parental home nor be adopted.

Placement Decisions

Children enter out-of-home care placements for many different reasons: due to being victims of child abuse or neglect, due to the illness of their parent and no other relatives to provide care, due to the incarceration of their parent and no other family members willing or able to care for them, or due to medical or behavior problems that require care above what their parent can provide. Foster care placements can be of short duration of a few days to lengthy placements of several years. Though in most cases the plan is for the child to remain in care only for a short period of time, it is not always feasible to return children to their parents. Most often children come into care due to child maltreatment such as physical abuse, sexual abuse, abandonment, or neglect. When the problems that required the placement of the child are unresolved, and when no other suitable placement (such as with relatives) can be found, the child must remain in foster care. Although current child welfare policy indicates that children should be reunited with their families within twelve months or less, for some children the length of time in foster care must continue for longer periods of time.

Of the hundreds of thousands of children in the foster care system the vast majority, if given the choice and regardless of the maltreatment they endured, still desire to return to their parents. For many children, this return will not happen. Some parents have abandoned their children, and an increasing number of parents are and will remain incarcerated for many years. In some situations the child's parents are deceased, and in many instances the parents are unable or unwilling to make the necessary changes to ensure the safety and well-being of the child. For these children a permanent living arrangement must be found.

The mandate of permanency for all children placed in out-of-home care does not sufficiently address the situation of an older child. Although the age at which a child is considered an older child can be debated, the reality is that many children have strong attachments to their parents, memories of their lives with their parents and families, and the desire to preserve their identities with their parents and past lives. They have an established position in their families and view the termination of their parents' rights as voiding their own existence. Not only do they want to preserve their identity, they are not interested in being adopted. These children are seeking a safe home rather than new families. They want to remain a part of and be known by their family of origin even if they will not be able to live with that family again. For these children a long-term arrangement may be the most appropriate choice of care.

Concurrent planning is used to curb lengthy placements and facilitate progress toward permanency for the child. While working to reunite children with their parents or a permanent placement with a relative, the child welfare agency also plans for the possibility of termination of parental rights with a goal of adoption. This planning is especially prevalent in situations of severe child maltreatment and in cases where parental drug abuse is the primary factor in the placement of the child. Severe and continued maltreatment is often grounds for criminal prosecution of parents. If the parent is convicted and sentenced for a lengthy period of time, the goal of reunification may not be appropriate and other plans have to be made. Out-of-home placement is also necessary when a parent's use of drugs escalates to the point that the child is endangered or neglected, and reunification is not likely to occur very soon because the parent will not likely succeed at addressing the addiction through short-term treatment.

The Adoption and Safe Families Act of 1997 shortened the timeframe for development of a child's permanency plan from eighteen to twelve months. During this twelve months of placement parents are provided services to make the necessary changes in their lives to have their children returned. The case plan outlining the services and what changes must be made are ordered by the court when the decision is made that the child must be placed outside the parental home. Unless these parents make significant progress on their reunification case plan, their parental rights may be terminated and the child placed permanently with relatives or adopted by another family. If the parents are showing progress, the court may allow the parent additional time to make required changes to provide a safe place for the child. If a child has been in placement for 15 of the last 22 months, however, child welfare agencies are obligated to consider the termination of parental rights and the adoption of the child.

The philosophy supporting the practice of concurrent planning says a child should not be deprived of the stability of a permanent home due to the inability of a parent to make progress on correcting the issues that threatened the safety and well-being of the child and made placement necessary. Through concurrent planning, both reunification and future permanency for the child are addressed. If the plan for reunification fails, steps toward the pursuit of other permanency options—such as legal guardianship and adoption—are already noted and can be advanced in a timely manner. The goal is for children to experience stability and permanence in a relatively efficient timeframe.

Not all children placed in foster care are victims of child abuse and neglect. Some children have medical or behavior problems that require a level of professional care their parents cannot provide. These children may have severe disabilities, chronic illnesses, or mental health disorders that require a high level of care. In most cases, the parents of these children have attempted to maintain their children in their homes and it is with great reluctance that they come to the decision that the child needs to be placed. Children who are placed in care because of their medical and behavior problems bring a different challenge to the goal of permanency. Often these children cannot remain in their homes because they require advanced therapeutic interventions that parents are unable to provide. The possibility of meeting the permanency mandates is eliminated by the level and length of care these children need. The termination of parental rights and possibility of adoption are not usually factors in such cases. These children are placed because of special needs. The parents do not usually lose custody. In most cases the decision to place the child is heart wrenching for the parents, who suffer guilt and feelings of inadequacy when out-of-home care arrangements must be made. Due to ongoing needs, most of the children placed because of special needs will never return home. Decisions surrounding their long-term care should be based on their safety, permanence, and well-being, with significant parental participation in the planning and implementation.

The decision of when to place a child, where to place a child, and for how long is complex and must be tailored to the safety, permanency, and well-being of the individual child. Although emphasis is now placed on reunification and permanency, significant numbers of children cannot go home, have no suitable relatives to live with, and are unwilling or unable to be adopted. These children need the stability of a long-term relationship with foster parents who have made a commitment to caring for them.

The Option of Long-Term Care

Placement in long-term care can meet the needs of children who cannot be returned to their biological parents or homes of relatives, or for various reasons are unlikely to be adopted. Typically, the older the child is when entering care or the longer the child is in placement, the more likely the child will remain in care until adulthood. The older the child, the less dependent the child is on the parent. Friends become more important in social aspects of the child's life. Older children also have a better understanding of the reasons for placement and often choose to remain in placement. As placements continue, the relationship between the child and the parent weakens. Visits between the parent and child become fewer, and the child becomes attached to the foster family. Parents are unable to answer the older child's questions regarding why they are unable to return home and when they will be able to return home. Parents who are having difficulty in meeting the demands for changing their lifestyles often give up and allow the children to remain in foster care.

For many adolescents, family reunification and adoption are often not feasible alternatives. Twenty years ago, less than 5 percent of adolescents were adopted and more than 80 percent of the adolescents in foster care reportedly returned to their parents (Hornby & Collins, 1981). Bussey and colleagues (2000) found, however, that of those teens exiting care only 52 percent reunify with their parents. This seems to indicate that over the past two decades there has been a significant decline in the reunification of adolescents with their parents. Although reasons for this decline have not been provided, the increased number of parents being incarcerated and the increased length of sentences may be a significant influence. Adolescents that come into care because their parents have been incarcerated may have no home to return to when they exit foster care.

Under the guidelines of policy, children are often returned to the parental home prematurely, or returned because they have "failed" their placements and no other resources are available. If the situation that brought the youth into care has not been substantively resolved, the cycle of maltreatment is apt to begin again and the child will enter foster care again. Tatara (1993) estimated that approximately 25 percent of children who enter care will exit and then return to foster care within a year. This supports the belief that premature reunification results in the revolving door syndrome of placement.

In the movement to establish permanency for children in the foster care system, long-term care appears to have been overlooked, insufficiently considered, and almost discarded. The goal to provide a permanent home for children was born out of concern for children who were drifting about the foster care system, enduring multiple placements, and losing contact with their birth parents and families. The children lacked the stability necessary for developing necessary bonds and support systems or appropriate social skills for success in day-to-day life. Clearly there was a problem. The popular thought behind the reform legislation was that every child should be placed in a permanent home. Since foster care was considered temporary placement, the concept of permanent foster care was not included on the roster for permanency planning. Therefore, the preferred permanency plans for children in out-of-home placements today focus on family reunification, permanent placement with relatives, or adoption.

Foster care has always been viewed as a temporary response to a child's need for protection and care, although many children have spent years in the foster care system. Under current policy, child welfare practitioners are required to develop a written permanent plan for a child within 12 months of placement. According to Fenster (1997), foster parents are often confronted with the dilemma of making a decision to adopt a child early in the placement or face having the child removed from their care and placed in a preadoptive home. Without adequate time, information, and experience with a child, foster parents cannot easily make a decision of this nature. Although prepared to care and provide for the child on a long-term basis, the foster parents may desire to establish a stronger bond with a child before taking the major step to adoption. This long-term placement arrangement can provide the stability and permanence needed by children who cannot return to their families. Fenster (1997) outlines the advantages of permanent or long-term care. They include (1) funding based on entitlement rather than a yearly or quarterly appropriation; (2) an ongoing relationship with the child welfare agency, thus the provision of supervision and training to foster parents; (3) the child's knowledge that the placement is permanent and the foster parents committed to providing care for the long term; and (4) the opportunity for the child and foster parents to form strong attachments to each other. Long-term foster care can provide much more stability than multiple placements, failed reunification with family members, or a disrupted adoption.

For children in long-term placements or those placed at an older age, we need to address the challenges they encounter as they reach young adulthood. As they are dismissed from the child welfare system, often with nowhere to go and few skills, we must provide the necessary supports and resources that help them reach self-sufficiency.

The Transition to Independence

Those children who do not return to the homes of their parents or relatives or are not adopted leave the foster care system upon reaching adulthood. Oftentimes they exit foster care ill prepared to meet the demands of adulthood and destined to a future of uncertainty (Mech, 1988).

Challenges to Independence

Even with solid preparation, the young adult that moves out of the family home to launch into independent living often falters and requires additional social and economic support from the family and community. By comparison, the move to independence is dauntingly challenging for the youths leaving our foster care system. Upon reaching the age of majority, typically 18, the youths in foster care are dismissed and expected to care for themselves. Often they have no family to provide financial and social supports and no home to return to if needed. The term used for this child welfare dilemma is *aging out*. Most states abruptly withdraw financial responsibility for a young person when the age of majority is reached. Many states do continue supports for the youth past the age of eighteen who continues in the education system. Although some youths forge a strong enough bond with foster parents to be assured of additional support if needed, most youths—especially the ones leaving group home and other institutional placements—have nowhere to go when they face the challenges of transitioning to independence.

The trauma that brought the youths into foster care, the experiences while in care, the lack of a stable family system to rely on, and in general a poor preparation for adulthood present a dismal picture for the future. These youths usually experience difficulties in establishing stable and productive lives. They are likely to be unemployed or work in low-paying jobs; fail to gain a high school degree or its equivalent; have a criminal record; engage in high risk behavior including alcohol and drug use, prostitution, and early pregnancy; and have a greater likelihood of experiencing physical and mental health problems and episodes of homelessness (Barth, 1990; Bussey, Feagans, Arnold, Wulczyn, Brunner, Nixon, DiLorenzo, Pecora, Wiess, & Winterfield, 2000; Holmstrom, 1998; Loman & Siegal, 2000; Nelson, 2001).

Characteristics of Youths Exiting Foster Care

In today's society emphasis is placed on education and the development of life skills for obtaining and continuing stable employment. Youths with poor reading, writing, and math skills face unending challenges during adulthood. Although in the past people with limited education could gain prosperity through hard work and perseverance, even minimal success in today's world requires a basic education and more mental proficiency than physical labor. A national study was conducted by WESTAT in the mid-1980s to identify how well adolescents from foster care were adapting to independence and community life. Approximately 800 youths were contacted and interviewed. Approximately one-half had completed high school, one-third were receiving public assistance, one-half were employed, and fewer than one-half had been able to maintain employment for at least one year. More than half (60%) of the females had given birth to at least one child, and all the youths reported experiencing housing problems (Cook, Fleishman, & Grimes, 1991). Barth (1990) had similar findings in a study of 55 youths discharged from foster care in the San Francisco Bay Area. More than half of the youths had exited foster care without completing high school, almost half were receiving public assistance, over a third were homeless or moved frequently, 35 percent had been arrested or incarcerated, and 40 percent of the females reported having been pregnant at least once since leaving foster care. In a multistage, longitudinal study of more than 500 adolescent youths' potential for independent living, Mech (2003) reported similar results. About 40 percent had completed high school or the GED and about 30 percent were enrolled in a postsecondary education program. Employment among the youths was inconsistent. The majority had periodic bouts of unemployment with average earnings about $4,100 per year. Female youths were more apt to be receiving public assistance (40%) and over half (56%) were either pregnant at the time of the interview or parenting one or more children. Again, housing was a problem for the youths, many needing to live with others on a transient basis.

These studies show that the young people who age out of our foster care system are faring poorly. They are not prepared to meet the challenges of independent living. Poor educational outcomes, high levels of early parenting, unstable housing, and unemployment are prevalent among them, as compared to youths who enter independent living from parental homes.

The Needs of Youths Exiting Foster Care

Of the approximately one-half million children in out-of-home care, it is estimated that one-third or more are adolescents. Of these adolescents, approximately 20,000 youth annually age out at 18 to 21 years of age (in some states youths attending school remain in care until age 21) and leave care to face the challenges of young adulthood (Caliber Associates, 1999). These youths come from unstable homes, are likely to be victims of abuse and neglect, and often experience multiple placements during their stay in the foster care system. Children placed in foster care face challenges that most children raised in their own homes do not experience. Children placed in foster care often miss the affection, protection and intimate contact of normal family life, experience differentiated parenting that includes biological parents, foster parents, and the child welfare agency, experience an isolation from their communities, and have no place they can actually call home (Mech, 1988). They are typically ill prepared at best to meet the demands of adulthood.

The care provided for these youths while in the foster care system is costly. It simply does not make sense to dismiss these youths when they reach 18 years of age, that magic year of adulthood, without preparing them for a stable life (Nelson, 2001). We have met a financial obligation to these youths and a social obligation as well in providing for them during their childhood. Our obligation does not vanish on the eighteenth birthday. A major emphasis of our ongoing obligation must be in preparing them for their future as adults.

Preparation for basic self-sufficiency requires a high school education, its equivalent, or some type of vocational training. This level of preparation is essential if the youths are to secure and maintain employment and obtain affordable and safe housing. To live independently, the youths must be able to manage finances and perform household activities such as cooking, cleaning, and laundry. They also need access to needed health and mental health care and other community services (Caliber Associates, 1999). Although these qualifications and services are of a basic level, the youths exiting foster care experience great difficulties in attaining them.

In a thorough review of the literature available on youths and independent living initiatives, Loman and Siegal (2000) identified several types of independent living services needed by youths exiting the foster care system. These authors emphasized the need for life-skills training and remedial educational programs. They proposed residential and transitional housing programs with less structured settings than the typical foster home, from which youths would move into independent living as they develop the needed skills. A serious concern was the lack of follow-up services for the youths who exit foster care. They proposed continued case management services based on a thorough service assessment to ensure coordination in service delivery. Fifteen years earlier, Barth (1986) identified a number of needed services by adolescents transitioning from foster care. He emphasized the need for training for foster parents to help them prepare adolescents for independent living. He also suggested less restrictive but supervised homes for youths preparing for independent living. Due to the difficulties of finding and maintaining affordable safe housing, Barth suggested independent living subsidies to assist youths in securing and maintaining housing. Additionally, scholarships and educational enrichment programs were identified as important to the successful entry into adulthood. He urged the use of community volunteer mentors to assist and guide youths in attaining independence. He suggested that when appropriate, contact with the birth family be promoted to provide a safety net for youth struggling with becoming independent.

Both scholars and child welfare practitioners have agreed upon and consistently identified the challenges for youths exiting foster care as well as the services needed to assist in their preparation for independent living. The mounting evidence that youths in the foster care system were faring poorly upon exit from the system was voiced and was eventually heard by the nation's policy makers.

Independent Living Initiative

The first federal approach to impacting the challenges faced by youths exiting foster care was the Independent Living Initiative (PL 99-272) enacted in 1986 as a part of the Consolidated Omnibus Budget Reconciliation Act of 1985 (Allen & Nixon, 2000; Stoner, 1999). This legislation appropriated $45 million for states to provide services to prepare foster care youths aged 16 or older for independent living. Upon passage by Congress, the legislation met with strong resistance from both the Reagan administration and the Department of Health and Human Services. A primary reason given for stalling the disbursement of funds to the states for implementation of independent living programs was the position that there were sufficient funds available for independent living services through other federal programs (Allen, Bonner, & Greenan, 1988). The funding was originally targeted for a two-year cycle, but thanks to efforts by child advocates, state officials, and service providers it was continued on a year-to-year basis. The funds were intended to provide assistance to youths in gaining a high school diploma or its equivalent, training in living skills, individual and group counseling, coordination of services to youths, outreach activities to bring youths into the programs, and the development of a plan for independent living for each youth participating in the program. Several states developed independent living programs that included mentors from the community to work with individual youths, training programs for both foster parents and youths in attaining life skills, and scholarships for youths to attend college. Local high school districts worked with the agencies to develop needed educational plans and services to address the educational challenges of foster youths.

More youths were receiving services and innovative programs were being developed. But the challenges faced by foster care youths seeking independence continued. In response, the Independent Living Initiative grew in scope. The growth allowed for the provision and continuation of services to youths for six months after exiting foster care. By 1992 the funding allocation had increased to $70 million. This averages to approximately $3500 per youth. Since states have different programs and provide additional services through other funding, it is difficult to determine how much money is actually being spent in the preparation for independent living of youths exiting foster care. In 1993, seven years after its original enactment, the Independent Living Initiative was granted permanent authorization, thus ensuring continued future funding (Allen & Nixon, 2000). By 1998 total funding (federal, state, local, and private dollars) had increased to $131.5 million, thus providing over $6,000 per youth.

Program Development and Successful Interventions

In 1989, the Child Welfare League of America issued a set of standards to guide the development of programs for independent living services. The standards required a written plan for independent living programs that included youth involvement in the program planning process. One goal was that services be provided earlier, so the youths would be more likely to master tasks such as budgeting, cooking, and employment skills. Since many of the youths lacked the security of a stable family for support, aftercare services were recommended. The standards also called for the inclusion of birth families as well as foster parents and caseworkers in the preparation of youths to meet the challenges of living on their own (Child Welfare League of America, 1989).

The foster youth services provided by the states have focused primarily on instruction in daily living skills, education, and employment assistance. A number of evaluations of the programs and services to determine effectiveness have been conducted. Although the studies had varied approaches there is a consistent pattern of outcomes. Youths who participated in independent living programs that offered training in practical living skills; community-based mentors for assistance and guidance; educational opportunities such as alternative high schools, tutoring, and GED classes; and transitional housing such as supervised apartment living were able to maintain suitable housing and employment after exiting foster care (Loman & Siegel, 2000).

Independent living programs for youths exiting foster care usually focus on education, employment, and basic life skills. The issues of early parenting and future plans for life have not been addressed. Nollan (2000) suggests that there are four effective approaches in preparing youths for independent living: a thorough assessment of the youth's skills, training in needed living skills, involvement of caregivers in the teaching of skills, and development of community support networks that include birth parents and other relatives.

During the crafting of the legislation that enacted the Independent Living Initiative, many reports distributed in support of the various programs and services. Caliber Associates in collaboration with the National Resource Center for Youth Development prepared one of the most extensive reports. They analyzed 10 years (1987–1996) of final reports submitted by the states on independent living services provided to foster care youths. These annual fiscal and program reports were a federal requirement for funding by the Independent Living Initiative. The program report was to include program outcomes that would be used as a means to determine future funding of the program (Tatara, Casey, Nazar, Richmond, Diethorn, & Chapmond, 1988). Although the range of services differed across the states, there is no question that the Independent Living Initiative and subsequent funding supported the development of policies, programs, and services to deal with youths exiting care and assist them in meeting the demands and challenges of adulthood. Services included educational supports, employment services, physical and mental health care, and life skills development. In addition, over the decade of service provision, more social skill development was emphasized including areas such as decision making, conflict resolution and communication. With the increased funding and enhanced services, it was expected that youths participating in these programs would experience positive outcomes. Few, if any, evaluations were conducted to determine the effectiveness of the independent living programs. Those studies that were conducted were based on very small samples and for the most part reported only process outcomes such as types of services provided and how many youths participated in programs.

A major criticism voiced, however, was that not all eligible youths were receiving the needed services. Even youths that received the services continued to struggle socially and economically when they left the system and attempted to live on their own. It was noted that the youths needed to receive independent living services earlier and also on a continuous basis through aftercare programs. Despite the limitation of prohibiting the use of the independent living funds for housing or room and board costs, a call was made for more hands-on skill building. In addition to classroom living skills instruction, youths needed to experiment with the skills needed for independent living. Suggestions were made to have youths develop and live on a budget while in foster care, to set up bank accounts that youths would be responsible for keeping in balance, and also to have mock interviews for employment with community business people. Other areas, such as youth involvement in the development of services, staff and foster parent training, collaboration among agencies providing various youth services, and the dissemination of information among the programs across the country, were reported as continuing challenges to the success of the Independent Living Initiative. The general consensus was, however, that through increased funding and an enhanced array of services the youths exiting foster care were being better served and experiencing more positive outcomes (U.S. DHHS-ACYF, 1999).

In 1999, Congresswoman Nancy L. Johnson, Chair of the Subcommittee on Human Resources, Committee on Ways and Means, requested the U.S. General Accounting Office (GAO) to review the federal Independent Living Program (ILP) to determine the scope and effect of the services provided. The GAO conducted a comprehensive study that included a review of relevant literature, a survey of all 50 states and the District of Columbia, a review of the 1998 annual state reports, interviews with state and federal officials and independent living experts, and site visits to four independent living programs. The GAO findings were similar to those by Caliber Associates: states were providing a wide range of services, including (1) education assistance, (2) development of living skills, (3) employment assistance, (4) personal interaction skills development, and (5) aftercare services. Although the states were providing education and employment assistance, there were few opportunities provided to foster youths in matching skills and interests to available employment. Connections between the program staff and potential employers had not been fully developed. Vocational programs such as technology, culinary arts, and medical assistance were too costly to be available to the youths. More than 80 percent of the states offered some type of transitional living opportunities, allowing youths to live independently and practice becoming adept in meeting the challenges of adulthood while still receiving some supervision and monetary support. It was noted, however, that the number of these services was limited. Typically, approximately 10 percent of youths in need of transitional housing were served.

The Department of Health and Human Services (DHHS), the federal agency with oversight of independent living programs, was taken to task in the GAO report for providing little leadership in the area of Independent Living. It was reported that DHHS had commissioned only one national study, conducted by WESTAT, Inc., on the outcomes of independent living programs and services, and had few strategies to determine the effectiveness of independent living efforts across the states. The WESTAT study indicated that youths who participated in a combination of skills training (managing money, obtaining a credit card, completion of education, and employment assistance) improved their outcomes for self-sufficiency. A call was made for DHHS to develop a system of standardized reporting and monitoring tools to assess the effectiveness of independent living programs and services (U.S. DHHS-ACYF, 1999). Although it was recognized that progress had been made, it was evident that there is much yet to be done in providing necessary supports and services for the youths exiting foster care.

The Chafee Foster Care Independence Act

In the late 1990s, with one of the largest populations of older youths in placement, California was in a prime position to bring more attention regarding the plight of youths leaving the foster care system to the forefront of the Clinton administration. After a number of invitational visits to child advocacy agencies in California, former First Lady Hillary Rodham Clinton met with a group of foster youths from across the nation to discuss the challenges they were facing when leaving care. She announced early in 1999 the intent of the administration to increase Independent Living funds and to propose continuation of Medicaid coverage for youths aging out of foster care. The House of Representatives and the Senate soon proposed expansions of the Independent Living Initiative. Throughout the subsequent hearings, youths participated and made it clear that more services were needed. These youths were instrumental in bringing a loud and moving voice to the policymakers of the country. Several legislators had been strong supporters of the inaugural Independent Living Initiative, and their continued interest and political presence moved the expansion of the programs and services quickly through the legislative process.

On December 14, 1999 President Clinton signed into law the Chafee Foster Care Independence Act of 1999. The signing of the legislation was witnessed by a group of current and former foster youths. The Act was named in memory of Senator Chafee, one of the original sponsors of the legislation and a longtime champion of abused and neglected children (Allen & Nixon, 2000).

The Chafee Foster Care Independence Act replaced the Independent Living Initiative and made significant increases in the funding and services available to youths in foster care and former foster care youths. Funding was doubled from $70 million to $140 million. All youths in foster care are eligible for independent living services including youths who expect to be reunified with their families and youths who are awaiting adoption. Former foster care youths between 18 and 21 years of age are also eligible for services. A portion of state funds (30%) can be used for housing and room and board for youths who have aged out of foster care, states are allowed to extend Medicaid coverage to youths up to age 21 who are exiting foster care, and foster children may accumulate up to $10,000 in assets (Allen & Nixon, 2000). With the expansion of funding and services also came additional directives to states regarding youths and community involvement in the planning and development of programs and services, allocation of training funds for foster parents providing care to adolescents, and participation in the outcome based evaluation of services (Hormuth, 2001).

The evolution and progress of child welfare policy addressing the challenges of youths aging out of the foster care system has been a hard fought battle. Although great strides have been made, child advocates must continue to keep the issues of young adults in the forefront to ensure progress. The funds from the Chafee Foster Care Independence Act have been allocated, and new and expanded programs are being developed and services provided. Over the next three to five years there will be keen interest in the outcomes these new initiatives bring. One thing is certain: services and supports for our young people exiting foster care can make a difference and need to be available to all of them. Anything less fails not only the youths, but their families and communities as well.

As we have seen in this chapter, significant changes have been made in child welfare practices that advance the permanency movement for our children who cannot go home. Although we are early into the process, preliminary positive outcomes are being reported. Hopefully, this success will continue and our children who cannot go home will reap the benefits through appropriate individualized permanency plans of adoption, long-term care and independent living.

REFERENCES

Allen, M. & Nixon, R. (2000, July–August). The foster care independence act and John. H. Chafee foster care independence program: New catalysts for reform for young people aging out of foster care. *Journal of Poverty Law and Policy,* 197–216.

Allen, M., Bonner, K. & Greenan, L. (1988). Federal legislative support for independent living. *Child Welfare, 67*(6), 515–527.

Barth, R. P. (1986). Emancipation services for adolescents in foster care. *Social Work, 31*(3), 165–171.

Barth, R. P. (1990). On their own: The experiences of youth after foster care. *Child and Adolescent Social Work, 7*(5), 419–440.

Bussey, M., Feagans, L., Arnold, L., Wulczyn, F., Brunner, K., Nixon, R., DiLorenzo, P., Pecora, P. J., Wiess, S. A., & Winterfield, A. (2000). *Transition from foster care: A state-by-state data base overview.* Seattle, WA: Casey Family Programs.

Caliber Associates. (1999). *Title IV-E independent programs: A decade in review.* Washington, DC: U.S. Department of Health and Human Services.

Child Welfare League of America. (1989). *Standards for independent living services.* Washington, DC: CWLA.

Clark, K. & Shute, N. (2001). The adoption maze. *U.S. News & World Report, 130*(10), 60–67.

Cook, R., Fleishman, E., & Grimes, V. (1991). *A national evaluation of Title IV-E foster care independent living programs for youth, final report* (Vol. 1). Rockville, MD: WESTAT, Inc.

Curtis, C. M. & Alexander, R. Jr. (1996). The Multiethnic Placement Act: Implications for social work practice. *Child and Adolescent Social Work Journal, 13*(5), 401–410.

Daley, K. J. & Sobol, M. P. (1994). Public and private adoption. *Family Relations, 43*(1), 86–94.

Dukette, R. (1984). Value issues in present-day adoption. *Child Welfare, 63*(3), 233–243.

Fenster, J. (1997). The case for permanent foster care. *Journal of Sociology and Social Welfare, 24*(2), 117–126.

Freundlich, M. (1998). Supply and demand: The forces shaping the future of infant adoptions. *Adoption Quarterly, 2*(1), 13–42.

Gallagher, S. (1998). The many roads to adoption. *Kiplinger's Personal Finance Magazine, 52*(4), 1–2.

Gendell, S. J. (2001). In search of permanency: A reflection on the first 3 years of the Adoption and Safe Families Act implementation. *Family Court Review, 39*(1), 25–42.

Holmstrom, D. (1998). The unadoptables: What happens to tens of thousands of teens who 'age out' of foster care each year? *Christian Science Monitor, 90*(239), 1–3.

Hormuth, P. (2001). *All grown up, nowhere to go.* Washington, DC: Center for Public Policy Priorities.

Hornby, H. C. & Collins, M. I. (1981). Teenagers in foster care: The forgotten majority. *Children and Youth Services Review, 3*(1&2), 7–20.

Loman, L. A. & Siegel, G. L. (2000). *A review of literature on independent living of youths in foster and residential care.* St. Louis, MO: Institute of Applied Research.

Mech, E. V. (1988). Preparing foster adolescents for self-support: A new challenge for child welfare services. *Child Welfare, 67*(6), 487–495.

Mech, E. V. (2003). *Uncertain futures: Foster youth in transition to adulthood.* Washington, DC: Child Welfare League of America.

National Adoption Information Clearinghouse. (2002a). *Adoption from foster care.* Retrieved June 30, 2002, from www.calib.com/naic/pubs

National Adoption Information Clearinghouse. (2002b). *Adoption: Numbers and trends.* Retrieved June 30, 2002, from www.calib.com/naic/pubs

National Adoption Information Clearinghouse. (2002c). *Persons seeking to adopt.* Retrieved June 30, 2002, from www.calib.com/naic/pubs

National Resource Center for Special Needs Adoption. (1995). *Multiethnic Placement Act requires expanded agency recruitment efforts, 9*(1), 1–3.

National Council for Adoption. (1999). *Adoption fact book III.* Waite Park, MN: Park Press Quality Printing.

Nelson, D. W. (2001). Gratified but not satisfied on foster care independence. *Advocasey, 3*(2), 1–4.

Nollan, K. A.. (2000). What works in independent living preparation for youth in out-of-home care? In M. P.. Kluger, G. Alexander, & P. A. Curtis (Eds.), *What works in child welfare?* (pp. 195–204) Washington, DC: Child Welfare League of America.

North American Council on Adoptable Children. (1995, summer). Multiethnic Placement Act policy guidelines issued. *Adoptalk, 2.*

Stoner, M. R.. (1999). Life after foster care: Services and policies for former foster youth. *Journal of Sociology and Social Welfare, 26*(4), 159–175.

Tatara. T. (1993). *Characteristics of children in substitute and adoptive care: A statistical summary of the VCIS national child welfare data base (FY 1982 through FY 1990 data).* Washington, DC: American Public Welfare Association.

Tatara, T., Casey, P. R., Nazar, K. L., Richmond, F. K., Diethorn, R., & Chapmond, T. (1988). Evaluation of independent-living programs. *Child Welfare, 67*(6), 609–624.

U.S. Department of Health and Human Services, Administration on Children, Youth and Families (U.S. DHHS-ACYF). (1999). *Title IV-E independent living programs: A decade in review.* Washington, DC: Government Printing Office.

U.S. General Accounting Office. (1999). *Foster care: Effectiveness of independent living services unknown* (GAO/HEHS-00–13). Washington DC: Government Printing Office.

U.S. General Accounting Office. (2002). *Foster care: Recent legislation helps states focus on finding permanent homes for children, but long-standing barriers remain.* Retrieved July 2, 2002, from www.gao.gov

CHAPTER **10**

Doing Child Welfare

A fat man with greasy, black hair and a tattoo on his left bicep was chasing a small boy, trying to hit him with a stick. A postal carrier delivering the mail to the house yelled at the man, "Hey, leave that kid alone, you big piece of crap."

The man stopped, turned to face the carrier, and said, "Just 'cause you're wearing a uniform don't make you a cop. Get outta here—and mind your own business 'fore I use this stick on you."

The postal carrier was frightened, and she did believe in minding her own business. She finished her route and tried to forget about what she had seen, but concern for the child—and guilt—kept nagging at her. Two months later, she called the child abuse hotline and reported that she feared something bad was going on at 239 Cornell Street.

231

So, on a cold and rainy March morning, social worker Anna Simms turned onto Cornell Street and faced the challenge of finding the right house. Apparently, few people on Cornell Street believed in house numbers. Anna finally located two adjacent houses with numbers: 204 next to 209. By figuring that the numbers increased by increments of five, she counted six more houses and located number 239.

Anna pulled her Jeep Cherokee to the curb in front of the house and scanned the area before unlocking her door. This was a high-crime neighborhood, in the heart of the drug trade district. Caution was in order. The houses on Cornell Street had been built shortly after World War II. In 1947, they were the starter homes of returning GIs, and in the 1950s, this had probably been one of those stereotypical American neighborhoods of working dads, stay-at-home moms, and lots of kids. By the 1960s, those residents would have become more prosperous and moved on to bigger houses in the suburbs, and this area would have become more commercial and industrial, with the residents poorer and poorer and increasingly transient. The houses now had the look of long-term rental property, with warped and cracked siding, rusty screens, and more than a few boarded-over window-panes. At the house next door to 239, a hand-painted sign nailed to a tree said, "FOR RENT— $79.95 PER WEEK—$100 MOVES YOU IN!"

Seeing no immediate reason for concern, Anna got out of the Cherokee and approached 239. The house had recently been painted yellow, but evidently, only one coat had been applied. The old color—pink—still showed, and the combination made for a sickly kind of hue that Anna imagined her 8-year-old niece would call "baby poop." The frontyard was enclosed in a chainlink fence that had been patched with brightly colored electrical wire. The fence corralled six semi–wild appearing dogs that were wandering around between pools of mud and patches of knee-high weeds, peeing on an old car and snapping at one another when they got too close.

Anna knew for sure she did not want to confront the dogs, so she yelled at the front door. "Hello, hello, is anyone home? Could you please come and get your dogs? I'd like to speak to you." In the six years she had been a child welfare worker, this approach had never worked, and it didn't work this time, either.

Anna had to decide whether to brave the dogs or return to the office without making contact with the family in 239. If she returned to the office, she would have to arrange to visit the home later that day, accompanied by the police and animal control, which would mean a huge scene. Such a disturbance could be depended upon to alienate the family, wipe out any possibility of establishing a positive relationship, probably making the family so uncooperative that she would be forced to ask the police to physically remove the children. This would mean Anna would be working until the middle of the night to get the required court order, locate an emergency foster placement, and advise the parents of agency procedures and their rights.

The decision-making model boiled down to this: Get her supervisor, the police, animal control, family court, the foster home placement unit, and at least one foster family involved in the case, making what might be a relatively simple matter into a huge deal that could take two years to straighten out—or brave the dogs.

Anna had a date that night, her first in three months, so the choice was easy. She cautiously put one hand over the fence and called to the dogs. All six ran up, jockeying for position, and slobbered on her hand and arm. Apparently, she was not going to be bitten—she was going to be a mess of dog spit and paw prints. She pushed open the gate, heaving against the weight of the dogs, and walked as gracefully as you can with 800 pounds of dogs jumping, barking, and licking you.

Anna knocked at the door and then knocked again and again. After about five minutes, a women opened the door a crack, enough to release a gust of superheated air that smelled of grease, garbage, dirty Pampers, a litter box, and unwashed bodies. A TV was blaring, a baby was crying, and it sounded like some other children were fighting. Anna peeked around the edge of the door and saw a young child, apparently a girl, lying on a ratty sofa and sucking her thumb. The appearance of the child—lethargic, with a bluish tint to the skin, bones clearly visible through the skin, and a distended stomach— reminded Anna of pictures in *National Geographic* of starving children in some famine-stricken land. Anna turned her head to get a gulp of fresh air before she spoke.

"Good morning. My name is Anna Simms, and I'm a social worker with the Department of Social Services. We received a call expressing concern about your children, and I have been assigned to investigate. If there is no problem, we can take care of this in only a short time, and then I'll let you get back to your day. Can I come in and speak to you for a few minutes?"

The woman said, "I'm sorry, but I'm sick. I can't talk to no one today. Come back next week." She began to close the door.

Anna stuck her foot in the door, thinking "I can't believe I'm doing this."

"Ma'am, I'm legally required to see your children and to speak to you today. If there is no problem, we will be done in a matter of minutes. If there is a problem, I'll try to help you. Please, can I come in so we can talk?"

In a surprising show of strength, the woman kicked Anna's foot out of the doorjamb and slammed the door. Anna heard the metallic sound of a deadbolt. She spent the next five minutes fighting off the dogs and pleading through the door for the woman to let her in. Finally, she returned to the car, wiped off the dog slobber, and used her cell phone to call her supervisor and the department's contact at the police department. She started the Jeep, turned on the heater, and busied herself with recording the incident while she waited for the police. When she saw the police car pulling up, she muttered to herself, "I guess tonight isn't going to be date night for Anna Simms after all."

Anna Simms is one of 10 child welfare social workers that met with us for a lengthy lunch and discussion once each week over a three-month period. Anna and her colleagues worked for the Kaye County Department of Family and Children's Services, a public child welfare agency in a midsized industrial city in the Midwest. Their work experience ranged from less than 2 to more than 20 years. They provided much of the information for this chapter about doing child welfare.[*]

---

[*]By agreement with the agency and the participants, the names of the social workers, clients, county, and agency are pseudonyms.

The Agency

Anna Simms and her colleagues are part of the approximately 65,400 social workers employed by public child welfare social agencies in the United States. These agencies are located in all political subdivisions in the country. The majority of the funding and legal mandate for their positions comes from the federal government, but a significant portion—legal and financial—comes from state and local jurisdictions. In 35 of the 43 states (81 percent) that responded to a recent survey, the child welfare system was run by the state government; in the remaining 8 states, the system was state supervised but administered on the county level (Alliance for Children and Families, 2001). The Kaye County Department of Family and Children's Services is one of the state-supervised, county-administered agencies.

Agency Functions

Public child welfare agencies, by law, are charged with the responsibility of protecting children from abuse, neglect, and exploitation. The task is generally broken down into two groups of functions. The first group is generally referred to as *intake,* which is further broken down into (1) screening, (2) investigation and substantiation, (3) risk assessment, and (4) service planning. The second group of functions is referred to as *ongoing services* and is broken down into (1) services to families and children at home, (2) foster care services, and (3) adoption or long-term care.

INTAKE The first intake function is complaint screening. *Screening* refers to the process of deciding if a complaint fits the agency's mandate for service. Child welfare agencies do not respond to all complaints—only the ones they are empowered to act on. State law specifies which problems are to be addressed. The particular problems involve child maltreatment, and although the definitions of maltreatment from state to state are not exactly the same, they are very similar. Some states define educational neglect as a reason for protective service intervention; some do not. Some require protective service intervention in all cases of positive drug screens on infants; some do not (Wells, 2000, p. 3).

Furthermore, before the agency can respond to a complaint, the problem has to be sufficiently serious to require protective service intervention. Anna recalled

> receiving a referral regarding an 8-year-old latchkey child who was at home by himself for two hours every day after school before his mother got home from work. The neighbor who made the referral was hell bent that we force the mother to place the child in an after school program. While it is not ideal for an 8-year-old to be home by himself, my agency concluded that this was not a situation requiring intervention.

At the end of the screening process, a case is rejected for service, referred to a more appropriate agency, or opened for investigation. In Anna's state, approximately 54 percent of complaints are screened in for investigation, closely approximating the national rate of 67 percent. (Child and Family Services Administration, 2000, p. 1; U.S. DHHS, 2003, p. 14).

When a case is opened for investigation, the investigators begin the process of substantiation: deciding whether there is sufficient evidence to conclude that child maltreatment has occurred. Once again, states differ regarding the procedures, guidelines, and evidence necessary to substantiate a case. According to Drake (1996), the substantiation decision depends on the answers to two questions: Is the harm to the child severe enough to constitute child maltreatment? and Is there sufficient evidence to support this being a case of child maltreatment? In order to substantiate a case, investigators must answer yes to both questions.

In some states workers choose between *substantiated* and *unsubstantiated,* and other states include a third category of *indicated,* which lets the social worker note belief or evidence that maltreatment has occurred, although not enough to substantiate the case. In 2001, 27.5 percent of cases investigated were substantiated and 4.4 percent were indicated (U.S. DHHS, 2003, p. 16). Concurrent with the investigation is the process of assessing risk, which was discussed in Chapter 4.

When a case has been substantiated and the risk assessment has been completed, the agency immediately begins the process of service planning. Initial service planning generally has one of three outcomes. The first potential outcome is that the case, although substantiated, will be immediately closed. Anna recalled such a case:

> A single father was leaving his two preschool age children in the care of his 9-year-old daughter when he had to work on weekends. This case was substantiated because this did violate state statutes, and the evidence clearly indicated that it was in fact happening. However, when I explained that this was a violation of state law, emphasized the risks to the children, and, most importantly, provided information on day care the father could afford that was available on weekends, he immediately made acceptable arrangements and the case was closed.

The second possible outcome of initial service planning is that the case will be opened for service but no court action will be taken. This occurs in cases that are serious enough to warrant ongoing agency involvement but where the imminent risk of serious harm to the children is low and the caretakers are open to receiving service. Daniel, one of Anna's colleagues and a focus group member, described a case involving a mildly retarded young mother, who clearly loved her child but was in need of much support and education regarding care for her child and other aspects of day-to-day living. The young woman was acutely aware of her needs and very receptive to help from Daniel and the agencies he recruited to help.

The final potential outcome of initial service planning involves situations where the agency files a court petition for custody of the child. The agency may be granted custody with the child remaining in the home under agency supervision; the agency may be given temporary custody and the child placed in foster or residential care while the agency works with the parents to correct their problems; or the parents' rights may be permanently terminated and the agency will plan for the child's long-term care.

ONGOING SERVICES   Once a case has been screened, investigated, and assessed and a service plan has been developed, the agency then provides *ongoing services*. Depending on the service plan, ongoing services can be either of two broad types: (1) services to families and children with the children at home or (2) services to families and children with the children in substitute care.

The most common means of service to children at home is traditional supervision. This means that the case is assigned to a social worker that has a number of other cases, and the social worker visits the family on a regular basis. The worker provides counseling to the family and makes referrals to other agencies for both supportive services, such as education and therapy, and concrete services, such as the provision of food, clothing, financial help, and so forth. The social worker regularly updates the risk assessment and service plan for the family and child, making adjustments where necessary. If the situation deteriorates, the worker may go to court to request that the child be removed. Hopefully, the situation will improve. If this happens, the worker tapers off the services being provided and eventually closes the case.

An approach to providing services to children at home that has been increasing in popularity is *family-based services,* also known as *family preservation.* This approach is based on the belief that in many cases where removal of the child from the home appears imminent, it is possible to prevent placement by providing intense services delivered in the child's home over a brief, time-limited period. Tracy (1995, p. 973) lists five primary goals of family preservation services:

- To allow children to remain safely in their own homes
- To maintain and strengthen family bonds
- To stabilize the crisis situation that precipitated the [referral]
- To increase the family's coping skills and competencies
- To facilitate the family's use of appropriate formal and informal helping resources

Family-based services begin, as do most child welfare interventions, when a child is referred to an agency as being in danger of serious harm. A social worker investigates the complaint and, if the complaint is confirmed, decides if the family is a good candidate for family preservation services. For a family to be considered appropriate, the child must be at risk of placement, but the social worker must be convinced that the child can remain safely in his or her own home if intensive services are provided. Depending on the model of family-based services being applied, the family is given services for periods ranging from four to six weeks in the most intensive models and three to six months in the less intensive models. The social workers providing services have small caseloads, sometimes as small as two or three families, and work with each family for many hours each week, sometimes 20 or more. After providing the brief intensive services, the agency withdraws to serve a supervisory role (as described earlier) and leaves the family to function, presumably with a greatly improved level of child care and problem-solving capacity.

In cases where the family situation is assessed to be dangerous to the child or the child is experiencing such severe behavioral problems that the family cannot cope, substitute care is provided in the form of foster care, group home placement, institutional care, or adoption. The placement of children in foster care involves two sets of specialized functions by the agency. The first is that of recruiting, training, licensing, and supervising foster homes and matching homes with children. The second set of functions involves working with the child in the foster home and, even more critical, working with the child's parents to address the problems that led to the place-

ment. With these functions, the objectives are to engage the biological family in the work of repair in order that the child may be returned to the home as quickly as possible; to engage the foster parents in the responsibility for the child, particularly at points of change in the child's circumstances; and to help the child cope with problems of identity and change (Meyer, 1983, pp. 488–491).

Children are placed in group care or institutional care by the protective service agency in cases where the child has special needs that cannot be met by a foster home. Group homes are often a helpful alternative in providing care for older children. As explained by Meyer (1983),

> The child in group care does not have to deal with identity issues in the same way as does the foster child cohort. Children in group care are not faced with confusion about their own names while living with a family of a different name; they do not have to make choices between their own family and the foster family upon whom they depend; children in small group care, by definition, because group homes are located within urban communities, are less likely to be placed outside their own family's community, so that ties to friends, school, and relatives can be maintained. (p. 489)

Institutional care is provided in cases where the child has special psychological, behavioral, or developmental needs that cannot be dealt with in a nonspecialized setting, such as a foster home or group home. With group care or institutional placement, the protective service agency's function consists of making an accurate assessment followed by a solid referral to the appropriate setting. Once the placement has been made, the protective service agency steps back and administers the legal and fiscal elements of the placement, keeps in close contact with the placement setting to monitor progress of the child, and works with the child's family to plan for reunification as soon as possible.

In situations where it is determined that the child will never again be able to live with the biological parents, protective service agencies make adoptive placements. Again, as described by Meyer (1983)

> The organizational power over children and families in this area of child welfare requires sensitive, delicate skills and extensive knowledge. The decision to place for adoption, the preparation of children, the selection of adoptive parents, the handling of "failed placements," the termination of biological parent rights, and the engagement with courts and other social agencies are among the most serious tasks social workers can do, partly because of their life long implications. The choice points involved in the adoption process rest in highly complex psychosocial dynamics. (pp. 490–491)

For these reasons, the adoption function is generally performed by the most experienced and highly trained social workers in protective service agencies. Generally, adoption workers hold the master's of social work (MSW) degree.

Agency Organization

Child welfare agencies can be organized in a number of ways to perform the functions described in the previous section. In a rural area, there is probably one unit—indeed, often one person—to handle all the tasks. Agencies located in urban settings are often organized into specialized units.

The Kaye County Department of Family and Children's Services is located in a medium-sized city and employs 40 social workers organized into six specialized units. One unit does intake and screening—that is, actually staffing the telephones and intake desk and receiving complaints and requests for service. This unit also provides immediate crisis response. This is a small unit that is assisted by the rest of the social work staff, who take turns providing evening and weekend coverage.

Although not in the intake unit, Anna provided coverage one weekend day and one weekday evening per month. She was required to carry a pager and cell phone when she provided coverage, and she had to remain within the county and have immediate access to her car. When she was on call, she usually received only a few calls, and most involved situations that could wait until regular office hours. However, she had spent evenings with the police removing children from a crack house and at the hospital's emergency room taking custody of children whose father had been shot by their mother.

The Kaye County Department of Family and Children's Services (DCFS) has several *protective services units.* They handle investigation, assessment, and initial case disposition, including court action. (Anna was a member of a protective services unit.) At the end of a protective services investigation, a case in Kaye County would be assigned one of the following classifications:

Category V: "Services Not Needed." No future risk of harm to the child. Cases are closed and no further action is taken.

Category IV: "Community Services Recommended." No evidence of child abuse or neglect, but the assessment indicates a low or moderate risk of future harm to the child. Cases are referred to appropriate agencies and resources, and DFCS closes the case.

Category III: "Community Services Needed." Evidence of child abuse or neglect is found. Assessment indicates a low or moderate risk of future harm to the child. DFCS assists the family in receiving community services. DFCS may reclassify the case as a category II if the family refuses to participate in community based services. The person who harmed the child is listed on the central registry.

Category II: "Child Protective Services Required." Evidence of child abuse or neglect, and assessment indicates a high or intensive risk of future harm to the child. DFCS must open a protective services case and provide necessary services. In situations where the child is left in the home for ongoing services and supervision, the protective service unit continues with the case.

Category I: "Court Petition Required." DFCS determines that child abuse or neglect exists and that one or more of the following are true:

1. A court petition is required under a provision of the child protection law.
2. The child is not safe and a petition for removal is needed.
3. The agency previously classified the case as a category II and the family does not voluntarily participate in services.
4. There is a violation of specific sections of the criminal code involving the child. (Child and Family Services Administration, 2000, p. 2)

Not all child welfare agencies use this exact five-level classification scheme, but all use some similar method of classification.

Another unit in the Kaye County agency is the *intensive family services unit*. It serves families that fit fairly narrow criteria: The child is assessed as being at risk of placement but not in danger of imminent harm, and the family is amenable to short-term intensive services. In Kaye County, the intensive family services unit uses the Homebuilders model. This model is very intensive: The social worker carries only two or three cases at a time, provides 10 to 20 hours per week service to each family, and keeps each case open for only four to six weeks. The family preservation workers help parents learn to shop, clean, physically care for their children, plan meals, cook, and do anything else necessary for successful parenting. While teaching parents these skills, the social workers also teach child development and childrearing skills, including communication, appropriate discipline, boundary setting, anger management, and others as indicated by the assessment.

Anna spent a year as an intensive family services worker, but she found it far too intense and at the same time boring. She felt that spending hours at a time with the same people discussing shopping, menus, and childrearing was, frankly, tedious. Anna also admitted that she has a strong aversion to physical labor, and as an intensive family worker, she often found herself having to do things she considered actual work. She far preferred the "no heavy lifting," fast pace, and variety in her work as a protective service worker.

Bill, by contrast, described himself as an "intensive family services junkie." He said,

I love the chance to occasionally put on jeans, a sweatshirt and work boots, instead of the dress shirt and slacks that social workers usually have to wear. I get a real high from helping a family learn to organize their garage, clean up their yard, or plant a garden, all the while gently talking to them, often modeling, ways to be an effective parent.

Before a child is removed from his or her home, the protective service unit social workers are charged with the responsibility of making a reasonable effort to prevent the placement. This point is a difficult one, because statutes and case law are very vague about what constitutes *reasonable efforts*. One judge may consider four appointments with parents that failed to show up for any of the appointments reasonable efforts, while another judge may expect the social worker to track the parents down, even if this involves days of effort, with little prospect of a payoff.

After reasonable efforts have been documented, if placement is still considered necessary, the Kaye County agency assigns the case to one of several *foster care units*. These units handle cases where the child is placed in a foster home with the intention of returning him or her to the parents. These are complex cases that involve severe abuse or neglect and sometimes abandonment; they are frequently complicated by drugs, alcohol, or mental illness. Although the goal is family reunification, such an outcome is not always possible.

With the child in temporary placement, the foster care unit proceeds with *concurrent planning*. This approach seeks to minimize the time a child spends in temporary placement. Social workers provide services and support to the parents and child in an attempt to resolve the problems that led to placement, yet simultaneously, they plan for adoption or another permanent placement in the event that satisfactory progress is not made toward reunification.

The foster home licensing unit in the Kaye County agency is responsible for recruiting, training, and licensing foster homes. It is also responsible for matching children with foster homes. This unit works closely with the media to publicize the needs of dependent children and make an appeal for foster parents to care for these children. In periodic information sessions, the workers explain the need for foster homes and the process of becoming licensed foster parents. They interview people who are interested, study their homes, and run thorough background checks. Throughout the process, the workers stress the realities of foster parenting. Prospective foster parents must understand that they are likely to receive children with severe problems who will manifest some very difficult behaviors. The social workers try their best to determine whether a person is up to the challenge of foster parenting, for they want very much to avoid placement where the child must subsequently be removed from the home.

When Anna investigated a case that resulted in the child being removed from the family home, she made a referral to the foster home licensing unit and asked them to find a foster home for the child. Anna and a foster home licensing worker collaborated in placing the child in the best available home. Then Anna transferred the case to the foster home unit, which worked with the child, the foster parents, and the biological parents to try to reunify the family.

Two social workers in the Kaye County foster home licensing unit are designated *adoption workers*. When the court determines that the agency has made reasonable efforts to reunify a child with the parents and also determined that there is no chance of reunification, the parental rights are terminated and the agency is charged with finding a permanent home for the child. In the past, some children were defined as not being adoptable due to age, illness, disability, behavioral problems, and so forth. Current philosophy is that every child is adoptable and has the right to a family. Due to this change in philosophy, the adoption workers in Anna's agency, as well as in every other child welfare agency in the United States, spend most of their time finding homes for special-needs children. This involves a lot of publicity work, doing things like preparing "Sunday's Child" features for the local newspaper, setting up public information meetings, addressing civic groups, and doing radio and television interviews.

When a couple applies to adopt a child, the social workers engage in a process similar to that with foster parent applicants only more thorough and detailed, due to the permanent nature of the planned relationship. As they are with foster parents, social workers are very careful to be sure that the applicants truly understand the realities of adopting a child and that they are entering the process for the right reasons. People investigate adoption for a lot of reasons, perhaps because they are lonely, or their marriage is deteriorating and they think a child will save it, or they feel their lives lack meaning. Obviously, reasons of this nature are not conducive to successful placements. The agency wants to screen out these applicants early in the process. One of the most difficult aspects of an adoption worker's job is dealing with failed placements, those situations where the adoptive parents decide they have made a mistake—that the placement is not working. They come to the agency to "give the child back."

Public child welfare agencies like that in Kaye County, which are organized into specialized units, experience a major problem: A case may be transferred to as many as four different social workers in a relatively short period of time. This creates confusion on the part of the children and families and duplication of effort on the part of the agency. It also makes the formation of a positive working relationship difficult. Given these issues, the trend now is for agencies to organize all of the functions into each unit and each worker's job description. A recent survey found that in 52 percent of the states, some counties were assigning the same caseworker from the beginning to the end of a case; of the total number of counties, only 15 percent had introduced this practice (Administration for Children and Families, 2002, pp. 3, 7).

The Child Welfare Worker

Anna's Job

Anna had worked for the Kaye County Department of Family and Children's Services for six years, most of that time in a protective service unit. When asked how she selected her career, she gave this answer:

> You know, I've come to think of child welfare social work as an "accidental career." Many of my friends have what I call "destination careers." They are teachers, lawyers, nurses, and the like. They all decided on their careers years before they actually began work and then embarked on a long series of steps that eventually involved their getting (or in some cases not getting) the career they wanted.
>
> As for me, I didn't have the slightest idea of what I wanted to do with my life, so I ended up majoring in criminal justice in college, mostly because I had to pick a major and crime sounded interesting. In my senior year, I took an introductory social welfare course as part of the requirement for my CJ major. I just loved this course and the professor, a wonderful man who drummed into our heads the statement "I don't care what a person has done, or how sorry he seems, that person has innate worth and is entitled to dignity and respect." This was so different than the perspective I was getting in my criminal justice courses, where people were referred to as "perps," "dirt bags," "animals," "skells" (I still don't know what that means, but I know it's not a compliment) and all sorts of other derogatory names. As one of the projects for this course, I met the director of the local child welfare agency and one thing led to another, until I eventually ended up with a job as a child welfare worker trainee.
>
> Three years ago, I went back to school in the part-time MSW program and got my master's degree last spring. So, I guess that this is now my lifetime career, although I can't remember ever making a real conscious decision that this was what I wanted to spend my whole life doing.

Anna's comments are insightful, and her experience is fairly typical. Rycraft (1991) conducted in-depth interviews with 23 child welfare workers and found this:

> These caseworkers entered a field of social work practice they virtually knew nothing about. For the most part, they just happened by and entered the field with little understanding or knowledge of what their jobs would entail. Most of them were naive and held an innocence of the problems addressed in child welfare. Public social services was often the only game in town when they first entered the job market. The agencies had openings in child welfare, and often that was the reason these caseworkers entered the field. (Rycraft, p. 5)

Child welfare agencies generally provide staff with extensive in-service training programs.

Unfortunately, Anna's lack of any specific training in social work, much less child welfare, is also typical. A recent study conducted by the American Public Human Services Association (Cyphers, 2001) and the Child Welfare League of America found that only one-third of the states require a social work license for employment as a child welfare worker. The remaining states require only a bachelor's degree in any position, and in some cases, it is possible to be employed in child welfare with less than a bachelor's degree (p. 9). The reason for the low entrance requirements imposed by state personnel systems on child welfare workers has less to do with a lack of recognition of the importance of social work education than it does with problems with recruiting job-ready candidates.

Once a person is employed in child welfare, most states, recognizing the general lack of preemployment child welfare education, make available numerous training opportunities. The average state requires 136 hours of pre-service training for child welfare workers and 23 to 28 hours per year of in-service training. A majority of the states (58 percent) provide educational financial support for workers to earn a bachelor's of social work (BSW) degree, and 80 percent provide support for earning a master's of social work (MSW) degree (American Public Human Services Association, p. 9).

As a master's-level social worker with six years of experience, Anna earned a little less than $42,000 per year in 2001, plus the standard benefits of a state employee. Anna worked in a heavily unionized midwestern state, and so her benefits were excellent, carrying a value of almost 30 percent of her salary. It is difficult to determine how typical Anna's salary is, due to the vast number of civil service systems (state, city, and county) that employ child protective service social workers and also due to the complexity of the salary structure within each system. The American Public Human Service Association (2001) survey just cited found that the average pay of the agencies responding was $33,436 in 2000. This figure was just an average and did not account for education, experience, rural or urban setting, or any other variables.

Thinking that this figure seemed very low, we surveyed a number of state and county civil service websites in 2002. For MSW-level child protective service social workers, Mecklenburg County, North Carolina (Charlotte), advertised a pay range from $34,957 to $59,426; Hennepin County, Minnesota (Minneapolis), advertised $35,520 to $58,980; and Orange County, California (Los Angeles), posted a range from $43,248 to $58,308, with an additional $2,300 for people hired into positions requiring bilingual skills. A 2005 job announcement from Washington, DC, advertised a salary range of $31,250 to $53,583 for BSW-level social workers, $43,964 to $72,289 for MSW-prepared social workers, and $62,268 to $81,246 for supervisory positions. On the downside, Randolph County, North Carolina (rural), indicated a pay range of $24,372 to $33,708. The low average pay found in the APHSA (Cyphers, 2001) survey can probably be explained as the result of a disproportionate number of rural agencies responding.

As these figures indicate, the stereotypical image of child welfare as a very low paying career is not entirely true. In fact, Rycraft (1991) found salary levels to be a problem for exactly the opposite reason as usually thought. Among her sample of child protective service workers, there were some who were burned out, no longer enjoying or productive at their jobs, who could not leave because they couldn't match the salary and benefits elsewhere. The workers cynically referred to this problem as the "golden handcuffs" (p. 17).

The Downside of Being a Child Welfare Worker

Although Anna loved her job and was not entirely unsatisfied with the pay and future prospects, she admitted that it did have a downside. In the focus group meetings I conducted with Anna and her colleagues, I found that their job concerns could be categorized into four general yet related groups: (1) role conflict, (2) job responsibility and job stress, (3) unsafe and unsanitary working conditions, and (4) worker safety.

ROLE CONFLICT   When Anna and her co-workers met socially, a favorite topic of conversation was the dumb things people say after learning they are child welfare workers. One of Anna's best friends in the office, Denise, a 15-year veteran of child protective services, said,

> My favorite is when I tell people I work for child welfare and they look at me with a sly smile and say "Neat! Can you get me some of that welfare?"—as though child welfare is part of public assistance and that people who receive welfare are doing so well that being on welfare is a good place to be. Even when I explain that I have nothing to do with public welfare, I still get held responsible for what people see as the sins of the system, and they proceed to lecture, sometimes even attack me about how we are helping deadbeats, wasting the taxpayers' money, ruining the motivation of

the poor to improve themselves, and generally harming the economy. Now when I'm asked what I do, I'm sure not going to use the word *welfare* anywhere in my answer. I now say that I work for the state and hope they don't pursue the matter. If they do, I say I'm a child protection investigator. This makes it look like I'm some kind of cop, but at least people don't go off on me.

Beth, a social worker in Anna's unit who had been with the agency a little over a year, said that when she tells people what she does for a living, they

sometimes begin to rant and rave about punishing the parents, saying things like we should jail them and throw away the key, that we should hang them up by their thumbs, and all sorts of punitive junk. If I explain that we are not really about punishing parents, that our main purpose is to see if we can help them get their lives together so they can care for their own kids, I get treated to a blast about not risking the lives of kids in the service of some half-baked liberal philosophy. I was talking to a guy in Sunday school last week who spent 10 minutes explaining free will and that children were a gift from God and we should only get one chance. He concluded by saying that there are plenty of loving homes for children whose parents have used up their one chance. I tried to explain to him that this was not true, but he didn't want to hear it.

Anna said her pet peeve was the way

people give me this doe-eyed look and say something like, "Oh, I think you are so wonderful. I could never do that kind of work, but I'm so grateful for people like you who do. I wish they would pay you more money, but, then, you don't really do it for the money, do you?" If I reply with something like "Well, yeah, I make a fairly good living doing this and hope to do better in the future," they look at me like I'm some kind of Philistine.

The problems that Anna and her friends discussed all relate to *role conflict*, which sociologists define as a feeling of unease that results when inconsistent prescriptions (or standards) are held for a person by himself or by others (Biddle & Thomas, 1996, p. 12). Kadushin (1974) noted the existence of role conflict in child welfare: "There tends to be some disparity between the ideology of the child welfare worker and that of the society in which he operates. . . . It contributes to a feeling of marginality, a feeling of being different, on the part of the worker" (p. 715).

The cause of this conflict is that the child welfare worker is caught between two contradictory orientations of American society. One orientation is Americans' belief in the idea of rugged individualism—that we are responsible for our own lives and obligations and that those who cannot handle these responsibilities are inherently weak. People who fail to meet their obligations, people like neglectful parents, should be punished. The extreme version of this orientation is *social Darwinism,* a philosophy that says that by helping people such as neglectful parents, we are allowing unfit people to continue to live and function in society and that this weakens the overall social structure. This thinking takes a harsh view of the role of child welfare, maintaining that social workers should investigate complaints and that when abuse is substantiated, they should remove the children, find another permanent living arrangement for them, and bring the parents to the criminal justice system for punishment.

The contradictory orientation is the Judeo–Christian ethic of *social responsibility:* to love and care for those that are dependent and in need. This orientation views all people as interdependent and draws no boundary between the fit and unfit. The Judeo–Christian view believes there are no superior people, only those who are lucky enough to have been spared. Everyone can potentially end up dependent and in need. This is the view of people who are fond of saying, "There but by the grace of God go you and I." Since everyone is seen as potentially dependent, the *humanitarian orientation* is pragmatic: Community support is ensured for us when we need it.

The social work profession in general and most of the agencies that employ social workers stand clearly and unequivocally with the humanitarian orientation. They believe that people are inherently good, that all people have the capacity for growth and change, and that at a pragmatic level, we have seen that punitive approaches to people with problems rarely if ever yield positive results. Social welfare agencies are given the responsibility of helping clients to deal more adequately with social problems. The only effective technical approaches that have been developed in discharging this responsibility are centered on understanding and accepting the client.

The source of the role conflict for child welfare workers is that neither social Darwinism nor humanitarianism has won a clear victory in our society. We will not permit the dependent child of the drug-addicted mother to die, and this is a result of the humanitarian orientation. However, we grant support grudgingly, hesitantly, and with considerable doubt about the wisdom and morality of what we are doing, and this is a result of the Puritan ethic and social Darwinism–based orientation. Society asks child welfare agencies to perform certain important tasks but denies them adequate resources and grants them only grudging support. Kadushin (1974) sums up the problem of role conflict for the child welfare worker:

> The child welfare worker, therefore, has to implement a policy that reflects society's ambivalence, and has to resolve, within himself and in contact with the client, the behavioral implications of that ambivalence. He has to implement a policy that conflicts, to some degree with the values of the profession. This conflict creates a stress for the worker in contacts with his peers. Acculturation to the professional ethos means that the worker is likely to be more understanding of deviancy than is true of the laymen with whom he associates. He finds himself "explaining" the delinquent child, the broken family, the neglectful parent, the [drug-addicted] mother to friends and relatives who feel punitive toward such groups. . . . Yet the worker is a member of that same society from which he differentiates himself in implementing his role as a social worker. As a member of the general society, he holds some of the same attitudes, and he might still not have resolved many of the moral dilemmas encountered in his work—dilemmas posed by the [drug-addicted] mother, the self-centered parents who neglect their children, the deserted mother living with a succession of "boy friends," the [welfare] mother who "cheats" on the agency, . . . the family's request for institutionalization of a mentally deficient child. The worker thus frequently faces the stress of making decisions and taking action in the face of moral, ethical, and value questions about which he is himself still undecided. (p. 717)

JOB RESPONSIBILITY AND JOB STRESS   Although as we have said a number of times that the pay of a child welfare worker is not nearly as bad as people popularly believe, the pay is for a job that involves an awe-inspiring amount of responsibility. A child welfare worker makes decisions and recommendations on an almost daily basis that can result in or prevent serious harm to children, parents, and families. Moreover, these decisions often have to be made without enough resources, time, or information, and they often come down to a choice between two bad alternatives, such as leaving the child in a dangerous home or placing the child in an inadequate foster home. As Kadushin writes in the *Encyclopedia of Social Work,*

> Admittedly, child welfare social work makes a number of egregious demands on the emotional life of its practitioners. Handling intractable situations with limited resources, in contact with demanding, often unwilling, clients, and having responsibility for significant aspects of children's lives can erode the idealism, conviction, and enthusiasm of many workers. (p. 274)

Anna and her colleagues could talk almost endlessly about the times when the responsibility of the job was almost overwhelming. As Denise recalled,

> I remember a Friday afternoon when I went on a home visit. It was to the apartment of a mother and her 12-year-old daughter. The father had been arrested for sexually abusing the girl and had been sent to jail, and he and the mother were now divorced. I went to the apartment thinking this would be a pleasant visit in preparation for closing the case, would not take too long, and I might finish early and get an early start on the weekend.
>
> When I got there, I found that the mother had a new boyfriend who appeared to be in the process of moving in. I couldn't really put my finger on anything, but there just seemed to be this weird sexual tension between this man and the daughter. When I pulled the mother aside and asked her about it, she seemed completely unconcerned. She insisted that this was a "nice guy" and finally accused me of having a dirty mind. I didn't have enough evidence to do anything (actually, I had no evidence), but I couldn't shake the feeling that the child was in serious danger. It completely ruined my weekend and resulted in my husband and I having a huge fight because he said I should just leave my work at the office. (He was right, of course.)
>
> On Monday when I returned to work, the first thing I did was call the mother to ask about the weekend. I found that my intuition had been exactly right. On Saturday morning, the boyfriend had "accidentally" walked in on the daughter while she was in the shower. She screamed bloody murder, and the mother came running and pulled a knife on the guy. She drove him out of the house and then threw his possessions into the yard.
>
> It actually worked out well because it gave me an opening to do some work with the mother on her responsibility for making better judgments about who she brings home, and on generally protecting her daughter. But it sure screwed up my weekend.

The other social workers in the group all had stories about children left in homes that they feared were dangerous, children removed from homes that may have been salvageable, parents with the potential to provide good homes for their children who became discouraged and drifted away when things did not move quickly enough, children that the worker was unable to free for adoption until they were too old and damaged to have any good options, and on and on. The workers felt constant stress: that they weren't doing enough to protect a child, that they might do something that harmed a child or family, that a decision could as well be the wrong one as the right one. Anna's colleague Bill referred to the job as "one big Maalox moment."

WORKING IN AN UNSAFE AND UNPLEASANT ENVIRONMENT   Child welfare workers, particularly those who work in investigations and protective services, spend a great deal of time in the homes of clients who are impoverished, disorganized, mentally ill, or exhibit unsavory sorts of social and behavioral problems. These homes are often in neighborhoods that are unsafe, or are at least perceived as such. Researchers (Mayer & Rosenblatt, 1978) interviewing social workers in New York City reported the following typical observation:

> The surroundings became dingier and dingier as I approached East Harlem. Moreover, my anxiety increased when I found the building in which the client lived. The front door was unlocked and open, the windows were broken, and there was a powerful stench. There were no names on the mailboxes and most of them had been broken into. (p. 229)

Once inside a client's home, the social worker frequently encounters all sorts of unpleasant conditions. The home is often hot or cold, smelly, and infested with bugs and rodents. Also, clients occasionally have dangerous or unpleasant pets. Members of the focus group listed helpful hints from the wisdom they have gained about how to deal with these conditions:

- Wear sturdy and washable clothes. Don't wear anything that you will be upset about if it gets dirty or even ruined.
- Wear pants and, if possible, socks to prevent bugs from running up your legs.
- If the smell is bad, breathe through your mouth.
- Look for a hard chair to sit on. Avoid upholstered furniture, as it may be wet and you don't know what may be living in it.
- Do not bring a bag of any kind into the house, as bugs may enter it.
- If you see evidence of a dog, ask the client to shut the dog in another room or put it in the backyard before you enter the house.

Sandy, a 20-year veteran of protective services, told the following story of the beginning of her career when she was in the intake unit:

> When I graduated from college, my husband had two years left of law school, so I decided to go directly on to social work graduate school. My first-year field placement was with a family-planning clinic where I mostly stayed in an office and counseled young women about birth control, and my second-year placement was with a private church-affiliated adoption agency where I did home studies for adoption applicants and did case management for the young birth mothers. So, I had an MSW, but virtually no experience with the kinds of clients and home conditions you encounter in protective service investigations.
>
> My first week on the job, we got a complaint from a man who reported that the woman living next door to him appeared to be seriously mentally ill and that she had three small children who appeared to be in danger. I immediately went to the home, and from the outside, it didn't look too bad. I knocked on the door. It was answered by a fairly normal-appearing woman who, after I explained the purpose of my visit, invited me inside.
>
> The house was a wreck. There were dirty dishes everywhere; ashtrays overflowed with old, foul-smelling cigarette butts, on seemingly every horizontal surface; and the floor was covered with dead bugs and dried dog poop. I could see into the kitchen

from the living room, and trash literally cascaded from the trashcan onto the floor. It was just a wreck! I was revolted by the scene, but I kept telling myself "You're an MSW; you're trained to handle this; you can do it."

I found one chair that appeared to be dry and not completely filthy and sat down and began to talk to the mother. Before I had one sentence out of my mouth, she began to scream and curse, calling me every foul name you can think of. Once again, I told myself that I was a professional, trained to handle this type of thing. I nodded my head and said things like "I can understand that you are upset" and "I know this must be hard for you" and "It's not easy when a complete stranger comes to your home and wants to discuss your family"—all the things that had worked well at the adoption agency. They did not work, however, with this woman. She just kept on and on and became increasingly hostile until I began to fear for my safety and started to consider exit strategies.

At the height of the woman's tantrum, this huge rat just strolled out from under the couch, lazily walked to the center of the room, turned around, and, fixing me in his beady little black eyes, sat down. Well, let me tell you, this was just too much. MSW or no MSW, I screamed, threw my pad and pencil into the air, and jumped up on the chair. The mother stopped her tantrum, became absolutely calm, almost serene, and said, "I'm sorry about that. You know, I think he belongs to the people next door."

WORKER SAFETY   An obvious extension of the previous discussion is that some situations in which child welfare workers find themselves are not only unpleasant but actually unsafe. A supervisor responding to a survey (Alwon & Reitzer, 2000) of child welfare staff turnover said, "Every day, we send caseworkers out by themselves, dealing with a potentially explosive issue, [the possible removal of a child], into the same homes a police officer wouldn't enter without backup" (p. 35). The findings of a similar study (Howe & McDonald, 2001) in Canada "demonstrate that child welfare staff are exposed to a significant degree of traumatic stimuli. Approximately 20 percent of staff in all job categories had been victims of assault on the job and 50 percent had been verbally threatened" (p. 1).

Members of the focus group recalled many incidents where they felt their safety threatened. Here is one such incident, as reported by the research assistant who did the interview:

One of Sandy's most frightening moments occurred when she was called out to investigate a domestic violence event that involved child abuse, as well. She was a protective service worker and on call at the time, and she was beeped to go out in the middle of the night. She met a policeman at the apartment door, and the policeman motioned for her to knock and to identify herself ("like a lamb to slaughter," she laughed). The door was opened by a woman standing stark naked who looked drugged out. The woman motioned Sandy to come in, and as Sandy stepped in, the woman grabbed her by the hand and bit her forearm. Luckily, the policeman was right behind Sandy and was able to intervene.

Sandy said this particular apartment seemed to have "bad karma" for her. Ten years after the first event, she returned there for another protective service investigation. A different family was living in the apartment, and this time, the investigation was for allegations of child neglect. The mother let her in, but when Sandy tried to discuss the condition of the house and the possibility of removal of the children, the woman picked up a butcher knife and chased her out of the door.

Fisher, Hartsough, and Heyn (1997) provide this account of a social worker's dangers encountered on the job:

> During the second year of her child welfare career, Nichole went to a mobile home park to investigate a complaint. Unknown to her, the drunk, spouse-abusing father of the children was in the mobile home. She called her supervisor on the phone to discuss whether she needed to act to immediately remove the children when the father emerged from the back, enraged, and began throwing dishes at Nichole and his wife. Luckily the dishes were Tupperware so no one was injured. The supervisor yelled at Nicole to hang up and he would call 911. As Nichole tried to get the children into the car to leave the scene, the father drove at them at high speed in his pickup truck. Nichole says that this is the only time in her three years as a protective service worker that she has truly feared for her safety. (p. 63)

In a recent discussion of future trends and influences on child welfare education and training, Tracy and Pine (2000) said,

> The increasing violence in society is on everyone's mind. Unfortunately, social workers are among those groups that are most at risk of violence at work. Among social workers, child welfare practitioners, especially direct service workers who work in some of the most high-risk neighborhoods, are especially vulnerable. Practitioners need knowledge and skills to avoid unnecessary risks on the job, while administrators need to know how to establish and implement comprehensive plans for workplace safety. (p. 98)

The Upside of Being a Child Welfare Worker

What we described in the previous section is a job that is misunderstood, dirty, stressful, and sometimes downright dangerous. It pays pretty well and is fairly secure but not to the extent that would seem to compensate for the downside. It is apparent that people must get other benefits out of this job.

DANGER AND DIVERSITY   For most people, a job that is dirty, stressful, and dangerous would be a negative, but not for everyone. For some people, these aspects of the job create an "adrenaline rush" and so are its most attractive features. As Beth told the focus group,

> Before I returned to school to get my MSW, I was a sales consultant at a BMW dealership. All my friends were really envious. I worked in a beautiful setting, wore a fancy business suit every day, made lots of money, and, the best part, I got to drive a new BMW for free. But I was bored to death. All I did, day after day, was to sit around the showroom waiting for customers to come in, give them test drives, and then try to get them to pay as much as possible for the car. It was mind numbing!
>
> Now, working for Family and Children's Services, I never know what my day is going to be like. I may go to a crack house with the police to remove the children of a dealer; I may try to make sense to a psychotic mother who needs to place her kids and seek treatment; I may have to talk my way past a teenage gang to gain entrance to a young mother's apartment to see if she needs help with her child; I may be on the witness stand in court, wearing one of my old $400 BMW sales consultant suits, with some sharp lawyer trying to trip me up so he can say I haven't made reasonable

efforts to save a family. Every day is a rush, and I love it. I could never go back to working in some sterile business or bureaucratic setting, where all anyone is concerned about is making money and acting important.

OCCASIONAL SUCCESSES   Child welfare work can be very frustrating. Social workers in the focus group were able to recite a seemingly endless series of cases where they worked for months, were finally making some progress, and then the case suddenly came apart. But occasionally, they had a success that made the job seem worth all the effort and frustration.

Denise recalled attending the wedding of a young woman from a very dysfunctional family who, with much help from the social worker and agency, graduated from college, began a career as a second-grade teacher, and was now marrying a fellow teacher and looking forward to a bright future.

Sandy told of a foster child who was labeled by the school system as developmentally delayed and placed in special education. Suspecting a mistake had been made, she spent almost a year advocating for the child for reevaluation and placement in a higher-track classroom. The school system finally relented. The child was retested and placed in a mainstream class. Now a young man, this individual had earned several computer system ratings and was working as a network administrator for a local bank.

Anna recalled buying a teddy bear for a foster child who had no toys of her own when she was first placed in care. While grocery shopping one Saturday, she ran into the young woman, now a high school freshman and living with her mother again, and was told how much the bear had meant to her and that she still slept with it every night.

The fact that these successes, infrequent as they were, had the effect of positively changing a whole life forever made them very satisfying. Kadushin (1974) captured this aspect of child welfare work well when he wrote the following:

> The Talmud, emphasizing the importance of each individual life, says, "If, during the course of your own life, you have saved one life, it is as if you have saved all mankind." Few occupations give us the opportunity of participating in the saving of a life. The everyday work of a child welfare worker is concerned with just that—reclaiming a child for life. It is to be expected that such a task would be very difficult. It is also to be expected that there are few, if any, tasks that offer the same degree of satisfaction and the same sense of accomplishment. (p. 728)

COMMITMENT TO KIDS, FAMILIES, AND SOCIAL JUSTICE   The ages of the workers in the focus group ranged from 28 to 57, meaning that a few of the members had not even been born before the 1960s ended. Regardless, literally all of these social workers identified themselves with this era in social history. The older workers described themselves as "children of the sixties," and the younger workers described themselves as "1960s sort of people." By this, they meant that their politics were liberal and that they were committed to equality, social justice, and empowerment of oppressed groups. This social and political orientation was the most frequent reason workers gave for staying with this very difficult job.

Career Orientations of Child Welfare Workers

For most of this chapter, we have been describing child welfare social workers as though they are all the same. This is obviously not true. The first thing to note in this regard is that many people who begin careers as child welfare workers, perhaps the majority, do not last very long. A study (Cyphers, 2001) of staff turnover in child welfare agencies found that the turnover rate was 22 percent for child protective service workers (p. 2).

Rycraft (1991) did an interesting study of child welfare workers who had lasted in the job at least two years. Four distinct categories of workers emerged from her data analysis. She labeled these different types of workers (1) the *crusaders,* (2) the *midway passengers,* (3) the *future travelers,* and (4) the *hangers-on.* The focus group workers fit these categories very neatly, certainly not confirming Rycraft's typology but lending strong support to it.

The Crusaders

This group of child welfare workers finds their job exciting and challenging. They are on a mission to protect children and to reform society to be more responsive to the needs of families and children. *Passion, commitment,* and *zeal* are words that are frequently applied to this type of worker. According to Rycraft (1991),

> They feel and see they are making a difference in the lives of the children and families they serve, which is both energizing and rewarding in and of itself. They have answered the call to action to protect children and strengthen families. Having accepted the call as a personal challenge, they are determined to succeed . . . These are the warriors who see the job as important to the very future of our children and society. (p. 9)

In Rycraft's sample, 22 percent were classified as crusaders. They were all women and had relatively brief tenure with the agency (less than 10 years), and a disproportionate number had professional social work training.

The focus group fit this profile. Anna, Beth, and Anne (30 percent of the focus group) were classified by this author as crusaders. Anna, with eight years' experience, was the senior member of the group. All had social work degrees—Anna, with an MSW, and the other two, BSW degrees. All were passionate about their jobs, a fact reflected in their willingness to take on additional responsibilities both in the agency, on committees and taskforces, and in the community, in professional and civic organizations.

The fact that crusaders are generally social workers who are relatively new to the job can be explained by the amount of physical and psychic energy required to maintain this orientation. These people are passionate and frequently become very angry at the agency and other elements of the system. They often have trouble leaving their work at the office. Unfortunately, the fate that often befalls crusaders is either burnout or being fired for defying agency rules on behalf of clients once too often. The happier outcome is that crusaders often evolve into midway passengers.

The Midway Passengers

Rycraft (1991) classified 43.7 percent of her sample of social workers as midway passengers. This group had significantly longer tenure with the agency than was the norm (all with 10 or more years). A disproportionate number (80 percent) held social work degrees. They were older than average and also disproportionately male.

Once again, the focus group members fit the profile. The workers classified by this author as midway passengers were Bill, Daniel, Denise, and Sandy. Their average number of years with the agency was nearly 12. Three (75 percent) had social work degrees, and 50 percent were male.

According to Rycraft (1991), midway passengers "represent the texture and fabric of public child welfare. Over the years they have found a way to balance the tremendous demands made upon them and currently view their jobs as more manageable if not easier" (p. 8). These workers have learned how to separate their professional from their personal lives so they can gain relief from the stresses and strains of their jobs. They emphasize the positive elements of their careers, especially the relative autonomy they enjoy, the job security, and the feeling that they are doing something important. They have become somewhat immune to the negative aspects, such as the constant frustration of working in a large bureaucracy and the public misunderstanding of what they do. They have largely ceased to participate in extraagency activities, such as committees and task forces, and their community activities on behalf of children have waned, although not completely ceased. They feel they have done their share and paid their dues. Midway travelers could just as appropriately be referred to as *careerists*.

The four midway travelers in the focus group all indicated that years ago, they would have been classified as crusaders. They were very conscious of the fact that they had had to tone down their level of zeal in order to last in this job. Bill had struggled with the decision a little more than the others, relating the following anecdote:

> For the first five or six years I had this job, I was a real firebrand. I was always butting heads with the administration or some other agency about some policy or the other, rushing off to some political rally for one cause or another. My wife began to keep score and pointed out to me that I was spending an average of two evenings every week attending community organization or committee meetings. The stress became so great that I spoke to my pastor about it, and he quoted a piece of poetry that really helped me to refocus my life. It went something to the effect of "My candle burns at both ends, it will not last the night, but to all my friends, and all my foes, gives such a lovely light."

The Future Travelers

Twenty-six percent of the social workers in Rycraft's (1991) study were classified as future travelers. All had been in child welfare for a limited period of time—all for less than 10 years and two-thirds for less than 5 years. The group was younger than average, fewer had social work training, and they were mostly female. In this author's focus group, two were classified as future travelers: Paul and Nichole. Paul had worked for the Department of Family and Children's Services (DFCS) for only two years and Nichole for three. Neither had a social work degree nor any interest in obtaining one.

Future travelers are workers who do not plan to continue their careers in child welfare social work. Sometimes, they identify with the social work profession but plan to enter another, generally more prestigious, area of practice, such as clinical mental health work. Sometimes, their desire is to enter a completely different profession. Some future travelers started out as crusaders, became disillusioned, and began to plan an exit strategy. Some future travelers have always had another career as their goal, and child welfare is just a way to pay the bills until the real plan can be implemented.

Paul had a bachelor of fine arts degree, and his goal had always been to open a fine art framing shop. Nichole had a bachelor of arts in psychology, and when she began at DFCS, she had planned to return to school for an MSW. She started out as a crusader but became disillusioned with the constraints of the system. Her new plan was to return to school in psychology, to earn a PhD, and to embark on a career in teaching and research.

Future travelers, then, are workers who plan to leave the agency soon. As Rycraft (1999) observes,

> Burnout is a distinct possibility for these workers, especially if they are unable to terminate their employment in the near future. They have reached a point of being unable to justify the costs of working in public child welfare to the sparse benefits. If they can not bring the costs and benefits into a greater balance they will continue to plan for their eventual termination of employment. . . . Until then, they are prepared to continue their employment and deal with the stress and demands to the best of their ability. (p. 11)

The Hangers-On

Rycraft (1999) classified 8.7 percent of her sample as hangers-on. These were workers with long experience—in all cases, more than 10 years. All were male, and half held social work degrees. In the focus group, one worker fit this category (10 percent). He had worked for the agency for 19 years and did not have a social work degree.

Hangers-on is the term Rycraft coined to describe workers who are burned out but for some reason cannot quit their jobs. These workers are disillusioned, retain little interest in the job, and are physically and emotionally worn out. "They resent any demands being made upon them, try to avoid contact with their clients and have disengaged themselves from the child welfare arena to every extent possible. They are depressed, angry and very unhappy with their jobs" (p. 10)

In the focus group, Randall clearly fit the profile of a hanger-on. It appeared that he had volunteered for the group for two reasons. The first and apparently main reason was that focus group members got an extended lunch hour, plus a free lunch once a week. The second reason was that the group gave him a forum to vent his seemingly inexhaustible feelings of anger and bitterness toward the agency, his colleagues, his clients, and the world in general. Randall had begun with the agency 17 years ago when, with a degree and certification in physical education, he was unable to find a

A homemaker is a paraprofessional aid who helps clients, like Mrs. Zalinsky, learn to organize and care for their home, and to provide good physical and nutritional care for their children.

job in his field. At first, he liked his job as a child welfare worker, and for a year or two, he would probably have been classified as a mild crusader. But when his passion began to wane, he became frustrated by the bureaucratic roadblocks to both his plans for clients and his attempts to advance in the agency, and gradually, he became a future traveler.

Randall decided he wanted to become a lawyer and transferred to an office in a city with a third-rate evening law school. After four years as an evening law student, he graduated and passed the bar exam on his third try. Unfortunately, Randall had no more luck finding a job in the legal field than he had had finding one in physical education. At age 46, Randall had given up hope of finding another job, could not afford to leave the pay and benefits he had accumulated after 17 years with the Kaye

County Department of Family and Children's Services, and was just waiting for retirement. He did not know if he could make it and had been referred by his supervisor to an employee assistance counselor.

In conclusion, let's return to where we left Anna at the beginning of the chapter. She had wiped away the dogs' slobber, was waiting for the police, and was not at all happy about the prospect of having to cancel her date for the evening. Let's tag along with Anna and learn the rest of the story.

At the end of the street where Anna lives, there is an old funeral home that has a clock rimmed in blue neon on the wall facing the street. As Anna turned onto her block, the clock told her it was 10:45 PM. The day had turned out to be as long and as big a mess as she had anticipated.

When the police arrived at the house on Cornell Street, they quickly intimidated the mother, whose name Anna soon learned was Corrie Zalinsky, into opening the door. When Anna and the police officer entered, her earlier brief observation was confirmed. The living room was littered with dirty clothes and dirty dishes; the only furniture was a couch and an overstuffed chair, both with stuffing hanging out of numerous rips. There were two television sets, stacked one on top of the other; apparently, the sound worked on the top set and the picture worked on the bottom one. Stacked in the corner were a coffee table and an end table; both appeared to have been smashed beyond repair.

It took all of Anna's skill to get the mother to stop cowering in a corner and sit down and talk. Mrs. Zalinsky kept asking over and over "Am I going to jail?" She pleaded, "Please don't take my kids. They're all I have anymore." Anna assured Mrs. Zalinsky that she would not be arrested but also informed her that she would not know what was going to happen with the kids until she had much more information. There were three children: two boys, ages 2 and 3, and a girl, age 5. The boys appeared to be okay, except for fitting a category Anna called F&P, meaning "frail and pale." The girl was another matter. She was extremely thin, gaunt, and lethargic and had a cough and a bluish tint to her skin.

As the investigation proceeded, Anna learned that Mrs. Zalinsky had been in a violent relationship with the children's father and that he had finally abandoned the family two months previously. All the family had was a few hundred dollars and a little food in the pantry. As is often true in such situations, Mrs. Zalinsky was isolated. She had not worked since the oldest child was born, was estranged from her family, and knew no one in the community. As the food ran out and the money ran low, she had sunk into a deep depression. She knew her daughter needed medical care but also knew that she owed the doctor several hundred dollars and so was afraid to call for an appointment. She had made an appointment with a public health clinic but got lost when she took the wrong bus and ended up having to walk several miles home.

Using the department's risk assessment procedure, Anna concluded that this was a situation that was probably salvageable. She took the mother and children to the local children's medical center for a pediatric evaluation. It was determined that all three children were malnourished and dehydrated. The girl had picked up a bacterial infection that she had been unable to shake off, largely due to her nutritional status and unsanitary home environment. The doctor, a friend of Anna's from several years of working together, loaded up Mrs. Zalinsky with samples of antibiotics, vitamins, nutritional supplement drinks and snack bars, disinfectant soap, and everything else he could find in the sample closet. He then made a referral to the public health department for a public health nurse to visit the next day to be sure the mother understood the directions and was following through.

Anna next took Mrs. Zalinsky and the children to the emergency food pantry and picked up a week's supply of food. She also called the utility company to be sure the power and water were not going to be shut off (a fear that had been nagging Mrs. Zalinsky for weeks) and made appointments for the next day to apply for food stamps, TANF, and Medicaid. Anna explained to Mrs. Zalinsky that job counseling would be provided as a condition of receiving TANF and that she would arrange for appointments at the public health clinic and mental health center to begin to deal with the woman's depression.

Following this whirlwind of activity, Anna took the family to a cafeteria for dinner. They then returned to the family's home, where she helped Mrs. Zalinsky give the children their medications and baths and helped to give the house a quick straightening up. For the third time, Anna went over the schedule for the next day, emphasizing how important it was for Mrs. Zalinsky to follow through on all of her commitments and explaining that a homemaker would come by later in the week to help get the house in good order.

As Anna was leaving, feeling exhausted and grubby, Mrs. Zalinsky took her hand, shyly looked at the floor and mumbled, "Thank God you came."

REFERENCES

Administration for Children and Families, Department of Health and Human Services. (2002). *National Survey of Child and Adolescent Well-Being (NSCAW), State child welfare agency survey: Report.* Washington, DC: Government Printing Office.

Alliance for Children and Families, American Public Human Services Association, and Child Welfare League of America. (2001). The child welfare workforce challenge: Results from a preliminary study. *2001 Finding Better Ways Conference Presentation Recap.* Washington, DC: Child Welfare League of America.

Alwon, F. J., & Reitz, A. L. (2000, November). Empty chairs: As a national workforce shortage strikes child welfare, CWLA responds. *Children's Voice.*

Biddle, B. J., & Thomas, E. J. (Eds.). (1966) *Role theory; Concepts and research.* New York: John Wiley & Sons.

Child and Family Services Administration. (2000). *Children's protective services.* Lansing, MI: Michigan Family Independence Agency.

Cyphers, G. (2001). *Report from the Child Welfare Workforce Survey: State and county data and findings.* Washington, DC: American Public Human Services Association.

Drake, D. (1996). Unraveling Unsubstantiated. *Child Maltreatment, 1*(3), 261–271.

Fisher, C., Hartsough, D., & Heyn, T. (1997). *Child welfare workers in Kalamazoo, MI: A field study.* Unpublished manuscript, Western Michigan University.

Howe, P., & McDonald, C. (2001). Traumatic stress, turnover and peer support in child welfare. *2001 Finding Better Ways Conference Presentation Recap.* Washington, DC: Child Welfare League of America.

Kadushin, A. (1974). *Child welfare services,* (2nd ed.). New York: Macmillan.

Kadushin, A. (1987). Child welfare services. In A. Minahan (Ed.) *Encyclopedia of social work* (18th ed.), pp. 265–275. Silver Springs, MD: NASW Press.

Mayer, J. E., & Rosenblatt, A. (1978). Encounters with danger: Social workers in the ghetto. *Sociology of Work and Occupations, 2,* 227–245.

Meyer, C. H. (1983). Staffing issues in child welfare. In B. G. McGowan and W. Meezan *Child welfare: Current dilemmas—Future directions,* pp. 479–503. Itasca, IL: F. D. Peacock Publishers.

Rycraft, J. (1991, September). The survivors—A study on the retention of public child welfare caseworkers. Paper present at the 9th National Conference on Child Abuse and Neglect, September 14–17. Denver, CO.

Tracy, E. M. (1995). Family preservation and home based services. In R. L. Edwards & J. G. Hopps, (Eds.), *Encyclopedia of social work* (19th ed.) (pp. 973–982).Washington, DC: NASW Press.

Tracy, E. M., & Pine, B. A. (2000). Child welfare education and training: Future trends and influences. *Child Welfare, 79*(1), 93–109.

U.S. Department of Health and Human Services (U.S. DHHS), Administration on Children, Youth and Families. (2003). *Child maltreatment 2001.* Washington, DC: Government Printing Office.

Wells, S. (2000). How do I decide whether to accept a report for child protective serves investigation? In H. Dubowitz and D. DePanfilis (Ed.) *Handbook for child protection practice,* pp. 3–6. Thousand Oaks, CA: Sage.

CHAPTER 11

Other Key Players in the Child Welfare System

Joyce Lee Taylor, Michael Schultz, and Jessica Noel

A child protection case involves many professionals in addition to the child protective services (CPS) social worker employed by the county or state. The CPS social worker strives to reduce the child's risk of harm by enhancing family functioning and improving conditions in the family's environment, with the goal of preventing further episodes of maltreatment. To accomplish the goal, the CPS social worker collaborates with professionals in three groups: (1) professionals that provide *refer-*

rals and important case information, (2) professionals that provide *authority,* and (3) professionals that provide additional *services* to help families achieve case goals.

In Chapter 10, the case example of Corrie Zalinsky began with a *referral* from a postal carrier, who was alarmed at the sight of a man chasing a little girl around with a belt. When the social worker, Anna Simms, arrived at the home, Mrs. Zalinsky refused to speak with her, so Anna needed the *authority* of the police to gain access to the home and conduct her investigation. If any of the three children had been at imminent risk (i.e., needed to be removed from the mother's care), Anna would have sought additional authority from the courts. As it was, she determined that the situation was salvageable: The children remained in their mother's care, and Anna introduced *services* for the family. To set up those services, she collaborated with other professionals in the community. The services provided for the Zalinsky family included a pediatric evaluation; a homemaker; mental health services to help with the mother's depression; the financial, nutritional, and health care coverage of TANF; food stamps; and Medicaid.

The CPS social worker carries the ultimate responsibility for conducting the child abuse and neglect investigation and overseeing the delivery of treatment services. To accomplish this huge task, the worker calls into play the services available in the community's network. Professionals from many areas of expertise become key players in any child protective services case. Skillful CPS social workers also call on the strengths of a family's natural environment, including relatives, religious organizations, cultural centers, and schools.

Previous chapters provided information on the types of services available within the child welfare field. These include the direct tasks of the CPS social workers, substitute caretakers (foster parents, youth shelters, group homes), and contractual service providers (parent aides, family preservation services, parent education programs, crisis nurseries and others). In this chapter, we examine the value of the collaborative process and note potential sources of tension between members of the team.

Collaboration is a critical aspect of promoting the child's safety, stability, and development. The CPS social worker tries to understand each client family by examining all areas—physical, mental, and social. Good case decisions are made within an overarching assessment process. Information is gathered via screenings, data collection instruments, decision-making tools, and consultations. This collaboration with other disciplines brings together various perspectives as a means of seeing the family more accurately and holistically. However, the bringing together of a number of professionals, with varying or opposing perspectives, sometimes leads to misunderstanding and tension between them. This subject, too, is part of our focus in this chapter, as we see how a CPS case entails the cooperation of professionals from a number of disciplines.

Working with Professionals Who Provide Referrals

Two years prior to the arrest of a father (Mr. Nelson) for allegedly dismembering the remains of his son, child welfare authorities in a neighboring state asked Connecticut to help them determine the well being of toddler Jerome Nelson. The boy's father was apparently a

convicted felon, and had received custody of his infant son approximately three years earlier in Connecticut Probate Court.

At the time of the hearing, the judge did not know that Jerome's 30-year-old father
was on supervised release from federal prison, or that he had more than a dozen previous
convictions, some of which included violent crime. Mr. Nelson's interest in gaining custody
of his 6-month-old son was apparently not opposed during the brief hearing.

According to a report in the *New Day* newspaper (p. 1), at the end of the hearing, the
judge asked Mr. Nelson under oath, "Do you have a good place for your son?"

"Yes, your honor," Mr. Nelson said.

"He is well taken care of?"

"Yes, your honor."

"All right," the judge responded. "And do you feel that this is in his best interest?"

"Without a doubt," Mr. Nelson said.

"All right," the judge said. "I'm satisfied."

He granted Mr. Nelson full custody.

Within two years, police say, Jerome would die at his father's hands.

Jerome's case was not contested. The baby boy's mother, Ms. Brown, of a neighboring
state, did not show up in court that day. She was not there to tell the judge about Mr. Nelson's troubles and his lengthy criminal record.

If she had appeared and argued for keeping her son, the court might have ordered an
investigation into Mr. Nelson and Ms. Brown. During the investigation, the judge would
likely have learned that less than a year before state authorities had taken another child
away from Ms. Brown. He might have learned that six months earlier a hospital worker
had filed a medical neglect complaint against Jerome's parents. And Jerome likely would
have been assigned his own lawyer.

Several child advocates say the current system places a parent's right to raise a child
over the child's right to a safe upbringing. The case, they say, shows just how easy it is for
a parent, particularly when unopposed, to gain custody without any proof that he or she
can give adequate care. Parents like Mr. Nelson, whose name was not on Jerome's birth
certificate, are not even required to provide proof that the child is theirs.

"When your choice is to bring a child into this world, we as a society have an obligation to the child as well as the two parents," said Judge Charles D. Gill, of Litchfield Superior Court, who advocates for children's rights. "Any time a child is in a courtroom and the
child's life or liberty or custody is at stake, that child should have a lawyer," he said. "In no
adult situation would we allow a decision to be made about life, liberty, or custody without that person being represented." Too often in the court system, he said, "children are
property, not people."

Police say Mr. Nelson confessed to having beaten the boy to death about a year after
receiving sole custody. His son's remains were dismembered and found by police about
three years later. He now faces a capital felony murder charge.

Since age 16, Mr. Nelson has led a life of crime. By age 29, he had been in and out of
prison. When Jerome was 6 weeks old, Mr. Nelson took him to a local hospital in Connecticut because the baby had pneumonia and rashes. According to Mr. Nelson's testimony, the
baby had primarily lived with Ms. Brown before his admission to the hospital.

The emergency room visit prompted a hospital worker to make a medical neglect call
to the state child abuse hotline. The Department of Children and Families (DCF) closed

Jerome's case without completing an investigation. After a four-day hospital stay, Jerome went home with his father.

Three months later, Mr. Nelson filed papers for custody of his son. The same day, local police arrested Ms. Brown for failing to appear in court on a breach of peace charge. She received notice of the custody case while she was incarcerated at a women's prison.

In seeking custody, Mr. Nelson didn't provide a birth certificate. He also never offered any documentation proving he was Jerome's father. He simply said so. According to court transcripts, Mr. Nelson briefly stated his charges against Ms. Brown, abandonment and medical neglect, in sworn testimony.

Mr. Nelson requested that Ms. Brown be given rights to visitation, but only under his supervision. Mr. Nelson explained that Ms. Brown had another son taken away by the state when she lived with him briefly. Mr. Nelson's comments did not prompt the judge to contact DCF or inquire further. Nor was the judge or anyone else obligated to contact any agency.

Who protects children? How does an abused child come to the attention of the child protective services system? People who are with children in the community may witness abusive events such as beatings; may notice injuries such as bruises, welts, burns, and other marks; and may hear children disclose abusive incidents. It is these concerned people who protect children by calling the authorities and reporting incidents of suspected abuse and neglect. The caller may be a private citizen—a family friend, relative, neighbor, or someone just passing by. Many referrals come from counselors, therapists, social workers, clergy, doctors, law enforcement officers, child care providers, and school staff. People who are in contact with children professionally are called *mandated reporters*. They are required by law to report suspected cases of child maltreatment. All 50 states have enacted mandated reporting statutes, which vary by state (National Clearinghouse, 2003).

Even though mandated reporting laws vary by state, they generally specify which professionals are mandated reporters. In the Zalinsky case, a postal carrier notified the CPS agency of children at risk of abuse, even though postal carriers are not included on the legal list of professionals who are obligated to report. A postal carrier would fall into the category of *voluntary reporters*, like relatives and neighbors. Although the majority of referrals come from mandated reporters, the system also relies on voluntary reporters. These reporters overcome their fears and reservations about making a referral when they contact the authorities and express their concern for a child without any obligation to do so.

Mandated reporters are required by state law to report incidents when they have reasonable cause to suspect that a child has been abused or neglected or is at imminent risk of harm. The mandated reporter states his or her personal knowledge from what he or she has observed or has been told. Observations may include physical and behavioral indicators that would lead one to believe that a child's injury or form of suffering was caused by maltreatment.

In the most serious cases, social workers seek legal authorization from the courts to intervene. Mandated reporters may be called on later to testify in juvenile or family court proceedings. Therefore, careful documentation of the injuries should include identifying information and details of the approximate date and time of the injuries,

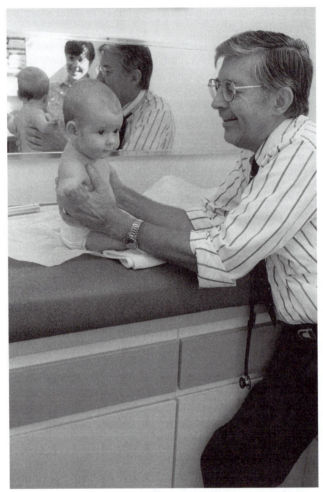

A great percentage of referrals come from counselors, therapists, social workers, physicians, law enforcement officers, child care providers, and school personnel. These people are called mandated reporters because they are required by law to report any suspicion they have of child maltreatment.

neglect, and imminent risk. It is important to include a full description of the extent of the injuries, the name and relationship of the perpetrator, and any types of treatment or efforts made to assist the child.

Mandated reporting laws encourage professionals to report incidents of abuse and neglect by guarding them from civil and criminal liability. Those who make the decision to report maltreatment in good faith are granted a form of legal immunity, usually with the exception of circumstances of professional misconduct or incompetence. If a mandated reporter makes a false report knowing that the information is false, he or she can be charged in criminal court or fined or imprisoned.

In the event that a mandated reporter neglects his or her duty to report suspicions, the state can impose a penalty in the form of a fine or imprisonment, depending on the statutes. Reasons some mandated reporters hesitate to make reports include lack of confidence in the CPS system, lack of training, fear of jeopardizing the therapeutic relationship with a client, fear of retaliation from the perpetrator, and unwillingness to get involved.

Those professionals who fail to report suspected child abuse or neglect are subject to criminal misdemeanor charges and fines. They are also vulnerable to civil litigation for neglect of duty, if their failure to report is directly cited in relation to later maltreatment—maltreatment that could perhaps have been prevented. Failure to report obviously allows the abuse to continue. Given this, a victim of continued abuse may be able to convince a court that the professional, who could have prevented further such trauma, knowingly ignored his or her suffering.

As we have pointed out, once a referral has been made, an investigation takes place. The investigation and subsequent case, if maltreatment is substantiated, require the attention of a number of professionals. The professionals in law enforcement and the courts provide legal authority. We now turn our attention to this portion of the child welfare process. In the final section, we will examine the coordination of services and the multidisciplinary team.

Working with Professionals Who Provide Authority

Social workers alone have no authority to make major decisions, such as removing children, terminating parental rights, and placing children for adoption. For this authority, they must go to the legal system and request an order for action. Likewise, social workers have no authority to force their way into the home of a resistant client, even in a situation they perceive as immediately dangerous. For this, they must call on the police for assistance. The courts and the police, however, heavily rely on social workers for guidance and recommendations as to the best decisions regarding children's well-being. Some social workers have advocated for a *law enforcement approach* to child welfare, which would give social workers certain police-like authority (Costin, Karger, & Stoesz, 1996; Lindsey, 2004).

The juvenile court or family court (this varies by state and county jurisdictions) handles child abuse and neglect matters. In this section, we present an overview of the important court participants and their roles and describe the various types of court hearings.

Child protection philosophies have evolved from child rescuing, to family preservation and reunification, and now to *concurrent planning*, since passage of the Adoption and Safe Families Act (ASFA) in 1997. At the same time, child protection courts have been evolving. The juvenile court concept dates back to 1899, beginning with a strong emphasis on juveniles who were accused of crimes. This was the start of a juvenile justice and delinquency system that later included other juvenile court actions, such as child protection.

The earliest juvenile court operated with a benevolent and rehabilitative vision. This was changed by a landmark decision in 1967, which brought due process and rights to the system. Juvenile court judges used to have unlimited discretion, but today's courts are more procedural—to protect the rights of parents and children. This creates an adversarial system, where lawyers on both sides fight as hard as they can and the court serves as a referee. The aim of the process is justice and the protection of each party's rights.

The manner in which the court handles child protection cases must not violate Section 1 of the Fourteenth Amendment to the U.S. Constitution:

> All persons born or naturalized in the United States and subject of the jurisdiction thereof are citizens of the United States and of the State wherein they reside. No State shall make or enforce any law, which shall abridge the privileges or immunities of citizens of the United States; nor shall any State deprive any person of life, liberty, or property, without due process of law; nor deny to any person within its jurisdiction the equal protection of the laws. (quoted in Nurcombe & Partlett, 1994, p. 19)

Parents have the right to raise a child as they see fit, and the family has a right to be together without interference—unless there is sufficient evidence to compel government action on behalf of a child's safety. It is appropriate for CPS workers to take immediate action to protect a child who is at risk of serious harm, but CPS workers must rely on the court's authority to remove a child from the care of his or her parents. CPS workers ultimately need help from witnesses to compile the evidence and prepare court petitions.

In the early days, the court's role was to judicially substantiate incidents of child maltreatment. This legal substantiation served as permission to provide services, but traditional services were not individualized to the child and family, and out-of-home placement was commonly the sole option for treatment intervention. This was the era of "foster care drift." Children were generally left in state custody, with no services provided to the family and no planning for the child's future.

The family preservation and reunification movement brought major change. Namely, the court gained the responsibility for monitoring the state's efforts at providing services, which led to two other significant changes: (1) the end of the custom of leaving children in foster care and (2) the beginning of case planning. Judges were required by law to examine each case to determine whether the state had made *reasonable efforts* to prevent removal or to reunify the child with the family and whether a child's removal and continued separation from the family was absolutely necessary. As mentioned in Chapter 10, the standard of reasonable efforts depends on a judge's opinion of whether sufficient services have been offered to the family by the state. There is no formula to determine what constitutes reasonable efforts, but the rule of thumb is to exhaust all possible avenues of helping the family and to remove any barriers that get in the way of helping them stay together or reunify.

The court's monitoring became even more involved with enactment of ASFA in 1997. The court now examines whether the state has applied the concurrent-planning concept. Concurrent planning mandates reasonable efforts to keep the child with or reunite the child with the family but requires at the same time an alternative plan for the child's future, in case reasonable efforts fail. Concurrent planning, in other words, means having a backup plan. The CPS social worker puts the state agency's alternative plan before the court for approval from the judge. The judge authorizes the state agency personnel to work toward a particular child's alternative plan with specific goals and timeframes for accomplishment; determines whether the state has made reasonable efforts to implement the plan; and follows the agency's progress in finalizing the child's adoption, transfer of guardianship, or independent living by holding permanency review hearings.

Child maltreatment cases are handled in civil court. Most states operate specialized juvenile courts; others operate general jurisdiction courts, where child maltreatment cases are heard along with other civil matters, such as car accidents, business contract disputes, and divorces. The civil court considers the extent to which the child is in danger and wants to see that a sufficient variety of services have been fully explored before authorizing that the child can be removed from the family.

When a child is at imminent risk of physical injuries, it may be necessary to remove him or her immediately. For extreme emergencies, CPS workers may do an emergency removal of the child by obtaining an administrative hold or court-ordered emergency custody order. The emergency removal allows the CPS worker to secure the child's safety during the time of preliminary investigations. Typically, the length of time for an administrative hold is limited to a couple of days and for an emergency custody order to a couple of weeks. The CPS worker conducts the investigation and subsequently decides which action to pursue, evaluating the merits of returning the child to the family against other legal options. The CPS worker may seek the court's assistance in gaining a family's cooperation in the investigation.

There are other reasons to initiate court actions, including the need for a legal decision that a child has been maltreated and requires substitute care to ensure well-being. If the court grants custody of the child to the agency, the legal term for the child's disposition is *commitment*. The court may instead order that the child remain in the home as long as family members participate in specified services and meet the expectations that address the concerns for the child's safety, as outlined in the treatment plan. This would be referred to as a *contingency order,* because the court has put conditions on the child's ability to remain in the family's care, and the child is under the court's *protective supervision.*

Once a child has been removed from the parents' care, the state is required to make diligent efforts to reunite him or her with the family. Chapter 10 provides essential information about the importance of family engagement when working toward reunification. But what if the attempt to engage the family in reunification services or visitation presents a significant risk to the child or presents another outcome that is not in the best interests of the child? As we have already emphasized, concurrent planning should be a continuous part of the process—at every stage of the case.

The state can seek an exception to diligent efforts under certain circumstances. ASFA allows for specific conditions where reasonable efforts are not required. Perhaps the parent has disappeared and failed to contact the social worker. Under certain circumstances, the social worker can seek the court's authorization to discontinue parent and child visitation. The CPS worker must keep in mind that ignoring the diligent efforts requirement or eliminating parent–child visitation without a judge's ruling can seriously jeopardize future legal efforts to free the child for adoption. Court improvement projects across the country have started testing the effectiveness of mediation to reach court agreements rather than litigating cases based on legal evidence and legal grounds. Thoennes (1994) suggests, "Mediation can be a valuable tool prior to hearings on the termination of parental rights. It will be most useful and effective if a voluntary relinquishment is being considered by one or both parents" (p. 42).

ASFA clarified three ultimate goals: (1) child safety, (2) well-being, and (3) permanence (stability). This new federal policy directs the states to keep child safety as a first priority and recognizes the importance of reunification or finding another permanent home (preferably, an adoptive home) for each child in as timely a manner as possible. The states have shortened the length of time for commitment orders, generally from 18 months to 12 months. By national standards, all 50 states are trying to reunify children with their parents within 12 months of the date they entered state custody. Of the children who are reunified, how many subsequently return to foster care? Of all children adopted within a certain time, how many were adopted within 48 months of the date they entered foster care? Reunification and adoption statistics such as these are measures of permanency.

The CPS social worker needs to understand current laws and court practices. Most social workers enter the child welfare field without any legal preparation or experience. The manner in which they conduct themselves and all they do should be guided by the law, the social work code of ethics and standards for practice, and their own competencies gained through training, education, and experience on the job. When entering the courtroom, the social worker encounters the court's traditional adversary system. The court formally applies the laws through rules that differ, depending on the type of case in question. CPS workers prepare petitions and testimony in juvenile court cases, and they interact with other courts where their clients are involved—for example, in cases involving restraining orders, criminal charges, divorce, or child support.

At all stages of involvement with a family, including the court phase, the CPS social worker's relationships with other professionals enhance the quality of services. From other professionals, the social worker gains information for assessing a family's risk factors, documents the information, and presents it to the court. The court relies on receiving comprehensive information and status reports from the social worker.

CPS workers need to understand the differences between a *criminal case* and a *child protection case*. A criminal case is held to establish guilt or innocence. A child protection case serves a number of purposes, including ensuring child safety and stability, providing services to strengthen the family, and achieving alternative permanent plans when necessary. In a criminal case, the deciding party is the jury, while in a CPS case, most states designate a judge as the deciding party. Access to the court proceedings is open to the public in criminal cases but is extremely restricted in child protection cases to protect confidentiality.

In every criminal case, the standard of proof must always be "beyond a reasonable doubt." This high standard is used in criminal cases because a guilty verdict could potentially deny the accused of the rights to life and liberty. In most states, child pro-

TABLE 11.1	Comparison of Criminal and Child Protection Cases

	Criminal Case	Child Protection Case
Purpose	To establish guilt or innocence	To provide child safety, services to strengthen family, alternative permanent plans when necessary
Deciding party	Jury	Judge (in most states)
Access to court proceedings	Open to public	Restricted
Standard of proof	Beyond a reasonable doubt	Reasonable cause, fair preponderance of evidence, clear and convincing evidence

tection cases require different standards of proof, depending on the case. For instance, the standard of *reasonable cause* is required in situations of emergency removals. Taking custody from a parent and committing a child to the state requires a *fair preponderance of the evidence*, which is a higher standard of proof than reasonable cause. When terminating parental rights, the standard of proof is raised even higher to *clear and convincing evidence*. Table 11.1 illustrates the differences between a criminal case and a child protection case.

Often, the intervention of a criminal court can increase the safety of a child within the family. For example, in a domestic violence situation, the father, who injured the mother and the child, is arrested and sent to prison. The child may be able to stay with the nonoffending parent if that he or she is responsible and can ensure the child's safety. CPS workers should consider alternative types of court actions, as illustrated in the example. Criminal courts, including domestic violence and drug courts, can help in procuring safety for children.

In a criminal court, a person may be charged with a crime, such as risk of injury to a minor, assault, or drug possession. Especially in domestic violence charges, prosecutors and judges often include family evaluations, mediation, mental health services, substance abuse treatment, or custody, guardianship, and visitation arrangements as part of plea bargaining or court orders in sentencing convicted offenders.

Parents and children have certain *due process rights* in the juvenile court: the right to know of legal actions and the schedule of hearings, the right to have proper legal representation, the right to a contested fact-finding hearing, and the right to confront and cross-examine witnesses. The judge determines whether all parties have received their due process rights and will not normally allow legal matters to proceed unless due process requirements have been fulfilled.

The first step is *proper notification* of the legal proceedings. Each parent who is named on the petition should be served a legal notice by the sheriff service immediately upon the filing of a petition. Enough time should be allowed for the parents to be able to participate in the court proceedings. The statutory timeframe for completion of the notification process varies by state and type of proceeding. In a case where it is difficult to locate the parents because the state does not have a current address, publication in a newspaper with general circulation in the town or city where the parent last resided qualifies as an attempt to notify the parents. Notification must be given to both parents of the child, even to an acknowledged, adjudicated, or putative parent.

Parents and children have the right to counsel and guardians ad litem. The majority of professionals involved in child protection cases have chosen this line of work out of a sincere desire to help children and families. These attorneys tend to be highly specialized and are genuinely committed to their clients, whether they represent the child or the parent. The American Bar Association (ABA, 1996) has issued standards of practice for lawyers who represent children in abuse and neglect cases. A child's attorney provides legal services to the child with the same "loyalty, confidentiality, and competent representation to the child as is due an adult client" (p. 1). In order to fully serve the child, the attorney will meet the child and extensively review his or her history, including dates, duration, and types of placements; family circumstances; psychiatric and substance abuse histories; and records of educational and physical development.

The child's attorney is responsible for advocating for his or her legal interests and representing his or her stated preference. In most cases, the child's attorney will fulfill both roles as attorney and guardian ad litem by also representing the child's best interest. If the child's attorney recognizes that the child has expressed a position that creates conflict or jeopardizes his or her well-being, the attorney can petition the court to appoint a separate guardian ad litem. In such a case, the child's attorney will continue to represent the child, but the new guardian ad litem will be responsible for representing the child's best interest.

Guardians ad litem are attorneys or (in most states) laypersons. The Court Appointed Special Advocates (CASA), a nonprofit organization, recruits, trains, and coordinates volunteers all over the United States and is authorized by law in nearly every state. After receiving the training, volunteers work with counselors, social workers, teachers, parents, foster parents, attorneys, and court administrators on behalf of children. The CASA guardian ad litem reports to the judge and represents the child's best interest in court proceedings.

There are several phases of child protection cases, including emergency removal orders, filing petitions, pretrial conferences (negotiating settlement), discovery, and the trial process. First, the judge must find that the child has suffered maltreatment, which requires state and court intervention. The trial process establishes whether a child has been harmed by the parents' acts of omission or commission. This is called the *adjudication,* a finding that the child needs help. The judge will then decide what level of intervention is most appropriate for the child's needs; this is called the *disposition.*

The judge may choose from any of several types of dispositions. If the judge orders *protective supervision,* the child may remain with the family as long as they participate in treatment and the child is not put in further jeopardy. If the judge feels that the family cannot guarantee the child's safety while receiving services, then he or she may order that the child protection agency place the child in *temporary care.* While a child is in temporary care, the child protection agency is responsible for facilitating parent and child visits and for providing services to the family to improve conditions. If conditions do not improve after the CPS agency has provided reasonable efforts to reunify the family, the judge may find that legal grounds for the *termination of parental rights (TPR)* have been met. In a TPR case, the child protection agency will file an alternative plan, as established in the concurrent planning for the child's future, such as adoption, transfer of guardianship, independent living (for older adolescents), or even permanent foster care in the most extenuating circumstances (based on the child's special needs).

Parents do occasionally consent to the commitment of their children to temporary placement or voluntarily agree to terminate their parental rights. In most instances, however, making a decision about temporary placement or termination of parental rights requires going to trial. Evidence is presented and the court participants engage in the adversarial process. Evidence includes narratives and documents contained in agency case records and the CPS worker's testimony. The CPS worker is sworn in and asked to discuss his or her professional credentials, including education, training, and experience. The worker is then asked questions from the attorneys in direct examination and cross-examination. The child is sometimes called as a witness. All the parties involved should then be mindful of a number of issues: (1) the child's age, developmental stage, and ability to recollect and communicate and (2) the child's emotional ability to cope with the court process and with sensitive questions.

One of the most valuable forms of evidence is *expert testimony.* The court relies heavily on professional observations as well as professional interpretations of a family's treatment needs, compliance with services, and prognosis. Such professional opinions may come from the normal course of services provided to the family (such as pediatric records) or from specific services the family was referred to for a targeted assessment. An example would be the court's request for a psychologist to conduct an evaluation of the parent–child interactions and relationship. Questions that might be asked include these: What is the strength of the bond between the parent and child? What is the parent's capacity to meet this child's individualized needs?

Another example would be the testimony of a sexual abuse specialist who examined the child. The specialist may have conducted a *forensic interview,* which produces documentation of whether sexual abuse occurred. During a forensic interview, the physical exam or the child's statements may have revealed a number of incidents, when and where the incidents occurred, the forms of sexual abuse, and the identification of the alleged perpetrator. The sexual abuse specialist may also be providing sexual abuse services to the child and will make treatment recommendations to the court. The recommendation might suggest a particular level or source of mental health services, or it might provide an opinion on the child's readiness, benefits, or potential trauma for family visitation or reunification.

As mentioned previously, mental health and medical professionals who have worked with the family may have mixed feelings about writing affidavits (i.e., sworn statements), testifying, or making treatment records available to the court in child maltreatment cases. These professionals may feel bound by confidentiality and privacy restrictions, which are set by their agencies or professional disciplines. However, the court has the authority to compel testimony and the power to subpoena documents and other records.

Unfortunately, not all child protection courts run smoothly and achieve the desired purpose. In a study of six groups of key decision makers from five Kentucky counties, Knepper and Barton (1997) described a misdirected court system that was more focused on clearing the daily docket (despite the number of continuances) than on making progress toward the case goals. The study concluded that although all parties within the court system had important official roles, the operational hierarchy and informal authority varied among court programs based on the court dynamics. These dynamics could inadvertently elevate the role of a court clerk so much that they influence the court process and case outcomes as much, if not more than, the combination of legal mandates, timeframes, and a presiding judge's discretion. Timely resolution of cases is an important factor, but the best child protection courts prioritize safety, permanence, and child well-being as their ultimate goals. Ensuring the best interests of the child becomes very difficult in busy courts that operate with too few staff, cramped space, and insufficient data systems. By providing enough resources and effective leadership, child protection courts can be more immune to courtroom dynamics and can operate without compromising the real issues at hand.

Working with Professionals Who Provide Services

In 1995, a 6-year-old child named Elisa was killed in New York. Her body was covered from head to toe with bruises and cuts. Elisa's mother admitted to smashing the child's head against a cement wall, forcing her to eat her own feces, and using her head to mop the floor before ultimately beating her to death. How did this tragedy occur? Elisa had been the subject of at least eight reports of abuse and had been previously investigated by government agencies. An extensive probe revealed that there had been an appalling lack of communication and coordination among the agencies involved.

In order to most effectively coordinate and manage a child welfare case, the CPS worker must develop and maintain effective professional relationships. The CPS social worker relies on highly specialized information and expertise from doctors, teachers, and mental health professionals. Professional relationships develop over time, with each new interaction building on the last. From each professional, the CPS social worker compiles documented observations, interactions, and treatment recommendations. As stated by Maluccio, Pine, and Tracy (2002), "Social workers need to build a collaborative informal professional support network, consisting of key contacts in their own and related agencies" (p. 195).

Given the many perspectives that may be engaged for a single case, friction can be expected, especially since the various professionals usually care deeply about the outcome for the child but represent particular disciplinary viewpoints about what is best for him or her. Awareness of the potential sources of tension and the rationale behind them will help the CPS worker better coordinate collaborations between service providers. The necessity of working collaboratively and the potential friction that is inherent in doing so are our subjects in this section.

The best way of addressing multidisciplinary issues is to bring all of the right people together at the right times. Multidisciplinary consultations are needed at critical points in a case—for example, when a child is removed from the home or hospitalized, when out-of-home placement is disrupted, or when there are intense barriers to reunification or adoption. If the same professionals meet frequently, they may decide to establish a standing team.

A multidisciplinary team consists of representatives from social services as well as medical and mental health staff, and it may include representatives from the police or the courts. Generally speaking, multidisciplinary teams may have a wide range of purposes. A hospital-based team intending to accurately diagnose patients should include multidisciplinary diagnostic members. Teams can facilitate case discussions to pool community resources, assess client progress, triage cases, expedite referrals, or manage flexible funds. Teams reach better decisions and certainly reduce the potential for redundancy, loss of time, and fragmentation.

Federal laws, as well as statutes in nearly every state, provide authorization for multidisciplinary teams. The team involves certain areas of expertise—CPS, medical, mental health, law enforcement, and the courts—with emphasis on child protection through joint investigations and criminal prosecutions. The team may also directly engage specific participants who are relevant to each case under consideration.

Without effective collaboration, the organizations involved in child welfare run a greater risk of missing critical information, failing to recognize the severity of risk, retraumatizing children, or tainting the accuracy of an investigation. In Connecticut,

The social worker relies on highly specialized information and expertise from physicians, teachers, and mental health professionals. The worker must develop and maintain effective professional relationships with all of these specialists.

for example, multidisciplinary teams work together locally, particularly on sexual abuse investigations. The child is spared the pain of repeatedly answering questions when the police and the CPS investigator conduct a joint interview. The court may permit the videotaped interview for use as evidence in the case. A pediatrician performs the physical examination, instead of sending the child to a crowded emergency room. A clinical social worker provides therapy, and a prosecutor may pursue a criminal court case. The Connecticut CPS social worker also works with the state's attorneys, paralegal staff, and attorney general's office in considering court petitions that assert neglect, abuse, or abandonment.

To have an effective impact on a case, all participants need to work as a team to achieve the established goals for the child and family. Areas of tension are inevitable, however, when case participants join forces. According to Maluccio et al. (2002), "Social work with children, youth, and families may involve highly intense personal contact with clients undergoing stressful and sometimes dangerous situations. Workdays may be long or unpredictable. Workers need to be highly flexible in the approaches and skills used" (p. 195). Besides intense interactions with case families, the CPS worker can expect stress in interactions with other key players on a case.

As an example of the tensions associated with a case, consider the role of a professional who is providing services to a family in the child welfare system. This professional may experience a number of conflicts related to making a referral. As a mandated reporter, the service provider must make a referral to CPS concerning child abuse or neglect. He or she may face conflict on many fronts related to the referral, including the act of making the referral, issues of confidentiality, and case decisions and outcomes. With the decision to make a referral, the service provider risks losing the trust established with the client, for doing so breaches the confidentiality between provider and client. Once the referral has been made, the service provider loses control of decisions regarding the child and family. And when the CPS agency makes a decision on the case—perhaps to remove the child from the family—the service provider may vehemently disagree with the decision.

Regardless of the tensions that surface, the CPS social worker's task continues: to coordinate the services in a case. The skilled social worker seeks to offset friction by maintaining strong interactive relationships with the other service providers. Small courtesies can go a long way in this direction—for example, a phone call or letter to follow up the referral made by the mandated reporter. This simple action not only verifies that what the service provider did was right, but it also shows appreciation for and understanding of the tough position he or she was in.

Conflict may also develop between the CPS social worker and those professionals that provide authority in child welfare cases. As discussed earlier, the criminal court and legal professionals seek to prosecute those who violate the law; they are concerned with protecting society. CPS courts and professionals, on the other hand, are responsible for protecting children and therefore focus on the child and family. Consider the following situation: A CPS social worker goes to court and presents documents asking for permission to remove a child from the family home. The judge does not grant the removal. The judge's decision generates anxiety for the social worker, who believes that the child is in imminent danger of harm. This situation could be avoided or at least improved upon if the CPS social worker and the judge had clear lines of communication and understood one another's professional viewpoints.

Different rules and protocols among various professionals' agencies can also create barriers that need to be carefully addressed. Imagine the frustration of sharing sensitive case information with agencies that have different rules of confidentiality. For example, suppose a CPS worker feels the pressing need to know how a child's mother is doing in her inpatient substance abuse program. The worker may be surprised to learn that he or she cannot just call and obtain that information, expecting a free-flowing conversation among professionals. Due to extremely high confidentiality requirements in the substance abuse field, programs normally require the client to sign a release of information using the program's specific legal language and limitations. The CPS agency's general release of information form would be insufficient for this purpose.

CPS workers and the various professionals involved in a case can best serve the child and family by building positive working relationships. To build such relationships, the players need to understand the limitations and responsibilities of one another's jobs. Maluccio et al. (2002) suggest that "most human service professionals will benefit from cross-disciplinary training, in order to better understand their own and other service systems" (p. 195). The familiar reality is that too often, there are shortages of resources, not enough services, and lengthy waiting lists. This reality frustrates both CPS workers and other service providers, as progress on the case will be delayed and a sense of urgency will be created for all involved.

CPS social workers must continually expand their skills and flexibility—and thereby, their comfort—in working within highly complex family, organizational, and social systems. Continuous supervision and training is necessary to the professional development of a CPS social worker. Maluccio et al. (2002) assert that high-quality, ongoing, and dependable supervision and support will prepare the worker for stressful situations. The quality of supervision for frontline social workers varies within agencies, and it is embedded within an organizational context of frequent change and perceived instability. The dynamics comprise a *parallel process* (Berg & Kelly, 2000; von Foerster, 1983, 1981; Keeney, 1983; Liddle & Saba, 1983; Liddle, Breunlin, & Schwartz, 1988; Schultz, 1991a, 1991b; Watzlawick, 1984), or a situation akin to what many children and their families experience as they enter the child welfare system. The term *parallel process* is used to denote the multiple-level challenges experienced by supervisors, parents, CPS social workers, and other key players.

Crisis-oriented feedback creates loops and patterns of interaction that cause deviation and amplification of problems (Maruyama, 1968), an effect common in CPS agencies, where change and transition are continuous. The less available experienced supervisors are for direct supervision and training, the more frustrated and overwhelmed frontline social workers feel. The more frustrated and overwhelmed frontline social workers feel, the more day-to-day crises seem to develop. The more day-to-day crises develop, the less time there is for proactive supervision and training. Thus, the loop that sustains crises within an agency can escalate rapidly and preclude timely supervision and support during those moments when these elements are most necessary.

Because those individuals with leadership roles in CPS agencies are expected to respond to constant shifts in social policy based on local crises and intense public scrutiny, the day-to-day operation of field offices may seem to be in perpetual flux, with little opportunity for preparation of frontline staff. The organizational stress associated with these inherent changes directly affects the interactions and interpersonal relationships that CPS social workers have with supervisors, colleagues, families, and other key players in the helping system. As a result, CPS social workers must build a tolerance for these factors and be willing to initiate contact with supervisors and more experienced colleagues on an ongoing basis in order to clarify current policies, procedures, and expectations. CPS workers that readily access and prepare for supervision are more likely to avert crises and to remain optimistic when working with highly complex client and organizational dynamics.

The families referred to the child welfare system are likely to be involved in multiple systems and with multiple professionals who hold conflicting views about their problems and solutions. These families often do not trust the so-called helping system. The configuration of relationships among various professionals has been referred to as the *meaningful system* (Imber-Black, 1988), the *significant system* (Boscolo, Cecchin, Hoffman, & Penn, 1987), and the *problem-determined system* (Anderson, Goolishian, & Windeman, 1986). Still others have indicated that as families show redundant patterns that maintain an equilibrium, so, too, do larger systems such as state agencies, community mental health centers, schools, and courts show similar tendencies toward homeostasis (Imber-Coppersmith, 1983; Matthews & Roberts, 1988; Schultz, 1991a, 1991b). Along these lines, Held (1982) and Minuchin, Colapinto & Minuchin (1998) suggest that the interventions used in family systems work are not only applicable to a larger system but may be necessary to ensure the success of the interventions and the effectiveness of the worker within the system.

The specific considerations, skills, and strategies needed by CPS workers and supervisors as they navigate complex social systems have been noted by researchers in a number of related fields, including behavioral health, child welfare, education, juvenile justice, pediatrics, medical science, and substance abuse. The primary principles and practices of brief, family-centered, solution-oriented and structural family therapy approaches have been predominant in the research (Berg & Kelly, 2000; De-Jong & Berg, 1998; Minuchin, 1974; Minuchin, Colapinto, & Minuchin, 1998). Here is a summary of the basic skills recommended for child welfare workers:

1. An ability to forge positive professional alliances with families, colleagues, supervisors, and other key players in the helping system
2. The capacity to tolerate and effectively manage intensive family and organizational stress
3. An ability and willingness to resolve interpersonal conflicts in constructive ways
4. An acute awareness and understanding of family organization and patterns of interaction
5. An ability to effectively intervene in these patterns of interaction through collaborative planning and revision of solution-oriented activities
6. An ability to accurately assess the influence of the larger system on family functioning

7. An ability to effectively coordinate professional activities with the family and the helping system
8. A willingness to use supervision and constructive feedback to become more aware of one's strengths and limitations while developing a professional style

Fragmented or conflicted case management can be detrimental to the child and the family. The complexity of a child maltreatment case requires skillful cooperation among many resources. CPS workers should first become familiar with their own agency's protocols that dictate the appropriate steps for making referrals, sharing case information, and providing case progress reports, and of course, workers should be aware of the fee structure and methods of payment for services. CPS workers must also work toward understanding the differing roles and perspectives that contribute to positive and negative case progress. Each professional brings expertise that sheds light on the totality of the case's circumstances. The result is a case picture that is much more complete than the CPS worker could produce independently.

REFERENCES

American Bar Association. *Section of family law standards of practice for lawyers representing children.* August, 2003.

Anderson, H. & Goolishian, H. (1988). Language systems and therapy: An evolving idea. *Journal of Psychotherapy, 24,* 529–538.

Anderson H., Goolishian, & Windeman, L. (1986). Problem-determined systems. *Journal of Strategic and Systemic Therapies 5,* 1–13.

Berg I. K. & Kelly S. (2000). *Building solutions in child protective services.* New York: Norton.

Boscolo, L., Cecchin, G., Hoffman, L. & Penn, P. (1987). *Milan systemic family therapy.* New York: Basic Books.

DeJong, P. & Berg I. K. (1998). *Interviewing for solutions.* Pacific Grove, CA: Brooks/Cole.

Children's Legal Rights Journal. (1990). Vol. 11, no. 2. ABA: Washington.

Costin, L., Karger, H., & Stoesz, D. (1996). *The politics of child abuse in America.* New York: Oxford University Press.

Held, B. (1982). Entering a mental health system: A strategic-systemic approach. *Journal of Strategic and Systemic Therapies, 1,* 40–51.

Imber-Black, E. (1988). *Families and larger systems: A family therapist's guide through the labyrinth.* New York: Guilford Press.

Imber-Coppersmith, E. (1983). The place of family therapy in the homeostasis of larger systems. In M. Aronson & R. Wolberg (Eds.), *Group and family therapies 1982: An overview.* New York: Brunner/Mazel.

Keeney, B. (1983). *The aesthetics of change.* New York: Guilford Press.

Knepper, P., & Barton, S. (1997). The effect of courtroom dynamics on child maltreatment proceedings. *Social Service Review, 71*(2) 288–308.

Liddle, H. A., & Saba, G. (1983). On content replication: The isomorphic relationship of training and therapy. *Journal of Strategic and Systemic Therapies, 2*(2), 3–11.

Liddle, H. A., Breunlin, D. C., & Schwartz, R. C. (Eds.). (1988). *Handbook of family therapy training and supervision.* New York: Guilford Press.

Lindsey, D. (2004). *The welfare of children.* New York: Oxford University Press.

Malone, M. J. (2004, March 21). Without a net: Alquan white case shows lack of safeguards in system. *The New Day*, pp. 1.

Maluccio, A. N., Pine, B. A., & Tracy, E. M., (2002). *Social work practice with families and children.* New York: Columbia University Press.

Maruyama, M. (1968). The second cybernetics: Deviation-amplifying mutual causal processes. In W. Buckley (Ed.), *Modern systems research for the behavioral scientist.* Chicago: Aldine.

Matthews, W. & Roberts, J. (1988). The entrance of systems family therapy into a residential treatment center. *Child Care Quarterly.* The Hayworth Press.

Minuchin, P., Colapinto, J., & Minuchin, S. (1998). *Working with families of the poor.* New York: Guilford Press.

Minuchin, S. (1974). *Families and family therapy.* Cambridge, MA: Harvard University Press.

National Clearinghouse on Child Abuse and Neglect Information. (2003). *2003 Child abuse and neglect state statute series statutes-at-a-glance reporting procedures.* Retrieved May 27, 2004, from http://nccanch.acf.hhs.gov

Nurcombe, B., & Partlett, D. (1994). *Child mental health and the law.* New York: Maxwell Macmillan International.

Schultz, M. J. (1991a). *Clinical supervision and training with multidisciplinary staff in a day treatment program.* Unpublished doctoral dissertation, University of Massachusettes at Amherst.

Schultz, M. J. (1991b). Program Development and training in residential treatment: Integrating milieu and systemic approaches. *Journal of Strategic and Systemic Family Therapies, 10*(2) Summer, 6–20.

Thoemes, N. (1994). Child protection mediation: A significant improvement over pretrial approaches. *The Judges Journal,* winter, 14–43.

von Foerster, H. (1981). *Observing systems.* Seaside, CA: Intersystems Publication.

von Foerster, H. (1983). *Plenary address.* Presentation at the Sixth Biennial MRI Conference: Maps of the Mind: Maps of the World. San Francisco, California.

Watzlawick, P. (1984). *The invented reality.* New York: W. W. Norton and Company.

CHAPTER 12

Concluding Thoughts on the Practice of Child Welfare

Child Welfare Agency
Anywhere, USA

Dear Staff:

I am very pleased to begin the position of Commissioner of the Department of Children and Families effective January 2005. It is a tremendous honor to be appointed commissioner and please know I very much look forward to our work together in the years ahead.

The advent of a new administration is an opportunity to contemplate the challenges and opportunities that face us. Let me begin by congratulating each of you on your important contributions to the children and families served by the child welfare system, even though you may at times find the daily challenges that characterize this work overwhelming. There is no doubt that overall, child welfare has experienced many advancements during the last century. Most dramatic is the change in mission: No longer do we merely rescue children from poverty; we now have a formal service delivery system organized by the government and sanctioned by the public to assist abused, neglected, and at-risk children and their families by protecting children and preserving families.

We continue to experience new and complex challenges, however, many of which arise from our dual responsibilities to protect children and preserve families. These two mandates, as I'm sure you understand, are not necessarily compatible. Ultimately, the continued dedication of individual child welfare professionals and advocacy by the community of concerned professionals will, I trust, effect positive changes in child welfare policy and practice.

As we prepare for our work together, I think we will do well to consider the major issues facing us. These major issues require considered discussion and thoughtful review. They center on the public perception of child welfare, the nature of the work, the outcomes of interventions, the research agenda, and resource availability. In brief, I would summarize the overall themes this way:

1. Child welfare practice is caught between conflicting value systems in society; therefore, it is not going to be popular and problem free.
2. Child welfare practice involves risk, a fact we just have to accept.
3. Although we know much more about how to protect children now than we did a few years ago, there is still much to learn; thus, continued research is a requisite.
4. Although we complain that too few resources are allocated for child welfare, we do not realistically expect a great deal more funding to be set aside for the protection of children—in part, because of other national priorities.
5. Even as we plea for more attention to a best-practice approach, we acknowledge that while not every case is a success, we see frequent and significant successes.

Again, I look forward to our work together and trust that the above points are helpful in identifying our areas of challenge.

Sincerely,

Child Welfare Commissioner

One might hope that in the real world, every child welfare commissioner would begin his or her tenure with a comprehensive understanding of the challenges in child welfare policy and practice. As we bring this text to a conclusion, we understand that many child welfare professionals do have a clear understanding of the points our imaginary commissioner made. In this final chapter, we revisit our five major themes, those often mentioned in previous chapters and set forth in the preceding letter. This concluding chapter gives us an opportunity to summarize what we believe are the most important issues relevant to understanding each of the five themes.

Conflicting Value Systems

As we explained in Chapter 1, according to the current social welfare policy in the United States, *child welfare* means services for children who are victims of abuse and neglect, and *social work* is the profession designated with the responsibility for implementing this policy. We, along with many others in child protective services (CPS), do not agree with this narrow definition of child welfare because it has diverted resources for supportive and developmental services to services for families in crisis.

The current child welfare system is expected to use a strengths perspective to serve the most serious cases of maltreatment and provide a continuum of services to respond to the complex needs of these children and families. While the definition of child welfare in the United States is narrow, there is also considerable tension in the country between the values of privacy and self-determination and the right of government to intervene in family life. An ongoing debate revolves around the question of how much involvement the government should have in protecting children from abuse and neglect. Child welfare is expected to accommodate the dual responsibilities of protecting children and preserving families. In practice, the twin mandates translate to an ongoing tension: whether to remove children from their families or to maintain children in their families and provide ongoing protective services.

As chronicled in Chapter 2, state-mandated child abuse reporting laws have been in place for more than 25 years. State definitions of physical abuse, emotional or mental abuse, sexual abuse and neglect are, with few exceptions, currently very similar (Orr, 1999). As long as the professional community continues to define child maltreatment as a social service problem, the emphasis will continue to be on intervention and on developing responses that are therapeutic. This emphasis translates to a focus on rehabilitating parents.

As explained in Chapter 3, parents often have serious mental health problems, including psychoses, clinical depression, and mental retardation. They are also likely to be substance abusers, to lack problem-solving skills, and to be emotionally immature. The goal that has been handed to child welfare social work is the rehabilitation of these parents—rehabilitation to the point that they are able to provide appropriate care for their children. As we have noted, the current role of CPS is contradictory. The agency is required to serve the function of policing families as well as the therapeutic function of providing social and rehabilitative services.

The explicit right of the agency to remove children from their families in cases of serious maltreatment will continue to be fiercely debated by parents' rights advocates, who argue that the agency oversteps the rights of parents to discipline their children (Waldfogel, 1998). The mandate to protect children also clashes at times with the right to religious freedom. All Americans are permitted to practice the religion of their choice; therefore, state agencies are cautious about interfering with parents who deny their children medical treatment due to religious beliefs. A child may be removed from the home temporarily, for necessary medical treatment, and then returned to the parents with no continued child protective supervision (Orr, 1999). Thus, although medical neglect is recognized as a reportable condition, the right to religious freedom is upheld unless the child's life is seriously endangered.

Another cause for concern is the impact of welfare reform in its explicit goal of moving parents into the workforce. Courtney (1998) argues that the goals of the welfare system and child welfare are competitive, even conflicting. The former Aid to Families with Dependant Children (AFDC) program was consistent with the child welfare goals of protecting children and preserving families because social workers could rely on AFDC financial resources (for rent, utilities, food) to support the goal of preserving families. The welfare reform law of 1996, which established Temporary Assistance to Needy Families (TANF), emphasizes employment and adult self-sufficiency—goals that are not necessarily compatible with the goal of preserving families. TANF may create more families who cannot care for their children and thus increase the demand for child welfare services. States can act to respond to these conflicting goals of the welfare system and child welfare by implementing strategies that reflect a commitment to protecting children while implementing welfare reform. For example, Courtney (1998) reminds us that states can provide welfare benefits to kin caregivers.

Another very bold example of how conflicting values influence decision making is evident in the patterns of federal funding. Chapters 6 and 7 provided examples of home-based programs that continue to be funded at lower levels than out-of-home care. This is ironic, considering that direct services preserve families and ultimately reduce the costs of care, as illustrated in Chapters 8 and 9. Conversely, funds for out-of-home placement are currently open ended.

This discrepancy is problematic because it creates an incentive for agencies to place children in foster care, rather than offer in-home services to keep the family intact (Courtney, 1998). We are especially troubled by this, given the trend in some states toward privatization of child welfare services (Snell, 2000). Many concerns are being voiced regarding a system where funding for prevention and direct services remain fixed, while unlimited funds are made available for out-of-home care. Can we expect agencies to consider the welfare of the child and family above the allure of higher federal reimbursements? (Courtney, 1998).

Inherent Risk

As societal and economic changes impact families, the child welfare system is increasingly called on to provide successful interventions. The complex role expected of the child welfare system puts child welfare workers in a double bind. They often get blamed for the unsuccessful delivery of services and for tragedies that occur in the community. The media exacerbate the public response when they magnify selected cases of child abuse and disparage child welfare by asserting that specific tragedies should have been prevented. The fact is, families that voluntarily request services are denied unless they are referred for maltreatment. The double bind for child welfare workers results from the double messages inherent in child welfare policy. CPS workers cannot become involved with families until there are allegations of maltreatment.

We agree with Waldfogel (1998), who reminds us that the child welfare system will always be subject to criticism because at the same time that some cases are being investigated unnecessarily, other children already known to the public child welfare agency are being repeatedly abused. Orr (1999) captures this tension in *Child Protection at the Crossroads:* "A child death translates into a policy of removing children too easily from their homes and keeping them in foster care too long. An overzealous removal rate then triggers the opposite reaction, dictating that too many children stay in dangerous settings as the agency tries to be more 'family friendly'" (p. 6).

Every year, about 1,000 children are murdered at the hands of their parents because agencies are not able to adequately investigate all reports of abuse (Orr, 1999). Lowry (1998) writes that the data reviewed from records in three cities show that involvement with the child welfare system does not guarantee protection from further abuse. In Milwaukee, 48 percent of families investigated for abuse had prior involvement with the child welfare system (National Council on Crime and Delinquency, 1995), and in Washington, DC, 32 percent of such families had been previously reported to protective services (T. J. Stein, as cited in Lowry, 1998). In New York City, in 43 percent of the families that had been the subject of an abuse or maltreatment complaint, the children were abused or maltreated again while under city supervision (Marisol Joint Case Record Review Team, 1997, as cited in Lowry, 1998). In 1995, 48 percent of the child abuse deaths in the United States involved children previously known to the authorities (National Committee to Prevent Child Abuse, 1996).

In the case of John Wallace of Chicago, who was killed by his mother (Snell, 2000), a family preservation worker recommended and a judge agreed that the child should be removed from the home. However, before the decision could be implemented, the family moved to another county, the case record was lost, the child was reunited with the family, and he was subsequently killed by his mother. The case review inaccurately assigned the cause of death to the failure of the family preservation intervention, not to the lost record and resulting gap in communication between two county offices that resulted when the family moved.

Another important lesson about risk can be learned from legislative actions in Florida in 1999, when the Kayla McKean Child Protection Act was passed in memory of Kayla, who died after repeated reports of abuse to the Department of Children and Families failed to result in her removal from the home. Although Snell (2000) does not indicate whether state agency workers were negligent in their practice, anger over the fact that this family had already been brought to the attention of child protective services inspired the above-named legislation. This act, which places caseworkers at risk of prosecution if they fail to remove a child who is later abused, has had the unintended consequence of creating a "foster care panic" and a 400 percent increase in foster care populations in some counties (Snell, 2000). This extreme response by child welfare workers—of placing children in foster care unnecessarily—has resulted in the unintended consequence of more harm and disruption to families and children. The McKean case and the consequences associated with the attendant legislative action illustrate in a huge way why all constituencies involved in child welfare need to accept this basic reality: Risk is inherent in child protection.

As we already noted in Chapter 4, the development and implementation of risk assessment tools has tremendously improved the accuracy of the assessment process.

Nevertheless, risk assessment tools are designed only to guide the decision-making process; we must not make the mistake of assuming that a risk assessment tool will ensure accurate assessments at all times and in all situations.

A final point with regard to understanding risk is that there will always be situations where the system cannot protect a child because there is no warning—situations in which the acts of parents or parental surrogates simply cannot be anticipated. In situations where we can intervene, we are obligated to achieve the highest possible level of assessment accuracy. The continuation of quality research is undoubtedly a requisite in our pursuit of accuracy.

The Need for Continued Research

Society has the right to hold all child welfare agencies to high standards (Waldfogel, 1998). The fact that the field of child protective services will always involve risk does not excuse and should never be used to excuse poor practice, such as the failure to provide required follow-up monitoring visits or the loss of or failure to transfer records when a family moves. Instead of poor practice or adequate practice, we want *best practice*. How can we keep moving toward the point where child welfare interventions are as effective as they can be? We can do so by continuing ongoing quality research in all areas of child welfare policy and practice.

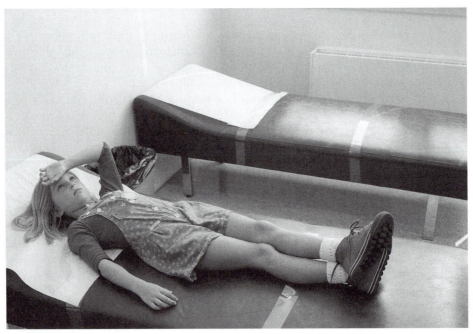

Although our base of knowledge has expanded greatly since the 1960s, continuing research in the areas of child development and child welfare practice is critical if we expect to influence the future directions of child welfare policy and practice.

Child maltreatment was first recognized as a serious problem in 1962, when C. Henry Kempe and colleagues' classic article "The Battered-Child Syndrome" appeared in the *Journal of the American Medical Association*. We now know considerably more than we did at that time. The definition of child maltreatment has expanded to include information about specific forms of child maltreatment, such as emotional abuse, neglect, and sexual abuse. Back in 1962, for example, no one realized the scope or extent of child sexual abuse. Our progress in understanding the scope of the problem has created complex challenges in terms of assessment and intervention.

The *ecological model* of practice (Bronfenbrenner, 1979) has made major contributions to understanding the complex and multifaceted etiology of maltreatment. In Chapter 3, we said that no single theory is adequate to explain the dynamics of child abuse and neglect. Child maltreatment results from the interaction of many individual personality factors and environmental stressors. We know today that most parents who abuse or neglect their children are not psychotic, and we recognize that personality characteristics such as low self-esteem, dependency, poor impulse control, lack of parenting skills, limited knowledge of child development, and social isolation can contribute to child maltreatment. The importance of understanding family factors, cultural factors, environmental/structural factors, and particularly the risk factors associated with poverty was emphasized in Chapter 3.

Leventhal (2003) has summarized many of the significant advances in the field. He notes that we now know that child maltreatment occurs in all societies and is more prevalent than anyone ever believed. We also know that family violence is being viewed as a major public health problem worldwide (Krug, Dahlberg, Mercy, Zwi, & Lozano, 2002). Leventhal identifies the need for continued research regarding the pathogenesis of child maltreatment, reminding us that trauma can affect the brain's development as well as the prognosis and consequences for long-term functioning in adulthood.

Research about child maltreatment has moved beyond description of the problem to evaluation of various modes of intervention. In Chapter 7, we identified the continued progress that has been made in establishing the contributions of home-based services. Research has shown that services such as home visiting, modeling of parenting, providing linkage to community services, and giving intensive support to high-risk first-time parents can successfully reduce the occurrence of maltreatment (Olds et al., 1997; U.S. Advisory Board on Child Abuse and Neglect, 1991). Additional research could help expand our knowledge of best practices for prevention, detection, and treatment. As McGowan and Walsh (2000) have argued, it is necessary to increase the qualitative research on program variables in order to develop viable preventive services. Program variables such as comprehensiveness, flexibility, client responsiveness, and continuity must be better understood.

Although many treatment advances focus on families, as described in Chapter 5, the established value of mental health counseling for victims of maltreatment needs to be underscored (Leventhal, 2003). Further research to substantiate the effectiveness of mental health counseling for abuse victims is crucial, given the demands of health insurers for proof of treatment efficacy.

Although our base of knowledge has expanded greatly since the 1960s, continued research in the areas of child development and child welfare practice is critical if we expect to influence the future direction of child welfare policy and practice. In a review of child maltreatment literature written over a period of 22 years, Behl, Conyngham, and May (2003) have concluded that the child neglect and child emotional abuse literatures need to be more developed. They recommend more research with adult males on the subjects of the perpetration and victimization of child physical abuse. They also point out that research participants must adequately reflect the characteristics of persons in the population affected by child maltreatment, so that research results can better inform clinicians and policymakers.

Research on maltreatment is substantially underfunded, given the frequency of the problem and its immense impact on children and families. This inequity will not be addressed unless society in general recognizes the importance of the problem. We agree that broadening the concerned community to include not only professionals but also the general population, along with marshalling the support of many constituencies, will make it far easier to continue the work ahead. The availability of research funding, plus sufficient funding for training and resources, will aid in recruiting young clinicians and researchers to enter the field of child welfare (Leventhal, 2003). This brings us to our next theme: resource availability.

Resources for Child Protection

When the Child Abuse Prevention and Treatment Act was passed in 1974, it provided a limited amount of funding (initially, only $22 million) to support child protection activities. The number of reports of child abuse and neglect, however, doubled between 1976 and 1986, and the number of children in foster care (following a brief decline in the 1970s) increased to record levels by 1996 and continues to increase.

In the years since 1974, federal and state governments have allocated increasing amounts of funding to public child welfare agencies. The complaint has been and continues to be that child welfare services are underfunded. The Urban Institute (2004), a nonpartisan economic and social policy organization that has tracked child welfare funding trends, reports that states spent $22.2 billion in 2002. This amount included federal, state, and local funds to serve the 4.5 million children referred for suspected abuse or neglect that year. Of this total spending, $2.6 billion came from localities, $8.2 billion from state funds, and $11.3 billion from the federal government. Growth in overall spending was 8 percent, but the increases were almost exclusively attributed to TANF (welfare) and Medicaid. Spending varied greatly across states.

Out-of-home services, such as foster care and kinship care, received the largest amount of funding: $10 billion (Urban Institute, 2004). In contrast, $3.1 billion was spent on child protection, maltreatment prevention, and family preservation and support services. (As we discussed in Chapters 6 and 7, this category of funding is an important one.) Adoption spending amounted to $2.6 billion, an increase of approximately $700 million over a two-year period. Administrative services totaled $1.7 billion, and $4.8 billion in state spending was not categorized.

Researchers suggest that the nature of the funding pattern points to the importance of understanding the relationship across the programs. In other words, we need to improve our understanding of where the gaps in funding are occurring. For example, in 1995, New York spent $111.94 per capita for child welfare services, while Georgia spent $11.81 per capita (Curtis et al., 1995, p. 96). Variations in state spending cannot always be attributed to caseload variations.

Urban Institute (2004) researchers are calling for the attention of legislators and policymakers to the variety of state-specific issues that may be influencing funding levels, such as state priorities and policy choices. Professionals, legislators, and policymakers are urged to learn more about how the programs (TANF, Medicaid, and child welfare) relate to the needs of families. We agree with the Urban Institute's recommendation to pay attention to how funding is being used. By analyzing how the states use existing funding, we may be able to improve the effectiveness of interventions for abused and neglected children and their families by getting more resources allocated for support and replication of exemplary programs.

Ensuring Best Practice

Throughout this text, we have maintained that best practice should be at the very heart of public child welfare policy. To that end, we continue to emphasize this primary point: Comprehensive assessments should guide interventions. Such an approach raises the level of care provided, for it helps us fit case decisions to the specific needs and resources of the family and to the level of risk to the maltreated child. Waldfogel (2000) calls for the provision of a differential response, tailored to the specific needs of each family with a child at risk of abuse or neglect. She cites such systems already in place in Iowa, Missouri, and Florida (pp. 54–55). The reforms reflect the integration of partnerships with community resources and approaches to families that are less adversarial.

In Chapter 7, we identified program models, particularly preventive services and home-based services, which had positive outcomes. We explained the need for continuing quality research to help us progress even further in developing successful programs. We also noted that collaborations with extended families and community resources are essential to achieving positive and meaningful changes.

It is tremendously important for us to continue to insist on improvements in the quality of foster and kinship care. Foster care and out-of-home care will continue to be necessary resources. CPS agencies must focus on the quality and appropriateness of placements while also seeking to decrease out-of-home placements. Attention to the complexities of managing the dual mandates to protect children and preserve families must necessarily be part of every case decision. Additionally, we must work toward doing a much better job of evaluating how children in foster care fare in terms of wellness (Altshuler & Gleeson, 1999). Strengthening adoption opportunities and reducing the number of adoption disruptions also remain on the list of important goals.

We have discussed the mutually interdependent relationship between policy and practice and the interplay among federal, state, and local policies. On this point, the relevant consideration in our end-of-text review is that states and localities have the discretion to determine and implement priorities, particularly in relation to the nexus

Best practices should be at the very heart of public child welfare policy.

of welfare reform and child welfare. The decisions made by individual states reflect the balance they strike between the implementation of welfare reform mandates (requiring the moving of parents into the workforce) and the implementation of public child welfare programs (requiring the protection of children). States that recognize the value of providing child care services for working parents create a complementary and mutually supportive arrangement between welfare reform and child welfare.

Finally, we would be remiss in this summary if we neglected to acknowledge the ongoing debate about privatizing child welfare. Briefly, we believe that it is important to continue to gather data on how children and families are doing in states that opt for privatizing the child protective function. We also look forward to seeing continued documentation of how children and families are faring with public child welfare agencies that are willing to make significant changes.

Ultimately, the question of who administers child welfare may not be as crucial as the question of how the work is approached. We believe quality of service depends on quality of assessment. That said, we can sum up by saying that child welfare—whether privatized or not—needs to be sure that its function is guided by a capacity for quality assessment and intervention plus the capacity for quality documentation of the effectiveness of services it provides.

REFERENCES

Altshuler, S., & Gleeson, J. (1999). Completing the evaluation triangle for the next century: measuring child "well-being" in family foster care. *Child Welfare, 78(1),* 25–147.

Andrews Scarcella, C., Bess, R., Zielewski, E., Warner, L., & Geen, R. (2004). *The cost of protecting vulnerable children IV.* Urban Institute. Retrieved January 11, 2005, from www.urban.org/urlprint.cfm?ID=9128

Behl, L. E., Conyngham, H. A., & May, P. F. (2003). Trends in child development literature. *Child Abuse & Neglect, 27,* 215–229.

Besharov, D. (1998). Commentary. *The Future of Children: Protecting Children from Abuse and Neglect, 8*(1), 120–123.

Bronfenbrenner, U. (1979). *The ecology of human development: Experiments by nature and design.* Cambridge, MA: Harvard University Press.

Courtney, M. (1998). The costs of child protection in the context of welfare reform. *The Future of Children: Protecting Children from Abuse and Neglect, 8(1),* 88–103.

Curtis, P. A., Boyd, J. D., Liepold, M., & Petit, M. (1995). *Child abuse and neglect: A look at the states: The CWLA stat book.* Washington, DC: Child Welfare League of America.

Kempe, C. H., Silverman, F. N., Steele, B. F., Droegemueller, W., & Silver, H. K. (1962). The battered-child syndrome. *Journal of the American Medical Association, 251,* 3288–3300.

Krug, E. G., Dahlberg, L. L., Mercy, J. A., Zwi, A., & Lozano, R. (Eds.). (2002). *World report on violence and health.* Geneva: World Health Organization.

Leventhal, J. M. (2003). The field of child maltreatment enters its fifth decade. *Child Abuse & Neglect, 27,* 1–4.

Lowry, R. (1998). Commentary. *The Future of Children: Protecting Children from Abuse and Neglect, 8*(1), 123–126.

McGowan, B. G., & Walsh, E. M. (2000). Policy challenges for child welfare in the new century. *Child Welfare, 79*(1), 11–27.

National Committee to Prevent Child Abuse. (1996). *Current trends in child abuse reporting and fatalities: The results of the 1995 fifty-state survey.* Chicago: National Committee to Prevent Child Abuse.

National Council on Crime and Delinquency. (1995). *An analysis of the Milwaukee County child protection and foster care systems: Results of case readings conducted for Milwaukee County Department of Human Services and the Children's Rights Project of the ACLU.* Washington, DC: National Council on Crime and Delinquency.

Olds, D. L., Eckenrode, J., Henderson, C. R., Kitzman, H., Powers, J., Cole, R., Sidora, K., Morris, P., Pettit, L. M., & Luckey, D. (1997). Long-term effects of maternal visitation on maternal life course and child abuse and neglect: Fifteen-year follow-up of a randomized trial. *Journal of the American Medical Association, 278,* 637–643.

Orr, S. (1999). *Child protection at the crossroads: Child abuse, child protection, and recommendations for reform.* Reason Public Policy Institute. Retrieved October 18, 2004, from www.rppi.org/socialservices/ps262.html

Snell, L. (2000). *Child welfare reform and the role of privatization.* Reason Public Policy Institute. Retrieved October 19, 2004, from www.rppi.org/ps271.html

Urban Institute. (2004). *U.S. spends more to protect vulnerable children despite sluggish economy.* Retrieved January 11, 2005, from www.urban.org/urlprint.cfm?ID=9127

U.S. Advisory Board on Child Abuse and Neglect. (1991). *Creating caring communities: Blueprint for an effective policy on child abuse and neglect.* Washington, DC: Government Printing Office.

Waldfogel, J. (1998). Rethinking the paradigm for child protection. *The Future of Children: Protecting Children from Abuse and Neglect, 8*(1), 104–119.

Waldfogel, J. (2000). Reforming child protective services. *Child Welfare, 79*(1), 43–56.

Index